T0189848

Communications
in Computer and Information Science

1619

Editorial Board Members

Joaquim Filipe ⓘ
  Polytechnic Institute of Setúbal, Setúbal, Portugal

Ashish Ghosh
  Indian Statistical Institute, Kolkata, India

Raquel Oliveira Prates ⓘ
  Federal University of Minas Gerais (UFMG), Belo Horizonte, Brazil

Lizhu Zhou
  Tsinghua University, Beijing, China

More information about this series at https://link.springer.com/bookseries/7899

Dmitrii Rodionov · Tatiana Kudryavtseva ·
Angi Skhvediani · Mohammed Ali Berawi (Eds.)

Innovations in Digital Economy

Third International Scientific Conference, SPBPU IDE 2021
Saint Petersburg, Russia, October 14–15, 2021
Revised Selected Papers

 Springer

Editors
Dmitrii Rodionov 🆔
Peter the Great St. Petersburg Polytechnic
University
St. Petersburg, Russia

Tatiana Kudryavtseva 🆔
Peter the Great St. Petersburg Polytechnic
University
St. Petersburg, Russia

Angi Skhvediani 🆔
Peter the Great St. Petersburg Polytechnic
University
St. Petersburg, Russia

Mohammed Ali Berawi 🆔
Universitas Indonesia
Depok, Indonesia

ISSN 1865-0929   ISSN 1865-0937 (electronic)
Communications in Computer and Information Science
ISBN 978-3-031-14984-9   ISBN 978-3-031-14985-6 (eBook)
https://doi.org/10.1007/978-3-031-14985-6

© Springer Nature Switzerland AG 2022
This work is subject to copyright. All rights are reserved by the Publisher, whether the whole or part of the material is concerned, specifically the rights of translation, reprinting, reuse of illustrations, recitation, broadcasting, reproduction on microfilms or in any other physical way, and transmission or information storage and retrieval, electronic adaptation, computer software, or by similar or dissimilar methodology now known or hereafter developed.
The use of general descriptive names, registered names, trademarks, service marks, etc. in this publication does not imply, even in the absence of a specific statement, that such names are exempt from the relevant protective laws and regulations and therefore free for general use.
The publisher, the authors, and the editors are safe to assume that the advice and information in this book are believed to be true and accurate at the date of publication. Neither the publisher nor the authors or the editors give a warranty, expressed or implied, with respect to the material contained herein or for any errors or omissions that may have been made. The publisher remains neutral with regard to jurisdictional claims in published maps and institutional affiliations.

This Springer imprint is published by the registered company Springer Nature Switzerland AG
The registered company address is: Gewerbestrasse 11, 6330 Cham, Switzerland

Preface

The International Scientific Conference on Innovations in Digital Economy: SPbPU IDE 2021 was held at Peter the Great St. Petersburg Polytechnic University (SPbPU), St. Petersburg, Russia during October 22–23, 2021. This conference was conducted jointly by the Graduate School of Industrial Economics (GSIE) at SPbPU and the Center for Sustainable Infrastructure Development (CSID) at the Universitas Indonesia (UI).

The spread of COVID-19 has been among the main factors affecting the global economy and has boosted the development of Industry 4.0 and the digital economy. On the one hand, COVID-19 has had severe negative effects on people, companies, and national economies. On the other hand, it has boosted the spread of digital technologies, which helped to overcome these effects and minimize damage. It has also supported the development of Industry 4.0 and the digital economy, since certain types of technologies have become more commonly used among a larger number of people and companies. Therefore, the aim of the conference was to discuss recent contributions to the understanding of innovations in the digital economy and its consequences for modern economies. We believe that the community of our conference is key to the dissemination of the most recent advances and promotion of new international collaborations. Professionals from Russia, Indonesia, Italy, France, the UK, Spain, and other countries took part in IDE 2021.

The conference started with an opening ceremony, and a welcome speech was given by the First Vice-Rector for Scientific and Organizational Activities and Corresponding Member of the Russian Academy of Sciences, Vitalyi Sergeev; Acting Vice-Rector, Yuriy Klochkov; Director of the Institute of Industrial Management, Economics and Trade, Vladimir Schepinin; Dean of Faculty of Engineering of the UI, Ir Hendri Dwi Saptioratri Budiono; Executive Director of the Center for Sustainable Infrastructure Development of the UI, Mohammed Ali Berawi; Director of the Graduate School of Industrial Economics, Dmitrii Rodionov; and the Head of Development and Strategic Planning of SPbPU, Maria Vrublevskaia. Yuriy Klochkov noted that SPbPU responds quickly to changes in science and everyday life, which allows it to develop rapidly, and the Institute of Industrial Management, Economics and Trade is a provider of such growth.

After the opening ceremony, a plenary session was held at which Roy Woodhead from Sheffield Hallam University (UK) spoke about the possibilities of, and approaches to, the implementation of the 'smart city' concept, Vincenzo Bianco from the University of Genoa (Italy) spoke about the development of PV power in Italy, Emma Juaneda Ayensa from La Rioja University (Spain) shared an omnichannel strategy for creating added value for users, and Jessica Lichy from IDRAC Business School (France) discussed the dark side of technological innovation for knowledge transfer.

During the conference, a master class was held by the editor of the IJTECH journal, Mohammed Ali Berawi, where the professor talked about strategies for writing articles for international journals and gave useful advice to authors on the publication process. Natalya Berestovskaia, a specialist in the promotion of business products from CJSC

Interfax-North-West, held a master class on identifying and assessing risks when working with legal entities using the SPARK-Interfax system.

During the two days of the conference, the participants spoke at six different sessions, participated in master classes, shared their experience with colleagues, and discussed issues related to innovations in the digital economy, including digitalization in education, the 'smart city' and 'smart home' concepts, the cryptocurrency market, eco-activism, risks of implementing infrastructure projects, etc.

The conference received a total of 153 submissions. All submitted papers underwent a four-stage review process. In the first stage, all papers were evaluated and reviewed by the conference or Program Committee co-chairs. In the second stage, papers were evaluated and reviewed by at least two reviewers or a Program Committee member. In the third stage, we conducted technical reviews and checked papers for plagiarism, mastery of the English language, and overall structure. This resulted in a pool of high-quality papers presenting the best practices and scientific results within the scope of the conference topics. Out of these papers, 23 were accepted for publication in CCIS after additional review and significant extension.

For the first section, 'Economic efficiency and social consequences of digital innovation implementation', three papers were selected. The first paper in this section, written by Maxim Kuznetsov, Alexander Gorovoy, and Dmitrii Rodionov, discusses a 120-year timeline of web innovation cycle development. The authors describe attributes and improvements of web development which can help strategize digitization initiatives among entrepreneurs, start-ups, investors, and governments. The second paper in this section, written by Elena Korchagina, Larisa Desfonteines, Samrat Ray, and Natalia Strekalova, describes the possibilities of using modern digital technologies for the transport system related to local environmental conditions and demographic characteristics. The authors note that the transport system could become the basis for improving people's quality of life if it undergoes digital development. The third paper in this section, written by Anuphat Thirakulwanich and Sudaporn Sawmong, studies how user-generated content on YouTube relates to customers' purchase decisions in regard to smartphones. The research also shows that perceived usefulness and perceived credibility have a positive effect on behavioral intention to purchase smartphones.

For the second section, 'Regional innovation systems and clusters as drivers of economic growth during the Fourth Industrial Revolution', three papers were selected. The first paper in this section, written by Ksenia Pereverzeva, Denis Tsvetkov, Konstantin Petrov, and Svetlana Gutman, aims to justify the selection of a region with the greatest potential for the bioenergy sector. The authors suggest developing a region's bioenergy sector in conjunction with digital technology, namely by introducing 'smart' greenhouses, applying digital technology to maintain the most favourable conditions for animals, and using the automated collection of biofuel. The second paper in this section, written by Mariana Petrova, Petya Popova, Veselin Popov, Krasimir Shishmanov, and Kremena Marinova, identifies the main characteristics, types, and components of the digital ecosystem concept and describes the business model to create value through this kind of system. In conclusion, the authors point out that a digital ecosystem should be related to the size and scope of a business organization because it will improve networks and gradually replace the supply chain model. The third paper in this section, written by Angi Skhvediani, Tatiana Kudryavtseva, Valeriia Iakovleva, and Igor Kuhotkin, is devoted to the issue of developing a database of clusters on Russian territory and a system for the visualization of statistical information for cluster policy decision-making. The results of this research paper show what the development of software tools will allow in terms of bridging the gap in the development of the analytical and predictive information systems of the regional economy.

For the third section, 'Industrial, service and agricultural digitalization', ten papers were selected. The first paper in this section, written by Lo Thi Hong Van, Liudmila A. Guzikova, and An Thinh Nguyen, explores the role of e-commerce development in sustainable economic growth through the example of the Socialist Republic of Vietnam. This article includes the authors' approach to assessing the contribution of e-commerce to the sustainable growth of GDP and the classification of e-commerce development policies based on level of regional development. In the second paper in this section, written by Mustika Sari, Mohammed Ali Berawi, Teuku Yuri Zagloel, Louferinio Royanto Amatkasmin, and Bambang Susantono, the authors explore the data preparation of energy-efficient and healthy buildings to be utilized in a machine learning (ML) model that can accurately predict the building variables. The outcome of this study shows that the predictive ML model could help decision-makers quantitatively predict healthy building variables to an adequate level of accuracy. The third paper in this section, written by Marina Bolsunovskaya, Nina Osipenko, Svetlana Shirokova, and Aleksei Gintciak, develops an innovative project model for digital wearable devices. This model illustrates the entire process of data transmission from a 'smart' device to a synchronized a mobile application and offers solutions to improve the transmission process and data protection.

The fourth paper in this section, written by Tatiana Bogdanova, Elena Rytova, and Ekaterina Krasilnikova, proposes an algorithm for choosing alternative technologies to implement a particular business process. The final assessment of technology implementation is carried out on the basis of a three-block pattern: assessment of technology risks, assessment of suppliers, and assessment of the financial and economic efficiency of the project. The fifth paper in this section, written by Alexander Babkin, Vadim Tronin, Anton Safiullin, and Alexander Alexandrov, explores the transformation of software project management in Industry 4.0. The authors note that a combined or hybrid model of software project management, combining traditional and agile methodologies, seems to be more sustainable. The sixth paper in this section, written by Ekaterina Abushova, Ekaterina Burova, Andrei Stepanchuk, and Svetlana Suloeva, develops an express method for assessing the current level of industrial enterprise digitalization. A feature of the proposed technique is to assess the level of digitalization of each of the key aspects of a modern competitive production enterprise and obtain a comprehensive indicator that allows further conclusions.

The seventh paper in this section, written by Maksim Pasholikov, Leonid Vinogradov, Tatiana Leonova, Vasily Burylov, and Eitiram Mamedov, tests the methods of multi-criteria optimization of quality criteria in the field of commercial water treatment. The proposed trained neural network model can become the basis for the development of a common methodology to create the optimal vector of business activity quality in any sector of the economy. The eighth paper in this section, written by Igor Ilin, Oksana Iliashenko, Victoria Iliashenko, and Sofia Kalyazina, proposes a method of integral assessment of the results of the implementation of an intelligent data analysis platform. This method makes it possible to assess the feasibility of the goals set for the development of a digital company and to form goals for further strategic development. The ninth paper in this section, written by Anastasia Levina, Alisa Dubgorn, Alexandra Borremans, and Evgenia Kseshinski, reveals a reference model for the use of information technology in terms of the need to simplify the management of geographically distributed organizations and improve the efficiency of medical services. This article discusses various ways in which modern healthcare information technologies can be used to improve the quality of direct care, increase benefits for commercial organizations, reduce costs for government enterprises, and improve user experience for patients. The tenth paper in this section, written by Galina Silkina, Natalia Alekseeva, Svetlana Shevchenko, and Lyudmila Pshebel'skaya, defines the digital management tools and information trends of the new industrialization. The results of this research substantiate the use of industrial knowledge graphs as a semantic basis for decision-making.

For the fourth section, 'Response of an educational system and labor market to the digital-driven changes in the economic system', four papers were selected. The first paper in this section, written by Viktoriya Degtyareva, Svetlana Lyapina, and Valentina Tarasova, discusses the problems of developing new educational program for universities and issues that need to be addressed by coordinating with various institutions in the system in the context of the spread of digitalization. The results of the work determine the following directions for the further development of educational program: normative and methodological development, the use of external expertise, and the expansion of cooperation with employers. The second paper in this section, written by Svetlana Evseeva, Oksana Evseeva, and Preeti Rawat, studies the modern features of the external environment of an organization and its impact on employee development. The results of this paper allow companies to design employee development program based on BANI (brittle, anxious, nonlinear, and incomprehensible) world characteristics. The third paper in this section, written by Aleksandr Kozlov, Alina Kankovskaya, Anna Teslya, and Artem Ivashchenko, researches regional labor digital potential through local organizations. The authors differentiate regions in terms of the intensity of use of digital skills of the population by employers. The fourth paper in this section, written by Marine Gurgenidze Nana Makaradze, Tatia Nakashidze-Makharadze, Anna Karmanova, Zhanna Nikiforova, and Victoria Sheleiko, identifies the strengths and weaknesses of distance training, evaluates its results, and defines ways to increase efficiency.

For the fifth section, 'Digital transformation trends in the government and financial sector', three papers were selected. The first paper in this section, written by Nikolay Lomakin, Aleksandr Rybanov, Anastasiya Kulachinskaya, Elena Goncharova, Uranchimeg Tudevdagva, and Yaroslav Repin, hypothesizes that an AI system can be used to obtain a forecast of the share of overdue loans in a bank's portfolio. As a result of this project, the perceptron program was developed to predict the dynamics of the share of overdue loans in the portfolio of a commercial bank, which was formed on the Deductor platform. The second paper in this section, written by Olga Chemeris, Victoria Tinyakova, Yaroslav Lavrinenko, and Xingyuan Sun, uses the Global Innovation Index as a tool to measure the level of innovation in a country's economy, determined in the current environment by digital transformation, as well as to identify the factors influencing it. The study reveals a strong correlation between the amount of public spending per student and the level of innovation in the economy. The third paper in this section, written by Svetlana Pupentsova, Alexandr Demin, Alina Kirilyuk, and Victoria Pupentsova, studies the development of tools for participatory design in the formation of urban public spaces and analyzes participatory design methods.

We want to thank our keynote speakers, panellists, and authors, who contributed to the conference and made this event possible by submitting and later reviewing their work according to the comments provided by the reviewers. We are also grateful to the members of the Program Committee for providing valuable and profound reviews.

We hope that the conference will continue to be an annual event at which scientists and practitioners can share recent developments in the sphere of the digital economy.

July 2022
Dmitrii Rodionov
Tatiana Kudryavtseva
Mohammed Ali Berawi
Angi Skhvediani

Organization

Conference Chairs

Vladimir Schepinin	Peter the Great St. Petersburg Polytechnic University, Russia
Hendri Budiono	Universitas Indonesia, Indonesia
Dmitrii Rodionov	Peter the Great St. Petersburg Polytechnic University, Russia
Mohammed Ali Berawi	Universitas Indonesia, Indonesia

Program Committee Chairs

Irina Rudskaya	Peter the Great St. Petersburg Polytechnic University, Russia
Tatiana Kudryavtseva	Peter the Great St. Petersburg Polytechnic University, Russia

Program Committee

Alexey Bataev	Peter the Great St. Petersburg Polytechnic University, Russia
Anderson Catapan	Universidade Tecnologica Federal do Parana, Brazil
Alberto Tron	Bocconi University, Italy
Andrey Zaytsev	Peter the Great St. Petersburg Polytechnic University, Russia
Angela Mottaeva	Moscow State University of Civil Engineering, Russia
Anis Alamshoyev	Tajik State Finance and Economics University, Tajikistan
Chen Fangruo	Shanghai Jiao Tong University, China
Cristina Sousa	Universidade Portucalense, Portugal
Diego Augusto de Jesus Pacheco	Universidade Federal do Rio Grande do Sul, Brazil
Antonio Petruzzelli	Polytechnic University of Bari, Italy
Ekaterina Abushova	Peter the Great St. Petersburg Polytechnic University, Russia
Ekaterina Koroleva	Peter the Great St. Petersburg Polytechnic University, Russia

Elena Rytova	Peter the Great St. Petersburg Polytechnic University, Russia
Elena Sharafanova	St. Petersburg State University of Economics, Russia
Evgenii Konnikov	Peter the Great St. Petersburg Polytechnic University, Russia
Gregory Porumbescu	Rutgers University, USA
Grogore Belostecinic	Academia de Studii Economice din Moldova, Moldova
Igor Lyukevich	Peter the Great St. Petersburg Polytechnic University, Russia
Isti Surjandari	University of Indonesia, Indonesia
James Chen	Asia University, Taiwan
Jessica Lichy	IDRAC Business School, France
Josef Windsperger	University of Vienna, Austria
Juan Montes	Universidad de Medellín, Colombia
Emma Juaneda-Ayensa	La Rioja University, Spain
Ksenia Pereverzeva	Peter the Great St. Petersburg Polytechnic University, Russia
Luis Borges Gouveia	Fernando Pessoa University, Portugal
Marco Avarucci	University of Glasgow, UK
Marina Ivanova	Peter the Great St. Petersburg Polytechnic University, Russia
Marina Järvis	Tallinn University of Technology, Estonia
Maxim Ivanov	Peter the Great St. Petersburg Polytechnic University, Russia
Magdalena Mißler-Behr	Brandenburg University of Technology, Germany
Natalia Victorova	Peter the Great St. Petersburg Polytechnic University, Russia
Natalya Kulagina	Bryansk State Engineering and Technology University, Russia
Olesya Perepechko	Peter the Great St. Petersburg Polytechnic University, Russia
Olga Kalinina	Peter the Great St. Petersburg Polytechnic University, Russia
Peeter Müürsepp	Tallinn University of Technology, Estonia
Peng Delei	East China University of Science and Technology, China
Lilia Sargu	University of European Studies of Moldova, Moldova
Sergey Demin	National Research University Higher School of Economics, Russia
Sergey Sosnovskikh	De Montfort University, UK

Susanne Durst	Tallinn University of Technology, Estonia
Yuri Zagloel	University of Indonesia, Indonesia
Tamara Shabunina	Institute for Problems of Regional Economics, RAS, Russia
Tatiana Mokeeva	Peter the Great St. Petersburg Polytechnic University, Russia
Valentina Lagasio	Sapienza University of Rome, Italy
Vincenzo Bianco	University of Genoa, Italia
Wang Yinchun	Shanghai Institute for Science of Science, China
Xiaorong Li	Nanjing University, China
Xinpeng Xu	Hong Kong Polytechnic University, Hong Kong
Yi Zhang	University of Technology Sydney, Australia
Yulia Dubolazova	Peter the Great St. Petersburg Polytechnic University, Russia

Organizing Committee Chair

Angi Skhvediani	Peter the Great St. Petersburg Polytechnic University, Russia

Organizing Committee

Anastasia Kulachinskaya	Peter the Great St. Petersburg Polytechnic University, Russia
Darya Kryzhko	Peter the Great St. Petersburg Polytechnic University, Russia
Viktoria Brazovskaia	Peter the Great St. Petersburg Polytechnic University, Russia
Valeriia Arteeva	Peter the Great St. Petersburg Polytechnic University, Russia

Contents

Response of an Educational System and Labor Market to the Digital-Driven Changes in the Economic System

Digital Transformation Trends in the Government and Financial Sector

Economic Efficiency and Social Consequences of Digital Innovations Implementation

Web Innovation Cycles and Timing Projections – Applying Economic Waves Theory to Internet Development Stages

Maxim Kuznetsov[1]([⊠]) [iD], Alexander Gorovoy[1] [iD], and Dmitrii Rodionov[2] [iD]

[1] ITMO University, Kronverksky Pr. 49, bldg. A, St. Petersburg 197101, Russia
max@raibo.net
[2] Peter the Great St. Petersburg Polytechnic University,
Polytechnicheskaya, 29, St. Petersburg 195251, Russia

Abstract. We combine the web evolution concept with the innovation waves and economic cycles theory to build up timing projections. Mostly used staging concepts involve tags for Web 1.0, Web 2.0, Web 3.0, Web 4.0. Web staging discussion is reviewed in historical order. Its influence on other industries is shown in confirmation of cross-cutting role of IT. We considered a wider timeline of 3 Kondratiev cycles related to information and web technologies to picture the 120 years' timeline. Attributes and improvements of web development have been described to help strategize digitization initiatives among entrepreneurs, startups, investors and governments. Blockchain and Artificial Intelligence integration, personal wearable devices and Internet of Things marked as the most forthcoming factors of Web 3.0 potential realization. Web 4.0 is positioned as an emotional web that will happen based on further convergence of communication and healthcare, neuro, nano and cognitive technologies that will result in Neuronet creation based on. 3 s-curved logistic trajectories of every web innovation stage are placed the timeline – technology, development, diffusion.

Keywords: Digitalization · Information communication technologies · Web evolution · Web 2.0 · Web 3.0 · Web 4.0 · Web 5.0 · Web 6.0 · Innovation management · Kondratiev waves · Economic cycles · Innovation logistic trajectory

1 Introduction

The Web and Internet as a techno-social system became the most influential essence that happened with society in this century. The evolution of the Web is happening every day and every second. There are 8 billion people that earn and are served. Some percentage of it is done using web technologies, yet there is a major field in expanding, and evolving more people. Let's define what role evolution of communication lawyer means and brings.

As digital information logistics changes and affects billions of people in a short period of time and becomes the de-facto most influential phenomenon, the attention

© Springer Nature Switzerland AG 2022
D. Rodionov et al. (Eds.): SPBPU IDE 2021, CCIS 1619, pp. 3–21, 2022.
https://doi.org/10.1007/978-3-031-14985-6_1

of the world community has been raised and allowed the creation of many structured projections and studies.

Information Communication Technologies (ICT/IT) get big attention from the financial market. 11 of the top 15 companies with the highest market capitalization were connected with IT in April 2021 [1].

The Internet, as the most influential part of IT, was in long development with roots in the military after World War II. The World Wide Web (WWW) since its formation in the early 1990s has been so far the most popular network on the Internet.

Thus, notions of the Internet, WWW, or, simply, web – nowadays are often used interchangeably. Even if such things as emails or bittorrents are related to other networks of the Internet rather than the WWW, mostly they're accessible through a web browser and web page. That's the most known part of the WWW and the Internet as we use it today.

So for further discussion, we stay on the term Web as a technical-social system with a wider meaning including both WWW and mostly synonymous to the Internet with its various forms and communication protocols.

1.1   Web 1.0

The first web has been presented as hyperlinked websites with static data where people could mainly read information. Website creation has been a harder task and mainly has been used for business purposes, or created by gig intentions.

And that action – finding information using browsers and hyperlinked websites – became the core value of the first web generation, coined after Web 1.0. It's built the necessary basis and Internet connections started to grow worldwide. Still, Internet penetration reached just 10% of the world's population in the early 2000s [2].

"Father" of WWW Tim Berners-Lee in 2001 suggested the future of the web in the form of an extension to what already existed – The Semantic Web, which should re-organize information on the web. The idea is that not only humans should be able to recognize the information on sites, but also that other programs and software should be able to interact with each other [3].

We can observe the lasting development of web technologies from many companies and their commercial results and actions.

Google, as one of the IT leaders, started with the core function as a search in 1998, became a leader in browsers and operational systems for mobile devices. Nowadays Google, with the Alphabet company name, is becoming a leading Artifactual Intelligence provider, opening vast Machine Learning possibilities for thousands of developers [4]. That's not the semantic web suggested, but a more elegant solution to the same challenge – teaching machines to interact and process the data.

1.2   Web 2.0

First coining the concept of Web 2.0 Darcy DiNucci in 1999 stated that further multiplying of web usage will happen not only through web browsers and desktop computers as the "front-end" of the system. But mainly by "countless permutations with different looks, behaviors, uses, and hardware hosts", shifting the meaning of the web from a hyperlinked text on screens to a transport mechanism through which interactivity happens [5].

Web 2.0 tag has been popularized by IT evangelist Tim O'Reilly since the same-named conference in 2005. Its purpose was to get the faith of stakeholders after the dot-com bubble. Developing the concept of Web 2.0 T. O'Reilly showed such differentiative advantages of Web 2.0 as:

- "Services, not packaged software, with cost-effective scalability
- Control over unique, hard-to-recreate data sources that get richer as more people use them
- Trusting users as co-developers
- Harnessing collective intelligence
- Leveraging the long tail through customer self-service
- Software above the level of a single device
- Lightweight user interfaces, development models, AND business models" [6].

Facebook as the great representative of Web 2.0, started in 2004. It's connected billions of people to the distance in a few clicks. Social networking and communication became the most attractive experience, with people spending hours a day scrolling through a newsfeed. And they contributed well in all ways – supporting acquired startups like Instagram and WhatsApp and open source technologies like React and PyTorch.

In 2019, the total number of Internet users passed 50% of the world population [7]. In 2020, Facebook reported more than 3.5 billion people using one of Facebook's products (which includes 8 independent brands such as Instagram, WhatsApp, Oculus, etc.) at least once a month. [8] Recently rebranding and Facebook now is part of Meta which aims to build a metaverse, deep dive into virtual and augmented communication, and build the next web [9].

Both Alphabet and Meta are in the top 10 largest companies in the world by market capitalization in 2021. Both companies were established based on Internet development, specifically the world wide web. And we can see how they improve technologies and reflect about further usage of IT and web.

Thinking about Web 2.0 as the web of social networks and collaboration, is accepted by all of the researchers as the new wave of Internet. Now, almost 20 years later, we can feel that affection by using Uber or Airbnb to move and live in different locations around the world. And see that web-native younglings producing data in web platforms like Tik-Tok adopting the micro-content concept and stepping into commercial and educational activities earlier.

1.3   Web 3.0 and Conceptualization of Future Internet

A massive study of online life took place at the Social Issues Research Center in 2006. Zoe Khor and Dr. Peter Marsh stated 2010–2020 to be the time of Web 3.0 as a "multi-media glocal network". For 2020, they projected that we will "no longer think of online communities and social networking sites as 'alternatives' to 'reality', but instead, they will provide additional forums for talking, shopping, working, playing and living." [10]

That's become a true reality with blogger popularization and influence market growth. And allowed people to work remotely during the COVID-19 lockdowns.

Nova Spivack in 2007 suggested not connecting Web evolution to a particular technology, but rather a decade "during which time several key technologies will become widely used. While Web 3.0 is not synonymous with the Semantic Web (there will be several other important technology shifts in that period), it will be largely characterized by semantics in general.". He argued that Web 2.0 is more focused on user experience and the front side of the web, while Web 3.0 will be a time to upgrade the "back-end" of the web [11].

Tim O-Reilly in his response to Nova Spivack agreed that Web 3.0 has already "been a recurrent theme of would-be meme-engineers who want to position their startup as the next big thing… "Web 3.0" to be meaningful we'll need to see a serious discontinuity from the previous generation of technology" [12].

Collective infographics were produced by TrendOne and Nils Mueller in 2008. The web evolutions were presented as stages including core techs and segmented by business, communication, and entertainment fields with timelines given:

- Web of Content (1993–2000) – catalog, forms; search, forum, mail; pictures, text.
- Web of Communication (2000–2008) – social commerce, auctions, eCommerce; social networks, blogs, wiki, instant messengers, crowdsourcing; UFC, viral, p2p audio, video, widgets
- Web of Context (2008–2012) – smart search, virtual shopping, smart advertising; semantic web, smart interface; MMORPG, virtual worlds, in media search
- Web of Things (2012–2020) – Smart Personal Assistant, location-based intelligence, AI robots, voice processing, immediate translation; wearable technology, connected space, enduring community, geospatial web; augmented reality, gesture technology, cinematic games, blurring boundaries
- Web of Thoughts (after 2020) – collective intelligence, agents, artificial brain, human-technology convergence; direct brain link, digital aura, brain wave control; 5 sense immersion, AV implant, active contact lens [13].

Janet Abbate in 2008 summarized the main problems of the Internet as "congestion and a scarcity of network addresses, and social dilemmas, including malicious and illegal activities and persistent digital divides based on income, location, age, gender, and education."

The technical development of the system has been characterized by a few trends.

- steady increase in the size of data and variety of services offered,
- layered architecture of web application behaves according to a lot of protocol as a set of rules for software and hardware,
- unusual decentralized and participatory design which led to a collaborative process for approving design changes and accounting for social goals.

As both social and technical Internet developments are supposed to provide values of increasing access, accommodating diversity, decentralizing authority, making decisions by consensus with a wide range of participants, and allowing users to take an active role in adding features to the network [14].

Being realistic about personal information sharing, Analee Newitz projected in 2008 that Web 3.0 would be about "making information less free. Privacy fears, new forms of advertising, and restrictions imposed by media companies will mean more digital walls, leading to a web that's safer but without its freewheeling edge" [15].

Ajit Kambil in 2008 showed Web evolution into 5 milestones:

– Web 1.0: The Basic Publishing and Transaction Medium
– Web 2.0: The Social and Co-created Web
– Web 3.0: The Semantic and Intelligent Web
– Web 4.0: The Mobile, Machine and Object Web
– Web 5.0: The Sensory-Emotive Web

For businesses, Web 3.0 promised differentiated insights from corporate and user-generated data. And more focus on transparency, "communicating and trust-building with multiple stakeholders". The main challenge for Web 4.0 proposed to be to "fully exploit the integration of physical and virtual objects with other user-generated content to create value" Web 5.0 projected to overcome "the lack of emotional awareness <that> limits the potential of the Web". As an example, the company can "sense neurological activity using non-invasive EEGs" [16].

The idea of the semantic web in different forms still was included in further research. In 2012 Sareh Aghaei et.al. described the web evolution as follows: "Web 1.0 as a web of information connections, Web 2.0 as a web of people connections, Web 3.0 as a web of knowledge connections and Web 4.0 as a web of intelligence connections." Focusing on specific techs, he summarized the future of "web as an information space <that> is moving toward using artificial intelligence techniques to be as a massive web of highly intelligent interactions in close future" [17].

Karan Patel continued this research in 2013 by comparing in more details Web 1.0 with 2.0 and 3.0, and adding Web 5.0 as still "an underground idea" that can be considered as "Symbionet web, decentralized" space where separate devices are interconnected and its sources are used to calculate data for a 3D virtual world with emotion recognition [18].

Russell Newman et al. in 2016 summarized the happenings of Web 2.0 as cloud computing, freemium and service marketplace business models, digital advertising, micro-transaction payments, social/casual cloud games. For Web 3.0 authors proposed such services as e-government, e-business, e-banking services, and improving virtual gaming [19].

The updated version of the infographic has been produced by Nils Mueller and TrendOne in 2017. They extended projections and timelines to 2030, placed differently named stages, summarized components, and made timelines as follows:

– The Web – since 1990 – WWW, search, e-mail, e-commerce
– Web 2.0 – since 2000 – Wikipedia & blogs, user-generated content, video & virals, BitTorrent, TOR

- 3D web – since 2005 – virtual worlds, e.g. Second Life, MMORPG e.g. WOW, head-mounted displays
- Outernet – since 2010 – Internet of Things (IoT), machine 2 machine (M2M), smart grid, wearables, augmented & virtual reality, Industry 4.0, digital twins, fog computing, blockchain
- Web of Thoughts – since 2015 – artificial intelligence, intelligent personal assistant, predictive intelligence, chatbots, voice processing, immediate translation, face identification, emotional intelligence, multipurpose robotics
- Bio Web – since 2020 – cyborgs, bioelectronics, artificial general intelligence, brain-computer interface, brain wave control, implants, wetware, active contact lenses, exoskeleton, digital tattoos, full-body prosthesis
- Super Intelligence – since 2030 – singularity, artificial life, self-replication machines, transhumanism, human enhancement, radical life extension, cryonics, artificial brain, whole brain emulation, brain scanning, brain upload, brain transplant, quantum computing, neuromorphic hardware, claytronics [20].

In 2019 Özgür Önday made an overview of previous authors and mentioned Web 6.0. Even its characteristics were described mainly in names of technologies owned by a corporate tech leader from the past century. He marked a great intention of where the web will go. "Web 5.0 is normal not just about helping people to be better at the things we would already be able to do; Web 5.0 is conceivably about helping people to do things which we can't as of now do… join Web for all to help individuals with uncommon needs" [21].

Khaleem Ibrahim in 2021 described Web 4.0 as making it "possible to connect all devices in a real and virtual world in real-time, such as services, virtual reality services, and natural language services where intelligent agents and sensors interact" after which emotionally sensitive machines are soon to come [22].

Another part worth mentioning is the development of neural science, nanotechnologies, and brain-computer interfaces. The Russian Federation stated Neuronet as the future of the Internet – Web 4.0 and made it one of the National Technological Initiatives with a 2035 year perspective. Neuronet market is projected as a total of 1800 bln USD and its effect covers 30% of services.

There are such sectors as NeuroCommunication, NeuroAssistants, NeuroEducation, NeuroEntertainment and Sport, NeuroMedTech, and NeuroPharma. Alongside Neuronet other markets and fields of innovation were described and named in analogy with the Internet: AeroNet, AutoNet, HealthNet, FoodNet, EnergyNet, TechNet, SafeNet, EduNet, SportNet, HomeNet, WearNet [23].

So the web transformed and there is a cyclic innovation we can observe. A variety of concepts arose and different technologies were in development simultaneously.

1.4   Implication of Web Stages to Specific Industries

While web staging came to scientific researchers, more specific industry studies started to appear about the edges of applying web staging development. For healthcare [24, 25], education [26–33], manufacturing [34–36] and tourism [37–40].

For the healthcare market, Donald Juzwishin in 2009 highlighted the importance of revealing political and social barriers for emerging opportunities of Web 2.0 and 3.0 in managing health-related information. [24] In the USA HIPAA compliance has been a standard for using personal data in telemedicine systems for a long time already. For the less sensitive information, as, for example, pharma training and education of staff and doctors – usage of modern communication and e-learning technologies is supposed to be the same well adopted as in other businesses [25].

In education, while questioning the Semantic Web and the future of research projects using web sources, Randall McClure in 2011 warned about a possible reduction in students' ability to make a choice and synthesize data. Yet believed that the web will solve this issue and suggested always questioning where the data comes from [26].

Other researchers considered web 2.0 and 3.0 tools as necessary to adopt among students to support lifelong learning and motivate it through the connection of learners with each other. They summarized such actions as accessing, managing, integration, evaluation, creation, and communication to be developed as basic elements of digital literacy [27].

Laura Varela-Candamio et al. in a study in 2014, noticed that a combination of web tools "for learning and social activities reinforces the academic attitudes related to collaborative tasks and group reports" [28].

Anastasia Atabekova et al. found that Web 3.0 non-formal learning using web tools provides more involving experience under study and proved that those tools are well suited for developing cross-curricular competencies [29].

Integration of web services for the group work, question & answer sessions, forming a course-based feed and tags, recording podcasts and videocasts, as well as applying AI to e-learning mechanics considered necessary to speed up the teaching/learning process and create a knowledge society [30].

By analogy with Web 4.0 and Industry 4.0, the concept of Education 4.0 is formed to reflect web integration into the education process [31]. An example of such environments for learning programming languages proved its efficiency [32].

Considering the era of sensory emotive Web 5.0 Diana Benito-Osorio et al. suggested higher education teachers focus on developing emotional competencies among learners to be more adaptable to new socio-professional contexts [33].

For manufacturing small and medium-sized enterprises (SMEs) H. Castro et al. in 2013 merged concepts of Web 3.0 development and meta-organization to form a ubiquitous virtual enterprise framework. "Meta-organizations comprise networks of firms or individuals not bound by authority based on employment". For the sides of the web, they marked social business, cloud computing, ubiquitous networking, open structure, adaptive information, adaptive service cloud, federated data, simulated intelligence. They believe that overdue of the limitations in IT integration among SMEs is the key to further sustainability [34].

Abdul Khan et al. in 2019 overviewed web evolution and mapped blockchain as an important part of it, which represents more social than technical vector of development. Even though it consists of a technically more complex way of working with databases, first, it solves the social issue of trust. They believed we are stepping into the Web 4.0 era and described Web 3.0 as "pure form and an example of the web which is using the database by altering the web" using artificial intelligence, Natural Language Processing, 3D graphics, virtual and augmented reality, big data and future prediction and advanced e-commerce. With the support of increasing speed of networks that will lead to emotional web 5.0. By analogy waves of blockchain evolution were described as 1.0 currency, 2.0 smart contracts, 3.0 DApps, 4.0 industry use [35].

Praveen Maddikunta et al. in 2021 overviewing enabling technologies for Industry 5.0. It was considered as the mass personalization stage and saw thought fields of application as intelligent healthcare, cloud manufacturing, supply chain management, manufacturing/production, education, human–cyber–physical systems, disaster management. Such technologies as edge computing, digital twins, collaborative robots, Internet of Everything, blockchain, 6G, extended reality, private mobile networks, and network slicing were considered as the most potential [36].

Tourism usage of web 2.0 and 4.0 tools in destination marketing were considered by Mariapina Trunfio and Maria Della Lucia in 2016. They considered best practices in digital marketing to promote the specific destination to tourists. Those include websites, social media, brand communities and e-participative platforms, smart tourism and augmented reality [37].

Application of netnography in tourism was considered by Rokhshad Tavakoli in 2018. With Web 3.0, "virtual, augmented and mixed realities allow customers/tourists to undergo highly immersive and multisensorial experiences… Web 4.0 is represented by phones' personal assistants, which may make tour guides obsolete in future holiday experiences". In Web 5.0, "emotional relationships between customers/tourists and machines could be explored" using "virtual reality headsets or/and brain wave detectors" and "the extremely immersive tourist experiences" [38].

The need for online maps was questioned in parallel with web evolution by Karol Król in 2020. While making an overview of map evolution, he noted that it is "difficult to say whether Web 6.0 will end up as one synthetic, self-conscious organism or a collective of "other identities, i.e., the personalities of individual devices integrated into the network" [39].

Effects of Web 4.0 and 5.0 technologies on tourist experience in Vietnam were measured by Nguyen Thien Duy et al. in 2020. Such tools as social robots, digitalized support by chatbots, IVRS support by robots, VR travel and sight-seeing experience enhancement, auto-data management by robots with AR were questioned. Even without great satisfaction, authors hope that "with their empathetic activities and information processing, promptness can win tourists loyalty in the long run" [40].

2 Materials and Method

More than 40 sources were considered in relation to the concept of web evolution. Chronological paper review of research articles, studies and conference publications, books, and media sources was placed at the introduction part. We considered both studies of the web staging concept itself, its implementation in other areas such as healthcare, education, tourism and manufacturing, and made parallels with other staging concepts that applied 1.0 2.0 3.0 4.0 5.0 type of name pointing.

Selection and aggregation methods were used to build projections for the dates and timelines of technology development. One of the aims of our research is placing reasonable expectations on the timelines of technology development. To complete that aim we challenged ourselves not to increase or add a next number of stages. But rather shorten stages to show how some technologies are going to collaborate with others at a time.

While considering different authors contributions, we paid attention to and asked ourselves questions:

– What is the end vision and description of the web authors suggest?
– What's the attribute of the web that will be important in transforming the paradigm of usage?
– How do authors segment web development into steps and milestones?

As a result, we formed our concept within 4 stages – Web 1.0, Web 2.0, Web 3.0, Web 4.0.

Methods of analysis of open statistical data have been used to place specific parts and match technologies with the stage of web technology development and diffusion. Synthesis of data was applied to fill in gaps in comparative fields for the Web technology development milestones Web 1.0 -> 2.0 -> all named the next web or Web 3.0, 4.0, 5.0, 6.0.

Comparison analysis was made to add details on specifics of every wave of Internet and web innovation.

The Internet, like any innovation, develops through technological cycles. So far more than 30 years have passed since mass adoption began, and we can not only see results but describe where it goes further.

Relying on innovation waves theory, we added missed timelines in Internet cycle development and full-fill descriptions of some core characteristics we believe are important to account for at every stage.

Thinking about waves of Internet development, we first noticed if any further projection is really changing the technical–economic paradigm or just aligned with some adjustment and improvement of the previous context.

We think it's necessary to note that the web isn't just technical but the same social system. As a socio-technical system, it has a huge effect on the technical-economic paradigm and likely is the way of changing last.

Also, we paid attention to the lack of timing projections in studies, which yet made the picture hard to understand and review. Thus in our study we paid to it the most attention, tracking the dates mentioned by researchers and applying innovation waves/cycles theory.

By that we mean we considered the length of:

- Kondratiev waves describing change of technological basis that last 40–60 years;
- Kuznets swing cycle caused by infrastructural investment that lasts 15–25 years;
- Juglar cycle influenced by investment in fixed capital of new businesses that lasts 7–11 years.

In 2020, the Sixth Kondratiev wave was predicted to begin. Structure changes connected with nano, bio, medical, additive, robots, information and cognitive technologies were described in works of Kondratiev (1925), Korotaev, Grinin, Akaev, Cirel (2002, 2010, 2011, 2012, 2013, 2016, 2017) [41, 42].

To review the innovation paradigm of the Web, we'll consider three logistic trajectories described by M. Hirooka in 2006 [43, 44]:

Technology – includes scientific achievements and further update

Development – covers commercial products launch and market creation

Diffusion – fact usage of technology among people

Following the mathematical explanation, Hirooka visualized those logistic trajectories as S-shaped fractals affected one on the other. This will help us place all Web stages on the timeline.

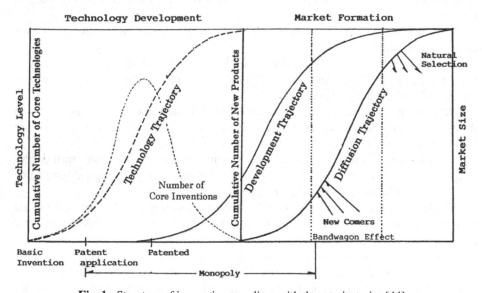

Fig. 1. Structure of innovation paradigm with three trajectories [44]

The same wave shape is used in Hype cycle research that Garthner makes on emerging technologies. This picture should help us to feel the current point of view – at the edge of Web 2.0 and 3.0 – most of the technologies related either to AI or blockchain and innovating through trust growth.

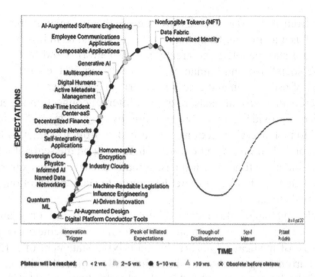

Fig. 2. Hype Cycle for Emerging Technologies, Aug 2021, Gartner [45]

3   Results

To pick up the end point and the basis for the next technology paradigm, we picked the most repeated direction of web evolution projections. Most of the researchers came at some point of web staging – emotional connectivity that would be possible to realize through a remote Internet connection. Emotional web matches with the concept of Neuronet, and nano-robots management systems applied to cognitive fields. That's likely the basis of the next big shift and we align this stage with Web 4.0 tag.

Our observations on the AR glasses market confirmed the statement that just displaying pictures on wearable devices isn't enough to create mass adoption and diffusion. Such products as Microsoft Hololens have some usage in manufacturing, while Magic Leap met difficulties with sales after their first release. The hardware market is harder to challenge due to increased risks of failure in finance/stock management. Thus, we put that as the last part of web development, which is shifting socio-technical paradigms. Web 4.0 likely will be a massive thing once truly interactive management is launched, though brain-connected interfaces and in emergence with AR/VR glasses/headsets.

Clearing out the path to this stage, we can see the convergence of all already developed fields of technologies. Even though the web3 tag is widely used in the crypto community, not only blockchain is the driver. First, those are Artificial Intelligence and Machine Learning technologies. And convergence of those two fields with each other and already existing web infrastructure.

By the shift from Web 1.0 to Web 2.0 we can see that the main increased parameter is interactivity of user actions and data management that results in involving consumers, customers, just ordinary people to co-create digital platforms and feel emotional connectivity. So the social part and human capital are drivers of the shift which matches with the concept of user-driven and community-driven economies.

Two parameters that we can measure are the Internet connection speed that infrastructure holders can provide and time spent online by the average individual user. Both parameters tend to increase. Connection speed transfers from less than 64 Kbps to up to Terabites per second. And time spent online is increasing on the scale of a few hours up to the whole day and night time. The last case already exists with an example of passive devices like rings that can track and share data about the health conditions of users and analyze data in real-time.

While developing nano and neuro technologies, we'll see only an increase in HealthTech dependence from web infrastructure. Such telemedicine concepts combined with the nano-size of medical robots are the underlying statement of a 120-years life. Accounting for current progress that may be realistically achieved within the current century. As the main technology shift ahead is related to healthcare, and the web comes to be a cross-cutting technology and the basis, reasonable questions of its security, privacy, reliability should have a place.

Seeing how companies can manipulate the data due to their commercial or political interests, the accents of the crypto-community on the need for decentralized authority and security become as rational as ever. Even currently, we massively rely on cloud-based services that share data with our mobile devices from remote servers, and our mobile devices tend to increase in processing capacity. With increase in the calculating power of personal devices and Internet connection speed – decentralized server architecture will be the one mostly used, combining both personal server-device and remote-provider servers for some parts of the data. In such systems, the core decision on sharing data will move to the user side. That's especially important when we oversee that data related to real-time health processes of our organism, and brain activity specifically, is collected and engaged. Rarely does one agree to share all the data on their brain activity with an attention-based commercial advertising enterprise, or with a government. Yet this trust issue is one of the same challenges faced by technically programmed platforms using both open and decentralized architecture and machine learning algorithms.

What technology providers are working on – results on diffusion of the technology. So the question of any marketer is always about how to easily explain the values of the products and vision. While observing previous studies about Web stages, we found a lot of noisy additions or specific technical abbreviations. So, our intent for the stage's description was to place basic terms and describe key value form for user, core action, relation nature, digitized process and commercial attention gainer.

You can overview comparative table with attributes description below:

Table 1. Attributes of web innovation [authors' work]

Attribute	Web 1.0	Web 2.0	Web 3.0	Web 4.0
Internet connection speed	GSM, 64 Kbps	3G–4G, 1 Mbps–1 Gbps	5G, 50 Mbps–20 Gbps	6G, 100 Gbps–1 Tbps
Time spent online	Less than 4 h	2–8 h	4–16 h	12–24 h
Value for users	Website, telephone, static data	Social communication	Machine learning and blockchain, Internet of Things	Emotional Web, Neuronet, eXtended reality
Core User Actions	Read Buy	Read Write Consume	Access Share Predict Delegate	Feel Act Augment
Relation	Business to Customer	Users to users to business	Communities to Web to Communities to Web	Human – Interface – Web – Communities
Process	Data sourcing	Communication	Learning and earning	Managing and engaging
Attention gainer	E-commerce companies and info websites, forums, desktops	Social networks, communities and mobile	Meta organizations, distributed AI, platforms and robots	Wearable devices, neuro interfaces and XR glasses/helmets

Moving to timing projection, we'd like to note that most of the researchers missed this part of staging – and those who did – overestimated short distance and underestimated what could be done for a few dozens of years. Basically, commercial planning rarely moves further than 10–25 years, which matches with Kuznets swing cycle. Yet for strategic planning and long-term investing it is better to have a maximum helicopter view and recognize the nature of social transformation and technology diffusion perspectives. With this reason we show the projected length of 3 core logistic trajectories for technology, development and its diffusion. Every trajectory in fact affects each other and can easily take up to several Kuznets cycles – thus we take as a length period of 40–70 years depending on when we can observe the fact usage and what complicity is underlying particular technology diffusion.

To show those trajectories on a timeline – we've built projections with graphs as suggested by Hirooks in S-shaped curves. 3 trajectories placed on the timeline from 1960 where the roots of the Internet came from to the 2080 till which active diffusion of Neuronet can happen. This fractal picture below can give some feeling on the developing field of digital communication and web technologies. What we'd like to mark is the increased time of initial technology and last diffusion stages. Every geography may

Table 2. Milestones of web innovation and timelines (projected) [authors' work]

Years (projections)	Web 1.0	Web 2.0	Web 3.0	Web 4.0
Technology trajectory	1960–2010	2000–(2030)	1990–(2040)	1980–(2050)
Development trajectory	1980–2020	2000–(2040)	2005–(2050)	2010–(2060)
Diffusion trajectory	1990–(2030)	2005–(2050)	2015–(2060)	(2025)–(2070)

build its own map of timing based on current social digitalization. Still, the upper half of this comparative graph – is the population of a planet where the Internet connection isn't the priority for survival. So the world is likely to receive further run of technocratic constructions upside the existing networks already used by half of Earth's population.

Combining web innovation paradigm trajectories with Kondratiev waves, we see the cross-cutting of technologies on the economic cycle. The same can be adjusted up to different geographies. In our example we took the wave cycle of 40–50 years and placed 3 waves over the timeline of web evolution. First Kondratiev wave is connected to computer development (previously – electronic and radio); the second wave within our horizon is connected with mobile and Internet development; and the third with neuro and nano sciences.

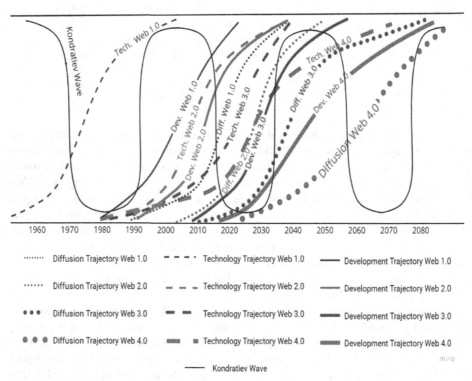

Fig. 3. Web innovation paradigm on timeline [authors' work]

4 Discussion

Ones describe the evolution of the web in pair with technologies it consists of. Others focus on the affection of web technologies known also as digital transformation, in particular fields like education, tourism, or healthcare. The influence of web technologies on social transformation is discussed in relation to business communication and virtual organization and community construction. Yet neither social effects, not a particular technology or field of appliance, were taken as the angle of our review. Any other researcher might have other points and insights, so we welcome the discussion and reuse of applied methods.

We tried to put down attributes of what web development milestones like Web 3.0, 4.0, 5.0 and 6.0 can include and form a shorter concept. First, to show interconnection between technologies and its diffusion. Second to form projections for the investment and organization cycles.

Another important limitation is the geographical implication of timelines and milestones. Internet usage is tend to cultural habits and particular service marketing campaigns and popularity. One service can be less or more popular among the same type of auditory in different counties. For example, Facebook – which is a friends-and-family-oriented social network in western countries, in Russia (mostly around Moscow) has been used as a platform for commercial contacts (like LinkedIn). And the greatest limitation is that half of the planet is not yet connected to the Internet.

We found that customer value became a declared priority, yet most studies focused either on business or government benefits, but not on customer value generation and retirement. That's another limitation that can be overworked in further researchers.

Recent studies consider various concepts of Internet, and web technologies separately – blockchain, Internet-of-Things, Augmented Reality, wearable devices. We analyzed their interconnection between each other and placed it within one stage as Web 3.0. What will be the way of all those technologies in development of Neuronet and how it will be approached – only the future shows. But we took the effort to consider some root studies to place overlaps on timing projections of every logistic trajectory. Those starting points can vary and are not strongly attached to the specific invention, but to the author's aggregated understanding of technology's trajectory. This may be the field of other studies for every separate innovation.

5 Conclusion

In the studies of social effects caused by the Web – a lot of other parts and projection came to life. Interactivity and connectivity already cover cell phones, TVs, cars, gaming devices, and many consumer electronic devices. Nowadays, we have many personal and home devices interconnected through Internet of Things (IoT) protocols – like vacuum cleaners, refrigerators, dishwashers. Personal devices spread out to watches, rings, and glasses.

Subscription-based business models known as Software-as-a-Service have become a massive thing in startups. Its main goal is to form recurring revenue through providing a convenient specialized self-service web platform.

On the other side, free services as most social platforms are, compete by their unique Machine Learning models built using massive user-generated data sets. They monetize through an advertising model. In such systems, users are the main creators of content on the platform. They build communities and adopt self-moderation.

Most of the current products work on multiple platforms and from any device and have an intuitive interface design. IT engineers and workers have become a class as hundreds of thousands of them are working in web development.

We can definitely say that the Proof of Concept, Minimal Viable Product and Proof of Value stages for the web as a whole are passed successfully. One can observe all the advantages and disadvantages and 3 waves of web evolution. Yet it's only the beginning and more pivots in history can happen during further technology development and diffusion. Competition on the market won't ever stop. New companies and organizations will be adding new things to the top of the list. Yet we see the common stake in bringing greater innovation into more fields that at the end of the day should make the lives of many people easier and better.

We aggregated more than 40 scientific sources to form the concept of 4 stages for the web development. While putting timelines projection, we applied innovation cycle and wave theories of Kondratiev, Kuznets and Juglar and recent works related to global economies development and economic waves. We confirmed direction and chosen topics through commercial companies' observation and practical evidence in attempts of different technologies to enter the market.

We describe core attributes of 4 web stages regarding core value form, user action, time spent online and connection speed, attention gainer and its relation with user as well as core value mining process.

To form web innovation, we mapped a graph of 3 logistic trajectories for every stage of web – technology, development and diffusion to see how they overlap each other and be able to place proper innovation at the right time. Overall timing perspective was taken as of 120 years ~ 60 years above and behind from current date.

Acknowledgements. The research was partially funded by the Ministry of Science and Higher Education of the Russian Federation under the strategic academic leadership program 'Priority 2030' (agreement 075-15-2021-1333, dated 30 September 2021).

References

1. The 100 largest companies in the world by market capitalization in 2021. https://www.statista.com/statistics/263264/top-companies-in-the-world-by-market-capitalization/. Accessed 6 Dec 2021
2. Internet growth statistics (2021). https://www.Internetworldstats.com/emarketing.htm. Accessed 6 Dec 2021
3. Berners-Lee, T.: "The Semantic Web" (PDF). Scientific American. S2CID 32015696. Archived from the original (PDF) on October 10, 2017. 13 March 2008. https://web.archive.org/web/20171010210556/https://pdfs.semanticscholar.org/566c/1c6bd366b4c9e07fc37eb372771690d5ba31.pdf. Accessed 6 Dec 2021

4. Blog post: Gartner names Google a leader in 2021 Magic Quadrant for Cloud AI Developer Services report, 2021. https://cloud.google.com/blog/products/ai-machine-learning/google-cloud-a-leader-in-gartner-mq-for-cloud-ai-developer-services. Accessed 6 Dec 2021
5. DiNucci, D.: Fragmented Future. (PDF). Print. **53**(4), 221–222 (1999). http://darcyd.com/fragmented_future.pdf
6. O'Reilly, T.: What is Web 2.0—Design patterns and business models for the next generation of software (2005). http://www.oreillynet.com/pub/a/oreilly/tim/news/2005/09/30/what-is-web-20.html. Accessed 6 Dec 2021
7. Individuals using the Internet (% of population). International Telecommunication Union (ITU) World Telecommunication/ICT Indicators Database. https://data.worldbank.org/indicator/IT.NET.USER.ZS. Accessed 6 Dec 2021
8. Cumulative number of monthly Facebook product users as of 3rd quarter 2021. https://www.statista.com/statistics/947869/facebook-product-mau/
9. Zuckerberg, M.: Founder's Letter (2021). https://www.facebook.com/story.php?story_fbid=10114026953010521&id=4. Accessed 6 Dec 2021
10. Khor, Z., Marsh, P.: Life online: The Web in 2020. A Study by the Social Issues Research Centre on behalf of Rackspace Managed Hosting (2006). http://www.sirc.org/publik/web2020.pdf
11. Spivack, N..: Web 3.0 -- The best official definition imaginable. Blog Post (2007). https://novaspivack.typepad.com/nova_spivacks_weblog/2007/10/web-30----the-a.html Accessed 6 Dec 2021
12. O'Reilly, T.: Today's Web 3.0 Nonsense Blogstorm. Blog post (2007). http://radar.oreilly.com/archives/2007/10/web-30-semantic-web-web-20.html. Accessed 6 Dec 2021
13. Mueller, N.: The web expansion – from web of things to web of thoughts. TrendOne (2008). https://blog.trendone.com/wp-C2A0content/uploads/2009/04/smartweb_web_50_evolution_confidential_-v004.pdf. Accessed 6 Dec 2021
14. Abbate, J.: The Internet: global evolution and challenges. In: Frontiers of Knowledge. Madrid: BBVA (2008). https://www.bbvaopenmind.com/en/articles/the-Internet-global-evolution-and-challenges/
15. Newitz, A.: Web 3.0. New Sci. **197**(2647), 42–43 (2008). https://doi.org/10.1016s0262-4079(08)60674-0
16. Kambil, A.: What is your Web 5.0 strategy? J. Bus. Strat. **29**(6), 56–58 (2008). https://doi.org/10.1108/02756660810917255
17. Aghaei, S., Nematbakhsh, M.A., Farsani, H.K.: Evolution of the World Wide Web : From Web 1.0 to Web 4.0. Int. J. Web Seman. Technol. **3**(1), 1–10 (2012). https://doi.org/10.5121/ijwest.2012.3101
18. Patel, K.: Introduced with Web 1.0 to recent web 5.0 – A Survey Paper. Increment. J. World Wide Web **3,** 10 (2013)
19. Newman, R., Chang, V., Walters, R.J., Wills, G.B.: Web 2.0—the past and the future. Int. J. Inf. Manage. **36**(4), 591–598 (2016). https://doi.org/10.1016/j.ijinfomgt.2016.03.010
20. Mueller, N.: The web expansion 1990–2030 (2017). TrendOne. https://blog.trendone.com/wp-content/uploads/2017/10/WEB_EXPANSION_TRENDONE.pdf. Accessed 6 Dec 2021
21. Önday, Ö.: Web 6.0: Journey from Web 1.0 To Web 6.0. J. Media Manag (2019). https://doi.org/10.47363/JMM/2019(1)102.
22. Ibrahim, KA.: Evolution of the Web: from Web 1.0 to 4.0. Qubahan Acad. J. **1**(3), 20–28 (2021). https://doi.org/10.48161/qaj.v1n3a75
23. Roadmap of NeuroNet (2021). https://nti2035.ru/docs/DK_neuronet_2021.pdf. Accessed 6 Dec 2021
24. Juzwishin, D.W.M.: Political, policy and social barriers to health system interoperability: emerging opportunities of Web 2.0 and 3.0. Healthc. Manag. Forum **22**(4), 6–10 (2009). https://doi.org/10.1016/s0840-4704(10)60136-6

25. Basset, H.: Enterprise 2.0 and Web 3.0. From Science 2.0 to Pharma 3.0, pp. 169–193 (2013). https://doi.org/10.1016/B978-1-84334-709-5.50006-5
26. McClure, R.: WritingResearchWriting: the semantic web and the future of the research project. Comput. Compos. **28**(4), 315–326 (2011). https://doi.org/10.1016/j.compcom.2011.09.003
27. Loureiro, A., Messias, I., Barbas, M.: Embracing Web 2.0 & 3.0 tools to support lifelong learning - let learners connect. Procedia. Soc. Behav. Sci. **46**, 532–537 (2012). https://doi.org/10.1016/j.sbspro.2012.05.155
28. Candamio, L.., Novo-Corti, V., Barreiro-Gen, M.: Do studies level and age matter in learning and social relationship in the assessment of web 3.0? A case study for 'digital natives' in Spain. Comput. Hum. Behav. **30**, 595–605 (2013). ISSN 0747-5632, https://doi.org/10.1016/j.chb.2013.07.048. https://www.sciencedirect.com/science/article/pii/S0747563213002872
29. Atabekova, A., Belousov, A., Shoustikova, T.: Web 3.0-based non-formal learning to meet the third millennium education requirements: university students' perceptions. Procedia Soc. Behav. Sci. **214**, 511–519 (2015). ISSN:1877-0428, https://doi.org/10.1016/j.sbspro.2015.11.754. (https://www.sciencedirect.com/science/article/pii/S1877042815061091)
30. Pattnayak, J., Pattnaik, S.: Integration of web services with E-learning for knowledge society. Procedia Comput. Sci. **92**, 155–160 (2016). https://doi.org/10.1016/j.procs.2016.07.340
31. Demartini, C., Benussi, L.: Do Web 4.0 and industry 4.0 imply education X.0? IT Prof **19**(3), 4–7 (2017). https://doi.org/10.1109/MITP.2017.47
32. Cabada, R.Z., Estrada, M.L.B., Hernández, F.G., Bustillos, R.O., Reyes-García, C.A.: An affective and Web 3.0-based learning environment for a programming language. Telemat. Inf. **35**(3), 611–628 (2018). ISSN: 0736-5853, https://doi.org/10.1016/j.tele.2017.03.005. (https://www.sciencedirect.com/science/article/pii/S0736585316304907)
33. Benito-Osorio, D., Peris-Ortiz, M., Armengot, C.R., et al.: Web 5.0: the future of emotional competences in higher education. Glob. Bus. Perspect. **1**, 274–287 (2013). https://doi.org/10.1007/s40196-013-0016-5
34. Castro, H., Putnik, G., Cruz-Cunha, M.M., Ferreira, L., Shah, V., Alves, C.: Meta-organization and manufacturing Web 3.0 for ubiquitous virtual enterprise of manufacturing SMEs: a framework. Procedia CIRP **12**, 396–401 (2013). https://doi.org/10.1016/j.procir.2013.09.068
35. Khan, A.G., et al.: A journey of WEB and Blockchain towards the Industry 4.0: an overview. In: 2019 International Conference on Innovative Computing (ICIC) (2019). https://doi.org/10.1109/icic48496.2019.8966700
36. Reddy, P.V., et al.: Industry 5.0: a survey on enabling technologies and potential applications. J. Ind. Inf. Integr. **2021**, 100257 (2021). ISSN:2452-414X, https://doi.org/10.1016/j.jii.2021.100257. https://www.sciencedirect.com/science/article/pii/S2452414X21000558
37. Trunfio, M., Lucia, M.: Toward Web 5.0 in Italian regional destination marketing. Symph. Emerg. Iss. Manag. **2**, 60–75 (2016). https://doi.org/10.4468/2016.2.07trunfio.dellalucia
38. Tavakoli, R., Mura, P.: Netnography in tourism – beyond Web 2.0. Ann. Tour. Res. **73**, 190–192 (2018). ISSN 0160-7383, https://doi.org/10.1016/j.annals.2018.06.002. (https://www.sciencedirect.com/science/article/pii/S0160738318300616)
39. Król, K.: Evolution of online mapping: from web 1.0 to web 6.0. Geomat. Landmanagd Landsc. **1**, 33–51 (2020). https://doi.org/10.15576/GLL/2020.1.33
40. Duy, N.T.: Study on the role of web 4.0 and 5.0 in the sustainable tourism ecosystem of Ho Chi Minh City, Vietnam. Sustainability **12**(17) (2020). https://doi.org/10.3390/su12177140
41. Akaev, A., Korotayev, A.V.: Global economic dynamics of the forthcoming years: a forecast. Struct. Dyns. **10**(1) (2021). https://doi.org/10.5070/SD9101033473 https://escholarship.org/uc/item/6r84f1b7
42. Grinin, L., Grinin, A., Korotayev, A.: The MANBRIC-technologies in the forthcoming technological revolution. Industry 4.0 - entrepreneurship and structural change in the new digital landscape: what is coming on along with the fourth industrial revolution, pp. 243–261 (2017). https://doi.org/10.1007/978-3-319-49604-7_13

43. Hirooka, M.: Innovation Dynamism and Economic Growth. A Nonlinear Perspective. Edward Elgar, Cheltenham (2006). https://doi.org/10.4337/9781845428860
44. Hirooka, M.: Complexity in Discrete Innovation Systems. Emergence: Complexity and Organization. 30 June 2006. https://doi.org/10.emerg/10.17357.d8cf2da38bebf8d00ec24a23ebdb3758, https://cjournal.emergentpublications.com/article/complexity-in-discrete-innovation-systems/. Accessed 16 Feb 2022
45. Hype Cycle for Emerging Technologies (2021). https://www.gartner.com/en/newsroom/press-releases/2021-08-23-gartner-identifies-key-emerging-technologies-spurring-innovation-through-trust-growth-and-change. Accessed 16 Feb 2022

Digitalization of Transport Communications as a Tool for Improving the Quality of Life

Elena Korchagina[1] (ID), Larisa Desfonteines[1]([✉]) (ID), Samrat Ray[2] (ID), and Natalia Strekalova[3] (ID)

[1] Peter the Great St. Petersburg Polytechnic University,
29 Polytechnicheskaya Street, St. Petersburg 195251, Russia
`lja2@yandex.ru`
[2] Maulana Abul Kalam Azad University of Technology, Kolkata, West Bengal, India
[3] Herzen State Pedagogical University of Russia, St. Petersburg, Russia

Abstract. One of the factors of improving the quality of life of the population is the digitalization of transport communications. The novelty and practical value of the research is connected with the combination of the development of the transport system in various natural conditions with the use of digital technologies to achieve an optimal solution. The article discusses the possibilities of using modern digital technologies for the transport system of the Russian Federation related to territorial, natural conditions and demographic characteristics. The purpose of the study was to prove that the transport system can become the basis for improving the quality of life of the population in case of its development, taking into account the unique territorial, natural and demographic characteristics of the country. As a promising direction in the development of the transport system, it is proposed to use digital technologies that ensure the convenience and comfort of using the transport system for citizens while maintaining environmental safety. To achieve this goal, the research used the methods of analysis of scientific research given in literary sources; the method of comparative analysis of statistical data on the use of various modes of transport in the Russian Federation and the EU countries; the method of comparative analysis of territorial, natural and demographic characteristics of the regions of Russia. As a topic for future research, we can suggest the use of the capabilities of modern digital technologies for the development of transport communications in areas with difficult natural conditions.

Keywords: Transport communications · Climate · Modes of transport · Digitalization · Quality of life

1 Introduction

Scientific studies are aimed at improving the quality of life of citizens with the help of an affordable transport system. At the same time, the concept of quality of life is associated with the preservation of the natural environment. Therefore, scientific approaches to the creation of an innovative transport system face contradictions. On the one hand, the key factor of improving the quality of life is improving people mobility. On the other hand, the

© Springer Nature Switzerland AG 2022
D. Rodionov et al. (Eds.): SPBPU IDE 2021, CCIS 1619, pp. 22–34, 2022.
https://doi.org/10.1007/978-3-031-14985-6_2

quality of life is associated with the concept of environmental friendliness of the habitat, which is ensured by reducing the destructive transport impact on the environment. A retrospective study of the resolution of the contradiction between technological progress in the transport sector and political goals was conducted on the example of the European Strategy for Sustainable and Reasonable Mobility 2020 [1]. The study helps to identify problems in solving transport problems at the political level. E. Ballantyne and G. Heron propose to create a single plan for all commercial air transportation, corresponding to the unified transport strategy of the northern region of Great Britain. The results of surveys and interviews with UK transport operators show the positive aspects of using a single strategy [2]. The importance of state regulation of airport activities is great in the context of declining economic, social and environmental sustainability in the region [3]. A study of transport characteristics (cost, transit time) and route choice between Ireland and continental Europe has showed the political decisions influence at the state level [4]. The role of public policy for restoring the public transport activity, railways and aviation after the Covid-19 pandemic is associated with the creation of conditions for innovation in the field of transport technologies [5]. A study of aviation in 10 Southeast Asian countries made it possible to predict the development of air transport and transport hubs of aviation routes using a growth expectation map that reflects a wide range of growth types, where individual countries and their public policies (Indonesia, the Philippines and Malaysia) play a leading role [6].

Changes in the urban transport system are associated with awareness of the city residents' responsibility for violating the ecological balance. In this regard, some citizens tend to live in the suburbs, where the environment is better, but there is a problem with transport mobility [7]. The study of factors influencing the demand for certain types of transport reveals the need of different transport types integration in the urban environment [8]. Some researchers consider fuel cell electric vehicles as the basis for the transport sector development [9].

Some researchers pay attention to the creation of a monitoring system as an instrument of EU transport policy to support transport research and innovation [10]. Radical solutions for the replacement of cars in urban conditions are proposed. Opportunities for the development of electric buses in Poland are considered as an alternative to traditional public transport [11]. 90% of transport-related emissions will be eliminated by 2050 for the European Union climate improvement. The Hyperloop transport system project is aimed at achieving this result, as the fastest and most environmentally friendly transport [12, 13]. Another area pursuing the goal of reducing emissions into the atmosphere is the project of unmanned aerial vehicles that will be used in the transport infrastructure of smart cities for monitoring and road safety [14], passengers and cargo transportation between airports and destinations [15], emergency medical services [16, 17]. An interesting direction in the urban transport future development is the concept of urban air mobility with a hybrid and fully electric motor, the so-called air taxis [18, 19] and the creation of an unmanned AirMetro to reduce the urban public transport congestion [20]. At the same time, there are doubts about the absolute positive impact of unmanned vehicles for individual use in the urban environment [21, 22]. The unmanned vehicles are also being considered for maritime transport. They can be used in the marine rescue search system or mine-fighting objectives in both above and underwater devices [23, 24].

The analysis of literary sources allowed us to identify the following areas of research:

- development of the urban transport system and its recovery after the Covid-19 pandemic;
- reducing the negative transport impact on the environment;
- using new technologies to create eco-friendly modes of transport;
- development of ultra-high-speed transport routes for the passengers and cargo transportation;
- creating conditions for the transport safe use.

The purpose of the study is to substantiate the main directions of various vehicles development in the conditions of the Russian Federation for improving the population quality of life.

To achieve this goal, the following tasks were set:

- to consider the features of various modes of transport in the Russian Federation;
- to identify the features of the vehicles operation in the territory of Russia;
- to determine the priorities and prospects for the transport system development in connection with the main characteristics of the operation of transport various modes.

2 Materials and Methods

The main hypothesis of the study is the assumption that the transport system of the Russian Federation can be the basis for improving the population quality of life, developing in accordance with the unique territorial, natural and demographic characteistics of the country, which should be combined with global requirements for the prospects of the transport industry. To confirm the hypothesis put forward, the following methods were used in the study:

- analysis of the scientific research results given in open literary sources;
- comparative analysis of scientific concepts and hypotheses about the transport of the future;
- comparative analysis of statistical data in the Russian Federation;
- comparative analysis of statistical data in the European Union;
- comparative analysis of territorial, natural and demographic features of Russian regions;
- analysis of global trends in the transport development.

The study used the statistical data on the transport development in the Russian Federation and European Union countries, statistical research data presented in the scientific literature, statistical data of the Russian Federation Official Statistics Service.

3   Results

All countries recognize the need for changes not only in the transport systems, but also in the vehicles themselves. The relevance of the changes is related to technological and digital changes in the life of society and the requirements for improving the quality of life as conditions for the future existence of mankind [25, 26]. Improving the quality of life is associated with the development of new technologies in transport, which will ensure high mobility of people, reduce travel time, reduce energy consumption and change the types of energy themselves [27–29]. The Russian Federation is characterized by features that determine the main directions of development of the transport structure:

1. A huge spatial territory creates difficulties for the transport infrastructure development. The Russian Federation is the largest country in the world. It occupies one-seventh of the Earth's landmass. Most regions of the country are located in the northern part of the continent and are characterized by the winter period significant duration. The geographical location determines the features of the vehicles use and the creation of transport hubs. The difficulties of creating transport routes are primarily associated with large territories and a harsh climate [30].
2. The nature of the country is very diverse, which creates problems in uniform requirements for both the operational characteristics of transport and infrastructure. The regions of the Far North have extremely complex natural conditions that require single, unique technical developments, the implementation of which requires large financial costs [31].
3. The analysis of the country's labor resources is determined by the peculiarities of demography [32, 33]. Despite the large territorial extent, the areas are populated unevenly. In addition, taking the first place in terms of territory, the country is only in ninth place in terms of population. This fact determines the problems for areas with difficult climatic conditions.

The peculiarities of Russia determine of development of transport. In order to create and implement the main vectors of the country's transport system development, a strategy of the Russian Federation Unified backbone transport network was built.

The transport system of regions with northern climatic conditions is considered separately, but these regions should also provide high mobility for the population.

The percentage of cargo turnover by type of transport is shown in Fig. 1.

Figure 1 shows that 87% of the total cargo turnover is accounted for by rail transport. In second place in terms of cargo turnover is road transport, 9.2%. The lowest percentage relates to air transport - 0.2%. The predominance of rail transport is explained by the territorial characteristics of the Russian Federation, the need to transport large loads over long distances in minimal time intervals. The low percentage of the use of inland waterway transport is surprising - 2%, in the presence of a large number of navigable river routes. In China, this figure is 7%, in Germany - 8%. Perhaps this is the result of a decrease in cargo turnover as a whole. In any case, the use of inland water transport resources is promising for providing remote territories with the necessary cargo.

The dynamics of cargo turnover of the Russian Federation is shown in Fig. 2.

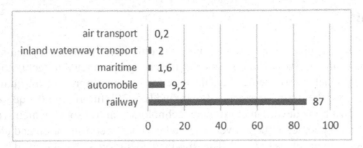

Fig. 1. Percentage of cargo turnover by type of transport

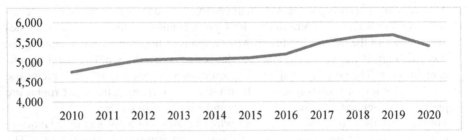

Fig. 2. Dynamics of cargo turnover from 2010 to 2020

As shown in Fig. 2, cargo turnover decreased in 2020 compared to 2019. The decline can probably be explained by the consequences of the covid-19 pandemic, which have reduced transportation of all types worldwide. This is a temporary decrease therefore it can be assumed that lifting of restrictions will increase cargo turnover. Automobile cargo transportation is used in Russia to deliver goods over short distances. The average distance of cargo transportation by road is 48 km. During the pandemic, this type of transport proved to be in demand for the delivery of goods in local territories. Sea transport was in demand in international transportation and cargo turnover by this type of transport was not subject to serious restrictions, since the main cargo is industrial raw materials.

The citizens' quality of life is ensured not only by optimizing the logistics chains of cargo delivery, but also by increasing mobility, ensuring the availability of territorial zones. For the Russian Federation, which has large territorial distances, this is a difficult task, which requires new technological developments to solve. The mobility of the population involves minimizing the time to move from one point to another. To reduce travel time and increase the accessibility of destinations, you can use the capabilities of high-speed railways. The introduction of new high-speed rail technologies is currently being used in providing commuter crossings. As an example, high-speed suburban trains "Swallow", "Ivolga" creation of a unified system of suburban and urban rail transport in Moscow.

As shown in Fig. 3, the main intercity transport in Russia is aviation and railways. This is due to the fact that air transport provides rapid movement over long distances compared to cars and rail transport. The percentage of passenger traffic by air is 63.3%

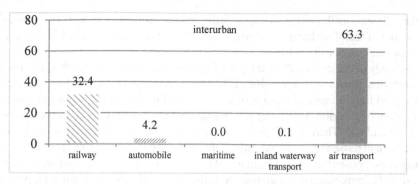

Fig. 3. Structure of passenger transportation by type of transport in 2020 (%)

of the total number of passenger traffic. This is almost 2 times more than passenger transportation by rail (32.4%).

It should be noted the low percentage of the use of river transport for passenger transportation. Despite the natural conditions, the presence of navigable rivers and channels connecting the territories, inland river transport is not used much. This type of transport is more often used for tourist and sightseeing purposes, for river cruises and river excursions. However, given the natural potential, it is possible to use the capabilities of this type of transport for passenger transportation of local importance.

The comparison of statistical data on the use of public transport by Russian citizens for the last 10 years has a significant importance. Figure 4 shows the dynamics of the public transport use.

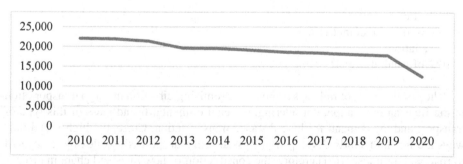

Fig. 4. Transportation of passengers by public transport from 2010 to 2020 (millions of people)

The use of public transport has been declining since 2010. The use of personal transport is preferable. The use of a personal car is considered an indicator of well-being and prosperity in Russia. Therefore, citizens seek to purchase a personal car in accordance with their own financial situation. From 2010 to 2020, the number of personal passenger cars increased by 30.8%. Thus, there are 307 cars per 1,000 people in Russia in 2020, in 2010 this figure was 240 cars per 1,000 people. Relative to European countries, this indicator is lower, which indicates the probability of growth of personal cars owners in Russia. On the one hand, this indicator indicates an increase in the quality of life of

Russian citizens, as the welfare and, accordingly, the number of owners of vehicles has increased. On the other hand, cars are sources of air pollution, especially in large cities where population density is high.

The study of the use of different types of transport in Russia for freight and passenger transportation allows us to generalize. Long-distance cargo transportation is carried out by rail, road freight transportation is mainly used within the region or for transportation to a neighboring region. Passenger transportation between regions and cities is carried out by air and rail. There is insufficient use of the potential of inland river transport for both cargo and passenger transportation within the country. The territorial features of the country presupposes the predominant use of rail transport and aviation to connect regions and cities. The percentage of cargo transportation by aviation is small, but aviation is used in critical situations: to provide especially important cargo for the restoration and repair of technical facilities, for the rapid transportation of medicines and medical equipment. The potential of aviation for cargo transportation has not yet been exhausted.

4 Discussion

The ecological situation in the world requires the replacement of traditional fuel for vehicles with alternative types – liquefied natural gas, hydrogen fuel. The European Union is committed to the transition to renewable energy sources, introducing bioenergy as a key technology based on renewable raw materials aimed at decarbonizing the energy and thermal sectors [34]. The use of alternative fuels and energy sources in transport systems will reduce atmospheric pollution and reduce fuel costs.

By 2035, transport with alternative fuels will appear in the world, which can be:

- 20% of cars;
- 20% of diesel locomotives;
- 2% aviation;
- 10% of water transport.

The development of railways is the most promising direction in cargo transportation in the Russian Federation, considering, the environmental friendliness of this type of transport and the demand for long-distance transportation. Currently, high-speed railways are not sufficiently developed in Russia. Rail transport is less flexible compared to road and air transport. Therefore, the construction of new lines and changing routes requires financial and time costs more than aviation and highways. The volume of passenger transportation by rail in long-distance destinations increased by 2% in 2020. The potential of railway lines is high-speed highways not only on the scale of a particular region, but also throughout the country.

The use of motor transport is growing, the use of personal cars in the urban environment is growing. Most likely, this growth will continue. However, this can lead to a lot of air pollution. In Russian cities, the level of harmful emissions (nitrogen dioxide (NO2) is 1.5 times higher than in large cities in European countries.

During the pandemic, the mobility of citizens decreased. The level of transport mobility of the population in the Russian Federation is 2–4 times lower in comparison with developed countries. Automobile mobility is high in cities and suburbs of large agglomerations, which leads to a deterioration of the environmental situation in large cities. The use of alternative fuels for public transport can solve this problem. However, residents of large cities prefer to use personal transport that runs on traditional fuel. Similar problems are reflected in the study of Qatar scientists. A study of the attitude of residents of Qatari cities to travel by public transport showed that the majority of respondents resisted using public transport because they had cars. Only 24% of respondents said they would consider using public transport in order to preserve the environment. The basis of the low popularity of public transport is the individual dependence on a car [35].

The Russian Federation is traditionally characterized by heterogeneity of population mobility over long distances. More than 70% of all long-distance trips account for 30% of the population living in the 20 largest agglomerations. In other regions, transport mobility is 40% lower.

Aviation mobility of the population of the Russian Federation is below the level of developed countries and is also uneven across regions. In the 20 largest agglomerations, it is at a level above the EU level and amounts to 2.6 trips per person per year. This shows the high centralization of business activity of the population in large cities. In other regions, the aviation mobility of the population is 10 times lower and amounts to 0.26 trips per person per year. The development of local air airlines is associated with the development of airport infrastructure, the use of digital technologies in the management of air lines, the improvement of the aircraft fleet.

The climate of North and the Arctic zone determine the need of air airlines use for the population mobility. Insufficient development of the local air transport system hinders the increase in residents' transport mobility in the Russian Federation Arctic and the Far East zone as well as the improvement of the quality of life.

The Covid-19 pandemic period has reduced the number of citizens' trips not only over long distances, but also within settlements. The decline in transportation and mobility is typical for all countries. A comparison of the reduction in commercial flights in the EU countries showed a reduction in flights by more than 40% only in the Czech Republic and Austria, in other countries a decrease by a third was recorded. The industry has not recovered until 2021. In absolute terms, the number of commercial flights amounted to 383,720 in December 2021, compared with 166,990 in December 2020 and 504,270 in December 2019 (Eurostat News - Eurostat, 2021).

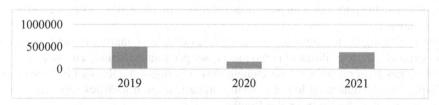

Fig. 5. Number of commercial flights in the EU countries, 2021.

As shown in Fig. 5, the recovery of commercial flights of EU air transport is slow. In the Russian Federation, the recovery after the pandemic of population mobility using all modes of transport also did not reach the indicators of 2019.

The use of sea transport makes it possible to expand the possibilities of cargo and passenger transportation. The Northern Sea Route has great potential for developing the economy and improving the quality of citizens life. The use of this transport corridor reduces transportation distances compared to routes passing through the Suez Canal.

The development of transport networks for all types of transport over long distances and in areas of difficult climatic conditions is associated with minimizing human participation in the transportation process. This will require the introduction of big data processing technologies in the management of traffic flows and individual vehicles, the use of digital technologies in diagnostics and monitoring. The use of unmanned vehicles for areas with a limited number of labor resources [36] or unfavorable natural conditions is very promising. To use the potential of maritime transport, it is necessary to create electronic navigation maps of waterways, the introduction of digital technologies in document management.

The development of digital fare payment systems on public transport can change the attitude of citizens to public transport, reduce traffic and improve the environmental situation in cities. Digitalization of payments is a promising direction in the field of passenger transportation and is very often considered as a condition for improving the efficiency of services provided [37].

The main conclusions of the study include the following:

- the diversity of the natural conditions of the regions creates a unique feature of the transport system, the development of which must be adapted to each region. To take into account all the peculiarities of the region, the possibilities of modern technologies can be used (for example, solving the problem of optimal design of a transport system using artificial intelligence);
- despite the fact that the level of transport mobility of the population in the Russian Federation is 2–4 times lower in comparison with European countries, the automobile mobility of the population in cities and suburbs of large agglomerations is high, which leads to a deterioration of the environmental situation in large cities. As a solution to this problem, it is proposed to use suburban high-speed trains, which are more environmentally friendly and able to improve the quality of life of citizens due to the high speed of movement to the suburbs or neighboring areas. To increase the comfort of buying a ticket, you can offer a digital payment system and electronic hotel booking systems in the region and neighboring regions. These technologies will increase the mobility of the population on weekends and make the suburbs of large cities attractive for tourism;
- the use of digital technologies in the logistics chains of maritime transport allows to expand the possibilities of cargo and passenger transportation. The Northern Sea Route has great potential for developing the economy of the Russian Federation and improving the quality of life of citizens. Digitalization of logistics will help expand the potential of the Northern Sea Route;
- the development of local air airlines will help to increase the business and recreational mobility of the population of individual regions. The creation of local airlines is connected with the development of airport infrastructure, which is impossible without the use of digital technologies in the management of air lines;

– the natural conditions of the far North and the Arctic zone determine the need to use air airlines for the mobility of the population. The use of digital technologies in this direction will ensure high speed of movement, quick purchase and registration of tickets, information about the availability of additional transport, which will increase the mobility of residents of the Arctic zone of the Russian Federation and the Far East and ensure their integration into the life of other regions.

The study of the transport structure of Russia made it possible to identify the potential of each type of transport for improving the transportation of goods and passengers, identify weaknesses and reveal promising areas of development in the special conditions of Russia.

5 Conclusions

The results of the study of the transport system of Russia allowed us to identify the main prospects for the development of transport for the future, ensuring an improvement in the quality of life of the citizens. Climatic features of Russia suggest priorities of the transport structure.

To increase the citizens' mobility, it is necessary to use rail transport with the use of high-speed technologies. Given the large territorial extent of the country, the main task of transport is to move quickly from one region to another. To solve this problem, it is optimal to use local aviation. To move over short distances, it is possible to use the resource of inland waterway transport with the creation of the necessary infrastructure.

Areas with difficult natural conditions, the Arctic zone have great economic potential, but have a weak transport structure and limited labor resources. In these conditions, it is possible to use modern technologies of unmanned vehicles, digital technologies to control traffic flows and improve traffic safety. In order to increase the connectivity of territories and ensure transport accessibility of remote and hard-to-reach areas, it is necessary to modernize the infrastructure of airports, railway stations and seaports.

To improve the quality of life, it is necessary to use the digital transformation of the transport complex with an information security system that ensures the protection of information resources and digital services of the transport system for the functioning of transport.

The following can be identified as promising areas of research:

– application of digital technologies for the transport system of the Far North and the Arctic zone;
– digitalization of logistics chains using the Northern Sea Route;
– the use of artificial intelligence for the development of the transport system while preserving the ecological balance and the unique natural conditions of each region;
– the use of digital technologies to increase the mobility of the population (accessibility of information about traffic flows, booking systems, digitalization of payments) and, as a result, improving the quality of life.

Improving the quality of life is possible with long-term planning for the creation and operation of the transport system, considering the peculiarities of the country and the use of the latest technologies.

Acknowledgments. The reported study was funded by RFBR according to the research project № 20-014-00029.

References

1. Gkoumas, K., Dos Santos, F.L.M., Stepniak, M., Pekár, F.: Research and innovation supporting the European sustainable and smart mobility strategy: a technology perspective from recent European Union projects (2021). https://doi.org/10.3390/app112411981
2. Ballantyne, E., Heron, G.: Can transport operator schemes deliver regional sustainability benefits? The case of the UK Northern powerhouse region. Sustainability **12** (2020). https://doi.org/10.3390/su12041662
3. Russo, F., Fortugno, G., Merante, M., Pellicanò, D.S., Trecozzi, M.R.: Updating national air passenger demand from traffic counts: the case of a secondary airport in an underdeveloped region. Sustainability **13** (2021). https://doi.org/10.3390/su13158372
4. Vega, A., Feo-Valero, M., Espino-Espino, R.: Understanding maritime transport route choice among Irish exporters: a latent class approach. Res. Transp. Econ. **90** (2021). https://doi.org/10.1016/j.retrec.2020.101025
5. Christidis, P., Christodoulou, A., Navajas-Cawood, E., Ciuffo, B.: The post-pandemic recovery of transport activity: emerging mobility patterns and repercussions on future evolution. Sustainability **13** (2021). https://doi.org/10.3390/su13116359
6. Joyce, S.C., Meeran, A., Agrawal, A.: A global population-driven perspective on South-East Asia's air transport growth prospects in the 21stcentury. In: IFAC-PapersOnLine. pp. 79–87. Elsevier B.V. (2020). https://doi.org/10.1016/j.trpro.2021.09.010
7. Liu, P., Xu, S.X., Ong, G.P., Tian, Q., Ma, S.: Effect of autonomous vehicles on travel and urban characteristics. Transp. Res. Part B Methodol. **153**, 128–148 (2021). https://doi.org/10.1016/J.TRB.2021.08.014
8. Reul, J., Grube, T., Stolten, D.: Urban transportation at an inflection point: an analysis of potential influencing factors. Transp. Res. Part D Transp. Environ. **92**, 102733 (2021). https://doi.org/10.1016/J.TRD.2021.102733
9. Tang, O., Rehme, J., Cerin, P.: Levelized cost of hydrogen for refueling stations with solar PV and wind in Sweden: on-grid or off-grid? Energy **241** (2022). https://doi.org/10.1016/j.energy.2021.122906
10. Tsakalidis, A., Boelman, E., Marmier, A., Gkoumas, K., Pekar, F.: Horizon scanning for transport research and innovation governance: a European perspective. Transp. Res. Interdiscip. Perspect. **11** (2021). https://doi.org/10.1016/j.trip.2021.100424
11. Połom, M., Wiśniewski, P.: Implementing electromobility in public transport in Poland in 1990–2020. A review of experiences and evaluation of the current development directions. Sustainability **13** (2021). https://doi.org/10.3390/su13074009
12. Noland, J.K.: Evolving toward a scalable hyperloop technology: vacuum transport as a clean alternative to short-haul flights. IEEE Electrif. Mag. **9**, 55–66 (2021). https://doi.org/10.1109/MELE.2021.3115542
13. Mitropoulos, L., Kortsari, A., Koliatos, A., Ayfantopoulou, G.: The hyperloop system and stakeholders: a review and future directions. Sustainability **13** (2021). https://doi.org/10.3390/su13158430

14. Outay, F., Mengash, H.A., Adnan, M.: Applications of unmanned aerial vehicle (UAV) in road safety, traffic and highway infrastructure management: Recent advances and challenges. Transp. Res. Part A Policy Pract. **141**, 116–129 (2020). https://doi.org/10.1016/j.tra.2020. 09.018

15. Lewis, E., et al.: Architecting urban air mobility airport shuttling systems with case studies: Atlanta, Los Angeles, and Dallas. Transp. Res. Part A Policy Pract. **150**, 423–444 (2021). https://doi.org/10.1016/J.TRA.2021.06.026

16. Steinhoff, C.: Einsatz von Drohnen für den Medikamententransport und das Rettungswesen. Unfallchirurg **124**(12), 965–973 (2021). https://doi.org/10.1007/s00113-021-01098-0

17. Alkinani, M.H., Almazroi, A.A., Jhanjhi, N.Z., Khan, N.A.: 5G and IoT based reporting and accident detection (Rad) system to deliver first aid box using unmanned aerial vehicle. Sensors **21** (2021). https://doi.org/10.3390/s21206905

18. Palaia, G., Salem, K.A., Cipolla, V., Binante, V., Zanetti, D.: A conceptual design methodology for e-VTOL aircraft for urban air mobility. Appl. Sci. **11** (2021). https://doi.org/10.3390/app 112210815

19. Keller, M., Hulínská, Š., Kraus, J.: Integration of UAM into cities - the public view. In: Transp. Res. Procedia **59**, 137–143 (2022). https://doi.org/10.1016/j.trpro.2021.11.105

20. Wu, Y., Low, K.H., Hu, X.: Trajectory-based flight scheduling for AirMetro in urban environments by conflict resolution. Transp. Res. Part C Emerg. Technol. **131**, 103355 (2021). https://doi.org/10.1016/J.TRC.2021.103355

21. Grindsted, T.S., Christensen, T.H., Freudendal-Pedersen, M., Friis, F., Hartmann-Petersen, K.: The urban governance of autonomous vehicles – In love with AVs or critical sustainability risks to future mobility transitions. Cities **120** (2022). https://doi.org/10.1016/j.cities.2021. 103504

22. Dhote, J., Limbourg, S.: Designing unmanned aerial vehicle networks for biological material transportation – the case of Brussels. Comput. Ind. Eng. **148**, 106652 (2020). https://doi.org/ 10.1016/J.CIE.2020.106652

23. Bays, M.J., Wettergren, T.A.: Optimization of waterspace management and scheduling for multiple unmanned vehicles. In: Autonomous Underwater Vehicles: Design and Practice. pp. 303–327. Institution of Engineering and Technology (2020). https://doi.org/10.1049/SBR A525E_ch11

24. Chen, M., Zeng, F., Xiong, X., Zhang, X., Chen, Z.: A maritime emergency search and rescue system based on unmanned aerial vehicle and its landing platform. In: 2021 IEEE International Conference on Electrical Engineering and Mechatronics Technology, ICEEMT 2021, pp. 758–761 (2021). https://doi.org/10.1109/ICEEMT52412.2021.9602734

25. Barykin, S., et al.: Digital logistics approach to energy service socio-economic mechanisms. Transp. Rese. Procedia **54**, 617–627 (2021). https://doi.org/10.1016/j.trpro.2021.02.114

26. Kharlamova, T.: Monitoring as an instrument of sustainable urban development. In: MATEC Web of Conferences, vol. 170 (2018). https://doi.org/10.1051/matecconf/201817002009

27. Kalinina, O., Firova, S., Barykin, S., Kapustina, I.: Development of the logistical model for energy projects' investment sources in the transport sector. Adv. Intell. Syst. Comput. **982**, 318–324 (2020). https://doi.org/10.1007/978-3-030-1975

28. Korchagina, E., Bochkarev, A., Bochkarev, P., Barykin, S., Suvorova, S.: The treatment of optimizing container transportation dynamic programming and planning. E3S Web of Conferences, vol. 135 (2019). https://doi.org/10.1051/e3sconf/201913502016

29. Teodorescu, M., Korchagina, E.: Applying blockchain in the modern supply chain management: Its implication on open innovation. J. Open Innov. Technol. Mark .Complex. **7**(1) (2021). https://doi.org/10.3390/JOITMC7010080

30. Korchagina, E., Shignanova, R.: Development of the North Baikal as a tourist destination: problems and perspectives. In: Proceedings of the 31st International Business Information Management Association Conference, IBIMA 2018: Innovation Management and Education Excellence through Vision 2020. 12 October 2018. https://ibima.org/accepted-paper/dev elopment-of-the-north-baikal-as-tourist-destination-problems-and-perspectives/. Accessed 3 Oct 2021

31. Karmanova, A., Kurochkina, A., Desfonteines, L., & Lukina, O.: Prerequisites and prospects for digitalization in the Arctic climate. In: ACM International Conference Proceeding Series (2020). https://doi.org/10.1145/3446434.3446461

32. Desfonteines, L., Korchagina, E., Evgrafov, A., Khnykina, T., Karmanova, A., Semenova, Y.: The future of information technology in the Russian Trade. IOP Conf. Ser. Mater. Sci. Eng. **940**(1) (2020). https://doi.org/10.1088/1757-899X/940/1/01

33. Korchagina, E., Desfonteines, L., Strekalova, N.: Problems of training specialists for trade in the conditions of digitalization. In: E3S Web of Conferences, vol. 164 (2020). https://doi.org/10.1051/e3sconf/202016412014

34. Koytsoumpa, E.I., Magiri-Skouloudi, D., Karellas, S., Kakaras, E.: Bioenergy with carbon capture and utilization: a review on the potential deployment towards a European circular bioeconomy. Renew. Sustain. Energy Rev. **152**, 111641 (2021). https://doi.org/10.1016/J.RSER.2021.111641

35. Al-Thawadi, F.E., Banawi, A.A.A., Al-Ghamdi, S.G.: Social impact assessment towards sustainable urban mobility in Qatar: understanding behavioral change triggers. Transp. Res. Interdiscip. Perspect. **9** (2021). https://doi.org/10.1016/j.trip.2020.100295

36. Desfonteines L., Korchagina E.: Potential of the "silver" generation of modern Russia. Psikholog. Zh. **42**, 137–146 (2021). https://doi.org/10.31857/S020595920015243-3

37. Frączek, B., Urbanek, A.: Financial inclusion as an important factor influencing digital payments in passenger transport: a case study of EU countries. Res. Transp. Bus. Manag. **41**, 100691 (2021). https://doi.org/10.1016/J.RTBM.2021.100691

Factors Influencing Shoppers' Behavioral Intention to Purchase Smart Phones: Digital Transformation Through YouTube User Generated Content

Anuphat Thirakulwanich$^{(\boxtimes)}$ ⓘ and Sudaporn Sawmong ⓘ

KMITL Business School, King Mongkut's Institute of Technology Ladkrabang, Bangkok 10520, Thailand

gunthira.t7@gmail.com, sudaporn.sa@kmitl.ac.th

Abstract. This study explored the factors that influence shoppers' behavioral intention to purchase smartphones based on User Generated Content on the YouTube platform. The study was underpinned by two critical theories which include; Extended Technology Acceptance Model (TAM) and Source Credibility Theory to understand how UGC on YouTube was applicable in influencing purchase decisions. The independent variables were UGC, perceived credibility, and perceived usefulness. The study adopted a quantitative descriptive survey research design. A questionnaire was used to collect data from a sample size of 442 YouTube users in Thailand and the data were analyzed using SEM. The findings revealed that user-generated content on YouTube has a positive effect on perceived credibility, perceived usefulness, and behavioral intention to purchase smartphones. It also showed that perceived usefulness and perceived credibility have a positive effect on behavioral intention to purchase smartphones. Ultimately, the study also found that UGC on YouTube has an indirect and significant effect on behavioral intention to purchase smartphones mediated for both perceived usefulness and perceived credibility. The study recommends that future studies should consider different social media platforms where UGC are available to test for consistency, and also incorporate a mixed method of research involving qualitative data that will allow respondents to provide clarifications for their decisions. A few imitations of the study could be highlighted. The first limitation is within the scope of the study, from the fact that the study's focus was on one social media channel – YouTube. The study focused more on the user-generated content on YouTube and added two more variables (perceived credibility and perceived usefulness).

Keywords: Digital transformation · YouTube · Smartphones · User-generated content · Thailand

1 Introduction

The swift development and acceptance of social media globally enhanced its application in commerce and human-centered solutions for sustainable development and

© Springer Nature Switzerland AG 2022
D. Rodionov et al. (Eds.): SPBPU IDE 2021, CCIS 1619, pp. 35–50, 2022.
https://doi.org/10.1007/978-3-031-14985-6_3

digital transformations. The Social media environment broadly encompasses online networks such as Line, Twitter, Pantip, Facebook, TikTok, LinkedIn, Pinterest, Twitch, and WeChat), wikis (such as Wikipedia), bookmarking sites (e.g. Del.icio.us and Digg), virtual worlds (e.g. Second Life), multimedia sharing (e.g., YouTube and Instagram), and blogs (TMZ) [1, 2]. Due to its wide use, firms and startups are designating resources towards finding out ways and means of profitably applying social media towards enhancing their business operations. Among the majorly used social media site is YouTube, which has been classified as a multimedia sharing site that enables users the ability to upload, view, and share videos whether the content is original or from other sources. The video-sharing activity on YouTube has significant impacts and has gone on to shape thoughts, opinions, and cultures online and offline, especially for content that is user-generated [3].

YouTube has a great significance to marketing and business activities due to its huge capacity to generate User-generated Content (UGC). It is considered the largest source of UGC because it allows for content uploaded to be rated by using the thumb up or thumb down feature as well as adding comments on the comments section underneath the video content [3]. The UGC serves as a source of information regarding the quality and trustworthiness of the information shared on the video. In making purchases, UGC on social media such as YouTube can provide explicit reviews that highlight the benefits and cons of products and services of interest to the interested users' [4], thereby exerting some influence on behavior. Potential consumers (buyers) rely in greater context on UGC than Producer Generated Content (PGC) because other users share their opinions from personal experiences; they share both positive and negative aspects of their product. Also, the lack of commercial interest by such users removes any conflict-of-interest issues and this allows them to provide an unbiased assessment of a product or the quality of service that is under consideration. This would be unlike the PGC which would be more focused on the positive characteristics while downplaying or skipping the negative aspects entirely because of their vested commercial interest. Research highlights that this is a global view of PGC which has made UGC more reliable and trusted, unlike the cynicism and skepticism with which PGC is viewed. This is one of the distinguishing properties of UGC and users' have come to regard it as being impartial, credible, and certainly more beneficial than PGC when viewing content about a product on YouTube [3]. The YouTube content posted about products/services that are user generated (UG), including views, reviews, and comments also impacts the trustworthiness, efficacy, and utility of UGC on the platform.

Individuals, commercial and non-commercial organizations use the platform to share their ideas, visions, goods, services, and generally improve the quality of life, enabling digital transformation. Thus, one can find information on health-related products, music, sports, cars, and so much more on the platform [5]. Users also use YouTube to communicate their views and experiences encountered in the use of products and services in video form. Examining the impact of UGC content on the purchase decisions of YouTube users can help in enhancing the quality of the content and how individuals and organizations alike perceive the videos. Consumers on the YouTube platform have a critical function in the creation, transmission, and perception of content, it becomes paramount to understand the influence of YouTube on the audience and how this affects the decision to purchase an item or its alternative, or not to purchase the product or service entirely based on user-generated content.

Based on this background, this research investigates the factors influencing the shoppers' behavioral intention to purchase smartphones from User-Generated Content (UGC). Specifically, the research investigates the credibility and usefulness of UGC about purchasing smartphones based on the number of views, quantity, and comments (reviews) posted on YouTube. Furthermore, the study investigates the effect of perceived credibility and perceived usefulness on consumers and responses to content generated by YouTube users, and the behavioral intentions to purchase such products and services. The research will be geared towards addressing three objectives: 1) to study the composition of User Generate Content, Perceived Credibility, and Perceived Usefulness; 2) to analyze the influence of User Generate Content, Perceived Credibility, and Perceived Usefulness; and 3) to develop the structural model of the shopper behavioral intentions toward YouTube User-Generated Content. This research will benefit marketers and social media managers as they analyze user data which can influence purchase decisions of potential customers and in some instances prevent public relations crises for the organization in the process of launching a product in the consumer market.

1.1 User Generated Content from YouTube

YouTube was founded by three former Google employees in 2005. With statistics showing that they were hosting an average of over two million videos per day and over 20 million daily active users under a year of production, Google acquired YouTube for $1.65 billion in 2006, this is quite inadequate considering that in 2020, YouTube ad revenue stood at $19.7 billion with over 2.3 billion users access YouTube at least once a month [6]. Video sharing platforms provide subscribers with low-cost transmission tools compatible with most web and mobile devices and allow for easy broadcast and sharing of content on YouTube pages (channels), which are convenient to use and allow consumers to share material on their accounts as well connect with other people. YouTube's number of users and videos has skyrocketed, and Time magazine named it the 2006 invention of the year, the statistics today show an even bigger platform for content creators, manufacturers, and advertisers. According to [7], TNS, a market research firm, YouTube is Thailand's favorite and most popular video platform, and that half of the time spent on the internet by 62% of the Thai population was spent on YouTube, found that Thais spend an average of 34 minutes per visit, they visit 3.3 times per day and they spend about 1.9 hours per day on YouTube. Other statistics indicate that 83% indicate YouTube is one of their favorite websites; 81% consider it the first place to visit for video content, and 61% favor it over television. Rural residents actively watch YouTube and spend more time on the platform than urban dwellers; the population aged between 16 and 24 years prefers the YouTube platform over television.

YouTube has seen an explosion in terms of usage as Thai users have shifted from the traditional platform of media content which is satellite television into digital spaces such as YouTube. [8] confirmed that Thailand had the most engaged mobile internet region in the world with 5 h and 13 minutes per day on mobile internet, ranking among the top 4 countries in Southeast Asia in mobile internet usage. A large part of the explosion of YouTube is credited to the emergence of smartphones that allows content creators the ability to conceive, create, upload and share content on the platform. This has added more flexibility and has led to more authentic content than the normal television shows [9]. YouTube globally has suggested content creators stay engaged, provide users a consistent stream of creative content and explore different content and stay in the content that is easy to assimilate. YouTube creator can better communicate with all groups of customers on YouTube, based on their passions, activities and interests, and the development of smartphone technology has been instrumental to their success. It also helps marketers find their target market with accuracy and precision. The platform crosses the line between being a direct communication space and being a space for brands to engage with consumers [10, 11].

1.2 Technology Acceptance Model

The Technology Acceptance Model (TAM) [12] was applied in this study to evaluate factors that influence consumer attitudes and purchase decisions from reviews and recommendations on the YouTube platform. TAM posits that what determines the audience's attitude toward the adoption of technology is the user's behavioral intention to embrace a certain technological device. Therefore, this study is built on prior research adopting TAM to justify the consumers' behavioral intention toward products and services recommended by YouTube reviews. [13] implemented and expanded TAM by the addition of user evaluations of satisfaction to perceived usefulness and perceived ease of use as predictors of future intention to repeat purchase. TAM has altered people's perceptions of digital commodities and the YouTube video viewing experience can be developed in the course of the procedure of user participation by identifying the potential customer on YouTube. To attain conviction and minimize risks associated with online shopping, users' are progressively searching for knowledge from internet sources including YouTube.

1.3 Source Credibility Theory

Source credibility is a crucial factor in marketing discussions that seek to influence opinion and attract a following, this is more critical in online settings. [14] stated that the online environment raises some concerns for customers in efforts to process and assess. To minimize risks that may be associated with online purchases, consumers tend to depend on sources they consider credible online, which imply that customers are pessimistic about the information from brands about their products, consequently, they seek validation of such information from sources they consider credible and familiar. They add that characteristics of sources affect their credibility and can affect customer's view and behavior towards a product, whether to purchase or not. The term source credibility infers a "communicator's positive characteristics that affect the receiver's acceptance of a message", and it has a substantial persuasive effect on consumers. [15] opine that Source Credibility Theory classifies persuasiveness of the information concerning the perceived credibility of the source. The theory believes that expertise and honesty are crucial influences that validate the perceived credibility of information source while asserting that source loyalty is the degree of confidence in the communicator's intent to communicate assertions, he considers most valid. Consequently, a communicator's in-depth knowledge, reliability, charisma, and pull embody the psychosomatic construct linked with source credibility. The way a message is received, as well as whether it changes behavior, is influenced by how the messenger is perceived [16]. By applying the principles of source credibility theory, this research seeks to understand the role of perceived source credibility in YouTube UGC and the influence it has on purchase decision by customers.

1.4 Empirical Literature

The emergent media ecosystem and technological advancements have reshaped the media landscape and the role of marketing in new media consumption. Innovative technology enables the public to boost their influence over what platform they expose themselves to; users have more influence over purchasing behavior because of the ability to share information quickly, at any time without geographical limitations. [17] online consumer reviews as favorable and unfavorable statements by probable consumers, current or past consumers about a product or organization, that are available to many people online. UGC is used to depict media content created by members of the platform community with personal experiences in the use of goods and services or at least are directly aware of the situations involving the application of such commodities, well enough to evaluate them. Considering that UGC is information and reviews created and uploaded by internet users, in this case, YouTube subscribers, such consumer reviews have greater relevancy in comparison to expert reviews because reviewers post positive or pessimist reviews based on their psychological motivations. UGC can also be considered free marketing for online entrepreneurs; it assists users to identify products and services that satisfy their needs [5, 18, 19]. Based on the above discussion and applying them to UGC about the features available in a smartphone, the following hypotheses are proposed:

H1: User generated content about smart phones on YouTube has a positive effect on perceived credibility.

H2: User generated content about smart phones on YouTube has a positive effect on perceived usefulness.

H3: User generated content about smart phones on YouTube has a positive effect on behavioral intention.

Perceived usefulness is "the degree to which a person believes that using a particular system would enhance his or her job performance." [20] opine that it is connected to the expectations that an individual is hopeful of achieving in the end. Perceived usefulness may be a consideration that affects the perception of online consumers and how they react to the information provided by others (UGC), it can also progressively produce positive purchase decisions [5, 18, 20]. [21] in their study on UGC on blogs, found out perceived usefulness has links aligned to the advantages of blogging and these benefits can avert losses on time and purchasing the wrong product because of the information accessible on the blogs and the different perspectives when the customer visits different blogs about the same product. Based on these assumptions and making the comparison to smartphones as the product, the following hypotheses are suggested.

H4: Perceived usefulness has a positive effect on behavioral intention to purchase smart phones based on YouTube UGC.

Online consumers today perceive and trust UGC as more credible than PGC [3], ascribing this function to YouTube content creators, users tend to consider each other as highly reliable and trustworthy information sources. [22] viewed credibility as a positive attribute of a communicator which is used to win influence and create receiver acceptance of the information promoted by the communicator because of the ability of such information to be factual and valuable, allowing users to make better decisions based on such information [15, 18]. Credibility is built on expertise which comes from knowledge and trustworthiness which comes from the quality of being reliable. [3] in their findings opined that consumer prefer UGC with regard to trustworthiness over traditional PGC due to the conflict of interest arising from PGC being a promoted effort. [15] opined that if consumers positively embrace and trust the information irrespective of its source, then, it will be easier to sway consumers into purchasing the items which are the subject of the UGC. Transposing this to content on smart phones, the next hypotheses are proposed:

H5: Perceived credibility has a positive effect on behavioral intention to purchase smart phones based on YouTube UGC.

H6: Perceived credibility mediates the relationship between user generated content and behavioral intention to purchase smart phones based on YouTube UGC.

H7: Perceived usefulness mediates the relationship between user generated content and behavioral intention to purchase smart phones based on YouTube UGC.

1.5 Proposed Conceptual Model

This study adopted the framework proposed in [13] where they modified and brought together different theories to produce a framework that incorporated the Extended Technology Acceptance Model. Studies conducted by other scholars such as [5, 18], and, found that User-Generated Content minimizes risk especially when the information will help potential users of a product in making good choices when shopping. The model contained four latent variables and three observed variables each: user-generated content (view, like, and comment); perceived credibility (message medium, expertise, knowledge & credibility); perceived usefulness (perceived usefulness, relative usefulness, outcome expectation); and behavioral intention (intention, prediction, and planning). The following model was proposed (Fig. 1).

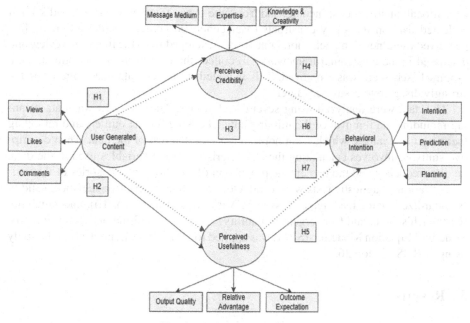

Fig. 1. Conceptual framework

2 Materials and Methods

This research employed the quantitative online survey design of YouTube users in Thailand, where the primary data which is collected from the representative sample will be analyzed using statistical methods and techniques. The justification for using YouTube to perceive characteristics of UGC on purchase decisions of smart phones stems from the understanding of the unique position occupied by YouTube in the social media landscape in Thailand. The study population included YouTube subscribers who log into YouTube at least once a month in Thailand. YouTube, according to [23] has about 7,822,000 million users in Thailand. The inclusion and exclusion criteria were the respondents' country of residence (must be Thailand), age (must be above 18), and YouTube usage.

A representative sample was selected from which the data was collected. This study used a stratified sampling method to select the study sample. This is a sampling technique in which samples were obtained from 10 districts in Thailand and a minimum of 40 respondents in each district. Using a confidence level of 95%, a 5% margin of error, and a population size of 7,822 million, the sample size of the study was determined to be 442 respondents. Only YouTube users who log into the platform at least once a month, are over 18 years of age, and reside in Thailand were selected to participate as respondents. Quantitative methodology was employed to carry out the study on variables that affect shoppers' intentions and attitudes towards user-generated content in Thailand. It involves collecting the data from the sample respondents using a questionnaire and then analyzed using the SEM technique, to answer the research questions.

Primary data was collected using a structured questionnaire, made up of 2 sections. The first part will collect data on demographic statistics, which include age, gender, educational qualifications, income, and YouTube usage frequency. The second section collected data on the study constructs (user generated content, perceived credibility, perceived usefulness, and behavioral intention) developed from the literature review and discussed in the conceptual framework. To collect the data using the questionnaire, a 5-point Likert scale was employed. This included measurements that range from 1 – strongly disagree to 5-strongly agree.

The data were analyzed using several techniques. The first step was data cleaning including the removal of the missing data, checking for the outliers and removing them, and any values, which seem not to align with the rest of the data. Then descriptive statistics involves calculating the characteristics of the variables used in the data, i.e. the frequency and the percentage proportion of the different categories of the variables. Various diagnostic tests were conducted including descriptive statistics, validity (standardized factor loadings and Average Variance Extracted (AVE)), and reliability (Cronbach's alpha and Convergent Reliability) tests, and confirmatory factor analysis. Structural Equation Modeling (SEM) was applied to evaluate the hypothesis of the study using AMOS version 26.

3 Results

3.1 Demographic Characteristics

This section conducted a descriptive statistical analysis of the demographic characteristics of the respondents. The demographic evaluated included age, gender, education level, and the number of hours the respondents spend on YouTube, the findings are presented in Table 1. Considering gender, the majority of respondents were female (56.6%) while men were the least (43.4%). Considering the age variable, the majority were aged 31–40 years (34.8%) followed by age-group 41–50 years (30.3%) while the least age group was 51–60 years (8.6%). The other variable was the hours the respondents spent watching YouTube videos. The majority indicated 1–2 h daily (45%) followed by 2–3 h daily. The least indicated 3–4 h daily (2.7%).

3.2 Model Evaluation

The proposed model was evaluated using several techniques, including Confirmatory Factor Analysis (CFA), reliability analysis, and validity analysis. The CFA was used to test the hypothesis that a relationship between observed variables and their underlying latent constructs exists. The CFA was conducted for the four latent variables of the study, which were User-Generated Content (UGC), perceived usefulness (PU), perceived credibility (PC), and behavioral intention to use (BI). The results for the CFA analysis are presented in Fig. 2.

The results indicated that the chi-square $X2 = 155.084$, df $= 48$, and CMIN/DF $= 3.231$ which was below 5.0 indicating an acceptable model fit [24]. The NFI $= 0.964$, RFI $= 0.951$, IFI $= 0.975$, TLI $= 0.966$, CFI $= 0.975$, GFI $= 0.944$, AGFI $= 0.909$. All these fitness tests were >0.90 indicating good levels of fitness between the model and the data [25–27]. Additionally, RMSEA $= 0.071$ and RMR $= 0.018$, which suggested

Table 1. Demographic characteristics of respondents

Demographics	Variables	Frequency	Percent
Gender	Male	192	43.4
	Female	250	56.6
Age	18–30 years	116	26.2
	31–40 years	154	34.8
	41–50 years	134	30.3
	51– 60 years	38	8.6
Education	High school or lower	35	7.9
	Certificate/Diploma	155	35.1
	Bachelor's degree	203	45.9
	Post-graduate or higher	49	11.1
YouTube hours	Less than an hour	84	19
	1–2 h	199	45
	2–3 h	147	33.3
	3–4 h	12	2.7
	Total	442	100

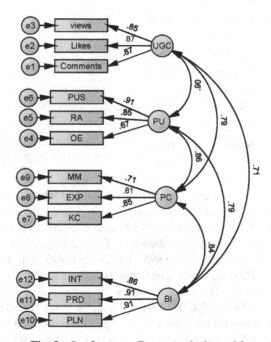

Fig. 2. Confirmatory Factor Analysis model

a reasonably good model-data fit [28, 29]. Since the model fitness with the data was satisfactory based on the result, it was considered suitable to evaluate the hypothesis using the model.

Before conducting the hypothesis evaluation, the model was evaluated for reliability and validity. The reliability of the constructs was evaluated using Cronbach's alpha and convergent reliability (CR) while the validity of the constructs was evaluated using the average variance extracted (AVE) and factor loadings.

Table 2. Validity and reliability evaluation

Latent variables	Observed variables	Validity		Reliability	
		Factor loadings	AVE	Cronbach's alpha	CR
User-Generated Content (UGC)	Comments	0.867	0.740	0.895	0.895
	Likes	0.868			
	Views	0.846			
Perceived Usefulness (PU)	Outcome expectancy	0.668	0.665	0.837	0.854
	Relative advantage	0.849			
	Perceived usefulness	0.910			
Perceived Credibility (PC)	Knowledge & creativity	0.852	0.631	0.831	0.836
	Expertise	0.812			
	Message medium	0.712			
Behavioral Intention to use (BI)	Planning	0.906	0.799	0.922	0.922
	Prediction	0.915			
	Intention	0.860			

The required threshold for composite reliability and Cronbach's alpha is that values between 0.6 and 0.7 are acceptable, while above 0.7 is considered good. The required threshold for AVE and factor loadings is 0.5 [30] (Hair et al. 2014). For the user-generated content (UGC), the factor loadings as shown on Table 2 ranged between 0.846–0.867, AVE = 0.740, Cronbach's alpha = 0.895 and CR = 0.895. The factor loadings for perceived usefulness (PU) ranged between 0.668–0.910, AVE = 0.665, Cronbach's alpha = 0.837 and CR = 0.854. The factor loadings for perceived credibility (PC) ranged between 0.712–0.852, AVE = 0.631, Cronbach's alpha = 0.831 and CR = 0.836. The factor loadings for behavioral intention to use ranged from 0.860–0.915, AVE = 0.799, Cronbach's alpha = 0.922 and CR = 0.922. From the results presented in the table above, the Cronbach's Alpha and CR values are greater than the threshold value of 0.7, and the AVE values are greater than the threshold value of 0.5. Therefore, the reliability and convergent validity of the instruments used are confirmed.

3.3 Structural Equation Modelling

The Structural Equation Modelling (SEM) was conducted to investigate the factors influencing shoppers' behavioral intention to purchase smart phones under an empirical analysis of YouTube user-generated content. SEM was used to study the hypothesis testing the relationship among the four variables under study. The SEM was conducted, and the results are presented in the following model output (Fig. 3).

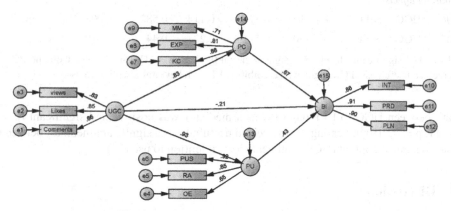

Fig. 3. Structural equation modelling results

The model fitness of SEM was first evaluated. The results indicated that X2 = 193.593, df = 49, CMIN/DF = 3.951 which was considered within the acceptable limit of below 5.0 according to [31]. The results for NFI = 0.956, RFI = 0.940, IFI = 0.966, TLI = 0.955, CFI = 0.966, GFI = 0.934, which were above 0.9 threshold [25–27]. The results also indicated that RMSEA = 0.082 which was <0.10 as recommended by [32] and [33]. These results satisfied the data-model fitness criterion. The relationship between the latent variables is summarized in Table 3.

The results in Table 3 present the direct and indirect paths. From the results, the path between user-generated content (UGC) and perceived credibility (PC) was significant and positive ($\beta = 0.862$, p = 0.000); the path coefficients between user-generated content (UGC) and perceived usability (PU) were significant and positive ($\beta = 0.656$, p = 0.000). Additionally, the path coefficients between perceived credibility (PC) and behavioral intention to use (BI) were significant and positive ($\beta = 0.661$, p = 0.000); the path coefficient between perceived usefulness (PU) a behavioral intention to use (BI) was significant and positive ($\beta = 0.627$, p = 0.002). In addition to this to the direct effects discussed previously, the indirect relationship was also conducted. The indirect path between UGC to BI though PC as a mediator was positive and significant ($\beta = 0.57$, p = 0.008) indicating that perceived credibility is a significant mediator between user-generated content (UGC) and behavioral intention to use (BI). As well, the indirect

Table 3. Structural equation modelling results

Paths				β	S.E.	C.R.	P-value	Decision
Direct effects								
H1	UGC	→	PC	0.862	0.048	17.804	***	Accept
H2	UGC	→	PU	0.656	0.045	14.491	***	Accept
H3	UGC	→	BI	−0.216	0.17	−1.269	0.204	Reject
H4	PC	→	BI	0.661	0.086	7.684	***	Accept
H5	PU	→	BI	0.627	0.201	3.125	0.002	Accept
Indirect effects								
H6	UGC ---> PC	→	BI	0.57	0.114	0.582	0.008	Accept
H7	UGC ---> PU	→	BI	0.511	0.27	0.44	0.019	Accept

*** = 0.01 significance level, ** = significance at 0.05, UGC = User-Generated Content, PU = perceived usefulness, PC = perceived credibility, BI = Behavioral intention to use.

path between UGC to BI though PU as a mediator was positive and significant ($\beta = 0.511, p = 0.019$) indicating that perceived usefulness is a significant mediator between user-generated content (UGC) and behavioral intention to use (BI).

4 Discussion

This research was conducted based on the findings of previous studies that helped to determine the research gap and study variables and based on various theoretical models such as the Technology Acceptance Model and Source Credibility Theory. The relationship between the variables has been explored through empirical tests, and the results have been presented in the previous section. The results of the hypothesis tests indicated that user-generated content on YouTube has a positive and significant influence on perceived credibility on the purchase of smart phones. In other words, the aspects of the user-generated content such as the comments, likes, and share activities in YouTube videos enhance the perceived credibility of the people towards the purchase of smartphones. These results are similar to previous studies such as [34], who indicated that the user-generated content has a significant influence on the other YouTube users, in belief about the authenticity and benefits of the concerned products. The positive and negative likes and comments left behind by the user or former customers concerning the company, their products, or services significantly influence the views and perceptions of future viewers or potential customers [35].

The results supported the hypothesis that user-generated content about smart phones has a significant and positive relationship with perceived usefulness. In other terms, if there is positive user-generated content such as likes, shares, and comments regarding a YouTube video, then the associated content of the video is considered or perceived as useful in Thailand. These results are supported by studies such as [36] who indicated that online consumers generally rely on the content which has been generated by other consumers regarding the product or service in question, to assist in the process of decision making. The results supported the hypothesis that perceived usefulness has a positive and significant influence on behavioral intention to use. These findings are in line with another previous research. For instance, [37–41] indicated that perceived usefulness is a critical factor that greatly influences online consumers to respond to the information provided by others regarding the concerned company, products, or services. Invariably, this influences their attitude and the resultant purchase or non-purchase of the concerned products or services [42, 43].

The research supported the hypothesis that perceived credibility has a positive and significant influence on behavioral intention to use information to purchase smart phones. These results are also supported by [44] Jonas (2010) who indicated that the current generation of online consumers perceive and consider that content generated by other users regarding the products or services is more credible compared to the content provided by the sellers. In addition to investigating the direct effects of perceived credulity and perceived usefulness on behavioral intention to use, this research also analyzed their mediating effect between the two variables on the effect of user-generated content on behavioral intention to use information to purchase smart phones. The research found that user-generated content has an insignificant direct influence on the behavioral intention to use information to purchase smart phones. This implied that independently, user-generated content (shares, likes, and comments) did not significantly influence users' intention, prediction, and planning to purchase smart phones. However, when perceived credibility and perceived usefulness were included as mediators, the user-generated content changed from insignificant to significant influence on behavioral intention to use. This confirmed the two hypotheses of the mediation effect of perceived credibility and perceived usefulness. It implied that user-generated content first influenced the perceived credibility and perceived usefulness of the concerned products and services, which in turn influenced the potential customers' intention, prediction, or planning to use information to purchase smart phones.

5 Conclusion

From the research results of this study, several conclusions were developed. Regarding the demographic statistics, the majority gender was female (56.6%). The results also indicated that the majority age group was 31–40 years, and the majority of respondents indicated that they spent 1–2 h watching YouTube videos. Normality and multicollinearity tests were confirmed to be satisfactory. The SEM results indicated that $X2 = 193.593$, $df = 49$, CMIN/DF $= 3.951$, NFI $= 0.956$, RFI $= 0.940$, IFI $= 0.966$, TLI $= 0.955$, CFI $= 0.966$, GFI $= 0.934$, AGFI $= 0.895$, RMR $= 0.025$, RMSEA $= 0.082$, the results which were considered satisfactory confirming that the proposed model fitted the data. The Structural Equation Modeling was the main analysis focused on evaluating the research objectives and testing the set hypothesis of the study. SEM was run to investigate the factors influencing shoppers' behavioral intention to purchase smart phones under an empirical analysis of the YouTube user-generated content. The results indicated that user-generated content significantly and positively affected perceived credibility (H1) and perceived usefulness (H2), but not behavioral intention to use information from UGC on YouTube about smart phones. Behavioral intention to use was found to be influenced by perceived usefulness (H5) and perceived credibility (H4). The results also indicated that the relationship between user-generated content and behavioral intention to use was significantly mediated by perceived credibility (H6) and perceived usefulness (H7).

The study is considered to have been conducted successfully from start to end. However, a few imitations of the study could be highlighted. The research focused on the factors affecting shoppers' behavioral intention to purchase smartphones in Thailand, with the focus on YouTube user-generated content. The first limitation is within the scope of the study, from the fact that the study's focus was on one social media channel – YouTube. There are other many social media channels that shoppers use to learn about user-generated content. Therefore, this research acknowledges that the findings of this research should be applied within the scope of this research. The second limitation of the study is the variables used in the study. The study focused more on the user-generated content on YouTube and added two more variables (perceived credibility and perceived usefulness). Therefore, the study had a total of four latent variables, which are considered not exhaustive. Based on these limitations, the study advocate for two future research recommendations; the first recommendation is that future studies should study different social media platforms on which user-generated content is found, and second, the future studies could be conducted by including more latent variables in the model applied in this study.

References

1. Naab, T.K., Sehl, A.: Studies of user generated content: a review. Journalism **18**, 1256–1273 (2016). https://doi.org/10.1177/1464884916673557
2. Kocabiyik, O.O.: Social media usage experiences of young adults during the COVID 19 pandemic through social cognitive approach to uses and gratifications. Intl. J. Tech. Edu. & Sci. (IJTES) **5**(3), 447–462 (2021). https://doi.org/10.46328/ijtes.226
3. Park, J., McMahan, C.: Exploring YouTube marketing communication among 200 leading national advertisers. J. Prom. Manag. **27**(4), 487–502 (2020). https://doi.org/10.1080/10496491.2020.1851845
4. Grewal, L., Stephen, A.: In mobile we trust: the effects of mobile versus nonmobile reviews on consumer purchase intentions. J. Market. Res. **56**(7), 791–808 (2019). https://doi.org/10.1177/0022243719834514
5. Bahtar, A.Z., Muda, M.: The impact of user – generated content (UGC) on product reviews towards online purchasing – a conceptual framework. Procedia Econ. Fin. **37**, 337–342 (2016). https://doi.org/10.1016/s2212-5671(16)30134-4
6. Iqbal, M.: YouTube revenue and usage statistics (2021). https://www.businessofapps.com/data/youtube-statistics/. Accessed 2 Jan 2022
7. Pornwasin, A.: Thailand is still number one for YouTube viewers in Southeast Asia (2016). https://www.nationthailand.com/business/30297423. Accessed 12 Oct 2020
8. Bangkok Post: Joint report bodes well for internet economy (2019). https://www.bangkokpost.com/business/1784259/joint-report-bodes-well-for-internet-economy. Accessed 12 Oct 2020
9. Bangkok Post. Thailand races ahead in the global digital revolution (2021). https://www.bangkokpost.com/business/2073087/thailand-races-ahead-in-the-global-digital-revolution
10. Kapoor, K.K., Tamilmani, K., Rana, N.P., Patil, P., Dwivedi, Y.K., Nerur, S.: Advances in social media research: past, present and future. Inf. Syst. Front. **20**(3), 531–558 (2017). https://doi.org/10.1007/s10796-017-9810-y

11. Lockett, A.R.: Online marketing strategies for increasing sales revenues of small retail businesses. Walden Dissertations and Doctoral Studies (2018). https://scholarworks.waldenu.edu/cgi/viewcontent.cgi?article=7175&context=dissertations. Accessed 15 Dec 2019
12. Davis, F.D.: Perceived usefulness, perceived ease of use, and user acceptance of information technology. MIS Q. **13**(3), 319–340 (1989)
13. Beldad, A.D., Hegner, S.M.: More photos from me to thee: factors influencing the intention to continue sharing personal photos on an online social networking (OSN) site among young adults in the Netherlands. Intl. J. Hum. Comp. Interac. **33**(5), 410–422 (2017)
14. Sinha, M., Fukey, L.N., Likitha, S.: Web user experience and consumer behaviour: the influence of colour, usability and aesthetics on the consumer buying behaviour. Test Eng. Manag. **82**, 16592–16600 (2020)
15. Wang, S.W., Scheinbaum, A.C.: Enhancing brand credibility via celebrity endorsement: trustworthiness trumps attractiveness and expertise. J. Advert. Res. **58**(1), 16–32 (2018). https://doi.org/10.2501/jar-2017-042
16. Ma, T.J., Atkin, D.: User generated content and credibility evaluation of online health information: a meta analytic study. Telemat. Inform. **34**(5), 472–486 (2017). https://doi.org/10.1016/j.tele.2016.09.009
17. Sharifi, S.: Examining the impacts of positive and negative online consumer reviews on behavioral intentions: role of need for cognitive closure and satisfaction guarantees. J. Hospital. Market Manag. **28**(4), 397–426 (2018). https://doi.org/10.1080/19368623.2019.1531804
18. Yüksel, H.F.: Factors affecting purchase intention in YouTube videos. J. Know. Econ. Know. Manag. **11**(2), 33–-47 (2016)
19. Goes, P.B., Guo, C., Lin, M.: Do incentive hierarchies induce user effort? Evidence from an online knowledge exchange. Info. Sys. Res. **27**(3), 497–516 (2016)
20. Ma, L., Feng, J., Feng, Z., Wang, L.: Research on user loyalty of short video app based on perceived value—Take Tik Tok as an example. In: Proceedings of the IEEE 16Th International Conference on Service Systems and Service Management (ICSSSM 2019), IEEE, Shenzhen, China, pp. 1–6 (2019). https://doi.org/10.1109/icsssm.2019.8887751
21. Nosita, F., Lestari, T.: The influence of user generated content and purchase intention on beauty products. J. Manag. Market. Rev. **4**(3), 171–183 (2019). https://doi.org/10.35609/jmmr.2019.4.3(2)
22. Ohanian, R.: Construction and validation of a scale to measure celebrity endorsers' perceived expertise, trustworthiness, and attractiveness. J. Advert. **19**(3), 39–52 (1990)
23. Online Marketing Thailand: The state of social media (2020). https://www.syndacast.com/infographic-online-marketing-thailand-the-state-of-social-edia/#:~:text=Youtube%20in%20Thailand,per%20visit%20is%2017.3%20minutes. Accessed 8 June 2021
24. Marsh, H.W., Hocevar, D.: Application of confirmatory factor analysis to the study of self-concept: first- and higher order factor models and their invariance across groups. Psychol. Bull. **97**(3), 562–582 (1985). https://doi.org/10.1037/0033-2909.97.3.562
25. Bentler, P.M.: Comparative fit indexes in structural models. Psychol. Bull. **107**(2), 238–246 (1990). https://doi.org/10.1037/0033-2909.107.2.238
26. Cole, D.A.: Utility of confirmatory factor analysis in test validation research. J. Consult. Clin. Psych. **55**(4), 584–594 (1987). https://doi.org/10.1037/0022-006X.55.4.584
27. Marsh, H.W., Balla, J.R., McDonald, R.P.: Goodness-of-fit indexes in confirmatory factor analysis: the effect of sample size. Psychol. Bull. **103**(3), 391–410 (1988). https://doi.org/10.1037/0033-2909.103.3.391
28. Browne, M.W., Cudeck, R.: Alternative ways of assessing model fit. In: Bollen, K.A., Long, J.S. (eds.) Testing Structural Equation Models, pp. 136–162. Sage, Newbury Park, CA (1993)
29. Jöreskog, K.G., Sörbom, D.: LISREL 8: Structural Equation Modeling with the SIMPLIS Command Language. Scientific Software International, Chicago (1993)

30. Hair, J.F., Tomas, G., Hult, M., Ringle, C.M., Sarstedt, M.: A Primer on Partial Least Squares Structural Equation Modeling (PLS-SEM). SAGE Publications, Incorporated, Los Angeles (2014)
31. Schumacker, R.E., Lomax, R.G.: A Beginner's Guide to Structural Equation Modeling, 2nd edn. Lawrence Erlbaum Associates, Mahwah (2004)
32. López, V.A., Iglesias, S.: A reputational-performance framework in an SME context: some empirical evidence from Spain. Irish J. Manag. **29**(2), 35–66 (2010)
33. Norzaidi, M.D., Chong, S.C., Salwani, M.I.: Perceived resistance, user resistance and managers' performance in the Malaysian port industry. Aslib Proc. **60**(3), 242–264 (2008)
34. Cheong, H.J., Morrison, M.A.: Consumers' reliance on product information and recommendations found in UGC. J. Interac. Advert. **8**(2), 1–30 (2008)
35. Hennig-Thurau, T., Gwinner, K.P., Walsh, G., Gremler, D.D.: Electronic word-of-mouth via consumer-opinion platforms: what motivates consumers to articulate themselves on the internet? J. Interact. Market. **18**(1), 38–52 (2004)
36. Bae, S., Lee, T.: Product type and consumers' perception of online consumer reviews. Electron. Mark. **21**(4), 255–266 (2011)
37. Horst, M., Kuttschreuter, M., Gutteling, J.M.: Perceived usefulness, personal experiences, risk perception and trust as determinants of adoption of e-government services in The Netherlands. Comput. Hum. Behav. **23**(4), 1838–1852 (2007)
38. Kim, H., Song, J.: The quality of word-of-mouth in the online shopping mall. J. Res. Interac. Market. **4**(4), 376–390 (2010)
39. Khalid, B., Chaveesuk, S., Chaiyasoonthorn, W.: MOOCs adoption in higher education: a management perspective. Polish J. Manag. Stud. **23**(1), 239–256 (2021)
40. Muangmee, C., Kot, S., Meekaewkunchorn, N., Kassakorn, N., Khalid, B.: Factors determining the behavioral intention of using food delivery apps during COVID-19 pandemics. J. Theor. Appl. Electron. Commer. Res. **16**(5), 1297–1310 (2021)
41. Kornpitack, P., Sawmong, S.: Empirical analysis of factors influencing student satisfaction with online learning systems during the COVID-19 pandemic in Thailand. Heliyon **8**(3), e09183 (2022)
42. Barykin, S., Borovkov, A., Rozhdestvenskiy, O., Tarshin, A., Yadykin, V.: Staff competence and training for digital industry. In: IOP Conference Series: Materials Science and Engineering, p. 012106, September 2020. https://doi.org/10.1088/1757-899x/940/1/012106
43. Barykin, S.Y., Bochkarev, A.A., Kalinina, O.V., Yadykin, V.K.: Concept for a supply chain digital twin. Int. J. Math., Eng. Manag. Sci. **5**(6), 1498–1515 (2016). https://doi.org/10.33889/ijmems.2020.5.6.111
44. Jonas, J.R.O.: Source credibility of company - produced and user - generated content on the internet: an exploratory study on the Filipino youth. Philippine Manag. Rev. **17**, 121–132 (2010)

Regional Innovation Systems and Clusters as Drivers of the Economic Growth During the Fourth Industrial Revolution

Revisiting the Question of Digitalization and Bioenergy Development in the Russian Federation Regions

Ksenia Pereverzeva(✉) ⓘ, Denis Tsvetkov ⓘ, Konstantin Petrov ⓘ, and Svetlana Gutman ⓘ

Peter the Great St. Petersburg Polytechnic University, St. Petersburg, Russia
pereverzeva_kv@spbstu.ru

Abstract. Bioenergy has been getting more and more popular as an alternative energy source in recent years. In Russia this type of energy generation has not become wide-spread yet, even though it seems potentially important for some regions of the country as bioenergy can be used to generate not only electrical, but also thermal power. This study is aimed at justifiably selecting a region that has the greatest potential for the bioenergy sector. The region was chosen in several steps using methods and tools that were suitable for meeting the objectives that had been set. At the first stage, a ranking score was used to choose several regions of the RF that have the most favorable natural, climatic and economic conditions for the bioenergy sector. At the second stage, Krasnodar Region was picked out of the formed pool of regions as it is a region with a low energy security level and high economic and agricultural potential for the development of bioenergy. At the third stage, the fuzzy logic method was applied for deciding if the region was ready for developing the bioenergy sector. The aggregate obtained showed a high state of readiness of Krasnodar Region for developing bioenergy according to the suggested ranking score. In their recommendations for further research, the authors of the paper suggest developing the region's bioenergy sector in conjunction with digital technology, namely by introducing "smart" greenhouses, applying digital technology for maintaining the most favorable conditions for animals, and using automated collection of biofuel.

Keywords: Bioenergy · Biogas · Biofuel · Digitalization · Smart greenhouses

1 Introduction

The need to search for new ways to develop alternative energy sources is obvious all around the world. For Russia, where hydrocarbon energy dominates and alternative energy is virtually absent, finding new solutions is especially important [1–3]. For example, the share of RES (excluding hydropower) in the total electrical power is 68% in Denmark, 32% in Germany, and 31% in the UK. These countries are the leaders. It should be noted that as for traditional RES, the bioenergy sector is also quite well-developed in these countries. Bioenergy is less popular alternative energy source in comparison with

© Springer Nature Switzerland AG 2022
D. Rodionov et al. (Eds.): SPBPU IDE 2021, CCIS 1619, pp. 53–70, 2022.
https://doi.org/10.1007/978-3-031-14985-6_4

electricity generated from wind or solar power, but it has a great potential. Energy can be produced using various resources:

- hard types of biofuel (chipped wood and wood waste from timber cutting processes, granules, straw, etc.);
- biogas;
- liquid biofuel;
- biomass that can be used for producing both electrical power and heat, similarly to traditional fossil fuel burning power stations.

Thus, when the process of using biomass is correctly organized, no additional pollution of the environment is caused by greenhouse gases [4].

Apart from environmental benefits, biogas has the following advantages:

- Abundance and replenishment of resources. There is plenty of biomass and it is a renewable energy source both in the vegetable form and in the form of waste products of living organisms.
- Waste disposal, prevention of methane emissions in the air. Applying organic waste and reducing the amounts of refuse in landfills. Less chemical fertilizers, which is the way to cushion the effects on soil and ground water.
- Versatility of biomass. Using various types of biomass and biological waste, electrical power and heat generation, biogas production.
- Making several end products: heat for buildings (from cooling reactors or gas burning); electricity (up to 2 kW of electrical power from one cubic meter of biogas); biogas itself.

The possibility of generating thermal energy from biomass is especially important for some regions of the Russian Federation [5]. The purpose of this paper is to validate the choice of the region that has a potential for introducing bioenergy. The paper considers not only the world experience in the bioenergy sector, but also suggest ways to develop it using digital technology. Finding new solutions for developing regions remains a key objective for Russia [6, 7].

The leading role in the amounts of gas generated in the European Union is played by technical crops and waste from the farming industry, which accounts for around 70% of biogas production; a considerable share is contributed by waste from private households and enterprises (around 20%); the remaining 8–10% comes from communal sewage treatment plants.

Germany is the leading producer of electrical power and gas generated from biological sources. The country has about half of all European bioenergy power plants. Supporting this sector ensures and stimulates a very significant factor – the state's commitment to buy electrical power at the "green tariff" [8, 9].

In Denmark biogas amounts for about one fifth of energy consumption inside the country. The biggest number of plants operate on animal farms where different types of waste are used as fuel.

It is worth highlighting the experience of Italy, where bioenergy has become widely spread over the last decade [10]. The growth of bioenergy can be explained by the focus on producing electrical power from biological sources (increase up to 90%), as well as 22% of increase in heat generated from biomass and 129% of increase in production of biofuel. To a large extent, these figures became a reality due to the commissioning of two electric power plants by the company Enel Green Power in Toscana. The power plants use the energy of biomass for primary heating of geothermal steam so as to increase the efficiency of air flows produced by geothermal heating [11, 12]. Toscana is an illustrative example of the improved socio-economic position of the region due to the power industry.

The USA has been using biofuel since 1910s [13]. Today about 80% of bioenergy power plants use biogas as fuel. Its production is based on dairy farms – cattle dung is used for producing natural methane that is further utilized for energy and electricity generation. The total capacity of all plants on such farms approximates 60 MW.

According to the Bioenergy International Journal, more than 86% of the potential of biogas production is in plant raw materials and animal waste while only 8% is accounted for industrial and communal waste. For this reason, producing biogas from organic agricultural waste and technical energy crops seems to be quite promising.

The development of the global and Russian alternative energy sector is closely related to energy security. A lot of research is conducted by the world scientific community. Energy security is studied from the perspective of economic aspects [13, 14] and sustainable development [15]. Special attention is given to risks [16], and the levels of energy security in different countries are compared [17]. One way or another, all this variety of scientific studies are aimed at searching for alternative ways of energy production, one of which is bioenergy [36–40]. The world academic literature touches upon the topic of bioenergy much more often [18–20] than the Russian one [21]. Thus the paper written by Vijayendra Singh Sankhla et al. [31] describes a refrigerating system working on biogas and using the absorption principle. The plant operates noiselessly and has no moving parts. The system can use any source of heat and operate anywhere without any engineering infrastructure. The above paper analyzes the losses of the plant and evaluates the productivity of the designed refrigerating system for more efficient use of renewable energy sources so that fridges could be fed using the principle of absorption. The paper by Rut Serra et al. [32] discusses the possibility of replacing fossil hydrocarbons with forest bioenergy, which can noticeably mitigate the effects on climate due to reduced emissions of greenhouse gases. However, it is calculated that no economy of greenhouse gases is achieved until the prevented fossil fuel emissions compensate the loss of atmospheric carbon that would be isolated if biomass was not used for bioenergy. The paper measures the potential for reducing greenhouse gas emissions and the time of receiving these benefits for the atmosphere in case usual natural gas is substituted for renewable natural gas that is obtained from various forest raw materials in three provinces of Canada. The article by N.E. Sokolinskaya et al. [33] presents a feasibility study of the technological scheme of a biogas plant on a pig breeding farm with a livestock of 1500 heads. The electrical efficiency of this plant reaches 26–30%, while the output temperature of the cooling liquid/water can be 95 °C, which suits to heat buildings. The discounted payback period is 8 years 8 months. If the suggested scheme of the biogas plant is widely used in pig-breeding enterprises of Russia, it will considerably mitigate the problem of production waste disposal and storage, which will have a positive effect on the country's environment and lead to simultaneous increase in autonomy and profitability of the energy sector. In addition, foreign publications study the area of digital bioenergy [22, 23], which is the further evidence that the research topic we have chosen is relevant and important.

2 Materials and Methods

In order to put forward recommendations upon the development of the bioenergy sector in Russia, at the first stage of this research study we chose a region that would satisfy the criteria that characterized it as favorable for this field. Such criteria can be: natural-climatic conditions, economic situation, internal level of development of the energy system. In addition, special attention should be paid to the energy security level and readiness of the region for developing the bioenergy sector.

In order to select a specific region, we ranked various regions of the RF based on the natural-climatic and economic indicators important for the bioenergy sector.

The world practice applies rankings for assessing, grading and classifying a wide range of parameters that are used for calculating complex aggregates. The most common types of ranking are sorting and classification.

The basis of any type of ranking procedure is a clearly devised system. Each basic system has the following main components:

The ranking score methodology includes the following stages:

- collect and process analytical and statistical information for the period under study;
- select and validate the system of indicators used in the ranking;
- choose the method and calculate the final ranking score coefficient;
- classify and grade enterprises according to the ranking [24].

At the second stage, the energy security level of regions was evaluated. The evaluation of energy security can embrace over 100 indicators [25]. The simplest methods suggest measuring energy security using just one indicator, for example, the share of the region's own energy resources in the total energy consumption [26]. The existing diversity of indicators make analytical estimations and comparison of regions more complicated. An essential problem of the assessment is the search for the necessary source data that can be used for measuring the energy security level, which is especially relevant to the RF regions. Given the existing constraints, the task was to select the assessment methodology relying on generally accessible information that would be sufficient for measuring the regional level of energy security and carrying out interregional comparisons.

This problem was resolved by using an approach that relies on the following list of indicators having a significant effect on the energy security level of the region [27]:

- availability of the region's own primary energy sources,
- efficiency of the energy supply system;

Human Development Index
This approach was chosen because it can be applied to measure the energy security level in the region using widely available information.

At the third stage, after selecting the region obtained as a result of the first two stages of research, a fuzzy logic method was applied to determine the readiness level of a specific region for developing the bioenergy sector.

Fuzzy set theory and fuzzy logic form the basis of the linguistic approach, in which variables in the analytical description of the model can take on linguistic values. Using fuzzy set models and obtaining aggregates based on a population of available indicators that differ by properties and measurement units can simplify the procedure of the analysis in order to classify the objects of the research by a set of essential parameters and compare them with a given accuracy degree [28].

The theory of fuzzy sets assumes the following sequence of actions:

– Define the list of quantitative and qualitative indicators that characterize the bioenergy development level of a region.
– Introduce a linguistic variable and form the scores for assessing the bioenergy development level of the region and compiling the ranking.
– Normalize the indicators and form a matrix of factor values.
– Calculate the aggregate of the bioenergy development level of the region.

Thus, the sequence of steps to be taken to achieve the aim of the research is as follows:

Define the list of quantitative and qualitative indicators that characterize the bioenergy development level of the region.

– Based on the ranking of the natural-climatic and economic indicators of various RF regions, select the region with the greatest potential for developing the bioenergy sector.
– Evaluate the energy security level of the regions through calculating the following indicators: availability of its own primary energy sources in the region, efficiency of the energy system, Human Development Index.
– Apply the fuzzy logic approach to measure the readiness level of the region for developing the bioenergy sector.

The information basis of the research study is statistics and ranking scores. System, comparative and content analysis can be highlighted as the major qualitative methods that were used for achieving the aim of this research.

3 Results

The method of region ranking is quite widely used. As noted above, the assessment is made according to the selected indicators and the positions of regions are determined by each of them. The final ranking score of a region is determined by summing the positions by each indicator. The highest ranking is obtained by the region with the least sum of positions.

At the first stage of the study, when the ranking is made and regions are compared to find out which of the socially and economically developed regions with agricultural specialization is the most suitable for developing the bioenergy sector, several regions were chosen from three largest districts producing agricultural goods – Central Federal District, South Federal District and Volga Federal District. These regions are listed in Table 1:

Table 1. List of regions for ranking

District name	Region name
Central Federal District	Belgorod region
	Voronezh region
	Kursk region
Southern Federal District	Krasnodar region
	Volgograd region
	Rostov region
Volga Federal District	Republic of Tatarstan
	Saratov region

* Compiled by the authors

The regions from this list were ranked according to the following indicators included in Table 2:

Table 2. Indicators for ranking the selected RF regions

	Indicator	Units of calculation
1	Population	Thousand people
2	Share of rural population	%
3	Rural labor force	Thousand people
4	Unemployment rate	%
5	Cost of a kW of electricity	Rub.
6	Electricity consumption	Million W/h
7	Agricultural area	Thousand Ha
8	Forest land	Thousand Ha
9	Emissions of pollutants into the atmosphere	Thousand tons
10	Capture of air pollutants	Thousand tons
11	Fixed capital investments	RUB mln
12	GRP	RUB mln
13	Agricultural produce volumes	RUB mln

* Compiled by the authors

The criteria were selected to meet the need for classifying the regions by indicators that reflect the significance of each region in terms of the economic and energy systems of the country, and are directly related to the possibility of developing the bioenergy sector in a specific region.

After the ranking was carried out for each indicator, all ranking scores were summed for every single region. The lower the sum of the aggregate ranking, the more preferable the region is for developing the bioenergy sector, because every ranking score showed the preference of each region by one or another indicator from the lowest to the highest.

The results of the study for all the regions are presented in Table 3 below.

Table 3. Final regional ranking scores

Rank no. region	1	2	3	4	5	6	7	8	9	10	11	12	13	Total
Krasnodar region	1	1	1	6	1	2	4	1	1	1	2	2	1	24
Volgograd region	4	8	3	8	2	4	1	4	5	6	5	6	7	63
Rostov region	2	5	8	6	5	3	3	6	3	2	4	3	2	52
Belgorod region	7	3	5	3	3	5	8	8	4	3	7	5	3	64
Voronezh region	6	4	6	2	7	7	6	5	7	7	3	4	5	69
Kursk region	8	2	7	5	6	8	3	7	8	8	8	8	6	84
Republic of Tatarstan	3	7	2	1	3	1	5	2	2	4	1	1	4	36
Saratov region	5	6	4	4	8	6	2	3	6	5	6	7	8	70

* Compiled by the authors

According to the results of the ranking assessment, it was concluded that Krasnodar and the Republic of Tatarstan are the regions with the greatest potential for developing the bioenergy sector. When these two regions are considered, it can be noted that Krasnodar Region is more preferable for developing the bioenergy sector by all key indicators except for the unemployment rate. Consequently, out of all the regions most suitable for developing the bioenergy sector, Krasnodar Region is the most suitable in terms of the level of its natural-climatic and economic indicators.

At the second stage of the research, the region was selected for introducing bioenergy projects in it based on the evaluation of its energy security level.

In order to validate the need for expanding the amounts of electrical power generated by the internal capacities of each region by setting up bioenergy power plants on the territory of the region, the energy security of several regions was estimated. The results obtained were compared in order to identify the region most suitable for this aim.

The following basic indicators were used to estimate the regions' energy security:

– Human Development Index;
– Resource Efficiency Index;
– energy availability level in the regions.

According to Rosstat, we defined the indices included in Table 4. The HDI of each region is a specific indicator, while the Resource Efficiency Index will be the same for all the regions, since they all are territorial constituencies of the Russian Federation.

Table 4. Statistical indices of the regions for 2018

Region	HDI	Resource efficiency index
Krasnodar region	0.885	0.640
Volgograd region	0.871	0.640
Rostov region	0.874	0.640
Belgorod region	0.908	0.640
Voronezh region	0.885	0.640
Kursk region	0.881	0.640
Republic of Tatarstan	0.921	0.640
Saratov region	0.865	0.640

[*] Compiled by the authors according to [34]

Then the Energy Availability Index was calculated. Table 5 contains the values obtained:

Table 5. Energy availability index

Region	Energy production, mln. W	Energy sold outside the region, mln. W	Total consumption, mln. W	Energy availability index	
				Real	Maximal
Krasnodar Region	10693237	5602 920.8	24772249.9	0.4317	0.2055
Volgograd Region	16894566.2	10481 118.9	16238913.7	1.0404	0.3949
Rostov Region	4456 407.4	26064 922.8	19324105.6	2.3061	0.9572
Belgorod Region	1111001.6	3611.9	16150319.4	0.0688	0.0686
Voronezh Region	23065739.1	15024 442	11974082.1	1.9263	0.6716
Kursk Region	25130171.5	16560 241	8706740.1	2.8863	0.9843
Republic of Tatarstan	2924 900.8	11623 838	30952529	0.9447	0.5692
Saratov Region	39462544.7	26474 407.8	13015604	3.0319	0.9979

[*] Compiled by the authors according to [34]

Then the estimations were used to calculate the final indicator – the energy security level of the RF regions.

A low energy security level of a region is the evidence of the need for modernizing the energy system of the region and using alternative energy sources. The maximal and actual energy security level for each region is given in Table 6 below:

Table 6. Energy security level of the RF regions

Region	Energy security level of region	
	Highest possible	Actual
Krasnodar Region	0.2445	0.1164
Volgograd Region	0.5893	0.2237
Rostov Region	1.3061	0.5422
Belgorod Region	0.0390	0.0388
Voronezh Region	1.0911	0.3804
Kursk Region	1.6348	0.5575
Republic of Tatarstan	0.5351	0.3224
Saratov Region	1.7173	0.5652

* Compiled by the authors

Thus, two regions that are the most preferable from the perspective of their potential for developing the energy sector and internal energy system as a whole are Krasnodar Region and Belgorod region. The preference was given to Krasnodar Region for the following reasons: the region already has an elaborate energy supply system; the electrical power capacities of the region make it possible to generate the amounts of electricity considerable for the region. These are the premises for the region's self-provision with energy as of today.

Eventually, 8 regions were ranked in terms of their economic development and energy security. As a result, Krasnodar Region was picked up. Krasnodar Region has a relatively low development level of the energy sector, but is economically advanced according to the results of the ranking (see Table 3). It has suitable natural-climatic conditions, which is the evidence that it has some potential for developing the bioenergy sector.

At the third stage, the region was investigated to find out about its degree of aptitude for developing the bioenergy sector.

This study was carried out using fuzzy sets theory in order to identify the aggregate indicator of the region as a territory having and considering the development of the bioenergy sector as a constituent part of the internal energy system.

When the estimation scale was built, the following indicators were determined by the inputs:

– Variable $\times 1$ reflects the ability of the region to meet the needs of the entire region and its population to provide them with a sufficient level of energy resources produced locally and ensure the sustainability of the whole socio-economic system of the region.

– Variable ×2 reflects the cost of one kilowatt of electricity according the average regional tariff, which allows introducing more advanced, but still more expensive ways of generating electrical power.
– Variable ×3 reflects the focus of the region on sustainable environmental development of the energy system as a share of the applied capacities of green energy in the total energy balance of the region's system.
– Variable ×4 reflects the share of rural population in total population, which indicates the level of population dispersal along the territory of the entire region and the need to develop a considerable extension of the effective power grid.
– Variable ×5 reflects the area of agricultural land, which illustrates the degree of the region's focus on this sector and the possibility of obtaining raw materials for synthesizing electricity for consumers from bioenergy.
– Variable ×6 reflects the share of captured harmful emissions from stationary sources, which illustrates the region's focus on more environmentally friendly operation of all sectors and industries.
– Variable ×7 reflects the share of contribution made by agriculture in the total GRP of the region, which indicates the significance of this type of activity for the region.
– Variable ×8 reflects the share of investment made in development of lands and industrial buildings, which concerns agricultural and energy sectors.
– Variable ×9 reflects the amount of agricultural produce in value terms, which indicates the significance of this type of activity and its development level in the region.
– Variable ×10 reflects the amount of investment in academic and research activities, which indicates the focus of the region on development both in the extensive and intensive direction.

In order to evaluate the region's readiness level for developing the bioenergy sector, let us introduce a linguistic variable "readiness level of the RF regions for developing the bioenergy sector" and describe it with a set of indicators:

$$Y = [x; T; D],$$

where x is the name of the variable "readiness level of the RF regions for developing the bioenergy sector; T is the range of values "low readiness level", "below average readiness level", "average readiness level", "above average readiness level", "high readiness average level"; D is the range of definition on the segment [0;1].

The value of function Y characterizes the readiness level of the RF regions for developing the bioenergy sector depending on a number of the chosen factors (x). This function is a parameter assessing this element. In order to measure the readiness level of the RF regions for developing the bioenergy sector, a fuzzy scale of variable Y is developed (Table 7).

Table 7. Scale of the regions' readiness level for developing the bioenergy sector

Range	Designation	Definition
0–0.333	"Low readiness level"	Ineffective use of resources available, too cheap traditional electrical power, low growth rates of the agricultural industry, weakly developed energy sector, continuous use of hydrocarbons, considerable emissions into the atmosphere, lack of investment into the production industry and scientific activities, sparse population throughout the territory
0.167–0.500	"Below average readiness level"	Rudimental development and use of renewable energy sources, low growth rates of the agricultural industry, considerable harmful emissions, low investment into the production industry and scientific activities, insufficiently developed energy sector
0.333–0.667	"Average readiness level"	Satisfactorily developed energy sector, low level of use of renewable energy sources, noticeably large population in the territory, considerable burden of the economy on the environment, average level of development and influence of the agriculture on the economy, average investment in the development and research activities
0.500–0.833	"Above average readiness level"	Highly developed and productive energy sector, practical application of green energy, low burden on the environment, considerable share of population spread in the territory, well-developed agriculture, electricity prices make it possible to introduce new technologies without causing damage to the consumers
0.667–1	"High readiness level"	Effective use of energy resources, large proportion of green energy, substantial funding of academic and research activities, electricity prices allow transferring to green energy, very low harmful emissions into the atmosphere, large population

* Compiled by the authors

Table 8 shows the indicators for all the ten x-variables for 2019:

Table 8. Values of indicators for Krasnodar Region. Final table

Indicators	Krasnodar region	Russia, mean value	Normalized value for Krasnodar region
X1, %	0.431662	1	−0.56834
X2, RUR	4.69	3,31	0.416918
X3, %	0.137793	0,21	−0.34384
X4, %	44.6	25,3	0.762846
X5, %	62.3	13	3.792308
X6, %	71.7	75	−0.044
X7, %	10.2	4.1	1.487805
X8, %	41	39.5	0.037975
X9, RUR mln	417201	69,896	4.968882
X10, RUR mln	5772.4	9090.423	−0.365

* Compiled by the authors

The values of the selected factors were normalized using the following formula:

$$x = \frac{x_i - \overline{x}}{\overline{x}} \tag{1}$$

Since the assessment of the region's readiness for developing the bioenergy sector is multi-component, and all the indicators used in the assessment were comparably significant for the final indicator, the weight of each factor is taken as equal. The model assumes that all the factors are equivalent. The authors chose 10 factors for the analysis. Hence, the significance of the factors ri is calculated using the formula: $r_i = \frac{1}{10}$. I.e. the significance level of each factor with their total quantity being equal to 10 is 0.1.

If there is a set of $i = 1..N$ individual factors with their current values xi, and each factor is corresponded by its M-level classifier, the quantitative value of the aggregate factor can be determined using the following double convolution formula [28]:

$$A\_N = \sum_{j=1}^{M} \alpha_j \sum_{i=1}^{N} d_i \mu_{ij}(x_i) \tag{2}$$

where αj is the nodal points, di is the weight of the i-th factor in the convultion, μij (xi) is the value of the membership function of the j-th qualitative level in relation to the current value of the i-th factor, M is the number of classifier levels.

The final formula for a five-level classifier will have the following form:

$$y = \sum_{j=1}^{5} y_j \sum_{i=1}^{N} r_i \lambda_{ij} \tag{3}$$

where yi is the nodal points of triangular numbers, λij is determined according to the matrix table.

The nodal points are calculating using the following formula:

$$y_j = 0.833 - 0.167 * (j - 1) \tag{4}$$

According to the data obtained, the value of the integral indicator of the readiness for developing the bioenergy sector in 2019 amounted to 0.66398.

It means that in 2019 Krasnodar Region was 66.40% above the average readiness level of the energy sector for developing alternative energy resources and is 33.60% higher in terms of list readiness for becoming "green", which is also a high level.

At the age of information technology, digital technology is forever developing, the same as AI based equipment that can be used in various sectors of production industry. Bioenergy is a relatively new sector that cannot do without advanced digital technology.

4 Discussion

Based on the literature review made in this study, it should be highlighted that there are a lot of articles dedicated to the technical aspect of the bioenergy sector, including digitalization. The study by RaúlTauro, RobertoRangel et al. [22] is about a web-platform set up in Mexico for facilitating decision-making in planning the bioenergy sector. The work by Mohammad Reza Ghatreh Samani, Seyyed-Mahdi Hosseini-Motlagh [23] considers digital technology in the bioenergy sector using the case study of Iran. The paper by J An and N E Sokolinskaya [33] studies the economic efficiency of building a biogas plant in large enterprises of the Russian Federation. Most commonly, studies consider the development of the bioenergy sector at the level of an individual country or several countries, but the specifics of regions are not taken into account. This paper attempts to combine these two areas of research: validating the choice of the region for developing the bioenergy sector given the possibilities of digital technology.

The region we chose – Krasnodar Region – has favorable natural-climatic conditions and so agriculture is well-developed. Some types of crops in the southern parts of the region are harvested two times a year, which is the way to obtain waste in the form of plant remains (later, silage) in larger quantities each year. Silage is a source of biogas that is biofuel.

A traditional biogas plant is a small heat power plant with a starting engine capable of operating on locally produced biogas. It feeds the pumps and the generator that produces electricity. When operating the generating power unit itself can produce large amounts of heat, which means it has to be continuously cooled. The heat collected through heat exchange process in water heating is used for bringing warmth to buildings and premises.

Small and medium-type power plants are the most realistic and preferable projects for implementation in Krasnodar Region. These plants have the following advantages [29]:

– enough raw materials both in the region and in the neighboring areas;
– affordability of raw materials;

– affordability of equipment manufactured domestically as an alternative to foreign analogs;
– strong focus of the region on agriculture and, as a result, simplified waste disposal process;
– big demand for electricity and rather high local electricity rates for consumers in comparison with the average country values.

According to the estimations made by a company that presents this kind of projects (small biogas plants) in Germany, the financial results are as follows [29]:

– The total annual revenue from selling biogas, electrical power, heat and recycling waste is about 4.5 million euros.

The total annual costs of a similar scale project are almost 3 million euros. This amount includes:

– 1.9 million on buying raw materials, waste disposal and electricity provision of the plant itself;
– 180 thousand on the cost of personnel labor;
– 460 thousand on technical maintenance;
– about 400 thousand on insurance and commercial aspects.

The full cost of building such a plant can be up to 14.5 million euros. Despite the initial expensiveness of such power plants, they have been erected abroad for several years already [58].

However, in order to operate a plant of this size has to meet certain requirements in terms of the amounts of waste, unless specially grown technical crops are used as raw materials.

The criteria of economic feasibility of biogas projects in terms of available waste as a necessary raw material are presented in Table 9.

Table 9. Criteria of the necessary amounts of raw materials (a day)

Waste source type	Livestock/amount of waste
Cattle complexes	From 8 000 heads
Pig farms	From 70 000 heads
Poultry farms	From 1 000 000 heads
Slaughterhouses and meat processing plants	Over 80 tons
Grain waste	Over 30 tons
Wastewater treatment plant	Over 150 tons

* Compiled by the authors according to [35]

However, all these requirements can be met inside the region, since the statistics show the following factors included in Table 10.

Table 10. Agricultural indicators of the Krasnodar Region

Indicator type	Livestock/production	Place in the country
Livestock of sheep and goats	212.2 thousand	22
Livestock of cattle	538.8 thousand	7
Livestock of pigs	626.9 thousand	9
Meat production	409.5 thousand tons	3
Grain harvesting	13,881.1 thousand tons	1

* Compiled by the authors according to [35]

In order to increase the agricultural indicators of Krasnodar Region, we suggest several areas related to digital technology: smart greenhouse, digital technology to maintain the best living conditions of animals, automated collection of biofuel.

The most efficient area for increasing the agricultural land indicators, i.e. yield, is the use of greenhouses where digital systems are introduced. Such greenhouses make it possible to install automated interval watering systems and grow harvest with specially controlled ultraviolet lighting. The introduction of smart greenhouses triples the yield [30]. This happens because crops can be grown round the year, which in turn, increases the amounts of plant remains that serve as fuel in the biogas power plant.

The cost of a smart greenhouse is about 5,000 euros per unit sized 4 × 4 × 12 m. Thus, in order to provide 1 hectare of land with such greenhouses, 1 million euros is needed. In combination with the cost of the power plant, the total amount is about 15.5 million euros with the recuperation period being 8–9.5 years.

Smart technologies can also be used on animal farms. There specialized devices can be installed to control food and water consumed by animals. These devices are based on artificial intelligence, which can adapt to the biological rhythm of an animal. In addition, artificial intelligence can be used on these farms for automated collection of biofuel.

All the above can help implement bioenergy projects, which are integral and harmonious in their processes, form biofuel production to electricity generation. The specific feature of such projects is the possibility of levelling off the load of the biogas power plant at the peaks of energy consumptions.

5   Conclusion

The course for developing environmentally safe power economy has been adopted in the countries all around the world. That is the reason why this paper discusses one of the types of green energy – biogas power plants.

The paper describes the mechanism used for selecting a region of the Russian Federation most favorable for developing the bioenergy sector, in particular, for introducing biogas power plants. At the first stage, the list of quantitative and qualitative indicators was defined to be used as a basis for ranking the natural-climatic and economic state of the RF regions. Krasnodar Region was determined as the region with the greatest potential for developing the bioenergy sector. At the second stage the energy security level was measured for the regions selected. Krasnodar Region was picked up again as the most favorable for developing the bioenergy sector. At the third stage the readiness of Krasnodar Region for developing the bioenergy sector was evaluated and recommendations on developing digital technology were given. The readiness of Krasnodar Region for developing the bioenergy sector was assessed using the fuzzy logic method.

The paper also considers the mechanism for improving the agricultural indicators of Krasnodar Region. In order to make these indicators grow, it is suggested using digitalization, namely smart greenhouses, due to which the yield of crops can be increased; digital technology for maintaining the best living conditions for animals, which increases their life expectance and, in turn, results in sufficient food supply in the region; automated collection of biofuel, which reduces the probability that the region can lack electrical power.

Acknowledgements. The research was partially funded by the Ministry of Science and Higher Education of the Russian Federation under the strategic academic leadership program 'Priority 2030' (agreement 075-15-2021-1333, dated 30 September 2021).

References

1. Bataev, A., Potyarkin, V., Glushkova, A., Samorukov, D.: Assessment of development effectiveness of solar energy in Russia. In: E3S Web Conference Energy Systems Environmental Impacts (ESEI 2020), vol. 221 (2020). https://doi.org/10.1051/e3sconf/202022103002
2. Bekbaev, A., Shakenov, K.B., Titkov, V.: Analysis of the roof of an autonomous house for efficient use of wind energy. EAI Endorsed Trans. Energy Web and Inf. Tech. **6**(21) (2018). https://doi.org/10.4108/eai.12-9-2018.155859
3. Pantskhava, E.S.: Biogas technologies (2008)
4. Bataev, A., Samorukov, D., Glushkova, A., Potyarkin, V.: Public-private partnership as a mechanism for the development of heat supply. In: E3S Web of Conference Energy Systems Environmental Impacts (ESEI 2020). vol. 221 (2020). https://doi.org/10.1051/e3sconf/202022103001
5. Rodionov, Dmitriy G., Konnikov, Evgenii A., Nasrutdinov, Magomedgusen N.: A transformation of the approach to evaluating a region's investment attractiveness as a consequence of the COVID-19 pandemic. Economies **9**(2), 59 (2021). https://doi.org/10.3390/economies9020059
6. Kudryavtseva, T., Skhvediani, A., Berawi, M.A.: Modeling cluster development using programming methods: case of Russian Arctic regions. J. Entrepreneurship Sustain. Issues **8**(1), 150–176 (2020). https://doi.org/10.9770/jesi.2020.8.1(10)
7. The EU experience in using biogas in the energy sector: Zeleneet.com: Journal "Green World" (2021). http://zeleneet.com/opyt-es-v-ispolzovanii-biogaza-v-energetike/2619/. Accessed 21 Jan 2021
8. Overview of biogas production in the world: Biowatt.com.ua: News website (2021). http://www.biowatt.com.ua/analitika/obzor-proizvodstva-biogaza-v-mire/. Accessed 21 Jan 2021
9. Bartolini, F.: Impacts of the CAP 2014–2020 on the Agroenergy Sector in Tuscany, Italy, Energies, № 8 (2015)
10. Enel Green Power: Enelgreenpower.com: Official company website (2020). https://www.enelgreenpower.com/it/chi-siamo

11. The first integrated power plant in the world: Energy-Fresh.ru: News journal «Energy Fresh» (2020): http://www.energy-fresh.ru/other-energy/geoenergy/?id=11631. Accessed 10 Oct 2020
12. American energy: The renewable path to energy security. Worldwatch Institute and Center for American Progress (2006)
13. Wang, J., Shahbaz, M., Song, M.: Evaluating energy economic security and its influencing factors in China. Energy **229**, 120638 (2021). https://doi.org/10.1016/j.energy.2021.120638
14. NjindanIykea, B., Thao, V., Paresh, T., Narayan, K.: Can energy security predict energy stock returns? Energy Econ. **94** (2021). https://doi.org/10.1016/j.eneco.2020.105052
15. Brodny, Jarosław, Tutak, Magdalena: The comparative assessment of sustainable energy security in the Visegrad countries. A 10-year perspective. J. Clean. Product. **317**, 128427 (2021). https://doi.org/10.1016/j.jclepro.2021.128427
16. Axon, C.J., Darton, R.C.: Sustainability and risk – a review of energy security. Sustain. Product. Consump. **27** (2021). https://doi.org/10.1016/j.spc.2021.01.018
17. Gasser, P.: A review on energy security indices to compare country performances. Energy Policy **139**, 111339 (2020). https://doi.org/10.1016/j.enpol.2020.111339
18. Sankhla, V.S., Sharma, D., Kothari, S., Jain, S., Agarwal, C.: Design and analysis of biogas powered refrigerator for dairy farmers. Int. J. Eng. Adv. Technol. **9** (2019). https://doi.org/10.35940/ijeat.E7321.109119
19. Serraa, R., Nikniab, I., Paréa, D., Brian, T., Bruno, G., Laganière, J.: From conventional to renewable natural gas: can we expect GHG savings in the near term? Biomass Bioenerg. **131** (2019). https://doi.org/10.1016/j.biombioe.2019.105396
20. Alsaleh, M., Abdul-Rahim, A.S. Abdulwakil, M.M.: The importance of worldwide governance indicators for transitions toward sustainable bioenergy industry. J. Environ. Manage. **294** (2021). https://doi.org/10.1016/j.jenvman.2021.112960
21. Nizhegorodtsev, R.M., Sekerin, V.D., Gorokhova, A.E.: Developing bioenergy as a solution to the problems of energy and environmental security. National interests: priorities and security, No. 42 (2012). https://cyberleninka.ru/article/n/razvitie-bioenergetiki-kak-reshenie-problem-energeticheskoy-i-ekologicheskoy-bezopasnosti
22. Tauro, R., et al.: An integrated user-friendly web-based spatial platform for bioenergy planning. Biomass Bioenergy **145** (2021). https://doi.org/10.1016/j.biombioe.2020.105939
23. Samani, M.R.G., Hosseini-Motlagh, S.-M.: A mixed uncertainty approach to design a bioenergy network considering sustainability and efficiency measures. Comput. Chem. Eng. **149** (2021). https://doi.org/10.1016/j.compchemeng.2021.107305
24. The essence and types of rankings: STUDBOOKS.NET: Student online library – Access mode (2021) https://studbooks.net/53682/ekonomika/suschnost_vidy_reytingovyh_otsenok. Accessed 13 July 2021
25. Litvak V.V.: The concept of energy security of the constituent entities of the Federation/V.A. Silich. Journal of the energy service company. Ecological systems, No.1 (2006)
26. Voikova, N.A.: Integral assessment of the electric power independence of the state [Text]/V.N. Belentsov (2007)
27. Vasikov, A.R.: Simplified assessment of the energy security level based on widely available information/A.R. Vasikov, T.P. Salikhov, Z.N. Garaev. Collection of articles of the symposium within the APEC project. Energy ties between Russia and East Asia: development strategies in the XXI century, Irkutsk, 30.08–02.09.2010. [Electronic resource]. https://sei.irk.ru/symp2010/papers/RUS/S6-12r.pdf
28. Nedosekin, A.: Fuzzy financial management [Text]. AFA Library (2003)
29. A biogas plant in Germany (2021). https://internationalwealth.info/best-offshore-services/buy-ready-made-business-in-germany-biogas-plant-2/. Accessed 30 Jan 2021
30. Alekseenkova, E.: Smart greenhouse: profitability and stop factors. (Electronic resource). https://cyberleninka.ru/article/n/umnaya-teplitsa-tempy-rentabelnost-i-stop-faktory/viewer

31. Sankhla, V.S., Sharma, D., Kothari, S., Jain, S., Agarwal, C.: Design and analysis of biogas powered refrigerator for dairy farmers. Int. J. Eng. Adv.Technol. **9**(1) (2019) https://doi.org/10.35940/ijeat.E7321.109119

32. RutSerra, I.N., Paréa, D., Titus, B., Gagnon, B., Laganière, J.: From conventional to renewable natural gas: can we expect GHG savings in the near term? Biomass Bioenerg. **131** (2019). https://doi.org/10.1016/j.biombioe.2019.105396

33. An, J., Sokolinskaya, N.E.: Economic valuation of biogas production in Russia. J. Phys. Conf. Ser. https://doi.org/10.1088/1742-6596/1399/3/033072

34. Federal State Statistics Service. https://rosstat.gov.ru/

35. Generating electricity from biogas and applying biogas technology. http://biogaz-russia.ru/ehlektroehnergiya-iz-biogaza/

36. Welfle, A., Alawadhi, A.: Bioenergy opportunities, barriers and challenges in the Arabian Peninsula, Resource modelling, surveys & interviews. Biomass Bioenergy. **150** (2021) https://doi.org/10.1016/j.biombioe.2021.106083

37. Ali, Z., Liaquat, R., Khoja, A.H., Safdar, U.: Sustainable Energy Technologies and Assessments. A comparison of energy policies of Pakistan and their impact on bioenergy development (2021). https://doi.org/10.1016/j.seta.2021.101246

38. Kung, C.-C., Lan, X., Yang, Y., Kung, S.-S., Chang, M.-S.: Effects of green bonds on Taiwan's bioenergy development. Energy **238** (2021). https://doi.org/10.1016/j.energy.2021.121567

39. Koondhar, M.A., Tan, Z., Alam, G.M., Khan, Z.A., Wang, L., Kong, R.: Bioenergy consumption, carbon emissions, and agricultural bioeconomic growth: a systematic approach to carbon neutrality in China. J. Environ. Manage. **296** (2021). https://doi.org/10.1016/j.jenvman.2021.113242.

40. Kaoma, M., Gheewala, S.H.: Sustainability performance of lignocellulosic biomass-to-bioenergy supply chains for Rural Growth Centres in Zambia. Sustain. Product. Consump. **28** (2021). https://doi.org/10.1016/j.spc.2021.08.007

Digital Ecosystem: Nature, Types and Opportunities for Value Creation

Mariana Petrova$^{(\boxtimes)}$, Petya Popova , Veselin Popov , Krasimir Shishmanov ,
and Kremena Marinova

Tsenov Academy of Economics, Svishtov, Bulgaria
m.m.petrova@uni-svishtov.bg

Abstract. The increased penetration of business organizations by information technology integrates products, services, and processes in a new way, changes existing business models and leads to their digital transformation. To successfully meet the challenges of the digital economy and create added value, organizations need to connect in the so-called digital ecosystem (DE) which became a key source of innovation for them. The article aims to define the concept of digital ecosystem, considering its multi-layered and multidimensional nature, to distinguish its main characteristics, types, and components and to identify a business model for creating value through digital ecosystem. The main method of research is the systematic review of the scientific literature on the subject. Through it, we identified and summarized selected publications, analyzed, and systemized them and made conclusions by applying a structural approach. We concluded that inclusion in an appropriate digital ecosystem, depending on the size and scope of the business organization, is essential both for it and the partner network in their efforts to create added value in the economy as digital ecosystem is gradually replacing the supply chain model. Our future research will focus on deriving clearer and more accurate criteria for selecting an appropriate digital ecosystem and defining different models for generating added value depending on the type and scope of the business organization.

Keywords: Digitalization · Digital ecosystem · Digital platform · APIs · Business ecosystem · Generativity

1 Introduction

The processes of change in business organizations that occur under the influence of digital technologies are generally called digital transformation. These processes are developing and can be studied in two directions - digitalization of products and services and digitalization of business models.

Modern IT integrates products, services, and processes in a new way and changes existing business models. The main trend in business development today, along with all other aspects of digital transformation, is the digitalization of the business environment. We are witnessing new models in the interactions with partners, suppliers, customers;

© Springer Nature Switzerland AG 2022
D. Rodionov et al. (Eds.): SPBPU IDE 2021, CCIS 1619, pp. 71–85, 2022.
https://doi.org/10.1007/978-3-031-14985-6_5

the models for organizing and managing business processes are changing, etc. Organizations' ITs become more externally oriented, enabling the spread of digital services and improving the customer experience [39]. Supported by technology, innovative business models expand the possibilities for creating value in a wide range - from operational optimization of processes and activities to radical changes in the business models used, which can be destructive for the organization or the industry [23].

The digital ecosystem model is gaining traction and is now the foundation of the most successful modern businesses. According to a McKinsey & Company study, "six of the world's top seven companies by market capitalization are ecosystem companies" [11]. The COVID-19 pandemic was a powerful motivator for consumer migration to digital technologies [15, 24, 40]. At the same time, it has played an important role for digital organizations that are hesitant to create or participate in digital ecosystems.

An in-depth study of the specialized literature on the digital ecosystem shows growing interest in both scientific [8, 16, 18, 20, 37] and practical-applied aspects [25, 31, 36, 43].

Scientific papers that describe the subject from several perspectives prevail, which is beneficial since it reveals a variety of viewpoints, but it also highlights the necessity for a holistic approach to defining the digital environment. All of this encourages us to investigate the nature of digital business ecosystems and their business potential.

2 Materials and Methods

The purpose of this article is to clarify the essence of the concept of the *digital ecosystem (DE)* and to derive *characteristics, types and components*, as well as to identify the *business model of DE* for creating added value, as well as to outline the steps and opportunities of value creating strategy based on an ecosystem approach.

As a methodological basis of the research, we apply the systematic literature review method of scientific publications on the topic [28, 29]. The scientific review was carried out in two stages: planning the literature review and its practical conduct. At the planning stage, we identified the need for a literature review and developed a research protocol for the selection of scientific sources. To achieve this goal, we needed to answer some questions: What is the purpose of the study? Which databases to research to find primary sources? Based on which criteria will we select the appropriate research? How will we extract, analyze, and synthesize the data in them? How will we formulate the conclusions and summarizes? The second stage of our study was conducted following the principles described by Jesson et al. [26] and supplemented by [17]. The authors propose 6 main principles that need to be observed in the preparation of a literature review: 1) Determining the scope of the study; 2) comprehensive and in-depth search; 3) evaluation of the quality of the publications; 4) extraction of the necessary data and information from the reviewed articles and their reliable storage; 5) synthesis of the extracted data and information and identification of the undeveloped fields in the scientific field; 6) writing a summary review. The principles defined above are reflected in the following steps we have taken: 1) we identified articles for primary research in Research Gate, Google Scholar, ScienceDirect, Scopus and other sources of scientific publications; 2) we selected publications that are relevant to the research problem; 3) we chose publications that we analyzed in detail and based on which we defined our conclusions; 4) we systematized the selected publications, made summaries, and defined conclusions by applying a structural approach. The study and definition of the digital environment takes a holistic approach.

3 Literature Review

The term *business ecosystem* refers to an organized partner network, the participants of which can vary in a very wide range of sectors to which they belong. The concept of the business ecosystem (BE) can be defined in many ways and very often overlaps with its semantically related terms innovation ecosystems (IE) and digital ecosystems (DE) [20]. It is also a very similar with the concept of industrial ecosystem which is a framework of implementation of digital technologies [5]. In DE, business participants use a set of technology standards and shared platforms. As a result, the offered products and services are compatible and interdependent, and the established relationships would be very difficult to maintain in other environments. In the digital age, business ecosystems are predominantly DE, becoming significantly more dynamic and complex, and increasingly becoming *a key source of innovation* [10]. Digital ecosystems are interpreted as the technological execution of business and innovation ecosystems [20].

The concept of DE is emerging as a new way of perceiving the increasingly complex and interconnected systems that are being built today. DE is a multidisciplinary and difficult to define category, which determines the many points of view and perspectives in its definition.

From an organizational perspective, it is seen as a digital duplicate of the biological ecosystem and in this regard is a stable, self-organizing, and scalable structure that can automatically solve complex and dynamic problems [8]. It is inspired by natural ecosystems, especially in terms of cooperation and competition between diverse entities [37]. A similar definition is given by Barikin et al. [7], which define DE as a self-organizing sustainable digital platform, forming a unified information environment in which its members can interact without building strong functional connections with each other.

According to Fu [18], the DE is a digital environment consisting of digital components, which can be software, applications, services, knowledge, business processes, models, training modules, laws, etc. It enables stakeholders to use digital technologies to access services and interact with each other to achieve better economic results [14].

The organizational point of view is essential because it helps the business to understand the possibilities for partner network integration and its dynamic expansion to generate value.

From a technological point of view, DE is an infrastructure based on peer-to-peer distributed software technology. That technology transports, finds, and connects services and information via Internet connections, allowing network transactions and distribution of all digital "objects" present in the infrastructure. Digital objects are all representations expressed in languages (formal or natural) that can be interpreted and processed by computer software and/or people, e.g. software applications, services, knowledge, training modules, contractual frameworks, laws, etc. [33]. It can be considered as a set of products or services that are interoperable within the platform and its interfaces, complement activities, and bring economies of scale [44].

The technological perspective helps us to explore the potential for digitalization of the information infrastructure.

The economic perspective explores the possibilities for innovating business models and in this sense, DE is a metaphor related to the dynamics of business networks at regional and sectoral levels, as well as their interaction with and through IT [16]. This perspective stands out in the definitions given by some authors and organizations.

Li et al. [31] define DE as a self-organizing, scalable, and sustainable system composed of heterogeneous digital actors and their interconnections. That System is focused on interactions between sites in order to increase the usefulness of the system, to promote and reap the benefits of information sharing, internal and external cooperation and system innovation.

Bakhtadze et al. [6] also define DE as a distributed, self-organized, and adaptive socio-technical system, consisting of automated systems and economic entities that are in competition and/or cooperation. It gathers independent players who share their experiences and resources for the deliberate development of products of greater economic value than those developed outside DE. The functioning of DE relies on an IT network infrastructure using intelligent management technologies.

According to Ojala et al., DE is "a loosely connected network of actors that interact and offer different kinds of resources, which together form a digital service around the platform" [35]. A key element in the structure of DE is the digital platform.

The DE is defined in the documents of the World Economic Forum in 2019 as "consist of interacting organizations that are digitally connected and enabled by modularity and are not managed by hierarchical authority (like in a supply chain)" [25, p. 14].

The digital ecosystem has three distinctive features of the digital business model defined by Weill [45]: a) high-quality content, provided to customers; b) fine-tuned customer experience, and; c) a digital platform that integrates internal resources with new content provided for the external environment. DE's business model stands out as a new way of providing services to end-users and many new features [4].

DE's business model is gradually displacing the supply chain model [9]. Traditional supply chain partners are now freelancers working closely together to generate value (Fig. 1), [43, p. 45].

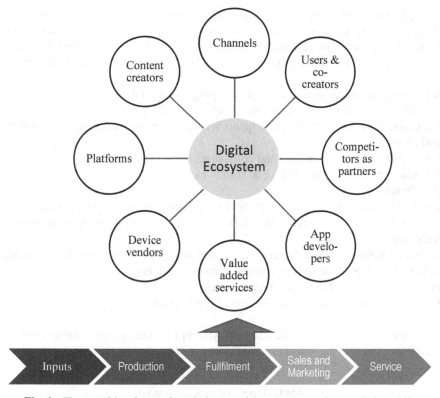

Fig. 1. The transition from value chains to value ecosystems. Source: [43, p. 45].

4 Results

4.1 Digital Ecosystem – Characteristics, Types, and Definition

The digital ecosystem is very close to the structure, the principle of operation and the way of interaction with the external environment of the biological, therefore the characteristics of ecosystems in general and biological ecosystems in particular are largely applicable to it.

The following are examples of common properties and characteristics [7]:

- It is situated in time and space;
- Internal consistency, geographical proximity, and interaction between ecosystem members;
- Adaptability to environmental changes;
- Systematic nonhierarchical link between members;
- Universality;
- Balanced environment that preserves homeostasis.

Despite their similarities, there is one significant difference between digital and biological ecosystems: a human has a significant role in building the digital ecosystem and making subsequent decisions. This is required for distinguishing the specific characteristics of the digital ecosystem [7, 31, 44], main of them are the following:

- it is a socio-technical system that is developing in a digital environment;
- consists of enterprises, organizations, developers and clients;
- the connections between the participants are based on the exchange of information and resources;
- develops based on cooperation and collaboration;
- is limited by social norms, laws, and resources;
- it is dynamic;
- it is scalable and changes its size to meet the growing number of elements and tasks;
- it is a self-organizing system, new global structures appear spontaneously based on local ones;
- is characterized by a high degree of resilience and productivity even during changes in the internal and external environment, errors and damage;
- creates additional value based on synergetics;
- brings economies of scale to the business organization.

The many perspectives in defining the concept of DE, suggest the existence of different types of DE, the subject of research by many authors (Table 1).

Table 1. Types of digital ecosystems.

Source	Criterion	Type	Features
[41]	Economic potential – how the DE supports the value creation process and contributes to the economic growth of companies	• Production DE	Production ecosystems consist of interdependencies, part of the value chain, such as the production and sale of a product or the provision of a service to a customer. By using digital technologies, manufacturers can significantly improve the performance of their products and services and thus strengthen their market position
		• Consumption DE	Consumption ecosystems consist of interdependencies that develop after the sale of a product or service and add value to the sale of related products that are not valuable enough in themselves
		• Digital envelopes and product-in use information	The digital envelope is a digital presentation of the product and the way it is used, achieved by collecting, analyzing, and implementing a product in real-time. Information is usually collected through sensors and analyzed through appropriate software platforms and analytical tools

(continued)

Table 1. (*continued*)

Source	Criterion	Type	Features
[7]	Functional feature – priority functions performed	• Process-oriented	They support the processes of creating innovations and venture capital enterprises
		• Resource-oriented	They focus on the search for resources (tangible and intangible)
		• Product-oriented	They aim to launch new products and services on the market
[30]	Tasks and goals set by the company	• Digitizer	The main goal is to transform the company's traditional product into a smart and connected one. These DEs are suitable for companies with a large product but few digital capabilities, mostly internally focused
		• Platform	This DE connects smart devices and their users in a common platform, providing them with higher levels of service and reducing disagreements between providers and users. It is suitable for digital companies and startups
		• Super platform	Integrate multiple digital platforms into one. They are suitable for established technology companies
[21, 42]	Ownership of the platform	• Centralized DE	The platform has one owner who defines the mechanisms for its management and control
		• DE of the consortium	The platform is owned by a group of participants who define the mechanisms for its management
		• Decentralized DE	Blockchain and Ethereum-type platforms managed by peer-to-peer communities
[6, 31]	Scope of application of DE	• Digital business ecosystems • Knowledge management ecosystems • Digital Service Ecosystems • DE, integrated with social networks • Educational DE • Industrial DE	

After analysing the existing points of view, definitions, characteristics, and types of DE for the needs of this article we can define DE as a self-organizing socio-technical system of heterogeneous entities (enterprises, organizations, developers, customers). They are integrated through a common digital platform and are focused on the potential of achievable synergies for designing a digital service for end users (or other innovation). As a result, the digital ecosystem benefits both the ecosystem itself and each of its participants.

4.2 Components of DE

The most important critical elements that enable the functioning of a reliable DE are: a) a stable and conducive political environment; b) stable and sustainable technological infrastructure; c) digital and service providers and IT staff; d) digital end-users [14].

The technological infrastructure of a digital ecosystem includes two main components - platform and application programming interfaces (APIs).

The digital platform is a special mobile or desktop application designed to be used by external users (customers and partners) and/or by internal users (employees). From a technical point of view, the digital platform is an extensible code base to which additional third-party modules can be added [12].

The digital platform is a special mobile or desktop application designed to be used by external users (customers and partners) and/or by internal users (employees). In practice, digital platforms connect people, organizations, and resources to facilitate the main interactions between business and consumers, as well as to ensure greater efficiency for business management [36].

The platform is the tool that enables the ecosystem partners to create their products or services. API is the technical tool through which the data flow is transmitted to components of the DE. It is based on a set of protocols that regulates the communication between the software components of the system and thus ensures interoperability between the various actors in the DE.

4.3 Business Potential of Digital Platforms и APIs

Based on the business potential of digital platforms и APIs, an analysis of opportunities for value creation by DE can be made. According to their purpose and the functionality they offer, digital platforms are communication platforms (for exchanging messages and ideas); an addition to the physical product (for additional services or product information); in the field of services - for data exchange and data aggregators, etc.

The specific characteristics of a platform on which the success of DE depends are openness and modularity. Openness is the ability to provide access to platform resources. It allows DE participants to develop their products and services. At the same time, modularity allows different organizations to build complementary products or services. Other important features of the platform are high availability, high reliability, security, etc.

The use of API provides DE with several technological opportunities such as access to various platforms and devices; internal and external interactions in the digital environment; technological and organizational flexibility; an alternative to the components of the digital environment; interoperability of applications and systems; improving internal integration and rapid data exchange between different departments and teams in the company; optimization of existing processes; integration with the systems of third countries - partners, external developers, etc. [22, 32, 45, 46]. At the same time, this software tool also creates DE risks, such as security risks associated with increased vulnerability, when systems are freely connected through APIs, without taking into account specific environmental conditions and often blind trust in APIs by users.

DE receives many economic and organizational advantages using digital platform and API, which can be systematized as strengthening cooperation at different business levels [32]; based on digital platforms and APIs develop new business strategies; stimulating innovation, especially in the following three areas: service delivery (multi-channel access, access to functionality, charge on a subscription base or transaction base); client interface (end customer access, support on user authentication); delivery system (product complementarity; revenue sharing); technology (security, stream connection) [46]; generate new sources of income as a result of providing access to corporate information assets; a tool for adherence of normative requirements and regulations.

4.4   Business Model and Strategies

Value creation in ecosystems, and in particular in platforms, is highly dependent on their structure and partnerships. It is considered from several aspects [19]: business, innovation, and the platform ecosystem. The platform DE is defined as an innovative ecosystem, which has many features in common with the business ecosystem. To be successful, it must be built by partners with similar business strategies, structures, and roles. This reduces the risk of joint innovations.

Value creation in DE can be in the context of IT business models and particular digital platforms. Value creation in DE is done through digital technologies that transform the way companies operate [2, 3]. It is facilitated by the protection of property rights, the dominant design used, and complementary assets. In terms of value creation, Akram introduces the concept of generativity, which has three dimensions: technological; organization; and business. Generativity is a function of the technological capabilities for solving certain tasks and is defined as the ability of DE for unexpected change through unfiltered input from the audience. From a business point of view, the concept defines the ability of the business model or the value of the partner network to generate a new technological solution.

The participants in DE form the so-called partner network [34]. Building a successful DE requires good knowledge of the partners who build it. They define the newly created value in the ecosystem as a compromise between benefit and sacrifice, and it can be tangible or intangible. From a functional point of view, value creation is determined by the activities that DE participants carry out to create added value for network members.

Spremić et al. [39] offer two models for value creation and implementation of innovations from DE: a) Introduction of innovations by customers through digital business models, which leads to optimization and digitalization of production processes and control and evaluation of the quality of digitalization in the enterprise; b) Interaction with universities and other educational institutions, using the experience and knowledge of students and scientists on technological trends and creating curricula focused on business needs.

Value models of ecosystems [19] can increase the chances of success and design the platform following the business models that build it. The first step in the value creation model in DE is to build an ecosystem strategy and risk assessment. Next, it is necessary to create a relevant integrative theoretical framework to ensure that DE participants have a similar structure and bring similar benefits and risks to the system. The first stage in this framework is an initiative by an ecosystem participant who wants to innovate their business processes. Depending on the type of innovation, it may need business processes, business models or IT to be provided by another ecosystem participant who accepts the idea and decides to participate in the ecosystem. For this purpose, it is necessary to integrate their platforms and unify their business strategies, and as a result, form an ecosystem strategy. All these stages are accompanied by an extensive analysis of expectations, risks, and additional conditions.

Creating value through DE is the subject of discussion and analysis by many authors who offer a variety of models and techniques for this purpose. The organizations' ecosystem strategy [1] is expected to clarify three issues: 1) to identify the ecosystems in which the organization has the potential and resources to participate or whose creation they will initiate; 2) to determine the roles he will perform (orchestrator; modular manufacturer; user); and 3) to determine the method and resources by which it will monetize its participation in the DE. Value generation strategies are heavily influenced by the role chosen. Researching the practice, Dietz et al. [13, 38] conclude that different types of participants (roles) take different approaches when developing their strategy for generating value from DE (cooperative approach, leaders, followers, etc.) and strategies (orchestrator strategy, dominator strategy, complementor strategy, protector strategy) [27]. In this regard, the authors define three major archetypes that businesses can navigate by selecting one or a combination of them. The choice is determined by factors such as the type of business and the specific local operational needs and characteristics such as geographical location, competition, regulations, and so on. These value-generating archetypes are: 1) expanding the core business through partnerships or establishing an ecosystem from the beginning; 2) expanding the partner network and portfolio with new products; and 3) developing an end-to-end solution for serving business customers and improving operational efficiency. The authors also outline six fundamental skills (advanced analytics, agile development and operations, governance that allows for a portfolio of bets, a strong middle platform that organizes core capabilities and maximizes synergies, entrepreneurial talent, partnership), The authors also outline six fundamental skills that participants must comprehend in order to develop different archetypes and strategies to accommodate them.

The main steps in the strategy for generating value from the implementation of an ecosystem approach are outlined in Fig. 2.

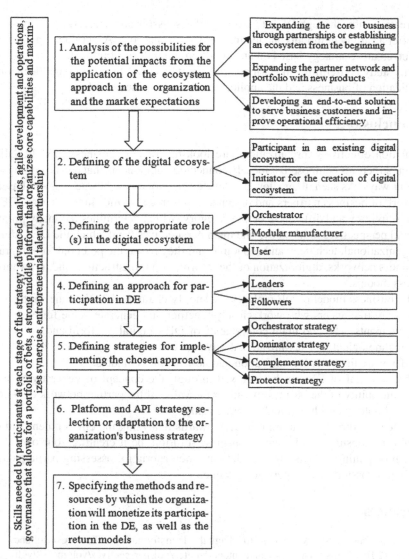

Fig. 2. Value creating strategy based on an ecosystem approach. Based on: [1, 13, 27, 38, 43]

5   Discussion

The contribution of the present research to the theory and practice is in the following directions: a) the essence of the concept of the digital ecosystem is clarified from organizational, technical, and economic points of view; b) the main characteristics are highlighted and the main types of DE are derived according to different criteria; c) the economic potential of the technological components of DE has been studied; d) the business potential of DE is commented and a strategy for DE development is outlined.

Creating value through DE is the subject of discussion and analysis by many authors who offer a variety of models and techniques for this purpose. A steps and opportunities of value creating strategy based on an ecosystem approach is outlined.

This study is useful for modern companies, which face the conceptual decision for digitalization of business and the application of new business models.

6 Conclusions

To function effectively, organizations are looking for new business models. DE are modular structures composed of loosely connected components that can be combined in different ways. As such, they allow the development of a new business model based on a network of business partners and organize economic activities in a new way. DE is a multidisciplinary and difficult to define category, which determines the many points of view and perspectives in its study. The main perspectives from which the DE is defined are organizational, technical, and economic and they reveal the potential for integration of business networks, digitalization of the information infrastructure, and innovation of business models.

The business model of DE replaces the supply chain model. Now the supply chain partners are freelancers who work closely together and generate value for each of the DE participants. The two main components of DE - digital platform and APIs define many technological and organizational advantages, which are followed by economic ones. They are the basis for innovation and new business models.

The potential of DE can be assessed through the concept of generativity, which defines the ability of the business model or the value of the partner network to generate a new technological solution and generate value.

We tend to direct our future research towards analyzing the environment and conditions for choosing the alternative business solution, be it creating your own digital platform or joining an existing one; defining the criteria for assessing participation in the DE and possibilities for generating value.

References

1. A Machine First Approach to Digital Transformation. Tata Consultancy Services (2019). https://www.tcs.com/content/dam/tcs/pdf/perspectives/volume-12/volume-12-Perspectives-Machine-First.pdf. Accessed 20 May 2022
2. Akram, A.: The influence of generativity on value creation–a study of digitized products. In: 8th IADIS International Conference on Information Systems 2015, 14–16 March, pp. 51–60. IADIS Press, Madeira, Portugal (2015)
3. Akram, A.: Value creation in digital ecosystem – a study of remote diagnostics. In: The 36th Information Systems Research seminar in Scandinavia. Oslo (2013)
4. Baber, W., Ojala, A., Martínez, R.: Transition to digital distribution platforms and business model evolution. In: 52nd Hawaii International Conference on System Sciences (2019). https://doi.org/10.24251/hicss.2019.600.
5. Babkin, A., Glukhov, V., Shkarupeta, E., Kharitonova, N., Barabaner, H.: Methodology for assessing industrial ecosystem maturity in the framework of digital technology implementation. Int. J. Technol. **12**(7), 1397–1406 (2021). https://doi.org/10.14716/ijtech.v12i7.5390

6. Bakhtadze, N., Suleykin, A.: Industrial digital ecosystems: predictive models and architecture development issues. Annu. Rev. Control. **51**, 56–64 (2021). https://doi.org/10.1016/j.arcontrol.2020.11.001
7. Barykin, S.B., Kapustina, I.V., Kirillova, T.V., Yadykin, V.L., Konnikov, Y.A.: Economics of digital ecosystems. J. Open Innov. Technol. Market Complex. **6**(4) (2020). https://doi.org/10.3390/joitmc6040124.
8. Briscoe, G.: Digital Ecosystem (2009). https://arxiv.org/abs/0909.3423. Accessed 18 Feb 2022
9. Bughin, J., Catlin, T., Dietz, M.: The right digital-platform strategy. McKinsey Digital (2019). https://www.mckinsey.com/business-functions/mckinsey-digital/our-insights/the-right-digital-platform-strategy. Accessed 04 Jan 2022
10. Burton, B., Blosch, M., O'Neill, M.: Hype Cycle for Business Ecosystems. Gartner (2017). https://www.gartner.com/en/documents/3766808/hype-cycle-for-business-ecosystems-2017. Accessed 9 Mar 2022
11. Chung, V., Dietz, M., Rab, I., Townsend, Z.: Ecosystem 2.0: climbing to the next level, (2020). https://www.mckinsey.com/business-functions/mckinsey-digital/our-insights/ecosystem-2-point-0-climbing-to-the-next-level. Accessed 15 May 2022
12. De Reuver, M., Sørensen, C., Basole, R.: The digital platform: a research agenda. J. Inf. Technol. **33**(2), 124–135 (2018). https://doi.org/10.1057/s41265-016-0033-3
13. Dietz, M., Khan, M., Rab, I.: How do companies create value from digital ecosystems? McKinsey Digital (2020). https://www.mckinsey.com/business-functions/mckinsey-digital/our-insights/how-do-companies-create-value-from-digital-ecosystems. Accessed 24 May 2022
14. Digital Strategy 2020–2024. USAID. https://www.usaid.gov/sites/default/files/documents/USAID_Digital_Strategy.pdf.pdf. Accessed 18 April 2022
15. Digital Transformation in the Age of COVID-19: Building Resilience and Bridging Divides, OECD (2020). https://www.oecd.org/digital/digital-economy-outlook-covid.pdf. Accessed 15 May 2022
16. Dini, P., Darking, P., Rathbone, N., Vidal, M., Hernandez, P., Ferronato, P., et al.: The Digital Ecosystems Research Vision: 2010 and Beyond (2005). https://op.europa.eu/o/opportal-service/download-handler?identifier=53e45e55-4bd2-42a4-ad25-27b339b051e0&format=pdf&language=en&productionSystem=cellar&part. Accessed 19 Jan 2022
17. Durst, S., Hammoda, B., Nguyen, H., Asl, M.: Sustainable business models and small- and medium-sized enterprises – a literature review. Sustain. Develop. Eng. Econ. **1**, 4 (2021). https://doi.org/10.48554/SDEE.2021.1.4
18. Fu, H.: Formal concept analysis for digital ecosystem. In: 2006 5th International Conference on Machine Learning and Applications (ICMLA 2006), pp. 143–148 (2006). https://doi.org/10.1109/ICMLA.2006.24.
19. González, A., Pfaf, M., Krcmar, H.: Value Modeling for Ecosystem Analysis. Computers, vol. 3 (2019). https://doi.org/10.3390/computers8030068.
20. Gupta, R., Mejia, C., Kajikawa, Y.: Business, innovation and digital ecosystems landscape survey and knowledge cross sharing. Technol. Forecast. Soc. Chang. **147**, 100–109 (2019). https://doi.org/10.1016/j.techfore.2019.07.004
21. Hein, A., Schreieck, M., Riasanow, T., Setzke, D., Wiesche, M., Böhm, M., et al.: Digital platform ecosystems. Electron. Mark. **30**, 87–98 (2020). https://doi.org/10.1007/s12525-019-00377-4
22. Heshmatisafa, S., Seppänen, M.: API utilization and monetization in finnish industries. In: Paasivaara, M., Kruchten, P. (eds.) XP 2020. LNBIP, vol. 396, pp. 23–31. Springer, Cham (2020). https://doi.org/10.1007/978-3-030-58858-8_3
23. Ibarra, D., Ganzarain, J., Igartua, J.I.: Business model innovation through Industry 4.0: a review. Procedia Manuf. **22**, 4–10 (2018). https://doi.org/10.1016/j.promfg.2018.03.002.

24. Iivari, N., Sharma, S., Ventä-Olkkonen, L.: Digital transformation of everyday life – how COVID-19 pandemic transformed the basic education of the young generation and why information management research should care? Int. J. Inf. Manage. **55** (2020). https://doi.org/10.1016/j.ijinfomgt.2020.102183.

25. Jacobides, G., Sundararajan, A., Alstyne, M.: Designing digital ecosystems. In: Jacobides, M., et al. (eds.) Platforms and Ecosystems: Enabling the Digital Economy, Briefing Paper, World Economic Forum (2019). http://www3.weforum.org/docs/WEF_Digital_Platforms_and_Ecosystems_2019.pdf. Accessed 23 April 2022

26. Jesson, J., Matheson, L., Lacey, F.: Doing Your Literature Review: Traditional and Systematic Techniques. SAGE Publications Ltd., Los Angeles (2011)

27. Kamalaldin, A., Sjödin, D., Hullova, D., Parida, V.: Configuring ecosystem strategies for digitally enabled process innovation: a framework for equipment suppliers in the process industries. Technovation **105** (2021). https://doi.org/10.1016/j.technovation.2021.102250.

28. Kitchenham, B., Brereton, O.P., Budgen, D., Turnera, M., Bailey, J., Linkman, S.: Systematic literature reviews in software engineering – a systematic literature review. Inf. Softw. Technol. **51**(1), 7–15 (2009). https://doi.org/10.1016/j.infsof.2008.09.009

29. Kitchenham, B.: Procedures for Performing Systematic Reviews. Joint Technical Report (2004). https://www.inf.ufsc.br/~aldo.vw/kitchenham.pdf. Accessed 29 April 2022

30. Lang, N., Von Szczepanski, K., Wurzer, C.: The emerging art of ecosystem management. Boston Consulting Group (2019). https://www.bcg.com/publications/2019/emerging-art-ecosystem-management. Accessed 7 Nov 2021

31. Li, W., Badr, Y., Biennier, B.: Digital ecosystems: challenges and prospects. In: International Conference on Management of Emergent Digital EcoSystems (MEDES 2012), p. 117–122. Association for Computing Machinery, New York, NY, USA (2012). https://doi.org/10.1145/2457276.2457297.

32. Maheshwari, A.: Digital Transformation: Building Intelligent Enterprises. Wiley (2019)

33. Nachira, P., Dini, P., Nicolai, A.: A network of digital business ecosystems for europe: roots, processes and perspectives. In: Digital Business Ecosystems, Luxembourg, Office for Official Publications of the European Communities, p. 232 (2007). https://op.europa.eu/en/publication-detail/-/publication/53e45e55-4bd2-42a4-ad25-27b339b051e0. Accessed 24 Feb 2022

34. Ojala, A., Helander, N., Tyrväinen, P.: Value creation and power asymmetries in digital ecosystems: a study of a cloud gaming provider. Measur. Bus. Value Cloud Comput. (2020). https://doi.org/10.1007/978-3-030-43198-3_6

35. Ojala, A., Lyytinen, K.: Competition logics during digital platform evolution. In: 51st Hawaii International Conference on System Sciences. Hawaii (2018). https://doi.org/10.24251/HICSS.2018.130.

36. Ruggieri, R., Savastano, M., Scaling, A., Bala, D., D'Ascenzo, F.: The impact of Digital Platforms on Business Models: an empirical investigation on innovative start-ups. Manage. Market. Challenges Knowl. Soc. **13**(4), 1210–1225 (2018). https://doi.org/10.2478/mmcks-2018-0032

37. Saleh, M., Abel, M.: Moving from digital ecosystem to system of information systems. In: 2016 IEEE 20th International Conference on Computer Supported Cooperative Work in Design (CSCWD), pp. 91–96 (2016). https://doi.org/10.1109/CSCWD.2016.7565969.

38. Sengupta, J., HV, V., Dietz, M., Chung, V.: How the best companies create value from their ecosystems, McKinsey & Company (2019). https://www.mckinsey.com/industries/financial-services/our-insights/how-the-best-companies-create-value-from-their-ecosystems. Accessed 22 May 2022

39. Spremić, M., Ivancic, L., Vukšić, V.: Fostering innovation and value creation through ecosystems: case of digital business models and digital platforms. In: Leadership. Management, and Adoption Techniques for Digital Service Innovation, pp. 25–44. IGI Global (2020). https://doi.org/10.4018/978-1-7998-2799-3.ch002.

40. Stalmachova, K., Chinoracky, R., Strenitzerova, M.: Changes in business models caused by digital transformation and the COVID-19 pandemic and possibilities of their measurement - case study. Sustainability **14**(1), 127 (2022). https://doi.org/10.3390/su14010127
41. Subramaniam, M., Iyer, B., Venkatraman, V.: Competing in digital ecosystems. Bus. Horiz. **62**(1), 83–94 (2019). https://doi.org/10.1016/j.bushor.2018.08.013
42. Tiwana, A., Konsynski, B., Bush, A.: Platform evolution: coevolution of platform architecture, governance, and environmental dynamics. Inf. Syst. Res. **21**, 675–687 (2010). https://doi.org/10.1287/isre.1100.0323
43. Valdez-de-Leon, O.: How to develop a digital ecosystem: a practical framework. Technol. Innov. Manag. Rev. **9**(8), 43–54 (2019). https://doi.org/10.22215/timreview/1260
44. Van der Boom, J., Samranchit, P.: Assessing the long run competitive effects of digital ecosystem mergers. SSRN (2020). https://doi.org/10.2139/ssrn.3746343
45. Weill, P., Woerner, S.: What is Your Digital Business Model? Six questions to help you build the next-generation enterprise. MIT CISR Research Briefing (2018). https://cisr.mit.edu/publication/whats-your-digital-business-model. Accessed 6 Mar 2022
46. Wulf, J., Blohm, I., Romualdi, T.: Designing Successful API Strategies. University of St. Gallen (2017). https://doi.org/10.13140/RG.2.2.29624.88322

Identification and Visualization of Regional Industrial Clusters: Case of Metallurgical Cluster in Russia

Angi Skhvediani$^{(\boxtimes)}$ (iD), Tatiana Kudryavtseva (iD), Valeriia Iakovleva (iD),
and Igor Kuhotkin (iD)

Peter the Great St. Petersburg Polytechnic University, Polytechnicheskaya, 29, 195251 St. Petersburg, Russia
`shvediani_ae@spbstu.ru`

Abstract. Currently, clusters are important elements of innovative development of constituent entities of the Russian Federation. In the context of rapid digitalization, a need to use information and analytical systems for decision-making in socio-economic development of regions arises. In Russia, only the Russian Cluster Observatory which contains information about state registered innovation clusters is dedicated to the issues of visualization of cluster development dynamics analysis results. The purpose of this study is to develop a database of clusters on the territory of Russia and a system for visualization of statistical information for decision-making in cluster policy as exemplified by the Metallurgy cluster identified on the basis of the Input-Output 2016 Table. Based on the functional approach, the cluster composition was determined by the maximum method. Using the calculation of the location quotient, the regions were identified where clusters and industries they comprised were found, and the dynamics of changes in the cluster location over the period from 2016 to 2020 was considered. In the course of the work, a database was formed in the MongoDB database management system which includes information on the average headcount and location quotients by constituent entities of the Russian Federation. The results obtained were visualized through generation of a cluster location map of Russia. In the future, it is planned to supplement the website with a region page where statistical data by clusters and industries concentrated in the selected region will be presented. The software solution developed will allow monitoring and modeling the cluster structure on the territory of Russia.

Keywords: Metallurgy cluster · Input-output · Location quotient · Visualization · Digitalization · Database · Software solution

1 Introduction

In the context of modern trends of transition to the digital economy, development, widespread dissemination and application of digital technologies to improve the efficiency of management decision-making in the economy is becoming increasingly popular [1].

© Springer Nature Switzerland AG 2022
D. Rodionov et al. (Eds.): SPBPU IDE 2021, CCIS 1619, pp. 86–98, 2022.
https://doi.org/10.1007/978-3-031-14985-6_6

Generation of information and analytical systems allows increasing the speed and quantity of data processed, responding more quickly and making important decisions. Thus, the use of digital twins of enterprises [2], cities [3] and industries [4] gets widespread.

The purpose of this research is to develop a database of clusters on the territory of Russia and a system for visualization of statistical information for decision-making in cluster policy as exemplified by the Metallurgy cluster identified on the basis of the Input-Output 2016 Table.

To achieve the goal the following objectives were set:

– to analyze intersectoral interactions using the Input-Output 2016 Table and identify the structure of the Metallurgy cluster;
– to determine the cluster spatial location and its industries in 2020, as well as to consider the dynamics of changes in the cluster location for the period from 2016 to 2020;
– to develop a statistical database in the MongoDB database system containing data on the constituent entities of the Russian Federation;
– to visualize a map of clusters on the territory of Russia.

Currently, cluster generation is a priority tool for development of regions. A need to develop information and analytical tools in the context of regional industry statistics is determined by the importance of identification and diagnostics of cluster performance indicators that could be used to justify management decisions. The system developed will make it possible to automatically identify potential regional clusters the officials could pay attention to in order to develop and support their performance. Today, such systems are implemented in the European Union [5] and the USA [6], but there is no such an integrated system accumulating statistical data in Russia [7].

The main signs of economy clusterization were established in *Principles of Economics* by A. Marshall [8] already. In his book, the author uses the term 'industrial areas' to refer to the spatial concentration of enterprises of similar industries. These provisions were developed in the works of M. Porter [9] who built his theory of the competitiveness of countries around the 'traded' industries exporting their products. Using the Input-Output Table, M. Porter identified strongly interconnected industries and their spatial concentration. Geographically adjacent and interconnected cluster organizations exchange knowledge, technologies and resources faster, which increases the competitiveness of organizations and strengthens the innovation component compared to companies from the same industry located outside the cluster environment. All this has an impact on the state of modern cluster theory which studies the concentration of types of activities in the selected area, the sectoral composition of clusters, as well as automated calculation of indicators and their mapping.

A large number of papers have been dedicated to the study of cluster formations. In particular, attention has been paid to the study of scientific clusters [10], pilot innovation clusters [11], industrial clusters in special economic zones [12], small-medium enterprise innovation clusters [13], high-tech clusters [14], cluster initiatives [15]. In addition, some researchers attempted to identify cluster structure in all regions of Russia [16–18].

In international practice, the following information and analytical resources can be identified that allow conducting the interactive cluster analysis—there is US Cluster

Mapping [5], a project of the American Cluster Observatory, and the European Cluster Initiative [6], a project of the European Cluster Observatory. In Russia there is a Russian Cluster Observatory [19], a project in the framework of which a Cluster Map of Russia was created, developed by NRU HSE (National Research University Higher School of Economics) specialists. The map provides information on such indicators as: specialization, cluster scale, maturity level, quantity, and others. The difference from the USA and European Union projects is that this project covers only the clusters that have been recognized at the state level. Thus, the Russian project does not focus on the analysis and identification of potential clusters, i.e. a general structure of the region economy.

2 Materials and Methods

2.1 Cluster Identification

To identify the Metallurgy cluster we used functional and spatial approaches. On the first stage of our research we have applied a functional approach using the maximum method. This method is based on the analysis of intersectoral chains in the Input-Output Table and was first used in the work of M. J. Montfort [20]. We used the Input-Output 2016 Table published on the Rosstat (the Federal State Statistics Service) website which contains information on 98 industries [21]. Descending and ascending cluster algorithms of the maximum method reveal the connections between the main suppliers and consumers of industries. The connection is considered strong if the supply value exceeds arbitrarily set thresholds [22, 23]. Industries that feature a sufficiently strong coherence are grouped into clusters.

The spatial approach has been implemented by calculating the location quotient based on the employment indicator which is a common indicator for identification of regions where individual industries and clusters are located. This indicator was used in the works of both domestic and foreign authors such as: E. S. Kutsenko [18], T. Yu. Kudryavtseva [15, 16], E. Feser [24], G. Lindqvist [25], M. Porter [9].

The location quotient in terms of employment indicator is calculated by formula 1:

$$LQ = \frac{Empig}{Empg} \Big/ \frac{Empi}{Emp} \tag{1}$$

where Empig is the number of employees in a cluster group (i) in region (g);
    Empg is the total number of employees in the region (g);
    Empi is the number of employees in the cluster group (i);
    Emp is the total number of employees.

The location quotient shows how many times the share of employees in the region cluster exceeds the average share of employment in the cluster across the country. Exceeding the location quotients of a certain level indicates cluster location in the region. As part of the ongoing research, we adhere to the position that the threshold value for the location quotient should be set at 1.3 mark.

In the course of the work, statistical databases on the average headcount by the constituent entities of the Russian Federation for 2009–2020 have been made in the

MongoDB database system. The data have been obtained from the portal of the Unified Interdepartmental Statistical Information System (EMISS) [26]. Due to the transition to OKVED-2, the authors have compared the old and new versions of the All-Russia Classifier of Types of Economic Activities.

When designing the database, the main emphasis has been placed on information division into cluster groups across the territory of regions of the Russian Federation.

The cluster contains data that allows assessing the region development level. The data is based on one factor, namely: a Location Quotient. The indicator is based on population employment data. The factor values are compared with a threshold value of 1.3 to determine the 'critical mass' which reflects a level of generation of positive externalities and connections.

2.2 Database Description

The database to be designed is supposed to determine a level of region development based on data on population employment in various types of activities. In particular:

- the database should be a flexible model where any number of new years and industries can be added;
- the database should provide a convenient access to data for their input and output;
- the database should simplify a storage of big data on the population employment in regions by year and industry.

Now therefore, a physical model of the developed database is non-relational and it is implemented in the MongoDB database system which offers a document-oriented data model due to which it operates faster and has easier scalability. The non-relational data model has been chosen based on the fact that data can be presented in different formats, the structuring of which, in turn, can impose significant restrictions. Accordingly, immediately allows achieving the goals set with regard to generation of our database. Instead of tables, collections are used here to contain a variety of objects with different structures and sets of properties. In our case, collections are clusters.

Figure 1 shows a physical model of the database as exemplified by the Metallurgy cluster.

As it has been mentioned above, each table is a specific cluster, the name of which is obvious from the collection name. Collections have a similar structure; they differ in the number of columns (documents) in them only which varies depending on the industries included in the cluster.

Let's take a closer look at the common names of columns (documents):

- year—a year by which the factor is calculated;
- total—an average headcount for all types of activities;
- region—a region where the factor is calculated;
- prefix d—an average headcount in a certain industry;
- prefix lq—a location quotient of a certain industry;
- prefix lq_cluster name—a cluster location quotient;
- prefix cluster_cluster name—an average headcount of the cluster.

Fig. 1. Clusters of Russian Regions—a physical model of a database as exemplified by the metallurgy cluster

3 Results

3.1 The Results of Identification of the Metallurgy Cluster

As a result of using a functional approach, namely descending and ascending cluster algorithms of the maximum method, it has been determined that the Metallurgy cluster consists of the following 8 industries, between closely tied with each other: Mining of Iron Ores (07.1); Mining of Non-Ferrous Metal Ores (07.2); Waste Collection, Treatment and Disposal, Materials Recovery (38); Manufacture of Coke Oven Products (19.1); Manufacture of Basic Precious and Other Non-Ferrous Metals, Processing of Nuclear Fuel (24.4); groups of industries—Manufacture of Basic Iron and Steel and of Ferro-Alloys (24.1, 24.51, 24.20, 24.3); Mining of Coal, Brown Coal and Peat (05, 05.20.1, 08.92.1) and Manufacture of Structural Metal Products (25.1–25.3).

According to the results of the spatial approach which involved calculating the location quotient, the Metallurgy cluster, as well as the industries included in the cluster in 2020, was located in the following regions (Table 1).

7 industries were located in the Chelyabinsk Region: Manufacture of Coke Oven Products (19.1), Manufacture of Basic Iron and Steel and of Ferro-Alloys (24.1, 24.51, 24.20, 24.3); Mining of Non-Ferrous Metal Ores (07.2); Manufacture of Structural Metal Products (28.1–28.3); Mining of Iron Ores (07.1); Waste Collection, Treatment and Disposal, Materials Recovery (38); Manufacture of Basic Precious and Other Non-Ferrous Metals, Processing of Nuclear Fuel (24.4).

6 industries were located in the Sverdlovsk Region: Manufacture of Basic Precious and Other Non-Ferrous Metals, Processing of Nuclear Fuel (24.4); Mining of Metal Ores (07.1); Manufacture of Basic Iron and Steel and of Ferro-Alloys (24.1, 24.51, 24.20, 24.3); Manufacture of Coke Oven Products (19.1); Mining of Non-Ferrous Metal Ores (07.2); Waste Collection, Treatment and Disposal, Materials Recovery (38).

6 industries were located in the Kemerovo Region—Kuzbass: Mining of Coal, Brown Coal and Peat (05, 05.20.1, 08.92.1); Manufacture of Coke Oven Products (19.1); Mining of Metal Ores (07.1); Waste Collection, Treatment and Disposal, Materials Recovery (38); Manufacture of Structural Metal Products (25.1–25.3); Manufacture of Basic Iron and Steel and of Ferro-Alloys (24.1, 24.51, 24.20, 24.3).

Table 1. Location quotients of the metallurgy cluster and the industries included in the cluster, in 2020

Regions	Cluster	OKVED 2 (All-Russia classifier of types of economic activities)							
		05, 05.20.1, 08.92.1	07.1	07.2	19.1	24.1, 24.51, 24.20, 24.3	24.4	25.1–25.3	38
Chelyabinsk Region	2.88	0.04	1.65	2.20	7.36	6.70	1.40	2.02	1.41
Kemerovo Region—Kuzbass	6.29	31.94	4.53	0.38	14.36	3.71	0.57	1.44	1.65
Sverdlovsk Region	2.89	0.03	5.24	1.50	2.52	4.20	8.61	1.24	1.30
Krasnoyarsk Territory	2.58	2.87	0.00	6.49		0.08	8.68	0.85	1.74
Murmansk Region	2.16		11.13	4.94		0.00	7.31	0.07	1.44
Orenburg Region	1.70	0.06		3.46	4.18	2.63	1.08	1.19	1.47
Irkutsk Region	1.61	2.19	3.18	4.06		0.18	3.35	0.59	0.87
Republic of Khakassia	3.70	10.11	4.06	6.48		0.39	9.62	0.34	0.50
Belgorod Region	3.09		33.73			2.93	0.16	3.36	0.96
Vologda Region	2.33				10.15	7.32	0.15	0.61	1.63
Chukotka Autonomous District	8.20	6.19		56.18					0.43
Magadan Region	7.15	0.53		54.15		0.02	0.01	0.06	0.20
Lipetsk Region	3.38	0.00	0.02			11.59	0.05	1.31	1.13
Trans-Baikal Territory	2.47	4.27	0.06	13.93		0.02	0.01	0.12	0.38

(continued)

Table 1. (*continued*)

Regions	Cluster	OKVED 2 (All-Russia classifier of types of economic activities)							
		05, 05.20.1, 08.92.1	07.1	07.2	19.1	24.1, 24.51, 24.20, 24.3	24.4	25.1–25.3	38
Amur Region	**2.46**	**3.43**	0.08	**13.28**		0.00		0.65	1.14
Republic of Sakha (Yakutia)	**2.33**	**5.90**	0.13	**10.95**		0.00	0.00	0.19	0.43
Volgograd Region	**1.45**					**4.14**	0.93	0.85	1.01
Republic of Tyva	**1.40**	**2.55**		**7.99**					0.09
Jewish Autonomous Region	**1.39**		**26.33**	0.43		0.08		0.11	0.39
Khabarovsk Territory	**1.32**	**1.49**		**4.64**		0.80	0.57	0.73	0.87
Republic of Mari El	**1.30**	0.09			0.06	0.02		**5.88**	**1.67**
Republic of Karelia	**1.30**	0.12	**14.74**			0.46	0.16	**1.86**	0.89
Sakhalin Region	**1.30**	**7.34**		0.73				0.32	1.10

In the Republic of Khakassia, 4 branches were located: Mining of Coal, Brown Coal and Peat (05, 05.20.1, 08.92.1); Manufacture of Basic Precious and Other Non-Ferrous Metals, Processing of Nuclear Fuel (24.4); Mining of Non-Ferrous Metal Ores (07.2); Mining of Iron Ores (07.1).

In the Krasnoyarsk Territory, 4 branches were located: Mining of Coal, Brown Coal and Peat (05, 05.20.1, 08.92.1); Mining of Non-Ferrous Metal Ores (07.2); Manufacture of Basic Precious and Other Non-Ferrous Metals, Processing of Nuclear Fuel (24.4); Waste Collection, Treatment and Disposal, Materials Recovery (38).

In the Belgorod Region, 3 industries were located: Mining of Metal Ores (07.1); Manufacture of Basic Iron and Steel and of Ferro-Alloys (24.1, 24.51, 24.20, 24.3); Manufacture of Structural Metal Products (25.1–25.3).

In the Vologda Region, 3 industries were located: Manufacture of Coke Oven Products (19.1); Manufacture of Basic Iron and Steel and of Ferro-Alloys (24.1, 24.51, 24.20, 24.3); Waste Collection, Treatment and Disposal, Materials Recovery (38).

In the Murmansk Region, 4 industries were located: Mining of Metal Ores (07.1); Mining of Non-Ferrous Metal Ores (07.2); Manufacture of Non-Ferrous Metals (27.4); Waste Collection, Treatment and Disposal, Materials Recovery (38).

In the Orenburg Region, 4 industries were located: Mining of Non-Ferrous Metal Ores (07.2); Manufacture of Coke Oven Products (19.1); Manufacture of Basic Iron and Steel and of Ferro-Alloys (24.1, 24.51, 24.20, 24.3); Waste Collection, Treatment and Disposal, Materials Recovery (38).

In the Irkutsk Region, 4 industries were located: Mining of Coal, Brown Coal and Peat (05, 05.20.1, 08.92.1); Mining of Metal Ores (07.1); Mining of Non-Ferrous Metal Ores (07.2); Manufacture of Basic Precious and Other Non-Ferrous Metals, Processing of Nuclear Fuel (24.4).

In the Chukotka Autonomous District, 2 industries were located: Mining of Non-Ferrous Metal Ores (07.2) and Mining of Coal, Brown Coal and Peat (05, 05.20.1, 08.92.1).

In the Trans-Baikal Territory, the Republic of Tyva, the Republic of Sakha (Yakutia), the Amur Region, 2 industries were located: Mining of Non-Ferrous Metal Ores (07.2) and Mining of Coal, Brown Coal and Peat (05, 05.20.1, 08.92.1).

In the Khabarovsk Territory, 2 industries were located: Mining of Non-Ferrous Metal Ores (07.2) and Mining of Coal, Brown Coal and Peat (05, 05.20.1, 08.92.1).

In the Lipetsk Region, 2 industries were located: Manufacture of Basic Iron and Steel and of Ferro-Alloys (24.1, 24.51, 24.20, 24.3) and Manufacture of Structural Metal Products (25.1–25.3).

In the Republic of Mari El, 2 industries were located: Manufacture of Structural Metal Products (25.1–25.3), Waste Collection, Treatment and Disposal, Materials Recovery (38).

In the Republic of Karelia, 2 industries were located: Mining of Metal Ores (07.1), Manufacture of Structural Metal Products (25.1–25.3).

In the Magadan Region, 1 industry was located—Mining of Non-Ferrous Metal Ores (07.2).

In the Jewish Autonomous Region, 1 industry was located—Mining of Metal Ores (07.1).

In the Sakhalin Region, 1 industry was located—Mining of Coal, Brown Coal and Peat (05, 05.20.1, 08.92.1).

In the Volgograd Region, the industry of Manufacture of Basic Iron and Steel and of Ferro-Alloys (24.1, 24.51, 24.20, 24.3) was located.

The results obtained make it possible for us to understand which industries need to be developed in the regions.

Further, we will analyze how the cluster location changed over the period from 2016 to 2020 (Table 2).

From 2016 to 2020, the Metallurgy cluster was steadily located in 17 regions. Since 2017, it has been concentrated in the Republic of Tyva and the Jewish Autonomous District; since 2019 and 2020 the cluster has been located in the Sakhalin Region, Khabarovsk Territory, the Republic of Mari El, and the Republic of Karelia. In the Kursk Region, the cluster was located in 2017 only.

The data obtained were uploaded to the developed database which allowed visualizing the spatial location of the Metallurgy cluster in the regions of the Russian Federation (see Fig. 2). The web application interface allows selecting the year, the cluster name

Table 2. Values of location quotients of the metallurgy cluster

Regions	Years				
	2016	2017	2018	2019	2020
Chukotka Autonomous District	9.29	8.38	8.67	8.54	8.20
Magadan Region	6.21	6.12	6.71	7.12	7.15
Kemerovo Region—Kuzbass	6.50	6.42	6.33	6.38	6.29
Republic of Khakassia	3.92	3.46	3.72	3.73	3.70
Lipetsk Region	3.70	3.01	3.26	3.36	3.38
Belgorod Region	3.61	3.37	3.26	3.01	3.09
Sverdlovsk Region	3.36	3.17	3.01	2.97	2.89
Chelyabinsk Region	3.50	3.27	2.97	2.91	2.88
Krasnoyarsk Territory	2.50	2.87	2.72	2.61	2.58
Trans-Baikal Territory	1.72	2.31	2.94	2.51	2.47
Amur Region	1.99	2.26	2.23	2.38	2.46
Vologda Region	1.86	2.80	2.04	2.25	2.33
Republic of Sakha (Yakutia)	2.04	1.73	1.98	2.10	2.33
Murmansk Region	2.37	2.57	2.30	2.14	2.16
Orenburg Region	1.88	1.68	1.73	1.68	1.70
Irkutsk Region	1.59	1.59	1.62	1.56	1.61
Volgograd Region	1.55	1.37	1.37	1.43	1.45
Republic of Tyva	1.22	1.55	1.53	1.63	1.40
Jewish Autonomous Region	0.39	1.35	1.37	1.45	1.39
Khabarovsk Territory	1.44	1.14	1.25	1.27	1.32
Republic of Mari El	0.60	0.63	1.02	1.16	1.30
Republic of Karelia	1.13	0.99	1.13	1.24	1.30
Sakhalin Region	0.80	1.13	1.12	1.32	1.30
Kursk Region	0.89	1.57	0.90	0.86	1.01

and the indicator. At the moment, the location quotient and the average headcount can be selected as indicators; in the future the list will be expanded.

The map is filled according to the color scale. The higher the indicator is, the brighter the area of the region is colored. When pointing a cursor bar over, the region name and the location quotient indicator are displayed.

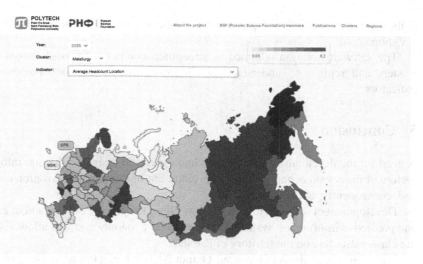

Fig. 2. Location of the Metallurgy Cluster in Russia in 2020

4 Discussion

In the article by O. V. Bazhenov, P. B. Kormachenko, A. E. Sheveleva, the main component in the structure of the metallurgical industrial cluster is the industries of OKVED-1, 27 class (OKVED-2, 24 class) [27]. Application of the maximum method based on the Input-Output 2016 Table has made it possible to establish that in addition to these industries, the production chain includes 7 others from various OKVED-2 classes. To analyze the Metallurgy cluster it is necessary to take all intersectoral interactions into account.

With the spatial approach the regions where the clusters are located have been determined. Besides, the results obtained coincide with the opinions of the authors who studied the clusters in the Belgorod Region [28] and in the Krasnoyarsk Territory [29].

When designing the interactive map the American Cluster Observatory project built on statistical information by state, industry and cluster category has been used as a basis. In turn, the Cluster Map of Russian of the Russian Cluster Observatory reflects pilot innovation clusters and industrial clusters. In 2012, the Ministry of Economic Development of the Russian Federation launched a national program for development of cluster support within which 25 pilot innovative territorial clusters were selected, and then their number increased. The clusters include a list of participating enterprises that have passed the procedure of selection by an expert commission for compliance with the requirements. Therefore, this project has been implemented using the 'bottom-up' approach, when clusters are searched for in a specific territory with the organizations and industry leaders under study previously identified. The purpose of our study was to create a software solution based on cluster identification using the 'top-down' methodology, where production spatial locations focused on certain types of economic activity are selected.

The software solution proposed can be used to build an automated system for identification and analysis of the state of clusters in the Russian regions. An important advantage of the generated interactive map is that it is publicly available on the portal: https://rscf-dev.spbpu.com/.

The software solution is aimed to strengthen competitiveness of Russia, to help clusters and regions to understand and improve their economic composition and indicators.

5 Conclusion

A need for the development of digital technologies and their introduction into the real sectors of the region economy entails development of the region innovation ecosystem and, consequently, of the entire country.

Development of software tools will allow filling the gap in development of analytical and predictive information systems of the regional economy and will allow visualizing the cluster structure on the territory of Russia.

Following the analysis of the Input-Output 2016 Table, it has been found out that the Metallurgy cluster includes 8 industries; the spatial location of clusters and their industries in 2020 has been determined, and the dynamics of changes in the cluster location for the period from 2016 to 2020 has been considered. To visualize the cluster spatial location a database has been designed in the MongoDB database system. Identification of clusters has been performed using the methodology of the Input-Output Table analysis. A high concentration of employees in related industries makes it possible to obtain information about the specializations of regions.

The results obtained can become the basis for development of a regional cluster policy in implementation of which visual representation of statistical information is particularly important.

The developed software solution allows getting a more complete picture of the cluster development in Russia, can become a basis for strategically important decisions made by state authorities in cluster policy of constituent entities of the Russian Federation, for recommendations on investments to adjacent and lagging industries of developed cluster groups of regions.

In the future, it is planned to supplement the web application with a region page where statistical data by clusters and industries concentrated in the selected region will be presented.

Acknowledgment. This research was funded by the Russian Science Foundation. Project No. 20-78-10123.

References

1. Janowski, T.: Digital government evolution: From transformation to contextualization. Gov. Inf. Q. **32**(3), 221–236 (2015)
2. Kuehn, W.: Digital twins for decision making in complex production and logistic enterprises. Int. J. Des. Nat. Ecodyn. **13**(3), 260–271 (2018)

3. Wan, L., Nochta, T., Schooling, J.M.: Developing a city-level digital twin–propositions and a case study. In: International Conference on Smart Infrastructure and Construction 2019 (ICSIC) Driving Data-Informed Decision-Making, pp. 187–194. ICE Publishing (2019)
4. Wanasinghe, T.R., et al.: Digital twin for the oil and gas industry: overview, research trends, opportunities, and challenges. IEEE Access **8**, 104175–104197 (2020)
5. Protsiv, S.: European Cluster Panorama 2016. Center for Strategy and Competitiveness, Stockholm School of Economics, Stockholm (2016)
6. Cluster Mapping: Mapping a nation of regional clusters. https://www.clustermapping.us/. Accessed 15 April 2022
7. Kozonogova, E., Kurushin, D., Dubrovskaya, J.: Computer visualization of the identify industrial clusters task using GVMap. Sci. Visualiz. **11**(5), 126 (2019)
8. Marshall, A.: Principles of Economics, 309 p. M.: Progress (1993)
9. Porter, M.E.: Clusters and Competition: New Agendas for Companies, Governments, and Institutions Editor M.E, pp. 197–299. Harward Business School Press, Porter, Boston, MA (1998)
10. Turgel, I.D., Bozhko, L.L., Pandzhiyeva, V.T.: Cluster policies of large cities in Russia and Kazakhstan. R-economy **6**(1), 28–39 (2020)
11. Kutsenko, E.: Pilot innovative territorial clusters in Russia: a sustainable development model. Foresight **9**(1), 32–55 (2015)
12. Sosnovskikh, S.: Industrial clusters in Russia: the development of special economic zones and industrial parks. Russian J. Econ. **3**(2), 174–199 (2017)
13. Bek, M.A., Bek, N.N., Sheresheva, M.Y., Johnston, W.J.: Perspectives of SME innovation clusters development in Russia. J. Bus. Indust. Market. **28**(3), 240–259 (2013). https://doi.org/10.1108/08858621311302895
14. Skhvediani, A., Sosnovskikh, S.: What Agglomeration externalities impact the development of the hi-tech industry sector? Evidence from the Russian Regions. Int. J. Technol. **11**(6), 1091–1102 (2020)
15. Kutsenko, E., Islankina, E., Abashkin, V.: The evolution of cluster initiatives in Russia: the impacts of policy, life-time, proximity and innovative environment. Foresight **19**(2), 87–120 (2017). https://doi.org/10.1108/FS-07-2016-0030
16. Kudryavtseva, T., Olaniyi, E.O.: Identification and analysis of the cluster structure of a territory and its impact on regional development: an example of Russia. J. Adv. Res. L. Econ. **10**, 1322 (2019)
17. Zemtsov, S., Barinova, V., Pankratov, A., Kutsenko, E.: Potential high-tech clusters in Russian Regions: from current policy to new growth areas. Foresight STI Govern. **10**(3), 34–52 (2016). https://doi.org/10.17323/1995-459X.2016.3.34.52
18. Kutsenko, E., Eferin, Y.: "Whirlpools" and "Safe Harbors" in the dynamics of industrial specialization in Russian Regions. Foresight STI Govern. **13**(3), 24–40 (2019). https://doi.org/10.17323/2500-2597.2019.3.24.40
19. Cluster Map of Russia. Russian Cluster Observatory. https://map.cluster.hse.ru/list. Accessed 15 April 2022
20. Montfort, M.J.: Les filières de production. In: Montfort, M.J., Dutailly, J.C. (eds.). INSEE Archives et Documents, pp. 1–193 (1983)
21. The official website of the Federal State Statistics Service [Electronic resource]. https://rosstat.gov.ru/
22. Peeters, L., Tiri, M., Berwert, A.: Techno-economic Clusters in Flanders and Switzerland: An Input-Output-Analysis. Cent. Sci. Technol. Stud. CEST, vol. 9 (2001)
23. Verbeek, H.: Innovative Clusters: Identification of value-adding production chains and their networks of innovation, international studies. na (1999)

24. Feser, E.J., Bergman, E.M.: National industry cluster templates: a framework for applied regional cluster analysis. Reg. Stud. Taylor Francis **34**(1), 1–19 (2000). https://doi.org/10.1080/00343400050005844
25. Solvell, O., Linqvist, G., Ketels, C.: The Cluster Initiative Greenbook. Stockholm School of Economics, Stockholm (2003)
26. The official website of the Unified Interdepartmental Statistical Information System. https://www.fedstat.ru/. Accessed 20 Mar 2022
27. Bazhenov, O.V., Kormachenko, P.B., Sheveleva, A.E.: Characteristics of the metallurgical industrial clusters an object of economic research. Econ. Sustain. Develop. **4**(40), 33–37 (2019)
28. Samarina, V.P.: Some Ecological Aspects of the Belgorod Mining and Metallurgical Cluster Activity. Malyshev Readings. pp. 116–120 (2019)
29. Bazhenov, O.V., Makhinova, N.V.: Identification of the arctic norilsk metallurgical cluster as an object of economic. Discussion. **4**(95), 22–29 (2019)

Industrial, Service and Agricultural Digitalization

Evaluation of E-commerce Impact on Sustainable Economic Growth: The Case of Vietnam

Lo Thi Hong Van[1]([✉]) [ID], Liudmila Guzikova[2] [ID], and An Thinh Nguyen[1] [ID]

[1] University of Business and Economics of Vietnam National University, 144. Xuan Thuy, 10000 Hanoi, Vietnam
hongvan289@gmail.com

[2] Peter the Great St. Petersburg Polytechnic University, 29. Polytechnicheskaya, 195251 Saint Petersburg, Russia

Abstract. Instruments for the sustainable growth attract a lot of attention. An assessment of e-commerce development through the example of the Socialist Republic of Vietnam allows determining the prospects for this branch of digital economy in most of the developing countries. The aim of this study is to assess the role of e-commerce in sustainable economic growth and to identify areas in which the strategy for e-commerce development in Vietnam until 2025 can be improved. The research methods include dynamic SWOT analysis, correlation analysis, and cluster analysis using IBM SPSS Statistics 23 software. Within the study the conditions for the development of the e-commerce market in Vietnam are identified; the role of e-commerce in ensuring sustainable economic growth is analyzed; the relationship between e-commerce and other economic and social factors affecting growth and development is analyzed; directions for the development of e-commerce in each Vietnamese province are proposed. The scientific novelty of this work consists in the approach proposed for assessing the contribution of e-commerce to the sustainable growth of GDP and the classification of e-commerce development policies based on the level of regional development. The authors provide recommendations for improving the government strategy for e-commerce development in Vietnam based on the grouping of administrative entities according to their technological and infrastructural development. The results of the study can be used in the elaboration of the government policy on the development of e-commerce and the digital economy in general – not only in Vietnam, but in other developing countries as well.

Keywords: Coronavirus pandemic · E-commerce · E-commerce development strategy · Sustainable economic growth · Vietnam

1 Introduction

The COVID-19 pandemic has changed the modus operandi in the economies of all countries. The development of Industry 4.0 plays an important role in ensuring the functioning of the economy in the framework of the coronavirus pandemic in Vietnam

© Springer Nature Switzerland AG 2022
D. Rodionov et al. (Eds.): SPBPU IDE 2021, CCIS 1619, pp. 101–111, 2022.
https://doi.org/10.1007/978-3-031-14985-6_7

[16]. From 2015 to 2020, the growth rates of the three largest Internet economies in Southeast Asia (Vietnam, Indonesia, and the Philippines) averaged 35–36%. According to the e-Conomy SEA 2020 report [14], Southeast Asia's Internet economy market volume reached USD 105 billion in 2020 and is expected to reach USD 309 billion in 2025. Southeast Asia may become one of the largest regions in the world in terms of the growth rate of online commerce. In Vietnam, the volume of the digital economy amounted to USD 14 billion in 2020. According to Google's forecast, the share of the e-commerce sector in Vietnam's digital economy should increase from 12.5% in 2015 to 55.77% in 2025 [14]. The digital economy is expected to grow 72.5 times – from USD 0.4 billion in 2015 to USD 29 billion in 2025.

E-commerce is one of the key areas of the digital economy and an important pre-requisite for the digital transformation of the economy as a whole [8]. E-commerce can be considered as a favorable environment for the application of new business models and the long-term development of national innovation systems from the strategic per-spective [41]. Today, Vietnam is at risk of falling into the middle-income trap, when the advantages of cheap labor and affordable raw materials are gradually being exhausted, so the country is constantly looking for new drivers of growth [15]. Accordingly, Vietnam seeks to actively use the opportunities for economic growth provided by digital transfor-mation and e-commerce development. Now, when the developed countries have already created a technical and human infrastructure in the field of information technology for the sustainable development of the e-commerce market, the question arises whether e-commerce can become a key factor for sustainable economic growth in developing countries?

Literature Review. Despite the great interest in the opportunities and challenges of the e-commerce market as an object of scientific analysis, most important issues remain insufficiently investigated. The main concepts of e-commerce development are discussed in the works of Kwilinski A., Volynets R., Shevchenko T., Berdnik I., Holovko M., Berzin P., Babenko V., Kulczyk Z., Davydova O. [3, 24]. These authors consider e-commerce as a factor transforming all economies across the world in the context of globalization. The issues of improving the regulatory framework for managing the growth of e-commerce and the restructuring of e-commerce in the digital economy need to be addressed in both developed and developing countries [11]. Of great importance for this study are the works of Western and Eastern scientists about the impact of e-commerce on the economic growth in various countries – for example, Indonesia [4], Nigeria [22], England [1], Malaysia [26], and China [13, 27]. The experience of different countries proves that there is a direct correlation between the growth of e-commerce and the growth of the digital economy, which the authors commonly view as an indicator of the influence of e-commerce on the growth rates of national economies [2, 6, 9, 25, 28, 36]. In recent studies, Southeast Asia's e-commerce market is viewed as a new emerging market with great potential (Nguyen H.P. et al. 2020). However, a strong cultural tradition of avoiding risk and change threatens the speed of e-commerce development in Vietnam and in other developing countries [10].

The subject of this study is the indicators of Vietnam's socio-economic development and the e-commerce index.

The aim of the study is to assess the role of Vietnam's e-commerce in sustainable economic growth and to improve Vietnam's e-commerce development strategy until 2025.

2 Methods

Please A logical diagram of the study is shown in Fig. 1 (see Fig. 1).

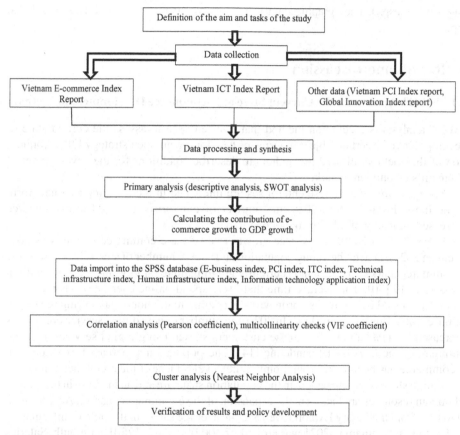

Fig. 1. Vietnam's e-commerce development study process (compiled by the authors).

The main research method is SWOT analysis with allowance for the dynamics.

The contribution of e-commerce growth to GDP growth was assessed by calculating the following indicators:

$$CE_t = \frac{E_t - E_{t-1}}{Y_t - Y_{t-1}} \times 100(\%) = \frac{gE}{gY} \times pE(\%) \qquad (1)$$

where: CE t is the contribution of e-commerce growth to GDP growth in year t; Y t is GDP in year t; E t is the e-commerce market value in year t; gE is the growth rate of e-commerce; gY is the growth rate of GDP; pE is the share of e-commerce in GDP.

Correlation analysis and cluster analysis were performed using IBM SPSS Statistics 23 software. The study is based on statistics available at the time of writing (before July 28, 2021). Data of Vietnamese and international research organizations and statistics agencies are used, available on the websites of the Vietnam e-Commerce and Digital Economy Agency of the Ministry of Industry and Trade of Vietnam (http://en.idea.gov.vn), United Nations Development Program (UNDP) (undp.org), Vietnam Provincial Governance and Public Administration Performance Index (PAPI) (https://papi.org.vn/eng/), Ministry of Science and Technology of Vietnam (http://www.most.gov.vn/en/Pages/home.aspx). Factographic data were obtained from online publications on the topic.

3   Results and Discussion

3.1   SWOT Analysis of the Current State of E-commerce Development in Vietnam

SWOT analysis is a common method that is often used to assess the current state of development of a certain object in terms of developing an open strategy [38]. Application of this method allowed the authors to describe conditions for the development of Vietnam's e-commerce market.

S – Strengths: Vietnamese enterprises are interested in e-commerce as a new form of business. From 2016 to 2019, the number of enterprises engaged in e-commerce increased almost twofold – from 244,635 to 477,014 [30].

From 2015 to 2020, the average growth rate of the e-commerce market was 26% (Statista 2021). Due to the young population and a large number of smartphone users, the e-commerce market in Vietnam is currently growing quite rapidly, and had 35.4 million users in 2019 [30]. The average time that users spend online every day has increased from 3.1 hours/day before the coronavirus pandemic to 4.2 hours/day during the origin of the coronavirus pandemic [14]. In 2020, the number of new digital service consumers increased by 41%, and 94% of these customers started using digital services after the outbreak of the COVID-19 pandemic [14]. The population's increased experience in e-commerce has become a strong point in the development of the e-commerce market.

A high share of young people in the population structure and an increase in the quality of human resources are factors in the expansion of the e-commerce market. According to statistics from the Salary Explorer website, the average salary in the field of information technology in Vietnam in 2021 was around 17,300,000 dong ($750) per month. Salaries in IT in Vietnam are about 12% of the same in Singapore and 45% in Malaysia.

Vietnam's technical infrastructure of e-commerce is gradually improving. As of January 2021, there are 68.72 million Internet users in Vietnam, which is 70.3% of the population [30]. In general, Vietnam has the lowest communication charges in the Asia-Pacific region, especially for fixed broadband Internet access [44].

Increased investment in the digital economy is a positive sign of digital transformation [40]. The volume of investment in Vietnam's digital economy increased from USD 156 million in 2016 to USD 935 million in 2019 [14].

Vietnam has a system of regulatory documents on e-commerce management. In 2007, the Vietnam E-Commerce Association was established [40] to create a favorable environment for the development of e-commerce. In October 2020, by Government Decision No. 645/QD-TTg 2020, the national strategy for e-commerce development was adopted. In accordance with the E-Commerce Development Strategy, the volume of B2C e-commerce sales should increase by 25% annually, reaching USD 35 billion by 2025, which will account for 10% of the total retail sales of consumer goods and services in the country.

W – Weaknesses: Vietnam's technical infrastructure varies greatly between large cities and mountainous provinces. In large cities, the percentage of households with Internet access exceeds 96%, whereas in the mountainous provinces the average value was 30% in 2020 [29]. The most noticeable and common limitations of e-commerce in Vietnam today are fraud risk and technology risk. According to the statistics of the Ministry of Public Security of Vietnam, 65% of frauds in 2020 were committed in cyberspace [31].

Websites of many Vietnamese businesses are not e-commerce websites: they are used only as a promotion channel, without taking full advantage of e-commerce. The share of enterprises investing in, creating, and operating websites/mobile applications tends to decrease. The share of enterprises investing in the development of websites/mobile applications over 20% of the total funds allocated for the development of e-commerce decreased from 40% in 2017 to 38% in 2020 [44].

Information security in Vietnam is still not up to par [20]. According to the survey of the heads of 30 banks and 16 financial and insurance companies in Vietnam conducted by the Vietnam Computer Emergency Response Center, frequent violation of information security policy by employees (70%) and difficulties in choosing a provider of information security solutions (over 40%) are considered to be the biggest obstacles to the information security of financial enterprises and banks.

Human resources are an important ground for the development of the digital economy [39]. Human resources for e-commerce in Vietnam are still limited. In 2020, 32% of enterprises had difficulties recruiting e-commerce specialists, which is more than in 2018, when only 28% of enterprises had such difficulties [44]. Today in Vietnam, on-demand e-commerce training has a 37% share; short-term training – 33%, long-term formal education –16%, online training – 9% [30]. These data show that currently the formal training of human resources for e-commerce only partially meets the actual needs.

O – Opportunities: The advantage of a "later entry" allows Vietnam to use the strengths of developed countries in e-commerce and to limit the shortcomings of the business models they have tested. Vietnamese enterprises have the opportunity to use successful e-commerce business models created around the world. For example, the business models of Vinabook and Nhommua are identical to the models of Amazon and Groupon [45]. Vietnam's entry into EVFTA in 2019 has opened great opportunities for the development of international e-commerce [43]. In the context of globalization, the development of sustainable business becomes more difficult [34]. The introduction of an e-commerce trading platform between Vietnam and the EU will facilitate the integration of digital solutions and the construction of a full-fledged digital ecosystem that will help enterprises operate efficiently, facilitating commercial activities via a single platform.

From 2016 to 2020, Vietnam's global innovation index gained 17 positions (rising from 59th place in 2016 to 42nd in 2020). With this position, Vietnam ranks first among

29 countries with low-middle income [29]. From 2017 to 2020, the score of information and communication technology (ICT) infrastructure increased from 52 to 62.8 points; the score of state online services – from 57.2 to 73.6 points (MIC 2017 & 2020). Improving the ICT infrastructure creates a foundation for the sustainable growth of e-commerce [5].

T – Threats: Ethical issues in e-commerce are becoming more common in Vietnam [37]. Business entities are virtual, goods are not stored at the place of business registration, there are no fixed warehouses, and trading operations are carried out without invoices and other documents, making it very difficult to identify and eliminate violations in e-commerce operations at the moment. Ultimately, unethical behavior in e-commerce reduces consumer confidence.

Competition from foreign e-commerce enterprises hinders the development of new domestic e-commerce enterprises. According to the report of iPrice Group, Thai e-commerce corporation Shoppee ranks first among the 50 largest e-commerce enterprises in Vietnam by the number of visits per month. During the first quarter of 2021, Shopee's customer traffic was around 64 million visits, which is twice as much as that of Vietnam's largest e-commerce corporation, thegioididong.

3.2 The Role of E-commerce in the Sustainable Growth of Vietnam's Economy

Calculating the contribution of e-commerce growth to GDP growth makes it possible to assess the role of e-commerce in the sustainable growth of the Vietnamese economy (Table 1).

Table 1. Contribution of e-commerce growth to GDP growth in 2015–2020 (Source: calculated by authors based on (VECOM 2015–2020).

Year	2015	2016	2017	2018	2019	2020
E-commerce market value, billion U.S. dollars	4.07	5	6.2	8	10.08	11.8
E-commerce annual growth rate, %	37.04	22.85	24.00	29.03	26.00	17.06
GDP, billion U.S. dollars	193.24	205.28	223.78	245.21	261.92	271.16
GDP annual growth rate, %	3.78	6.23	9.01	9.58	6.81	3.53
Percent E-commerce in GDP, %	2.11	2.44	2.77	3.26	3.85	4.35
Contribution of E-commerce growth to GDP growth, %	20.63	8.93	7.38	9.89	14.68	21.05

From 2015 to 2020, Vietnam's e-commerce market consistently experienced double-digit growth. It is noteworthy that, despite the COVID-19 pandemic, Vietnam experienced a 17% growth of the e-commerce market in 2020. Thus, e-commerce is an important factor for sustainable economic growth. Over five years, the share of e-commerce in GDP has increased from 2.11% to 4.35%. The average contribution of the e-commerce market growth to economic growth was 13.76%.

E-commerce not only played an important role in GDP growth, but also enhanced the restructuring of the economy by sectors of production and by forms of ownership. From 2016 to 2018, the share of private enterprises engaged in e-commerce operations was consistently above 96%. The share of enterprises with foreign investment engaged in e-commerce operations increased twofold – from 1.8% in 2016 to 3.6% in 2018 [30]. While economic restructuring in terms of forms of ownership in Vietnam is leaning towards increasing the share of the private sector and reducing the share of the public sector, private enterprises (which make up the majority in the field of e-commerce) are becoming the driving force of economic restructuring by forms of ownership. The restructuring of Vietnam's e-commerce by economic sectors in 2016–2019 moved towards increasing the share of enterprises engaged in e-commerce operations in agriculture from 1.08% to 1.31% [30]. Therefore, participation in transactions on e-commerce platforms should facilitate the active use of technology among farmers, cooperatives, and agricultural enterprises, gradually performing a digital transformation of production and sale of agricultural products. E-commerce should ensure national food security and a stable basis for sustainable agricultural development in Vietnam.

3.3   Factors Affecting the Growth of E-commerce in Vietnam

The correlation analysis based on the results of e-commerce development assessment in 55 out of 63 administrative entities of Vietnam published by VECOM allowed the authors to identify the main factors affecting the development of e-commerce in Vietnam. The Pearson correlation coefficient between the e-commerce development index and the ICT index is 0.487, which indicates a relationship between the level of ICT development and the level of e-commerce development (EBI). However, a Pearson correlation coefficient below 0.5 means that this relationship is weak [35]. In other words, the level of e-commerce development is determined by the development of ICT technologies in Vietnam only to a small extent. In contrast, the level of e-commerce development does not determine the level of ICT development. Considering the different pace of changes, it can be concluded that the information technology platform does not yet meet the demand for the development of e-commerce. In addition, the results of the correlation analysis show that there is no significant relationship between the Governance and Public Administration Performance Index (PAPI) and the E-Commerce Development Index (EBI). This shows that e-commerce in the G2B sector is limited and does not contribute to improving the efficiency of e-government. Thus, the main indicators of the PAPI index – the quality of the business environment and e-government – have not made a substantial contribution to the development of e-commerce.

The results of a multicollinearity test with a variance inflation factor (VIF) coefficient below 2 confirmed the reliability of the results of the correlation analysis. Cluster analysis was used to divide the provinces of Vietnam into four clusters based on the nearest neighbor analysis method.

The first cluster includes Hanoi and Ho Chi Minh with a high EBI level (above 85), an average level of technical infrastructure development (0.6–0.7), a high level of human infrastructure development (0.7–0.8), and a low level of information technology application (0.2–0.4).

The second cluster includes Hai Phong, Da Nang, Binh Duong, Dong Nai, and Bac Ninh with an average EBI level (53.1–60.6), an average level of technical infrastructure development (0.6–0.7), a low level of human infrastructure development (0.4–0.6), and the lowest level of information technology application (0.18).

The third cluster includes Quang Ninh, Hai Duong, Nghe An, Vinh Phuc, Bac Giang, Ben Tre, Khanh Hoa, Ninh Binh, Long An, Thanh Hoa, Binh Dinh, Hung Yen, Ha Nam, Thua Thien Hue, Lam Dong, Nam Dinh, Tien Giang, Thai Nguyen, Quang Nam, Phu Tho, Tay Ninh, An Giang, Dong Thap, Thai Binh, and Kien Giang with a low EBI level (38–49), a low level of technical infrastructure development (average value is 0.4–0.6), an average level of human infrastructure development (average value is 0.5–0.7), and a very low level of information technology application (0.18–0.2).

The fourth cluster includes the remaining provinces with a very low EBI level (27–37), a low level of technical infrastructure development (0.3–0.5), a low level of human infrastructure development (0.2–0.5), and a very low level of information technology application (0.12–0.2). For this group of provinces, a program for the development of information technology infrastructure in all three aspects – human, technical, and applied – is proposed.

4 Conclusions

Most studies stop at considering the internal development of e-commerce or the impact of e-commerce on rural development or the development of small and medium enterprises, but do not analyze the contribution of e-commerce and its impact on the economy and society in the framework of a sustainable economic development model [7, 12, 17, 18, 23, 32, 33]. The analysis of strengths and weaknesses, combined with the identified threats and opportunities for the development of e-commerce in Vietnam, shows that Vietnam belongs to the group of Southeast Asian countries with a unique potential for e-commerce growth. E-commerce is an advanced area of Vietnam's digital economy and plays an important role in sustainable economic growth. In 2015–2020, e-commerce accounted for an average of 14% of GDP growth. E-commerce also contributes to the restructuring of the economy in terms of forms of ownership and the sustainability of growth in the agricultural sector.

The analysis of conditions for the development of e-commerce, the correlation analysis of the relationships between the development of e-commerce, information technology, and public administration, cluster analysis of the indicators of administrative entities make it possible to propose the following solutions to overcome the weaknesses of the e-commerce sector in Vietnam and respond to upcoming challenges in 2021–2025.

1) In Vietnam, administrative entities vary greatly in terms of the level of e-commerce development. Only 13% of provinces have an EBI above 50. Therefore, when implementing the E-Commerce Development Strategy, it is necessary to develop executive programs for each group of provinces. It is also necessary to develop a policy for allocating financial and human resources in accordance with the selected groups of administrative entities to minimize the gap in e-commerce development. Logistics links between provinces need to be developed to facilitate the development of e-commerce.

2) Increasing the operational efficiency of e-government, improving e-commerce management mechanisms and institutions to create a favorable environment for G2B e-commerce transactions.

3) Increasing investment in the creation of technical infrastructure systems, developing application infrastructure systems based on the promotion of application development training and identification of priorities for the development of the software industry.

4) Encouraging the development of information security, building an ethical code and a system for protecting the interests of consumers in the e-commerce space.

5) Training and development of human resources in the field of e-commerce should become a key factor in the development of e-commerce. This requires giving priority to the creation of training programs and e-commerce majors; providing career guidance for high school students; developing a model of educational institutions at enterprises to meet modern requirements for e-commerce.

The experience of e-commerce development established in Vietnam at the national strategy level can be used in other developing countries.

Acknowledgements. This research is partially funded by the Ministry of Science and Higher Education of the Russian Federation under the strategic academic leadership program 'Priority 2030' (Agreement 075-15-2021-1333 dated 30.09.2021).

References

1. Allen, J., et al.: Understanding the impact of e-commerce on last-mile light goods vehicle activity in urban areas: the case of London. Transp. Res. Part D: Transp. Environ. **61**, 325–338 (2018)
2. Anvari, R.D., Norouzi, D.: The impact of e-commerce and R&D on economic development in some selected countries. Procedia Soc. Behav. Sci. **229**, 354–362 (2016)
3. Babenko, V., et al.: Factors of the development of international e-commerce under the conditions of globalization. SHS Web Conf. **65**, 04016–04021 (2019)
4. Barata, A.: Strengthening national economic growth and equitable income through sharia digital economy in Indonesia. J. Islamic Monet. Econ. Finan. **5**(1), 145–168 (2019)
5. Barykin, S.Y., et al.: Developing the physical distribution digital twin model within the trade network. Acad. Strateg. Manag. J. **20**, 1–18 (2021)
6. Baytar, C.U.: The Impact of e-commerce on economic growth: a Bibliometric study. In: Global Business Research Symposium, pp. 1–7 (2015)
7. Bich, N.N.T., et al.: Inclusive and implementable legal rules for E-Commerce: a comparative study of Indonesia and Vietnam. Indon. L. Rev. **10**, 314–319 (2020)
8. Bresciani, S., et al.: digital transformation management for agile organizations: a compass to sail the digital world. Digital Business Models, pp. 28–32 (2021)
9. Bukht, R., et al.: Conceptualising and measuring the digital economy. Development Informatics Working Paper, vol. 68 (2018)
10. Choi, Y., et al.: The sustainable role of the e-trust in the B2C e-commerce of Vietnam. Sustainability **10**(1), 291–293 (2018)
11. Janow, M.E., et al.: Digital trade, e-commerce, the WTO and regional frameworks. World Trade Review. **18**(S1), S1–S7 (2019)

12. Dung, D.T., et al.: E-commerce in Vietnam: opportunities and challenges. Socio-economic and Environmental Issues in Development, pp. 244–249 (2019)
13. Fang, Y.: Current situation, obstacles and solutions to China's cross-border e-commerce. Open J. Soc. Sci. **5**(10), 343–351 (2019)
14. Google & Temasek: E-Conomy SEA 2020 Report, p. 594 (2020). https://www.bain.com/glo balassets/noindex/2020/e_conomy_sea_2020_report.pdf. Accessed 21 July 2021
15. Guzikova, L.A., et al.: Sustainable development as national doctrine: experience of Vietnam. Economic and Social Development. In: 37th International Scientific Conference on Proceedings "Socio Economic Problems of Sustainable Development, pp. 1011–1021. Baku (2019)
16. Guzikova, L.A., et al.: Sustainable economic growth in Vietnam: challenges and opportunities of the coronavirus pandemic. In: the 2nd International Scientific Conference on Innovations in Digital Economy on Proceedings SPBPU IDE 2020, pp. 1–7. ACM (2020)
17. Ha, N.T.V.: The development of the digital economy in Vietnam. VNU J. Sci. Econ. Bus **36**(5E) (2020)
18. Ha, N.T.: Middle economic growth towards to development of e-commerce in Southeast Asia. J. Econ. Empower. Strat. **4**(1), 1–6 (2020)
19. Hossin, M.A., et al.: Development dimensions of e-commerce in Bangladesh: scope, challenges and threats. In: Proceedings of the 2018 International Conference on Information Management & Management Science, pp. 42–47 (2019)
20. Hsu, Y., et al.: The factors influencing customers' repurchasing intention in B2C-E-commerce in Vietnam and Taiwan. Int. J. Bus. Commerce **7**(3), 77–93 (2019)
21. Irina, A.: Contribution of the e-commerce to the economic development. In: International Conference on Business Excellence, pp. 3–8. Brasov, Romania (2017)
22. Khan, H.U., et al.: Possible impact of e-commerce strategies on the utilisation of e-commerce in Nigeria. Int. J. Bus. Innov. Res. **15**(2), 231–246 (2018)
23. Kim, H.B., et al.: E-Commerce in the Vietnam Legal System: review legal framework to be improved to promote e-commerce. J. Legal **24**(2), 9–19 (2021)
24. Kwilinski, A., et al.: E-Commerce: concept and legal regulation in modern economic conditions. J. Legal Ethical Regul. Issues **22**, 1–6 (2019)
25. La Rocca, M.: General Management: Business Model e Business Plan. Entrepreneurship, Business Modelling and Business Planning, vol. 12 (2020)
26. Lim, S.C., et al.: Factors influencing continuance intention of ecommerce among SMEs in Northern Region of Malaysia. In: International Conference on Computer & Information Sciences (ICCOINS) – IEEE, pp. 53–58 (2020)
27. Li, F., et al.: E-commerce and industrial upgrading in the Chinese apparel value chain. J. Contemp. Asia **49**(1), 24–53 (2019)
28. Mandel, M.: How ecommerce creates jobs and reduces income inequality, pp. 3–9. Progressive Policy Institute (2017)
29. MIC - Ministry of information and communications: Vietnam ICT Index Report (2021). Accessed 02 June 2021
30. MOIT Vietnam: Ministry of Industry and Trade. Developing e-commerce to become one of the pioneering fields of the digital economy (2020). https://moit.gov.vn/bao-ve-nen-tang-tu-tuong-cua-dang/phat-trien-thuong-mai-dien-tu-tro-thanh-mot-trong-nhung-linh.html. Accessed 23 July 2021
31. Nguyen, H.K., et al.: Improvement of service quality in the supply chain of commercial banks-a case study in Vietnam. J. Risk Finan. Manage. **14**(1), 357–359 (2021)
32. Nguyen, H.P., et al.: Logistics revolution for e-commerce in Vietnam: a brief review. Int. J. E-Navig. Maritime Econ. **13**, 50–62 (2021)
33. Nguyen, T.H., et al.: Developing Vietnam electronic commerce in the period 2020–2025. J. Contemp. Issues Bus. Govern. **27**(2), 953–966 (2021)

34. Nikolova, L.V., Rodionov, D.G., Litvinenko, A.N. Sustainability of the business in the conditions of globalization. In: Proceedings of the 30th International Business Information Management Association Conference, pp. 417–421 (2017)
35. Okagbue, H.I., et al.: Trends and usage pattern of SPSS and Minitab software in scientific research. J. Phys. Conf. Ser. **1734**(1), 012017–012022 (2017)
36. Pamungkas, B., et al.: Proposing a key model e-commerce towards digital economy for coastal areas in Indonesia. IT Convergence and Security, pp. 98–105 (2018)
37. Phan, S.: The effect of PESTLE factors on development of e-commerce. Int. J. Data Network Sci. **5**(1), 37–42 (2021)
38. Puyt, R., et al.: Origins of SWOT analysis. Acad. Manage. **1**, 17416–17428 (2020)
39. Rodionov, D., Rudskaia, I.: Problems of infrastructural development of "industry 4.0" in Russia on sibur experience IBIMA 2018-Vision 2020, pp. 3534–3544 (2018)
40. Rodionov, D., et al.: Modeling changes in the enterprise information capital in the digital economy. J. Open Innov. Technol. Market Complex. **7**(3), 166–169 (2021)
41. Samarasingha, T., Perera, J.: E Business Evolution. Perspective and Strategy, pp. 67–84 (2020)
42. Tang, W., et al.: Informality and rural industry: rethinking the impacts of E-Commerce on rural development in China. J. Rural. Stud. **75**, 20–29 (2019)
43. Trang, N.T.L.: EVFTA—A Review of Opportunities and Challenges for Vietnam. Shifting Economic, Financial and Banking Paradigm, pp. 131–151 (2021)
44. VECOM (Vietnam E-commerce Association): Vietnam E-commerce Index 2021 Report. http://en.vecom.vn/documents. Accessed 23 July 2021
45. Yang, Z., et al.: Ethics of retailers and consumer behavior in E-Commerce: context of developing country with roles of trust and commitment. Int. J. Asian Bus. Inform. Manage. **11**(1), 107–126 (2020)

Machine Learning Predictive Model for Performance Criteria of Energy-Efficient Healthy Building

Mustika Sari[1,3] , Mohammed Ali Berawi[1,3(✉)] , Teuku Yuri Zagloel[2,3] ,
Louferinio Royanto Amatkasmin[3] , and Bambang Susantono[3]

[1] Civil Engineering, Faculty of Engineering, Universitas Indonesia, Depok 16424, Indonesia
maberawi@eng.ui.ac.id
[2] Industrial Engineering, Faculty of Engineering, Universitas Indonesia, Depok 16424, Indonesia
[3] Center for Sustainable Infrastructure Development, Universitas Indonesia, Depok 16424, Indonesia

Abstract. Energy efficiency and occupant wellbeing are complex concepts increasingly becoming a mainstream building and construction industry focal point. These concepts demand deciding not only the appropriate building materials, techniques, and systems but also abstract qualities, which are challenging to quantify. As recent automation technologies have advanced, the building and construction sector is experiencing rapid progress, bringing about efficient building development methods. However, building design needs an efficient computerized design tool that enables designers to make more reliable decisions to help achieve the intended quality objectives of the buildings. This paper aims to explore the data preparation of energy-efficient and healthy buildings to be utilized in a machine learning (ML) model that can accurately predict the determination of the building variables. The generalized data used in this study were quantified, analyzed, and processed before being utilized in the machine learning model developed using Support Vector Regression (SVR) and Multi Layer Perceptron (MLP) algorithms. The accuracy of the models was evaluated using the Mean Absolute Error (MAE). The outcome of this study shows that the predictive machine learning model could help decision-makers quantitatively predict the healthy building variables to an adequate level of accuracy.

Keywords: Machine learning · Predictive model · Healthy building · Performance criteria

1 Introduction

Building practitioners have tried to develop various approaches to address issues caused by the buildings to the environment, as it consumes more than one-third of the world's primary energy and accounts for 40% of the world's greenhouse gas emissions global [33, 34]. Moreover, the fact that people spend more than 85% of their lives in buildings [9] has

© Springer Nature Switzerland AG 2022
D. Rodionov et al. (Eds.): SPBPU IDE 2021, CCIS 1619, pp. 112–132, 2022.
https://doi.org/10.1007/978-3-031-14985-6_8

raised concerns not only about the increased energy demands for the building operation but also about the occupants' health. Therefore, a high-quality built environment that is less energy consuming and less harmful to the wellbeing of its occupants has been highly considered as the solution.

A healthy building is a concept that strives to lower the negative impacts of the buildings on the environment while increasing the positive effects on the occupants' health and wellbeings [7]. A healthy building is designed to support the occupants and the environment by highlighting the quality of the indoor environment through restorative materials and promoting healthy living principles. Even though the healthy building concept has attracted the world's attention, its development is still considered low due to insufficient research, lack of awareness, and flawed building standard systems [35]. Hale [25] argued that advanced technology could help foster and elaborate the development of healthy buildings.

Advanced technologies play a crucial role in developing data-driven design by presenting designers with more design options and providing insights into the issues they are trying to solve [11]. The benefits of technology advancement have been embraced in the building and construction industry through the employment of digital technologies, intelligent systems, and smart materials in the project life cycle [27]. The implementation of these technological innovations has created enhanced systems that make the value creation and decision-making processes in the industry more efficient [13], as well as strengthens the interaction between humans and technology [30].

The development of smart digital technologies such as Artificial Intelligence (AI), blockchain, and big data brings about more competent working approaches in the building design process. It can help assess and predict the conditions of humans and the surrounding environment in the location of the building, which can further improve the environmental requirements for the people to live and increase the building design quality [36]. Machine learning, a section of artificial intelligence (AI), helps solve problems in a wide range of areas by providing a system the ability to learn and improve on its own [31]. Machine learning techniques have been adopted in the building sector for these past few years, primarily on the aspect of energy and carbon efficiency [28]. However, research on machine learning models for healthy building design has not been done yet. Therefore, this study aims to develop a model that predicts the design criteria of a healthy building that puts forward energy efficiency and occupant health as the crucial aspects of the buildings. The result of this study is expected to alleviate the decision-making process by providing an approach to efficiently determine the design criteria of a healthy building in the conceptual design phase with a certain level of accuracy.

2 Literature Review

2.1 Healthy Buildings

Engineers in the 1970s have solved the issues by alleviating the energy crisis in buildings by sealing up the buildings. However, this approach caused a phenomenon where the pollutants were built up indoors, known as Sick Building Syndrome (SBS), which is used to define situations where building occupants experience health and comfort concerns related to their time in the building [6, 40].

Healthy buildings have been viewed as the solution to these problems [45]. A healthy building is designed so that it does not affect the health of its occupants or the wider environment. The concept of a healthy building does not only emphasize the design and materials that are friendly to the occupants' health but also promotes a healthy lifestyle to people to increase their awareness of living healthily. The study carried out by MacNaughton et al. [39] proved that buildings influence our health, wellbeing, and productivity. Their study results showed improved indoor environmental quality is associated with better health outcomes.

There are nine focal determinants of health in a building, including ventilation, air quality, thermal health, moisture, water quality, dust and pests, acoustics and noise, lighting and views, and safety and security [5]. On the other hand, Loftness et al. [37] viewed the design of healthy buildings from three perspectives: (1) sustainable development that emphasizes the aspects that must be considered in the design and land use; (2) the occupants' effects on the indoor air quality that links the building operation to its design; and (3) the developments in products and materials and their certification and labeling.

From the first point of view, sustainable design and engineering development are essential for improving health, productivity, and quality of life. The analysis results were done on building components to reveal the benefits for human wellbeing from high-performance buildings designed to deliver high-quality air, thermal control, light, ergonomics, privacy, interaction, and access to the natural environment. The second point of view discusses the role that human plays in maintaining the quality of their indoor environment quality (IEQ). Moreover, the third point provides an overview of recent developments in low emitting products and materials becoming the primary way to control indoor air quality and achieve an excellent indoor environment.

IEQ is complex because it deals with the combined effects of stress factors on the users, their interactions, and their movements in buildings of different types. Therefore, instead of individual components and only preventing people from getting sick, occupants' situations and improving the quality of life should be the focus of the indoor environment's design [16]. The performance indicators of healthy buildings can be seen from three different angles that include; (1) the environmental parameters: concentrations of certain pollutants, ventilation rate or CO_2 concentration, temperature, and lighting intensity; (2) the occupants or end-user: such as sick leave, productivity, number of symptoms or complaints, health adjusted life indicator or specific building-related illnesses; and (3) the building and its components: specific characteristics of a building and its components.

According to Tao et al. [54], the occupant wellbeing is correlated with occupant satisfaction measured by the defining human factors, such as essential comfort (lighting, temperature, and acoustics), healthy necessity (good air quality, clean water, pleasant interior design, etc.), convenience (human building system interaction, service access, etc.) and other contextual factors, such as community, school district, transportation, etc. However, the consideration of these human factors complicates the decision-making process. Therefore, the conceptual framework was developed with humans, the built environment, the wellbeing and building interface metrics, and the wellbeing-centric life cycle assessment metrics as the interrelated aspects. The framework aimed to address the missing links and potential pathways that connect energy efficiency and occupants' wellbeing in a building-level sustainability framework; therefore, human wellbeing can motivate adopting a healthy building concept for the building design and operation.

Sustainability rating systems have already been established for nearly 20 years; however, the procedures for identifying healthy buildings are still being developed and are not mature yet. McArthur and Powell [42] studied the defining health and wellness categories in buildings. The credit requirements of primary types were analyzed and synthesized to identify trends across healthy building systems and alignment with existing literature. The level of similarities or consistencies between contemporary research on the effect of the built environment on human health and in the process has identified relevant gaps within the systems.

One of the gaps identified is the absence of explicitly noting toxic chemicals within the workplace with toxins like lead, mercury, and asbestos, which are all present in common building materials and can have significant environmental and health impacts. Another gap directly related to indoor environmental quality is the lack of a standard to improve resistance to mold and mildew. Furthermore, equipping the built environment with operable windows is another gap that can improve indoor air quality and provide occupants with more thermal comfort control. Coverage on lighting was still limited, though it holds great potential to improve visual comfort in offices. Lastly, other problems like the design for thermal comfort (e.g., thermal zoning, humidity control, and air diffusion design) and vibration minimization must be considered in the rating systems to optimize its health benefits for the occupants.

2.2 Machine Learning

Machine learning refers to a collection of methodologies that can automatically detect patterns in data used to develop forecast models and support decision-making on things that are in uncertain conditions [43]. It is a process in which a model is trained using historical data of input-output to adapt to new data independently [27, 29]. The focus of machine learning development is to automatically generate a pattern, plan, representation, or description from data designed to show a system's main work or concept.

There are three types of learning in machine learning: supervised, unsupervised, and reinforcement learning. Supervised learning is a method used to develop predictive models by mapping and studying a series of inputs (features, attributes, or covariates) to one or more outputs (response variables) which become training data, where the inputs are labeled. On the other hand, the input to training data in unsupervised learning is not labeled. Algorithms are built to learn and generate their own data structures to find the underlying relationships in the data [38]. Both types of learning can be achieved using parametric and nonparametric models. The third type of learning is reinforcement learning, an approach used to learn how to act or behave under uncertainty by adapting to different environments using learning control policies through direct interaction with the environment [52, 53].

By leveraging the statistical analysis of large datasets, machine learning algorithms can be trained to efficiently identify patterns of correlation in contexts with a high number of features and complex relation functions. Moreover, machine learning algorithms are pervasive in recognizing patterns in contexts with multiple variables that could affect specific variables of interest. When large labeled datasets are accessible, supervised learning becomes a tangible, potent method for pattern recognition by performing classification or regression analysis [23].

Machine learning has easily replaced simulation programs and has become the desired tool to evaluate and predict building performance due to its efficacy and better computation for data analytics [11]. The schematic building design is developed in the preliminary and conceptual design stages, where estimated ranges of values can be obtained from many sources, such as national building design guidelines, legal thresholds, and designers' expectations despite the unspecified detailed design frameworks [30]. Machine learning techniques are helpful in the design process of sustainable and healthy buildings, where a clear understanding of the complex relationship between the effects of building specifications and the interaction of building elements is required [12].

Furthermore, the machine learning model was developed based on the importance of universality as an analyzing tool that can assess various environmental irregularities present in the early stages of the built environment. This method yields multiple advantages. It allows building designers to analyze potential early design options in the early design stage. Furthermore, it also provides results that specify the impacts early design would have on environmental performance and examines the early frameworks for performance uncertainty to ascertain their relative importance.

Successful pilot studies on machine learning models for many aspects of the buildings, such as fault detection and diagnosis of heating, ventilation, and air conditioning (HVAC) equipment and systems, load prediction, energy baseline estimate, load shape clustering, occupancy prediction, and learning occupant behaviors and energy use patterns, have been conducted. However, the building sector has not implemented these studies [27]. It had to do with the challenges that include: (1) lack of large scale labeled data to train and validate the model; (2) lack of model transferability, which limits a model trained with one data-rich building to be used in another building with limited data; (3) lack of solid justification of costs and benefits of deploying machine learning; and (4) the performance might not be reliable and robust for the stated goals, as the method might work for some buildings but could not be generalized to others.

Furthermore, different machine learning models are validated on specific datasets in various studies, making it hard to compare results. A large-scale open-source dataset is needed to enhance comparability by testing different methods on the same dataset. Another limitation is the interpretability of results because of machine learning's data-driven black-box approach [2].

3 Methods

This study was conducted in two phases to develop a predictive machine learning model for the healthy building design criteria. The identification of the healthy building performance variables in healthy building criteria and indicators that will be used later as input and output features for the machine learning models was conducted in the first stage. These variables were obtained by analyzing relevant research on healthy building research published in the last five years in journals, proceedings, and textbooks. Archive analysis and sourcing from the guidelines were conducted to obtain the range of values of the healthy building's performance metrics. Furthermore, the ranges for the value of each variable were determined [25] based on the building standards and regulations applied in countries worldwide.

In the second stage, the development of the machine learning models was performed using the design variables and indicators obtained as the features for the machine learning model. The machine learning model development dataset was collected from the UCI repository and then completed by conducting the data syntethization as a data acquisition method [48]. Synthetic data for machine learning model training and testing generated by adding actual or entirely synthesized data should represent the original dataset and be based on existing standards [21, 24, 26].

A preprocessing step in the form of data cleaning using regression and data transformation using normalization was performed to prepare the data. This preprocessed data was then used for model development using k-folds cross-validation and mean absolute error measurement. Two algorithms were employed for model development: linear Support Vector Regression (SVM) and Multi Layer Perceptron (MLP). Subsequent sections explain the data collection, machine learning algorithms, and model accuracy measurement.

3.1 Data Collection

The raw datasets used for the machine learning development are secondary data obtained from existing sources through the UCI Machine Learning Repository, an online archive of databases, domain theories, and data generators. The repository was created in 1987 by David Aha and fellow graduate students at UC Irvine and is widely used by the machine learning community to obtain machine learning datasets for the empirical analysis of machine learning algorithms [56].

Aside from the repository, additional necessary data will be retrieved to complete the missing quantitative data to the datasets retrieved from the UCI repository through data synthetization. The synthetic data added was built based on the ranges of data parameters obtained from the existing standards and guidelines on healthy buildings, which include: (a) the Building Research Establishment Environmental Assessment Method (BREEAM) [17]; (b) the RESET Standard that provides a data quality standard for continuous monitoring sensors in the built environment [58]; (c) the European standard EN 12464-1 that underlines the minimum illuminance requirements for a working area [18]; (d) EN-15251 that details indoor environmental input parameters for design and assessment of buildings' energy performance focusing on the indoor air quality, thermal comfort, lighting and acoustics [44], and BASIX.

Furthermore, in-depth interviews with experts in the field of healthy building were conducted with questions related to the composition of the dataset and the most relevant standards and guidelines for this study's intended purpose. The in-depth interviews were also performed to validate the variables generated from the archive analysis and obtain recommendations for data composition, standards, and guidelines.

3.2 Machine Learning Algorithms

The machine learning model development was then carried out with the data obtained from the previous step. However, since the research goal is to determine values using regression quantitatively, the variables will have to display a weak correlation to be considered independent variables. Therefore, prior programming was done a correlational study measuring the correlation in the dataset between independent input and output variables. The nonparametric test method Spearman's correlation coefficient was used, in which the correlation degree between two variables can be determined according to the grading standards of ρ, as shown in Table 1 [51].

Table 1. Spearman's correlation degree standard (ρ)

Grading standard	Correlation degree
$\rho = 0$	No correlation
$0.00 < |\rho| \leq 0.19$	Very weak
$0.20 < |\rho| \leq 0.39$	Weak
$0.40 < |\rho| \leq 0.59$	Moderate
$0.60 < |\rho| \leq 0.79$	Strong
$0.80 < |\rho| \leq 1.00$	Very strong

Collected datasets were then normalized to be used for further model development. Normalization is an essential process of transforming data by scaling each variable column within the range of 0 to 1, mainly since the scale of the columns is varied, and the distribution of data generated from standards and guidelines in this study is unknown.

The dataset was imported into the Python environment, where data preprocessing began. Python 3 programming language was used to develop the predictive model for healthy building design, coupled with Anaconda 3 distribution software used to abridge the programming process due to its ability to manage packages and libraries in programming environments. The code written into the Jupyter notebook integrated within the Anaconda made the process of loading, writing, and saving programming documents much easier and faster. The packages used in this study are NumPy, pandas, Scikit-learn, Tensorflow, Keras, and Openpyxl. The machine learning algorithms used in this experiment are the Support Vector Regression (SVR) and Multi Layer Perceptron (MLP).

SVR is an application form of Support Vector Machines (SVM), learning machines that implement the principle of minimizing structural risk minimization to obtain appropriate generalization on a limited amount of learning patterns. SVM applies a learning algorithm to recognize subtle patterns in complex datasets by performing classification learning by example to predict classifications of previously unseen data.

SVR is generated from SVM through generalization by introducing ε-tube, an insensitive region around the function. It is formulated as an optimization problem by initially defining a convex ε-insensitive loss function to be minimized and then identifying the flattest tube that includes the best of the training cases [10]. Compared to other regression techniques, the SVR algorithm is recognized as the technique demonstrating high predictive and accuracy performance [47]. Furthermore, it can model nonlinear relationships and solve regression functions by selecting the necessary support vectors. It can be employed even though there are only a few samples than the variables [1].

MLP is a feedforward artificial neural network (ANN) class, a modeling mechanism known to be skilled in solving nonlinear problems. ANN has a high pattern recognition ability and is a robust classifier that can generalize and make decisions from large and fuzzy input data [20]. Furthermore, the feedforward ANN yields a distinguishable benefit through its representative and universal function estimation capabilities [49], hence its ability to learn a continuous function that acts more smoothly when changes occur in the input and output [19]. MLP plots sets of input data onto a set of suitable outputs using historical data so that the model can be used to generate the output when the preferred outcome is not identified [22]. The equation for MLP regression is shown in Eq. (1) below.

$$Y_j = f\left(\sum_i w_{ij} X_{ij}\right) \tag{1}$$

where:

Y_j = node j output.
$f()$ = transfer function training an MLP with one hidden layer.
w_{ij} = connection weight between node j and node i in the lower layer.
X_i = input signal from node i in the lower layer.

3.3 Model Validation

Validations were carried out during the model's training and after the model had been developed. K-fold cross-validation was used to validate the training dataset during the data training to develop the model. It was performed to randomly divide the data into the training set and the testing set into a preferred subset of k. K-fold cross-validation then repeats k-times to separate a set randomly into the freest set of sections [8].

Once the model has been developed and predicts the output values from a data sample's input, accuracy measurement was then done using a Mean Absolute Error (MAE) interpretation on the model prediction. MAE calculates all the absolute errors and then finds the mean value for all. It first calculates the mean of all the datasets present, then subtracts the mean value with each data individually, adds all the resultant value, and finally divides it by the total number of datasets present. The formulation of MAE is expressed in Eq. (2).

$$MAE = \frac{1}{n}\sum xi - x \tag{2}$$

where,

xi = the actual value.

x = the predicted value.
n = the total number of values.

Figure 1 shows the workflow of the research in obtaining its two objectives: identifying healthy building performance metrics and developing a predictive machine learning model for healthy building performance criteria.

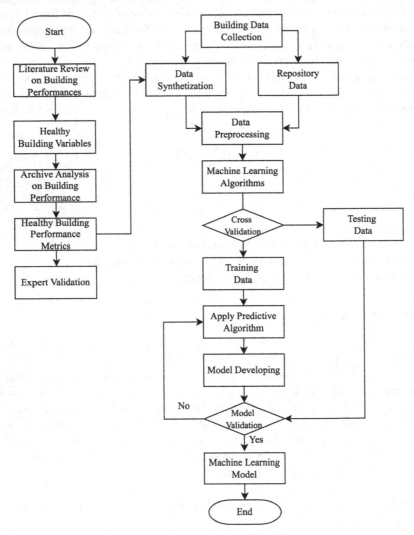

Fig. 1. Research flowchart

4   Results and Discussion

4.1   Healthy Buildings

The healthy building performance criteria used in developing the machine learning model were obtained from the literature study. Indicators for healthy building performance can be considered from several perspectives: the built environment, the occupant or end-user, and the dose parameter, such as indoor air pollutants concentrations, indoor temperature, lighting intensity, and ambient noise level [16]. However, standards and guidelines for healthy buildings are still focused on dose-related indicators rather than considering the different viewpoints integrated into the design process [14]. Therefore, the subject of human health and wellbeing from a built environment perspective should be discussed and researched extensively [7]. There are three main objectives in healthy building design frequently discoursed in the scientific publications and standards, which include human wellbeing from a building situation perspective, human wellbeing from a dose exposure perspective, and human wellbeing from an occupant effect perspective (see Table 2).

The variables for these three perspectives in Table 2 were derived from the journals regarding the healthy building. The variables for human wellbeing from the perspective of building situations include materials characteristics, control systems, processes, psychosocial factors, age, interactions, building infrastructure, and community [11, 16, 50, 54]. The variables for human wellbeing from the perspective of doze exposure include acoustic comfort, thermal comfort, air quality, visual comfort, environmental factors, time, interaction, energy reduction, and disease satisfaction [4, 16, 37, 42]. More-over, human wellbeing from the perspective of occupant effect: symptoms, productiv-ity, behavior, physiological markers, physical markers, personal factors, history/future, interactions, social wellbeing, and psychological wellbeing [16].

Since the focus is on target variables that have measurable outcomes in the indoor environment that can be quantified, some of the variables shown in Table 2 can not be used to develop a machine learning model. Therefore, a selection was conducted over analyses and in-depth interviews with the experts. Only variables from the dose exposure perspective were selected as the results since it highly influences the indoor environmental quality of a healthy building, including visual comfort, indoor air quality, thermal comfort, and acoustic comfort. These variables were then manifested into five variables for machine learning development, namely: (X1) Daylighting: a method used to bring natural light into the home using glazing on the exterior (windows, skylights, etc.) to reduce the need for artificial lighting and saving energy; (X2) Indoor Air Quality that refers to the air quality within and around buildings and structures that relates to the health and comfort of building occupants; (X3) Thermal Comfort that expresses satisfaction with the thermal environment; (X4) Acoustic Comfort that conveys the wellbeing and feeling of the occupants about the acoustic environment; and (X5) Energy Use that refers to all energy used to perform an action, manufacture something, or simply inhabit a building. Table 3 summarizes the healthy buildings' variables for machine learning model development.

Table 2. Healthy building performance and indicators

No.	Objectives	Variables	Indicators	References
1	Human Wellbeing from a building situation perspective	Materials characteristics	Mold resistant materials	[5, 16, 42]
			Non-toxic materials	[16, 42]
2		Control systems	Furnishing and decoration	[16, 37]
3		Processes	Building materials	[16, 37]
			Control systems	[16]
			Furnishing and decoration	[16, 37]
4		Psychosocial factors		[16]
5		Age		[16]
6		Interactions		[16]
7		Building		[54]
8		Infrastructure		[54]
9		Community		[54]
10	Human Wellbeing from a dose exposure perspective	Acoustic comfort		[16]
11		Thermal comfort	Operable windows	[16, 37, 42, 54]
			Thermal zoning	
			Humidity control	
			Mechanical ventilation	
			Air diffusion design	
12		Air quality	Operable windows	[16, 37, 42, 54]
13		Visual comfort	Lighting	[42, 54]
14		Environmental factors		[16, 37]
15		Time		[16]
16		Interactions		[16, 42]
17		Energy reduction	Daylighting	[37]
18		Emission reduction	Active commuting	[42]

(continued)

Table 2. (*continued*)

No.	Objectives	Variables	Indicators	References
19	Human Wellbeing from an occupant effect perspective	Non-communicable diseases		[16]
20		Satisfaction/annoyance		[16]
21		Symptoms		[16]
22		Productivity/performance		[16]
23		Behavior/activity		[16, 37]
24		Physiological markers		[16]
25		Physical markers		[16]
26		Personal factors		[16, 37]
27		History/Future		[16]
28		Interactions		[16]
29		Social wellbeing		[42]
30		Psychological wellbeing		[42]

Table 3. Healthy building variables for machine learning model development

Variable	Reference	Indicator		Data Source
X1	Lighting [3–5, 37, 42, 54, 57]	X1.1	Illuminance levels (E_v)	EN 12464-1 and BREEAM
		X1.2	Unified glaring rate	
		X1.3	Colour rendering index (R_a)	
		X1.4	View out	
X2	Indoor air quality [5, 15, 32, 37, 42, 54]	X2.1	Particulate matter PM2.5	Reset air standard
		X2.2	Total volatile organic compounds	
		X2.3	CO_2 and CO	
X3	Thermal comfort [5, 15, 37, 42, 54]	X3.1	PMV/PPD	EN 15251:2007
		X3.2	Operative temperature (TOP)	
X4	Acoustic comfort [5, 16, 54]	X4.1	A-weighted sound pressure level (dB(A))	EN 15251:2007
X5	Energy use [4, 46, 50, 57]	X5.1	Heating and cooling load	UCI repository

4.2 Data Collection

Machine learning models require extensive data to acquire good accuracy and robustness; therefore, the numerical data collection for adequate size and usable existing datasets was conducted. Data retrieved online from UCI Machine Learning Repository (2012) was altered and applied to the research. The original data was utilized in a study by Tsanas & Xifara [55] to quantify the residential buildings' energy efficiency using machine learning methods. The data consisted of eight input variables (X1–X8) and two output variables (YI and Y2), which include the heating and cooling load of the building (heating, ventilation, and air conditioning system) related to energy efficiency (see Fig. 2). The dataset consists of 768 samples of simulated residential building data, in which X1 to X8 were initially used as an input to determine Y1 and Y2, heating and cooling load, which have a relation to energy efficiency.

For this study, the data was altered by adding several more variables in conjunction with all existing data. Table 4 summarizes the input variables, the range of values, and the descriptions.

X1	X2	X3	X4	X5	X6	X7	X8	Y1	Y2
0.98	514.50	294.00	110.25	7.00	2	0.00	0	15.55	21.33
0.98	514.50	294.00	110.25	7.00	3	0.00	0	15.55	21.33
0.98	514.50	294.00	110.25	7.00	4	0.00	0	15.55	21.33
0.98	514.50	294.00	110.25	7.00	5	0.00	0	15.55	21.33
0.90	563.50	318.50	122.50	7.00	2	0.00	0	20.84	28.28
0.90	563.50	318.50	122.50	7.00	3	0.00	0	21.46	25.38
0.90	563.50	318.50	122.50	7.00	4	0.00	0	20.71	25.16
0.90	563.50	318.50	122.50	7.00	5	0.00	0	19.68	29.60

Fig. 2. Excerpt of UCI machine learning repository: energy efficiency dataset [56]

Table 4. Identification of input variables

Input variables		Range of values	Description
X1	Relative compactness	0.62 to 0.98	Volume to surface ratio compared with the most compact shape with the same volume
X2	Surface area	514.5 to 808.5	External surface area from which heat can escape
X3	Wall area	245 to 416.5	Area of a wall, including any openings
X4	Roof area	110.25 to 220.50	Area of a roof or ceiling assembly separating conditioned space from the outdoors or unconditioned spaces
X5	Overall height	3.5 to 7	The vertical distance between the finished grade and the highest point on the building

(continued)

Table 4. (*continued*)

Input variables		Range of values	Description
X6	Orientation	2 to 5	The positioning of a building concerning seasonal variations in the sun's path and prevailing wind patterns
X7	Glazing area	0 to 0.4	The interior surface area of the entire assembly, including glazing, sash, curbing, and other framing elements
X8	Glazing distribution	0 to 5	Distribution of glazing area within the whole building

The output variables for the machine learning model were also identified during the literature review. The healthy building variables mentioned in Table 3 become the output variables with sub-variables based on the building standards and guidelines used. While machine learning datasets for YI and Y2 were from UCI Repository, datasets for Y2 to Y14 were built from the used standards and guidelines. The output variables, range of values, sub-variables, and references are summarized in Table 5.

Table 5. Identification of output variables

Output variable		Range of values	Subvariable	Reference
Energy use	Y1	6.01–43.1	Heating load	BASIX
	Y2	10.9–48.03	Cooling load	
Lighting	Y3	500	Illuminance levels	EN 12464-1
	Y4	19	Unified glaring rate	EN 12464-1
	Y5	80	Color rendering index	EN 12464-1
	Y6	1	View out	BREEAM
Indoor air quality	Y7	<35 mg/m^3	Particulate matter (2.5)	RESET
	Y8	<500 mg/m^3	Total volatile air compounds	
	Y9	<1000 ppm	Carbon dioxide	
	Y10	<9 ppm	Carbon monoxide	
Thermal comfort	Y11	$-0.2 < PMV < 0.2$	Predicted mean vote	EN 15251
	Y12	0–6	Percentage predicted dissatisfaction	
	Y13	21–25.5 °C	Operative temperature	
Acoustic comfort	Y14	26–32	Decibel(A)	EN 15251

4.3 Machine Learning Model Development

Upon programming, plotting the correlation in the dataset between independent input and output variables using Spearman's scale was done (see Fig. 3). The results showed that the variable correlates the best with itself, and most variables as plotted independently correlate weakly with each other. It implies that no independent variable correlates strongly with another one, meaning that all variables are independent and proper for the regression case.

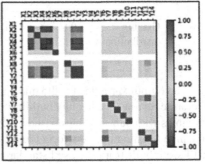

```
import numpy as np
import pandas as pd
import matplotlib.pyplot as plt
data = df
corr = data.corr()
fig = plt.figure()
ax = fig.add_subplot(111)
cax = ax.matshow(corr,cmap='coolwarm', vmin=-1, vmax=1)
fig.colorbar(cax)
ticks = np.arange(0,len(data.columns),1)
ax.set_xticks(ticks)
plt.xticks(rotation=90)
ax.set_yticks(ticks)
ax.set_xticklabels(data.columns)
ax.set_yticklabels(data.columns)
plt.show()
```

Fig. 3. Inter-variable correlation

4.4 Support Vector Regression

Chained multiple-output regression is when a sequence of dependent models is created to match the number of target variables to be predicted. The model takes the input variables and predicts the first output variable. The second output variable is determined using the first output variable and the input variables. The third output variable is determined using the first and second output variables and the input variables, and so forth until all output variables are predicted. Figure 4 shows an excerpt of the programming code for the SVR method.

```
# example of evaluating chained multioutput regression with an SVM model
from numpy import mean
from numpy import std
from numpy import absolute
from sklearn.model_selection import cross_val_score
from sklearn.model_selection import RepeatedKFold
from sklearn.multioutput import RegressorChain
from sklearn.svm import LinearSVR
# define base model
model = LinearSVR()
# define the chained multioutput wrapper model
wrapper = RegressorChain(model)
```

Fig. 4. Defining the model with SVR and RegressorChain

4.5 Multi Layer Perceptron

The second model was developed using MLP, that is capable of learning a continuous function to support outputting multiple variables for each prediction [19]. The number of nodes in the output is set equal to the number of target variables in multi-output regression. A linear activation function is applied to each node. The input layer was specified to have eight inputs for the "input_dim" argument in the first hidden layer and 14 nodes in the output layer. The activation function used for the hidden layer is the rectified linear unit (ReLU). The code for the MLP model development is shown in Fig. 5.

```
# mlp for multi-output regression
from numpy import mean
from numpy import std
from sklearn.model_selection import RepeatedKFold
from keras.models import Sequential
from keras.layers import Dense
from tensorflow.keras import Sequential
from tensorflow.keras.layers import Conv2D, Flatten, Dense

# get the model
def get_model(n_inputs, n_outputs):
        model = Sequential()
        model.add(Dense(20, input_dim=8, kernel_initializer='he_uniform', activation='
        model.add(Dense(14))
        model.compile(loss='mae', optimizer='adam')
        return model
```

Fig. 5. Defining the model with MLP

4.6 Accuracy Evaluation of Machine Learning Predictive Model

MAE was used to evaluate the accuracy of the models, where a small MAE score indicates that the model is great at prediction, while a large score implies that there might be issues. Moreover, an MAE score of 0 means perfect output prediction provided.

In both methods, the dataset was fitted to the defined model. K-fold cross-validation was performed to reduce bias and leave enough data for model training and validation by dividing the datasets into smaller subsets into ten subsets, taking one of the subsets for validation and the nine others for training. This process was repeated, and the error estimation was averaged. The evaluation codes are shown in Figs. 6 and 7.

```
# define the evaluation procedure
cv = RepeatedKFold(n_splits=10, n_repeats=3, random_state=1)
# evaluate the model and collect the scores
n_scores = cross_val_score(wrapper, X, Y, scoring='neg_mean_absolute_error', cv=cv,
# force the scores to be positive
n_scores = absolute(n_scores)
# summarize performance
print('MAE: %.3f (%.3f)' % (mean(n_scores), std(n_scores)))

MAE: 0.177 (0.004)
```

Fig. 6. SVR predictive model evaluation

128   M. Sari et al.

```
# evaluate a model using repeated k-fold cross-validation
def evaluate_model(X, Y):
        results = list()
        n_inputs, n_outputs = X.shape[1], Y.shape[1]
        # define evaluation procedure
        cv = RepeatedKFold(n_splits=10, n_repeats=3, random_state=1)
        # enumerate folds
        for train_ix, test_ix in cv.split(X):
                # prepare data
                X_train, X_test = X[train_ix], X[test_ix]
                Y_train, Y_test = Y[train_ix], Y[test_ix]
                # define model
                model = get_model(n_inputs, n_outputs)
                # fit model
                model.fit(X_train, Y_train, verbose=0, epochs=100)
                # evaluate model on test set
                mae = model.evaluate(X_test, Y_test, verbose=0)
                # store result
                print('>%.3f' % mae)
                results.append(mae)
        return results
# evaluate model
results = evaluate_model(X, Y)
# summarize performance
print('MAE: %.3f (%.3f)' % (mean(results), std(results)))
```

Fig. 7. MLP predictive model evaluation

The SVR model first developed using raw data in order to determine the effect of preprocessing on model development has an MAE score of 16.818 with a standard deviation of 4.230. Besides, the model developed with preprocessed data has promising prediction results in determining the output variables. The prediction evaluation from the chosen 400th-row sample has the MAE score of 5.66, implying the prediction's distance from the expected value. The progression in the accuracies through decreased MAE of the models is shown in Fig. 8.

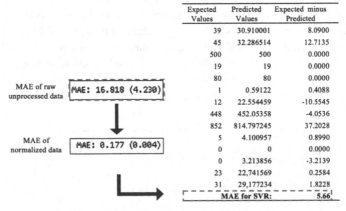

Fig. 8. MAE for SVR prediction

On the other hand, the MLP model first developed using raw data has an MAE score of 16.574 with a standard deviation of 0.932. Meanwhile, the MAE score from the model developed with preprocessed data is 3.02, showing significant improvement in the model accuracy. Figure 9 shows the accuracy of the developed MLP model.

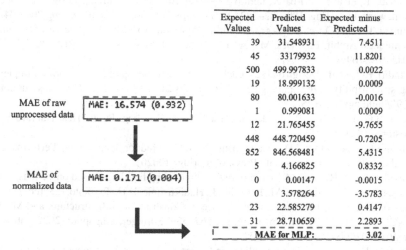

Expected Values	Predicted Values	Expected minus Predicted
39	31.548931	7.4511
45	33179932	11.8201
500	499.997833	0.0022
19	18.999132	0.0009
80	80.001633	-0.0016
1	0.999081	0.0009
12	21.765455	-9.7655
448	448.720459	-0.7205
852	846.568481	5.4315
5	4.166825	0.8332
0	0.00147	-0.0015
0	3.578264	-3.5783
23	22.585279	0.4147
31	28.710659	2.2893
MAE for MLP:		3.02

MAE of raw unprocessed data   MAE: 16.574 (0.932)

MAE of normalized data   MAE: 0.171 (0.004)

Fig. 9. MAE for MLP prediction

The accuracy evaluation of the predictive models developed with SVR and MLP algorithms indicates that the MLP model has a lower MAE score of 3.02 than the SVR model. This outcome aligns with the study [41], where the built MLP neural networks estimating the building's IEQ condition obtained a significant error and generated a high accuracy.

5 Conclusion

This research aimed to identify the relevant variables of healthy buildings considering the occupant wellbeing and the energy efficiency to be used in the development of a machine learning model that quantitatively predicts the values for these target variables. Based on an extensive literature study, the identified variables to include when designing a healthy indoor environment are lighting, indoor air quality, thermal comfort, acoustic comfort, and energy use. The variables were then used as the input and output features to build the machine learning models using SVR and MLP algorithms; the MAE scores are 5.66 and 3.02, respectively. The result of this study signifies that a data-driven approach can contribute to assisting the decision-making and estimation planning process of healthy buildings.

Acknowledgements. The authors would like to thank the Ministry of Education, Culture, Research, and Technology, Republic of Indonesia, for the support given to this research.

References

1. Adinyira, E., et al.: Application of machine learning in predicting construction project profit in Ghana using support vector regression algorithm (SVRA). Eng. Constr. Archit. Manag. **28**, 5 (2021). https://doi.org/10.1108/ECAM-08-2020-0618
2. Ahmad, T., et al.: BIM-based iterative tool for sustainable building design: a conceptual framework. Proc. Eng. **180**, 782–792 (2017). https://doi.org/10.1016/j.proeng.2017.04.239
3. Ahmad, T., et al.: Developing a green-building design approach by selective use of systems and techniques. Archit. Eng. Des. Manag. **12**, 29–50 (2015). https://doi.org/10.1080/17452007. 2015.1095709
4. Akadiri, P.O., et al.: Design of a sustainable building: a conceptual framework for implementing sustainability in the building sector. Buildings **2**(2), 126–152 (2012). https://doi.org/10. 3390/buildings2020126
5. Allen, J.G., et al.: The 9 Foundations of a Healthy Building. Public Heal Harvard School, Boston (2017)
6. Allen, J.G., Macomber, J.D.: Healthy Buildings: How Indoor Spaces Drive Performance and Productivity. Harvard University Press, Cambridge (2020)
7. Amatkasmin, L.R., et al.: A literature review on healthy buildings based on various perspectives. In: Lie, H.A., Sutrisna, M., Prasetijo, J., Hadikusumo, B.H., Putranto, L.S. (eds) Proceedings of the Second International Conference of Construction, Infrastructure, and Materials. LNCE, vol. 216. Springer, Singapore, pp. 567–583. Springer, Singapore (2022). https://doi. org/10.1007/978-981-16-7949-0_51
8. Anguita, D., et al.: K-fold cross validation for error rate estimate in support vector machines. In: International Conference on Data Mining, June 2014 (2009)
9. ASHRAE: ASHRAE Guideline 10–2011: Interactions Affecting the Achievement of Acceptable Indoor Environments (2011)
10. Awad, M., Khanna, R.: Efficient Learning Machines: Theories, concepts, and Applications for Engineers and System Designers. Apress Media LLC (2015). https://doi.org/10.1007/978-1-4302-5990-9
11. Ayoub, M.: A review on machine learning algorithms to predict daylighting inside buildings. Sol. Energy. **202**, 249–275 (2020). https://doi.org/10.1016/j.solener.2020.03.104
12. Azar, E., et al.: Integrating and optimizing metrics of sustainable building performance using human-focused agent-based modeling. Appl. Energy. **183**, 926–937 (2016). https://doi.org/ 10.1016/j.apenergy.2016.09.022
13. Berawi, M.A.: Managing artificial intelligence technology for added value. Int. J. Technol. **11**(1), 1–4 (2020). https://doi.org/10.14716/ijtech.v11i1.3889
14. Bluyssen, P.M.: A different view on indoor environment: focus on people and situations rather than single-dose response relationships. In: 10th International Conference on Healthy Buildings 2012, pp. 163–168 (2012)
15. Bluyssen, P.M.: The Healthy Indoor Environment: How to Assess Occupants' Wellbeing in Buildings. Routledge, Milton Park (2013).https://doi.org/10.4324/9781315887296
16. Bluyssen, P.M.: What do we need to be able to (re)design healthy and comfortable indoor environments? (2014). https://doi.org/10.1080/17508975.2013.866068
17. BREEAM: Technical Standards | BREEAM - Sustainability Assessment Method. https:// www.breeam.com/discover/technical-standards/. Accessed 14 Feb 2022
18. Britsh Standards Institute: BS EN 12464–1:202, Light and lighting. Lighting of work places. Indoor work places (2021). https://www.en-standard.eu/bs-en-12464-1-2021-light-and-lig hting-lighting-of-work-places-indoor-work-places/
19. Brownlee, J.: How to Develop Multi-Output Regression Models with Python. https://machin elearningmastery.com/multi-output-regression-models-with-python/. Accessed 9 May 2022

20. Carpenter, G.A., Grossberg, S.: A massively parallel architecture for a self-organizing neural pattern recognition machine. Comput. Vision. Graph. Image. Process. **37**, 54–115 (1987). https://doi.org/10.1016/S0734-189X(87)80014-2
21. Dalsania, N., et al.: An application of machine learning for plasma current quench studies via synthetic data generation. Fusion. Eng. Des. **171**, 112578 (2021). https://doi.org/10.1016/j.fusengdes.2021.112578
22. El-Bendary, N., et al.: Cultivation-time recommender system based on climatic conditions for newly reclaimed lands in Egypt. Proc. Comput. Sci. **96**, 110–119 (2016). https://doi.org/10.1016/j.procs.2016.08.109
23. Ferrando, C.: Towards a Machine Learning Framework in Spatial Analysis (2018)
24. Geyer, P., Singaravel, S.: Component-based machine learning for performance prediction in building design. Appl. Energy. **228**, 1439–1453 (2018). https://doi.org/10.1016/j.apenergy.2018.07.011
25. Hale, L.A.: Business model innovation for smart, healthy buildings. In: IOP Conference Series: Earth and Environmental Science (2020). https://doi.org/10.1088/1755-1315/588/3/032067
26. Heyburn, R., et al.: Machine learning using synthetic and real data: similarity of evaluation metrics for different healthcare datasets and for different algorithms (2018). https://doi.org/10.1142/9789813273238_0160
27. Hong, T., et al.: State-of-the-art on research and applications of machine learning in the building life cycle. Energy Build. **212**, 109831 (2020). https://doi.org/10.1016/j.enbuild.2020.109831
28. Huang, W., et al.: carbon footprint and carbon emission reduction of urban buildings: a case in Xiamen City. China. Proc. Eng. **198**, 1007–1017 (2017). https://doi.org/10.1016/j.proeng.2017.07.146
29. Jordan, M.I., Mitchell, T.M.: Machine learning: trends, perspectives, and prospects. Science **349**(6245), 255–260 (2015). https://doi.org/10.1126/science.aaa8415
30. Karan, E., Asadi, S.: Intelligent designer: a computational approach to automating design of windows in buildings. Autom. Constr. **102**, 160–169 (2019). https://doi.org/10.1016/j.autcon.2019.02.019
31. Kubat, M.: An Introduction to Machine Learning. Springer International Publishing, Cham (2017). https://doi.org/10.1007/978-3-319-63913-0
32. Lagesse, B., et al.: Performing indoor PM2.5 prediction with low-cost data and machine learning. Facilities (2022). https://doi.org/10.1108/F-05-2021-0046. (ahead-of-print)
33. Lee, P., et al.: Probabilistic risk assessment of the energy saving shortfall in energy performance contracting projects-a case study. Energy Build. **66**, 353–363 (2013). https://doi.org/10.1016/j.enbuild.2013.07.018
34. Li, D.H.W., et al.: Zero energy buildings and sustainable development implications - a review. Energy **54**, 1–10 (2013). https://doi.org/10.1016/j.energy.2013.01.070
35. Lin, Y., et al.: A review on research and development of healthy building in China. Buildings **12**, 3 (2022). https://doi.org/10.3390/buildings12030376
36. Liu, Z., et al.: Building information management (BIM) and blockchain (BC) for sustainable building design information management framework. Electron. **8**(7), 724 (2019). https://doi.org/10.3390/electronics8070724
37. Loftness, V., et al.: Elements that contribute to healthy building design. Environ. Health Perspect. **115**, 6 (2007). https://doi.org/10.1289/ehp.8988
38. Luckey, D., Fritz, H., Legatiuk, D., Dragos, K., Smarsly, K.: Artificial intelligence techniques for smart city applications. In: Toledo Santos, E., Scheer, S. (eds.) Proceedings of the 18th International Conference on Computing in Civil and Building Engineering. LNCE, vol. 98, pp. 3–15. Springer, Cham (2021). https://doi.org/10.1007/978-3-030-51295-8_1

39. MacNaughton, P., et al.: The impact of working in a green certified building on cognitive function and health. Build. Environ. **114**, 178–186 (2017). https://doi.org/10.1016/j.buildenv. 2016.11.041

40. Mannan, M., Al-Ghamdi, S.G.: Indoor air quality in buildings: a comprehensive review on the factors influencing air pollution in residential and commercial structure. Int. J. Environ. Res. Public. Health. **114**, 178–186 (2021). https://doi.org/10.3390/ijerph18063276

41. Martínez-Comesaña, M. et al.: Use of optimised MLP neural networks for spatiotemporal estimation of indoor environmental conditions of existing buildings. Build. Environ. **205**, 108243 (2021). https://doi.org/10.1016/j.buildenv.2021.108243

42. McArthur, J.J., Powell, C.: Health and wellness in commercial buildings: systematic review of sustainable building rating systems and alignment with contemporary research. Build. Environ. **171**, 106635 (2020). https://doi.org/10.1016/j.buildenv.2019.106635

43. Murphy, K.P.: Machine Learning - A Probabilistic Perspective. MIT Press, Cambridge (2012)

44. Olesen, B.W.: Revision of EN 15251: indoor environmental criteria. REHVA Eur. HVAC J. **49**(4), 6–14 (2012)

45. Palacios, J. et al.: Moving to productivity: the benefits of healthy buildings. PLoS One. **15**(8), e0236029 (2020). https://doi.org/10.1371/journal.pone.0236029

46. Pardo-Bosch, F., et al.: Holistic model to analyze and prioritize urban sustainable buildings for public services. Sustain. Cities Soc. **44**, 227–236 (2019). https://doi.org/10.1016/j.scs.2018. 09.028

47. Pham, D.T., Afify, A.A.: Machine-learning techniques and their applications in manufacturing. Proc. Inst. Mech. Eng. Part B J. Eng. Manuf. **219**(5), 395-412 (2005). https://doi.org/10. 1243/095440505X32274

48. Rankin, D., et al.: Reliability of supervised machine learning using synthetic data in health care: Model to preserve privacy for data sharing. JMIR Med. Informatics. **8**, 7 (2020). https:// doi.org/10.2196/18910

49. Shalev-Shwartz, S., Ben-David, S.: Understanding Machine Learning: From Theory to Algorithms (2013).https://doi.org/10.1017/CBO9781107298019

50. Solaimani, S., Sedighi, M.: Toward a holistic view on lean sustainable construction: a literature review. J. Clean. Prod. **248**, 119213 (2020). https://doi.org/10.1016/j.jclepro.2019.119213

51. Statstutor: Spearman's correlation. http://www.statstutor.ac.uk/resources/uploaded/spearm ans.pdf. Accessed 08 May 2022

52. Sun, H., et al.: Machine learning applications for building structural design and performance assessment: state-of-the-art review. J. Build. Eng. **33**, 101816 (2021). https://doi.org/10.1016/ j.jobe.2020.101816

53. Sutton, R.S., Barto, A.G.: Reinforcement Learning: An Introduction. MIT Press, Cambridge (2018)

54. Tao, Y.X., et al.: Modeling and data infrastructure for human-centric design and operation of sustainable, healthy buildings through a case study. Build. Environ. **170**, 106518 (2020). https://doi.org/10.1016/j.buildenv.2019.106518

55. Tsanas, A., Xifara, A.: Accurate quantitative estimation of energy performance of residential buildings using statistical machine learning tools. Energy Build. **49**, 560–567 (2012). https:// doi.org/10.1016/j.enbuild.2012.03.003

56. Tsanas, A., Xifara, A.: UCI Machine Learning Repository: Energy Efficiency Data Set. https:// archive.ics.uci.edu/ml/datasets/energy+efficiency. Accessed 22 Mar 2022

57. Zabihi, H., et al.: Sustainability in building and construction : revising definitions and concepts. Int. J. Emerg. Sci. **2**(December), 570–578 (2012)

58. RESET® Standard. https://www.reset.build/. Accessed 08 May 2022

Innovative Project Model Development for the Use of Digital Wearable Devices to Improve the Quality of Life

Marina Bolsunovskaya⑩, Nina Osipenko⑩, Svetlana Shirokova(✉)⑩, and Aleksei Gintciak⑩

Peter the Great St. Petersburg Polytechnic University, Saint-Petersburg, Russia
swchirokov@mail.ru

Abstract. In the modern world, the digital space is becoming more complex and detailed. Many digital devices are already becoming extremely important and necessary in everyday life. Recently, "wearable" gadgets have become increasingly popular in the market of IT devices. This trend is explained by their ease of use and fairly accurate measurements. The functional characteristics of these devices greatly simplify the control of the main indicators of human activity and health, and also allows the analysis of this data array in the treatment of chronic diseases. However, "smart" devices are not yet so perfect in terms of secure transmission of complete and encrypted data.

In this article, the market of digital "wearable" devices is considered, a comparative characteristic of the most popular manufacturers is carried out, a design model is built that clearly illustrates the entire process of data transmission from a "smart" device to a mobile application synchronized with it. The paper also offers solutions to improve the transmission process and data protection.

Keywords: Digitalization · Wearable devices · Bluetooth · BLE · Market of wearable electronics

1 Introduction

In the era of ubiquitous digitalization, consumers are trying in every possible way to facilitate the performance of their own routine actions. In this matter, various electronic devices come to the rescue. It should be said that digital devices are already quite actively being introduced into our daily lives not only as "assistants" on household issues, but also as a means of controlling general physical condition and health.

Wearable devices are a kind of miniature computers: bracelets, glasses, watches and even clothing items - with wireless local or remote connection to other computers.

According to statistics, the volume of the market of wearable electronics in Russia in 2020 increased by 17% in pieces (according to the calculations of analysts of M.Video-Eldorado) [1]. This trend has been maintained for several years and only increases the growth rate (Table 1). This economic aspect is explained by the fact that wearable devices are increasingly attracting consumers with their functionality and ease of use, and also serve as some alternative to visiting medical institutions.

© Springer Nature Switzerland AG 2022
D. Rodionov et al. (Eds.): SPBPU IDE 2021, CCIS 1619, pp. 133–142, 2022.
https://doi.org/10.1007/978-3-031-14985-6_9

Table 1. Sales of wearable devices [2]

Company	Shipments, million things		Market share, %		
	3Q 2021 г.	3Q 2020 г.	3Q 2021 г.	3Q 2020 г.	Year-over-year growth
Apple	39.8	41.3	28.8%	32.8%	−3.6%
Samsung	12.7	11.2	9.2%	8.9%	13.8%
Xiaomi	12.7	16.7	9.2%	13.2%	−23.8%
Huawei	10.9	10.5	7.9%	8.4%	3.7%
Imagine marketing	10.0	3.3	7.2%	2.6%	206.4%
Others	52.2	42.9	37.7%	34.1%	21.6%
TOTAL	138.4	125.9	100.0%	100.0%	9.9%

From the above data, there is an increase in sales of devices from manufacturers such as Apple, Xiaomi. Such devices are equipped with sensors. Sensors monitor various characteristics of the external environment or parameters of human activity. Almost all wearable devices integrate with a smartphone. But in the future, wearable devices will be able to use their own processors and connectivity and will become independent. This can happen when the size of the device components will decrease significantly, the battery life of wearable devices will increase, the power of their processors, and other technical limitations will be solved.

Pairing of a mobile phone and wearable devices is carried out using Bluetooth Low Energy technology. It is important that there is a big difference between classic Bluetooth and low-power Bluetooth in terms of technical specifications. This indicates that they are incompatible with each other. The comparative characteristics of the two technologies are presented in Table 2.

Table 2. Comparative characteristics of technologies

Bluetooth classic	BLE
Used for streaming applications such as audio streaming and file transfer	It is used in sensors, wearable devices and application management (related to the Internet of Things)
It is not optimized for low power consumption, but supports a high transfer rate (maximum 3 MBit/s, while BLE 5 has a maximum of 2 MBit/s)	It is intended for use in low-power devices with some intervals between data transmission
Uses 79 radio channels	Uses 40 radio channels
Detection occurs on 32 channels	Detection occurs on 3 channels, which leads to faster detection and connection setup compared to Bluetooth Classic

To transfer data from a device that supports only a BLE connection, you need another device that supports both BLE (will act as a gateway) and IP connections. It will receive the data and send it to the Internet.

The paper analyzes the market of wearable devices and analyzes the mechanisms of data transmission and processing (from wearable devices). To do this, it is necessary to analyze the prospects for using wearable devices, to investigate the structure of storing and transmitting their data (using the mobile application database). Further, based on a comparative analysis using the project model, conclusions about the prospects for the development of the market of these devices are formed.

2 Material and Methods

The authors analyzed scientific sources and statistical data on various classes of digital wearable devices and their application options. Based on the analysis, we see that the market for wearable devices is quite extensive and diverse. It covers not only fitness trackers and smart watches, but also more sophisticated wearable devices designed to diagnose chronic diseases and pathologies. Currently, there is a trend towards changing medical techniques. The treatment of patients with acute diseases is replaced by the treatment of "chronic" patients [3]. Experts agree that wearable devices will allow better monitoring of patients' condition over a certain period of time. So, wearable devices allow you to monitor pulse, pressure, breathing and other health indicators, as well as notify the patient about the need to take medications or make a visit to the doctor.

During the pandemic and the spread of the new coronavirus infection COVID-19, pulse oximeters are becoming particularly popular. Their functional characteristics make it possible to measure saturation (oxygen saturation of the blood), as well as blood pressure and pulse rate. Modern wearable devices reliably register the pulse wave shape. The accuracy of blood pressure measurement is at least 98%. They work on the principle of an electrocardiograph [4]. The electrodes are wetted with water or coated with a special gel for better skin contact, and the data is transmitted to the receiver. The data received from the device can be used both for remote consultation with a doctor and self-diagnosis.

The range of applications of wearable devices is quite wide and extensive. Many of them are used not only for medical purposes (for health monitoring), but also help in maintaining physical health and daily activity. Smart watches and fitness trackers are currently gaining the greatest popularity. The bracelet can accurately measure: heart rate, number of steps, calories consumed, stress level, sleep quality, travel speed and distance length, amount of direct sunlight, changes in oxygen in the air [5]. It should be noted that fitness trackers and smart watches are synchronized with a mobile application. The processed data is immediately sent to the application, which allows you to save information in a single system and keep sleep and nutrition diaries. Many programs associated with wearable devices are able to analyze the information received, build control schedules and make recommendations for maintaining health.

Many experts note that digital wearable devices can also be used in professional sports. Active development and design of "smart" devices that can detect and analyze the dynamics of movements are already underway. It is important that the devices can analyze human interaction with the environment, sports equipment, medical devices.

More importantly, it is possible to evaluate the effectiveness of this interaction. For example, the possibility of fixing, "capturing" movements with the help of "smart" clothes is being tested. In many sports, such IT solutions find their response and are applied. In addition to research and development in sports, there are already ready-made digital "wearable" solutions. This is, for example, a "Smart paddle" for swimming [6], which evaluates the nature of the athlete's interaction with the aquatic environment: registers the strength of the swimmer when rowing, the momentum of this force and other parameters. The device "Smart ski Concept" is used in alpine skiing. The skis are equipped with sensors that allow you to analyze the distribution of body weight between the legs, the load on different segments of the skis.

The most popular system for sports wearable devices is "Catapult". With its help, it is possible to analyze such indicators as distance, average speed and meters per minute, the amount of mechanical and linear running work in minutes and percentages of the total time, pulse cost, maximum and average pulse, time distribution by pulse zones [7].

Thus, the market of wearable devices is not limited only to the medical field. In the modern world, this digital orientation is actively developing in other spheres of life of consumers. From the analysis of scientific papers, we see that the market for wearable devices is quite extensive and diverse. It covers not only fitness trackers and smart watches, but also more complex wearable devices designed to diagnose chronic diseases, pathologies and monitor general health.

2.1 Analysis of Types of Wearable Devices

In general, wearable devices can be classified according to their functional applicability in the field of medicine – for pulse measurement, electrocardiogram recording, asthma attack control, sugar control. The most popular devices from the listed categories are considered below and their functionality is analyzed.

1. "Smart" wristwatch. The most famous device of this class is the Apple Watch bracelet. The gadget can measure the pulse, count the number of steps taken during the day and even record an electrocardiogram. All these functionalities are implemented using several sensors located on the back of the watch. Many smartwatch models support third-party applications and are controlled by popular mobile operating systems, but recent platform updates already allow some watch models to receive phone calls, connect to Wi-Fi and respond to SMS and email [8].
2. ADAMM is a device for controlling asthma attacks. The device is attached to the torso in the chest area and reads the necessary set of characteristics: pulse, temperature, respiratory rate and the presence of wheezing when breathing. The device is designed to prevent an attack so that you can prepare for it. The application, synchronized with the gadget, keeps a log of the listed indicators and seizures, in addition, you can configure notifications about taking medications.
3. Blood glucose meter. "iHealth Smart" connects as a peripheral device via Bluetooth to a smartphone and analyzes blood samples in a few seconds. The strip is inserted inside the device, where optical sensors that record the reaction to blood are included in the operation. The device has a companion app that stores information about all changes.

4. Devices for monitoring the general condition. This category includes a set of general-purpose devices: a thermometer, a stethoscope, an otoscope. The most popular brand for the release of these devices is "TytoCare". The device connects via Bluetooth to a mobile phone and sends information to cloud storage, and can also arrange a video call with a doctor if the indicators deviate from the norm. To do this, the gadget and its application must be associated with a specific clinic. Thus, data collected from devices can be stored in an application or cloud storage.

2.2 Advantages and Disadvantages of Wearable Devices

The use of "smart" wearable devices has both advantages and disadvantages. In particular, an increase in the level of patient involvement in taking care of their own health, the possibility of using this device as an online consultant can be considered a plus. Statistical studies have shown the effectiveness of wearing many "smart" gadgets even in the treatment of diseases [9].

At the same time, when evaluating the effectiveness of telemedicine technologies, it should be borne in mind that the main disadvantage of wearable devices remains the mechanism of data protection and transmission. So, for the most part, data is transmitted and stored without the use of encryption, PIN codes or user authentication mechanisms [10, 11].

Unfortunately, manufacturers and users underestimate the importance of protecting personal data in smart devices. The low degree of protection of the collected data may have a bad effect on their owner. After all, many attackers can use them for their own selfish purposes. For example, remotely hack a pacemaker, or change the recommendations of the diagnostic system. Therefore, wearable devices must be reliably protected from external attacks.

3 Results

Analysis of the synchronization mechanism of a wearable device and a mobile application. In order to understand the structure of storage and transmission of data received from wearable devices, it is necessary to consider the basic mechanism of operation of the wearable devices. The algorithm of intelligent monitoring of a "smart" gadget was considered on the example of a fitness tracker.

Any "smart" bracelet is equipped with an accelerometer - a spatial positioning sensor, as well as a heart rate sensor, magnetometer, gyroscope, pedometer. The background mode is set when the patient's condition corresponds to the normal state. In this mode, no more than two indicators that are most significant for diagnosis are evaluated, and the state of the norm is monitored [11]. The principle of heartbeat monitoring is determined using photoplethysmography technology.

The data of the wearable device is transmitted to the smartphone via Bluetooth. But since fitness bracelets do not have a full-fledged operating system in the usual sense, they are synchronized with mobile devices that are presented with the most common operating systems based on iOS or Android [12]. The tracker cannot function without a smartphone, so it is important that the operating system of the bracelet is compatible with the operating system of the smartphone. The mechanism of functioning and synchronization of a wearable device and a mobile phone application is shown in Fig. 1.

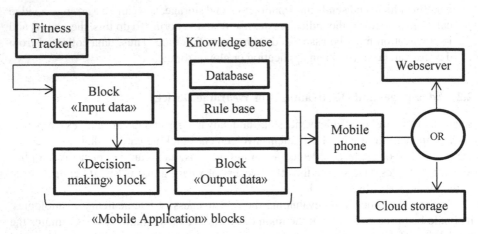

Fig. 1. The mechanism of synchronization of a wearable device (tracker) and an application in general.

Analysis of the data storage and transmission process.

It is known that wearable devices and sensors are part of the ecosystem of the Internet of Things. IoT makes it possible for medicine to reach a new level of diagnosis of diseases – "smart" devices track indicators, compare them with the norm and report deviations [13].

All smart devices allow you to remotely receive and analyze information.

In older simple devices, such as step counters and heart rate monitors, data is stored on the wearable device itself, so to ensure data security, it is enough to know where the fitness tracker is located and not lose it. However, modern fitness trackers and smartwatches are usually connected to external applications to track, publish and analyze activity. All fitness bracelets are paired with smartphones using a regular Bluetooth connection.

According to the conducted research, it was revealed that the Bluetooth connection can be manually deactivated on Garmin Vivosmart and LG Lifeband Touch devices. After pairing, trackers from Sony, Polar and Withings become invisible to Bluetooth devices. To connect, authentication using PIN or any other methods is not required - the bracelet simply connects and voluntarily transfers all its data. The data is sent to the smartphone in an unsecured and encrypted form. The current fitness data is automatically transferred to any paired device that has the appropriate application [14].

Thus, there is a problem of secure transmission and processing of large amounts of information collected from wearable devices. It should be noted that the final "receiver" of data received from wearable devices can serve as a server or cloud storage.

Devices are data sources with low computing power that continuously transmit a lot of information in various formats to the gateway. The sensor of the end device generates an analog signal, which is converted into a digital (discrete) value using an ADC - analog-to-digital converter. This value is marked with a timestamp and classified (tagged) by the local processor of the end device. The gateway, in turn, sends data to the cloud cluster.

On a cloud server, data from various peripheral devices are integrated (summarized by tags), systematized and analyzed using Machine Learning and other artificial intelligence methods. The results of data mining are visualized in the form of graphs, diagrams in the dashboards of the user interface (see Fig. 2).

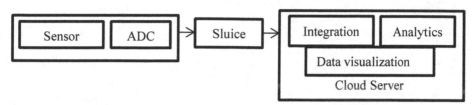

Fig. 2. Transferring information from the end device to the cloud

In order to analyze consumer behavior and integration of cloud storage with a wearable device, we will build a project model for data transmission and processing (see Fig. 3).

This design model reflects the user's path, as well as the transmission and storage of data received from wearable devices. Initially, the user is considered in the category of "potential", after that, under the influence of advertising and other factors, he passes into the category of "buyer". It is necessary to focus on two main segments of the target audience – people who lead a healthy lifestyle and those who, on the contrary, have health problems [15]. After purchasing a wearable device, the user downloads an additional application for the phone.

Only with its help, a wearable device (in this case, a fitness tracker) will work correctly. Next, the data is synchronized and transmitted using a wireless network (Bluetooth). The synchronization process allows you to connect a fitness bracelet with a mobile phone. Thanks to this, the user can view activity data through the installed application. After authorization in the application, the process of pairing with the bracelet does not start automatically, for this you need to find in the application the option to start pairing (search for a device to pair). Then the data is displayed in the mobile application. In the considered case, the application acts as a "gateway" in the data transfer stage. With the help of a request, the received data array is sent to the cloud storage [16]. The user should be given free access to the resources allocated to him (such as networks, virtual disks, memory, processor cores, etc.) and these resources should be provided automatically - that is, without interference from the service provider.

Further, an analysis of the consequences of exposure to viral software was carried out and ways to reduce and block them were proposed. Situations with the impact of hacker attacks on the system are considered. It is concluded that the transmission of network data between the cloud and the phone application occurs in encrypted form with TLS1.2. It was revealed that there is no quick check of the cache code of a suspicious file, as well as checking IP packets using antivirus protocols. To improve the encrypted

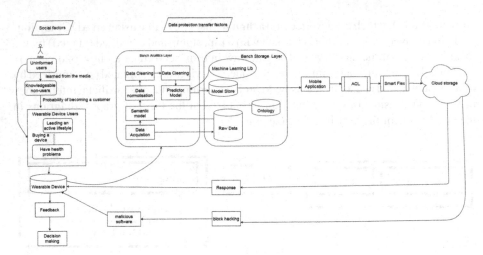

Fig. 3. Project model

input, additional use of access control lists ACL (Access Control List) and Smart Flex protection is possible.

Thus, a project model was built, as well as tools for its improvement were proposed and integrated.

4   Discussion

In the modern world, wearable devices are quite actively integrated into everyday life. "Smart" gadgets make it possible to significantly simplify and speed up the performance of routine operations by a person. Wearable devices are able to measure heart rate, blood oxygen saturation, prevent and alleviate the course of chronic and acute diseases. It should be noted that health monitoring devices are available in almost all price categories and in different versions - from simple fitness bracelets to blood sugar analyzers. According to statistics, the demand for these goods is steadily growing. If we analyze the overall situation on the market of wearable devices, we can see an increase in the number of devices sold by 12.8%. At the same time, forecasts for the profit of the global market of wearable devices by 2027 exceeded $ 104 billion. Such indicators are associated with an increase in demand among consumers of wearable devices.

However, it is worth noting that not all researchers and experts share optimistic sentiments about wearable devices. Many of them believe that rather unprotected access to the personal information of the owner of a technological device and the risk of its loss does not justify all the useful properties of this device. Research in the field of transmission and storage of big data received from wearable devices is still ongoing. Perhaps, after some time, more accurate results of the advantages and disadvantages of using wearable devices will be obtained and more reliable data transmission and storage mechanisms will be proposed. The paper analyzed the device market and showed an increase in the share of "smart bracelets", considered the compatibility problems of a wearable device and a mobile phone application, identified ways to improve data integration options when synchronizing a device and an IT application. When transmitting data, solutions aimed at improving the reliability of the transmission mechanism in order to avoid their loss are important.

In the course of the work, agent and project models were developed, which allowed us to conclude about the trends in the development of the wearable devices market and their impact on the quality of life, as well as problems were identified in the transmission and preservation of data integrity from the wearable device to the mobile application and a mechanism was proposed aimed at improving the reliability of the transmitted information [17].

5 Conclusions

The main result of the study was the conclusion about the increased applicability of wearable devices. These digital devices, previously used in medicine, are now being used to improve the quality of life. These include smart watches, fitness bracelets, smart wireless headphones, head-mounted displays, and so on.

A significant dynamic of change is observed in the increase in the market share of smart wireless headphones. This is due to the fact that manufacturers deliberately removed the 3.5 mm jack, which is used for wired headphones, from the smartphone configuration. Thus, smartphone manufacturers managed to increase the demand for "smart" components for their own smartphones. The analysis of the situation showed that there is an increase in the number of devices sold by 12.8%. This is due to the increasing demand and use of wearable devices in everyday life. In the first quarter of 2020, there was also a high demand for fitness trackers, as these devices are among the most popular gifts [18].

The target audience of wearable gadgets is young people aged 18 to 34. Mintel's research only confirms the statistics. Owners of fitness trackers aged 16–34 years are 3 times more common than people over 35 years old [19].

According to the publication, 71% of buyers of "smart" watches are men and only 29% are women. However, the fair sex compensates for the difference with fitness bracelets: 54% of the owners are ladies. Americans and Chinese were recognized as the most active buyers of watches and bracelets. The market of the latter shows the most rapid growth [19].

The population actively cares about the state of their own health and physical development. But since 2020, a sudden pandemic has made adjustments to the usual way of life. Thus, COVID-19 has also affected the consumer frequency of using the health and fitness app.

References

1. Wearable electronics (Russian market)/Tadviser. https://www.tadviser.ru/index.php/Article. Accessed 22 Nov 2021
2. IDC Reports Strong Growth intheWorldwideWearables Market, Led by Holiday Shipments of Smartwatches, Wrist Bands, and Ear-Worn Devices. https://www.idc.com/promo/wearab levendor/vendor. Accessed 15 Nov 2022

3. Bogomolov, A.I., Nevezhin, V.P., Zhdanov G.A.: Artificial intelligence and expert systems in mobile medicine. https://cyberleninka.ru/article/n/iskusstvennyy-intellekt-i-ekspertnye-sis temy-v-mobilnoy-meditsine. Accessed 15 Jan 2022
4. Terentyeva, N.G., Terentyeva, E.V.: Innovative aspects of science and technology development. https://cyberleninka.ru/article/n/perspektivy-primeneniya-nosimoy-elektroniki-dlya-opredeleniya-fizicheskogo-sostoyaniya-sotrudnikov-na-osnove-fiziologicheskih/viewer. Accessed 15 Jan 2022
5. Gold, N.A., Chistyakova, S.V., Stepanova, I.P.: Digital economy for a healthy lifestyle. https://cyberleninka.ru/article/n/tsifrovaya-ekonomika-dlya-zdorovogo-obraza-zhizni. Accessed 15 Jan 2022
6. Bykov, D.Y., Vasyuk, V.E., Paramonova, N.A.: Intelligent sensors of sports movements: the state of the issue and prospects for use. https://cyberleninka.ru/article/n/intellektualnye-dat chiki-sportivnyh-dvizheniy-sostoyanie-voprosa-i-perspektivy-ispolzovaniya. Accessed 15 Jan 2022
7. Koryagina, Y.V., Kopanev, A.N., Nopin, S.V., Abutalimova, S.M.: Analysis of online testing systems for sports and fitness. https://cyberleninka.ru/article/n/analiz-onlayn-sistem-testirova niya-dlya-sporta-i-fitnesa. Accessed 15 Jan 2022
8. Huarng, K.-H., Yu, T.H., Lee, C.: Adoption model of healthcare wearable devices. https://www.sciencedirect.com/science/article/pii/S0040162521007204. Accessed 15 Nov 2022
9. Gartner Says Worldwide Wearable Device Sales to Grow 26 Percent in 2019. https://www.gartner.com/en/newsroom/press-release/2018-11-29-gartner-says-worldwide-wearable-dev ice-device-sales-to-grow. Accessed 15 Nov 2022
10. Thomason, J.: Big tech, big data and the new world of digital health. https://www.sciencedi rect.com/science/article/pii/S2414644721000890. Accessed 15 Nov 2022
11. Wu, J., Li, H., Cheng, S., Lin, Z.: The promising future of healthcare services: when big data analytics meets wearable technology. https://www.sciencedirect.com/science/article/pii/S03 78720616300775. Accessed 15 Nov 2022
12. What is the Internet of Things: how it works and usage examples. https://blog.calltouch.ru/chto-takoe-internet-veshhej-princzip-raboty-i-primery-ispolzovaniya/. Accessed 15 Dec 2021
13. WHO Global Recommendations on physical activity for Health. World Health Organization. https://www.who.int/dietphysicalactivity/factsheet_recommendations/ru/. Accessed 4 Dec 2021
14. Distance learning in extreme conditions/Interfax education. https://academia.interfax.ru/ru/analytics/research/4491/. Accessed 4 Dec 2021
15. Yeager, S.: The big book of 15-minute workouts for women. Potpourri, 400 p. Minsk (2013)
16. Yeager, S.: The big book of 15-minute workouts for men, 391 p. Potpourri, Minsk (2013)
17. Milko, M.M.: Research of physical activity of students in conditions of distance learning and self-isolation. In: Milko, M.M., Guremina, N.V. Modern high-tech technologies, vol. 5, pp. 195–200 (2020). http://top-technologies.ru/ru/article/view?id=38056. Accessed 12 Dec 2021
18. Uspenskiy, M.B., Smirnov, S.V., Loginova, A.V., Shirokova, S.V.: Modelling of complex project management system in the field of information technologies. In: Proceedings of 2019 3rd International Conference on Control in Technical Systems, CTS 2019, pp. 11–14, 8973245 (2019)
19. Orlova, V., Ilin, I., Shirokova, S.: Management of port industrial complex development: environmental and project dimensions. In: MATEC Web of Conferences, vol. 193, p. 05055 (2018)

Digitalization of Business Processes in the Automotive Industry

Tatiana Bogdanova(ID), Elena Rytova(✉)(ID), and Ekaterina Krasilnikova(ID)

Peter the Great St. Petersburg Polytechnic University,
Polytechnicheskaya, 29, St. Petersburg 195251, Russia
rytova_ev@spbstu.ru

Abstract. The main goal of this study is to develop a methodology for introducing digital technology aimed at improving of the business processes of a company in the automotive industry. As part of this study, an algorithm for choosing alternative technologies for implementing a particular business process is proposed, which includes a comparative assessment of alternatives for three blocks of indicators. To achieve the goal of the paper, a system analysis was used including comparative analysis and expert procedures. A comparative analysis of existing methods of digitalization of business processes is carried out. Based on the study of existing scientific approaches to the digital transformation of enterprises and the world experience of digitalization of business processes of manufacturing enterprises, a new methodology for digital transformation of an automobile industry enterprise were proposed. This new approach is taking into account the risks and also the need to return to the previous stage based on the results of the values of the benchmarks. The final assessment of technology implementation is carried out on the basis of the pattern in three blocks: assessment of technology risks, supplier assessment and assessment of the financial and economic efficiency of the project. Approbation was carried out through the digital transformation for the process of checking the quality of body cars for Toyota Company. The application of the methodology is possible at enterprises of any industry and is aimed at creating sustainable competitive advantages through the consistent digitalization of business processes.

Keywords: Digital transformation · Business processes · Digital technologies · Production process · Competitive advantages · Risks

1 Introduction

The growing availability of digital technologies, their active development and application there is a need to develop sound approaches to the digitalization of business processes of an enterprise in any industry to create and maintain long-term competitive advantages in a constantly changing external environment (changing consumer preferences, heightened competition in the industry, the adoption of various laws that directly affect the activities of companies, etc.). Many companies, due to the lack of systemic information about this process, are losing their competitive advantages, since they either introduce digital technologies with a great delay or with great costs. Due to the specifics of production

© Springer Nature Switzerland AG 2022
D. Rodionov et al. (Eds.): SPBPU IDE 2021, CCIS 1619, pp. 143–158, 2022.
https://doi.org/10.1007/978-3-031-14985-6_10

activities, company's managers do not know where to start: which processes should be changed priority, how to do it, who should participate in the transformation process, how the processes could be integrated into the organizational, industrial and economic environment of the enterprise.

Digital transformation means not just the transformation of company processes from manual to digital, but also a holistic, systemic transition (or transformation, improvement) of the company's activities into a digital environment, including integration with partners along the value chain into the digital ecosystem [1–3].

As for the automotive industry, since the 1990s, new technologies have been actively developed and introduced in this area. Today, production has become much more complicated, the number of electronic components has increased, costs of digital technologies in the final product reached 50% [4]. According to a study by A.T. Kearney [5], German mechanical engineering companies, while reducing the complexity of production, could save up to $ 30 billion annually, which would lead to a five percent increase in operating profit for these companies. Applying a sound approach to the implementation of digital transformation projects will create additional competitive advantages for the automotive industry participants, as it will allow maintaining a high level of product quality and speeding up the decision-making process. This is especially important in today's competitive environment in the automotive industry.

2 Literature Review

While working with global brands analysts at Altimer have identified six stages of digital transformation, which have become widespread [6]:

1. Business as usual. The company works with an established vision of customers, business processes, technologies, believing that this will remain relevant in the digital age.
2. Presence and activity. The company starts smooth small-scale experiments in digitalization, stimulating workers' digital literacy and creativity.
3. Formalized stage. The company' experiments becomes systemic, initiatives are more daring and promising. Management support is sought to provide resources for further changes.
4. Strategy. The company is ready for the transformation: strategic plan for digital transformation with an indication of those responsible, the amount of investment and the desired results is created.
5. Convergence. Separate digital transformation team is formed.
6. Innovative and adaptive. Digital transformation is becoming a way of doing business for the company as leaders recognize that change is happening all the time.

This technique has several problems. The first problem is that the stages are described too superficially. For many companies, the main difficulty is that they do not know where to start, what the first step should be. This method does not give an answer to this question. The second problem is that according to this technique, digital transformation should come from the bottom, but not from the top, which has a low probability of success [7]. In this case everything can end at the second stage - the stage of scattered, unsynchronized attempts to digitize a certain process pointwise, which will eventually end because of the lack of consistency and support from top. The third problem of this technique: it is not clear how the company should determine (and should it at all?) what changes need to be implemented and when, whether they need to be controlled and, if necessary, how and to whom.

According to Hewlett Packard Enterprise, there are three stages of digital transformation that are common to all companies [8]:

1. Create a plan. The plan should take into account all the needs of the company; determine the direction of development and technologies which will cause changes.
2. Training of employees. For a successful digital transformation of a company, all employees must be prepared in advance to work with new technologies and must be able to think creatively.
3. Rejection of outdated technologies. Maintaining and maintaining the functionality of old technologies is very costly and hinders the further development of the company.

This methodology, unlike the previous one, assumes a systematic approach to the digital transformation [9] of the company, but it is also too superficial. Moreover, the stage of determining the sphere from which it is necessary to start the digital transformation is not indicated, there is no control stage.

Eastern Peak, company which creates digital solutions for companies, identifies the following key steps in a successful digital enterprise transformation [10]:

1. Assessment the current state of digital technologies in the company.
2. Definition of the goals of digital transformation.
3. Describing of a digital transformation plan.
4. Selection of the necessary tools and technologies.
5. Establishment clear leadership.
6. Setting of a budget for transformation.
7. Training of employees.

This methodology quite broadly and consistently describes the process of digital transformation, in contrast to the previous ones. But it is also has a lot of drawbacks. So, according to this methodology, the digital transformation process is considered separately from the strategy of the company, while the digital strategy must necessarily be coordinated with the corporate strategy [11]. There is also no stage of analyzing the industry where the company operates, its position in it. So, not only the digital transformation process itself is considered separately from the rest processes of the company, but the company is considered separately from the industry, which is also not true. Also, the team responsible for the digital transformation of the company is formed only at the fifth of seven stages, which is too late. There is no control stage also.

Research firm Gatner also offers companies its plan for digital business transformation [12]:

1. Gathering information. It involves studying the experience of digitalization of other companies, analyzing of the industry and the position of the company in the industry, collecting of all relevant indicators of the organization and industry.
2. Transitional stage. At this stage, qualified personnel are sought for digital transformation of the business, the results are predicted, and the existing IT departments in the company are divided into two: the first is responsible for the technologies traditionally used in the company, the second - for new technologies.
3. Directly implementation. At this stage, digital technologies are being introduced into the company's activities, new policies and instructions for various processes are being developed.

There is also a search for new technologies for implementation. The Gatner methodology, unlike the others, paid attention to the analysis of the industry and the position of the company, but the subsequent stages are blurred - some aspects are highlighted in detail (personnel search), some are given in general terms (technology implementation).

N.D. Evans, the author of the book "Mastering Digital Business" [13], believes there is a lot of talk about digital transformation, but very little in practice. Everyone is trying to develop a strategy, but no one comes up with concrete actions. For this reason, Evans lists the following six steps of digital transformation, with the help of which, in his opinion, one can finally move from the theoretical development of a digital strategy to practical implementation.

1. Determination of the goal of transformation. It is critical that the strategy reinforces the desired business outcome. Typically, the desired transformation goals are associated with the following areas:

    increasing customer loyalty, their retention; reducing costs; increasing productivity; integrating supply chain partners;

    simplifying service management, solving problems before they arise, increasing transparency;

    optimization of infrastructure for increased flexibility;

    obtaining information in large volumes and at a higher speed for making more effective decisions and gaining a competitive advantage.
2. Studying of the factors influencing the development of technologies in the market. There is a need to achieve full awareness and use of market-based instruments to support technologies. A holistic view can help maximize business benefits.
3. Presentation of the future platform for digital business. The company must select the combination of technologies that maximizes the targeted business outcome. This platform (in other words, the model) can be used as a benchmark for digital business transformation in terms of key IT capabilities.
4. Lifecycle management of digital services. It is not enough just to have an innovative set of products and services; you also need to skillfully deploy, manage, personalize and continually evolve them. Ownership of the lifecycle of digital products and services will be a key competence for business development and creating sustainable competitive advantage in the coming years.
5. Creation of favorable conditions for digitalization. Having created a platform for digital business (point 3), a company must select the most appropriate technologies

("building blocks") based on specific business results. Instead of a single monolithic platform holding everything together, the future platform will consist of a highly virtualized and distributed ecosystem of services from the best providers. From a practical point of view, managers will be able to choose from all the options for grouped services, those that are most suitable for their goals.

6. Making a flexible transition to a new digital platform. Businesses need to move to digital platforms while maintaining their existing applications and infrastructure. Some elements may be decommissioned and upgraded, while some may coexist with the digital platform. Since the company will have such a hybrid environment, it will be important to maintain interoperability between the two "sections".

An important aspect of this methodology is that the initial stages of digitalization of the company are clearly identified - a clear definition of the goal, research of the technology market. For the first time, the importance of controlling the life cycle of digital services is mentioned. However, the method completely ignores the internal environment of the company, the process of its restructuring, adaptation. It is not clear who and how should be responsible for the transition to the digital level of doing business, whether there is a connection with the corporate strategy of the company [13].

Archer Point, the company based in US, dedicated to providing business innovation solutions to companies, believes that when enterprises are unable or unwilling to recognize the need to change their business model or the technologies they use, they suffer negative consequences [14]. Technology plays an important supporting role as a tool to achieve a higher goal. Due to the fact that all companies are different (industry, size, etc.), the path to digital transformation is also different for everyone. Archer Point has compiled its own digitalization methodology, based both on the study of theoretical material and practical experience. The methodology is a rough digital transformation framework that companies can rely on when creating their own plan, and consists of 7 steps:

1. Creation of an innovation-friendly culture. Digital transformation is an iterative process - there will be stops, returns to previous steps, and that's normal way. Before starting practical introduction of new technologies, it is necessary to create an appropriate culture within the organization that provides freedom of action: involving all employees, creating a dynamic environment for collaboration, encouraging feedback, etc.

2. Assessment of company's current condition. Before creating and implementing a digitalization plan, it is necessary to have a solid understanding of the current position both the company in the industry and internally. It is necessary to analyze the desires of the target consumers and the market: what current needs are not yet met and how can digital transformation help to achieve the company's goals?

3. Determination of the business processes that need to be transformed, creation of digitalization strategy, determination of the budget. After analyzing the situation, it is necessary to determine the most relevant business processes for revision. The budget should include not only technology, but also training, support, the cost of lost productivity during the plan is implemented.

4. Definition of technologies, which are going to be used. It should be remembered that technology is a tool that contributes to the goal achievement, not the goal itself. Technologies need to be assessed based on the processes that are planned to be optimized.
5. The right people attraction. People with the skills to help bring all ideas to life with an actionable plan are needed. This applies not only to employees within company, but also to external partners such as technology providers.
6. Creation of a plan for digital transformation. After defining the processes, technologies, people, position of the company, it is necessary to create a roadmap for the implementation of the digital transformation plan. It is recommended to break the roadmap into stages. The ability to test each idea on a smaller scale and ability to train employees are important for each stage.
7. Define goals by setting KPIs. Each stage of the plan should have clear goals, key performance indicators to be achieved. It is also necessary to introduce mechanisms to reduce risks throughout the entire process [15].

This technique has fulfilled its goal - a superficial description of the structure of the digitalization process. Important aspects are touched upon - the formation of a favorable internal environment; assessment of the market, technologies, business processes for digitalization; setting goals. However, a too superficial description makes this technique too scientific and unsuitable for most companies wishing to digitalize their business processes. It is not clear the decision-making criteria at each stage, also difficult to understand who should prepare for the digitalization process, how to implement technologies, what risks may be, how to determine the need for digital transformation of the business process, etc. [15].

All the methodologies discussed above describe digital transformation as a sequential process without the possibility of returning to the previous stage, do not imply the choice of a direction of activity in general (for example, the choice of zones for the initial implementation of transformation), do not describe a method for assessing digitalization options, organizing control. In fact, the digital transformation process cannot be a simple list of sequential actions, but can be an algorithm in which the progress through the stages directly depends on the result of the previous stage, and the steps involve multiple choices. Table 1 provides a comparative analysis of various methodologies of digital transformation of companies proposed by various authors above [6–15].

All the considered methodologies describe digital transformation as a sequential process without the possibility of returning to the previous stage. In all these cases there is no considering the process of digital transformation as an algorithm in which the progress through the stages directly depends on the result of the previous stage, and the steps involve multiple choices. These methodologies do not imply the choice of direction of activity (for example, the choice of zones for the initial implementation of digital transformation). Also there is no describing of a method for assessment of digitalization options [16], control and monitoring organization.

The main goal of this study is to develop a methodology for introducing digital technology aimed at improving of the business processes of a company in the automotive industry. As part of this study, an algorithm for choosing alternative technologies for implementing a particular business process is proposed, which includes a comparative

Table 1. Methodologies of digital transformation of the companies analysis.

Methodology	Advantages	Disadvantages
Altimer [10]	- Digital technologies smooth introduction -Appointment of those responsible for the transformation	- Superficial description of digitalization stages - No clear first step -Digitalization should come from the bottom - No clear criteria of digitalization and risk assessment
Hewlett Packard enterprise [11]	System approach to digitalization of the company	- Superficial description of digitalization stages - No stage of determining the sphere, - No control and monitoring stage - No clear criteria of digitalization and risk assessment
Eastern peak	- Consistent description of the digitalization process -Analysis of the current digital technologies state in the company	-Digitalization of each process is isolated from the digitalization of company as the whole -The process of digitalization of the company is isolated from the industry digitalization trends - No clear criteria of digitalization
Gatner [12]	- Industry analysis stage and company position added	- Vague and incomplete description of digitalization process - No clear criteria of digitalization and risk assessment
Evans	- Clear highlighting of the first stage of digitalization -Control of the technology life cycle	- Digitalization of each process is isolated from the digitalization of company as the whole - No clear criteria of digitalization and risk assessment

assessment of alternatives for three blocks of indicators: technology risks, technology supplier assessment, financial and economic efficiency of the project.

3 Materials and Methods

To achieve the goal of the paper, a system analysis was used including comparative analysis, morphological analysis and expert procedures.

Morphological analysis is a method of decision making, based on the selection of possible solutions for individual parts of the problem and the subsequent systematic obtaining of their combinations. It refers to heuristic methods. The method was developed by the Swiss astronomer Fritz Zwicky. He was able in a short time to obtain a significant number of original technical solutions in rocketry using this method.

An exact formulation of the problem for the system under consideration is required to carry out morphological analysis. As a result, an answer is given to a more general solution by searching for all possible options for particular solutions, regardless of the fact that in the original problem only one specific system is discussed.

The main stages of the method:

1. The goal of the study is clarified - the search for variants of functional schemes, or principles of operation, or structural schemes, or constructive varieties of the system being developed. It is possible to study on several grounds at the same time.
2. Nodal points (separate parts of the problem) are allocated, which characterize the developed system using formulated goal. These can be the particular functions of subsystems, the principles of their work, their shape, location, characteristics and properties. It is convenient to preliminarily (for example, from the analysis of a similar system) construct an appropriate block diagram, the elements of which form the nodes. The number of nodes is usually selected on the basis of the visibility and reality of the analysis of the subsequently obtained options (with manual processing from 4 to 7 nodes). It is convenient to solve the problem in a number of stages: first, for a limited number of the most important nodal points, and then for additional, secondary, or new nodes identified during the analysis.
3. Solutions are proposed for each nodal point: either based on personal experience, or taking them from reference books and databases. The options should cover the entire range of possible solutions for a given nodal point. But in order for the solution to be visible, it is recommended to first single out the enlarged or generalized groups of options, which, if necessary, are subsequently concretized. The options can be not only real, but also fantastic.
4. A complete enumeration of all solution options is carried out with checking the combinations for compliance with the problem conditions, for the incompatibility of individual options in proposed general group, for feasibility and other conditions. If necessary, for the selected solutions morphological analysis can be repeated specifying the nodes and options.

It is more convenient and clear to carry out morphological analysis using morphological tables (boxes). Formal combination of options gives the impression of automatism in the application of the method. However, its heuristic nature is very significant and depends on the following subjective factors:

- Intuitive selection of nodes and their features, composition of options. Lack of confidence that all nodes and options have been taken into account;
- A specific decision is a consequence of the analysis of the combinations being viewed, the emergence of productive associations and images.

4   Results

The new approach to digitalization of the company's business processes is shown in Fig. 1. It includes the following stages:

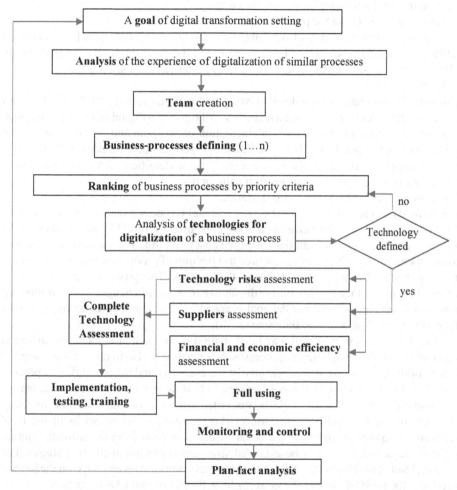

Fig. 1. The methodology of the company's business processes digitalization (Compiled by the authors)

1. The goal of digital transformation determination.

At the first stage it is necessary to determine the corporate strategic goal: cost reduction; market share increasing (by increasing the quality of a product or service, increasing customer loyalty, etc.); the existing market share maintaining; differentiation of activities, etc. Strategic analysis could be used to take into account industry trends (for example, using the A. T. Kearney methodology).

It is not so important what kind of digital technology the company wants to use, but important how much this technology use corresponds to the company's strategy: is this digital transformation carried out with a clear expectation of achieving the company's strategic goal or is it caused by the influence of trends, without much understanding of the meaning of the transformation for the company?

2. Market analysis (from the point of view of digital transformation).

An analysis of the efficiency of digitalization of other companies which are aimed at achieving of similar goal should be carried out at this stage: the level of digitalization, advantages and disadvantages, the availability of alternative technologies.

3. Team creation.

This stage is associated with a detailed work on the digitalization plan for the business processes. It is necessary to create a team that will develop a digital transformation plan, and will be responsible for direct implementation of this plan and further control. The team could be recruited from both existing employees of the enterprise and outsiders, possibly suppliers (if the suppliers have already been identified for some reason and if the company has a long-term partnership with them).

4. Business process defining for digitalization.

The formed team has to determine the most relevant business processes of the company for the transformation. Various indicators could be used for this [17]: the duration of the process cycle (time spent); material costs ; the cost of eliminating the marriage; training costs for employees; efficiency of resource use per unit of production (rate of equipment use, raw materials, etc.); added value of the process. The processes are assessed in terms of their adaptability, flexibility (the ability to adapt to changes in environmental conditions), efficiency (whether the goal is achieved at all), and repeatability (whether the process can always lead to the same result).

The full process of production and distribution of the final product is considered in the context of individual business processes. It is necessary also to take into account the impact of the process on the strategic goal of the company and the possibility of process digitalization. For example, business processes that do not affect the achievement of the company's strategic goal could be discarded from transformation at the first step (for example, if the goal is to increase market share, then the processes of the legal department, equipment maintenance department, labor protection department, internal logistics department, etc. can be excluded from consideration at the first stage). The existing level of digitalization of remaining business processes is analyzed on the second step from the point of view of the need for their further digital transformation.

5. Ranking of business processes by priority criteria.

A survey of specialists and engineers experience and expertise directly related to business processes, analysis of their ideas and proposals help us to assess the level of influence on the achievement of the set goal. Further, an assessment the social (for example, job cuts may lead to a certain involvement of public services) [18] and environmental consequences (disposal of old equipment, the need for large amounts of energy, etc.) is made of the digitalization of business process.

6. Analysis of the technologies for digitalization of a business process.

The existing technologies of digitalization for the priority business process are investigated. The possibility of using the equipment with the existing production volume or with its possible expansion is assessed. The prospects of the technology development, the time of its existence on the market are analyzed. If the market does not have suitable technologies for the first priority business process, the technologies for the second priority business process are analyzed, etc. The participation of the engineers involved in the team and related to the business process being transformed is the great importance at this stage.

7. Complete technology assessment.

But it's not the last assessment stage, when a suitable technology was found. It is necessary to carry out further assessment: an assessment of the risks of technology implementation, an assessment of the technology supplier and an assessment of the financial efficiency of the project. The complete assessment could be given based on the pattern (Fig. 2).

Different groups of risks have to be taken into account depending on the specific features of the business process: operational risks (perhaps the introduction of technology will require the involvement of highly qualified workers, will increase the production time of one product, lead to the occurrence of defects, etc.), security risks (for example, the impact on the safety of employees, on the security of information, if the technology assumes its output to cloud systems), risks of the external environment (if the technology is supplied from abroad, there may be risks of a change in the exchange rate, a ban on the import of technology, etc.) and others.

Assessment of the technology supplier. Potential suppliers are assessed by the proposed cost of technology, quality, technology development and delivery time, reliability (time of existence, financial position, quality of implemented projects, etc.). The supplier with the highest assessment score is taken into calculating the final technology grade.

Assessment of the financial and economic efficiency of the implementation of the technology includes the calculation of the financial and economic indicators of the project (NPV, IRR, DPP, PI, etc.).

All technologies acceptable for the digitalization of a specific business process are evaluated in a similar way. The result of the assessment is a summary table (Fig. 2) with the pattern for each technology. This pattern helps company's management to make further decisions.

If the final efficiency of the project is negative, and the use of a similar technology remains relevant, then it is necessary to return to the sixth stage. If the final efficiency of the project is positive, then it makes sense to consider the application of this technology in other business processes of the company. So the final stage of the business process digitalization is the choosing the next process for digitalization based on the successful experience.

As an example of the implementation of this algorithm, the Russian division of Toyota, Toyota Motor LLC, was chosen. Based on the analysis, we can consider the strategic goal of Toyota in Russia as an increase in market share in the D segment

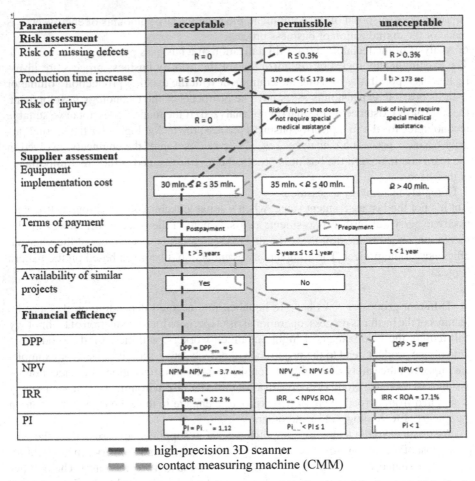

■ ■ high-precision 3D scanner
■ ■ contact measuring machine (CMM)

Fig. 2. Results of the final technology assessment for digitalization of the process of the body components quality control: morphological box (Compiled by the authors)

(Camry) and in the C segment of crossovers (Rav 4). Stable growth in demand allows Toyota to aim at increasing (not just maintaining) the company's market share. The growing competition forces to focus on improving its own cars. Toyota has focused on the high quality of its products and the improvement of production technologies throughout the entire period of its existence. The company has even developed its own production system, which pays great attention to quality and optimization of the production process [19].

The business processes of any organization could be divided into three main groups: managing, operational, and serving. But the attention was focused only on the operational business processes of Toyota in the framework of this study, since these processes directly generate profit of the company [20].

The main operational business processes of an automotive company are: procurement of materials and equipment; acceptance of materials and equipment; storage of materials in the warehouse; stamping; molding of plastic parts; welding; coloring; assembly; quality control. The production processes have already reached a sufficiently high level of digitalization and are not currently a priority (the level of automation of the welding shop has reached 67%). But the procurement processes (procurement of materials and equipment, acceptance of materials and equipment, storage of materials in a warehouse) and the quality control process, either slightly digitalized in the company, or not digitalized at all.

The following sequence of digitalization of business processes for a given automobile company was proposed as a result of ranking business processes by priority: the process of control of acceptance of body components, the process of quality control of the external paintwork of the body, automation of individual processes of the assembly shop. An analysis of the technologies existing on the market showed that improving the business process of checking the quality of body parts is possible through the introduction of a number of alternative technologies, the priority ones being: a high-precision 3D scanner and a contact measuring machine (CMM). The use of high-precision 3D scanners [21] requires their fixation either on robotic arms or on pedestals, which makes it possible to obtain the most accurate result than the use of hand-held scanners. At the same time, the installation of several scanners on a pedestal allows you to increase the scanning speed without losing accuracy. Moreover, this will allow not purchasing expensive robotic manipulators, while it will remain possible to change the configuration of the scanners by rearranging the pedestals.

Figure 2 shows the stage of the final assessment of the compared technologies according to the proposed methodology, which shows that the best option for the company will be the introduction of 3D scanning technology. This technology use does not carry significant risks, the supplier of this technology is assessed according to the parameters as "ideal", and the assessment of the financial efficiency of the technology introduction is positive.

5 Discussion

Various studies indicate that digitalization improves financial performance through many mechanisms [22]. It facilitates product commercialization and introduces new methods of trade and marketing, diversifies communication channels and sales methods [23]. Digitalization contributes to entering international markets - in addition to the emergence of new opportunities, contacts with new customers, partners and suppliers around the world are facilitated [24]. Efficiency and productivity are increased by automating certain processes, improving production control and human resource management.

According to analytical studies [25], the most significant positive consequences of digital transformation of companies in the automotive industry, respondents include an increase in operational efficiency and the ability to meet constantly changing consumer needs. Significant disadvantages are [26] the high cost of investment; the availability of relevant competencies of employees (the need to either hire new specialists or train existing ones); a decrease in information security: physical systems integrated with the

Internet and associated production systems become vulnerable to cyberattacks (there is a need to develop secure networks that ensure the invulnerability of these processes and complete protection from outside interference) [27]; the automation of enterprise processes will lead to a reduction in jobs and, as a consequence, to an increase in unemployment [28].

6 Conclusion

The efficiency of digital transformation of business processes of a company depends on awareness of the importance of continuous improvement of technologies and conscious choice of algorithm of digitalization: goal-setting, team building, ranking business processes by priority for the digital technologies implementation, risk assessment, testing and training, control and monitoring of results.

As a result of the analysis of existing scientific approaches to the issue of digitalization of business processes of companies and the study of world experience, it was revealed that the existing methods have a number of disadvantages, which makes it difficult for companies to use them: the stages are described incompletely and vaguely, it is not clear where the process begins; often digitalization of business processes of companies are considered separately from the company itself and the company is considered separately from its environment; clear criteria for assessing technologies and business processes for digitalization are not proposed; there is no consideration of risks, etc.

The developed methodology for digital transformation of business processes takes into account the advantages and disadvantages of existing approaches and algorithms, and also offers a final assessment of the technologies being implemented in three blocks (assessment of the risks of technology implementation, assessment of the technology supplier and assessment of the financial efficiency of the project for the implementation of the selected technology) by building pattern.

The developed methodology was tested on the business process of quality control of body parts (panels of the central and rear floor) on Toyota Motor LLC plant in St.-Petersburg. A qualitative and quantitative assessment of alternative technologies was carried out and the introduction of 3D scanning technology was justified. In the future, the methodology can be improved by taking into account the specific for each industry indicators of the final assessment of the technology, formalizing each criterion, including the time factor.

Acknowledgments. The research was partially funded by the Ministry of Science and Higher Education of the Russian Federation under the strategic academic leadership program 'Priority 2030' (agreement 075-15-2021-1333, dated 30 September 2021).

References

1. Amarala, A.: SMEs and Industry 4.0: two case studies of digitalization for a smoother. Comput. Ind. **125**, 103333 (2021)
2. Andreja Rojko Industry 4.0 Concept: Background and Overview. Int. J. Interact. Mob. Technol. (iJIM). №5 (2017)

3. Bataev, A.V.: Analysis and development the digital economy in the world. In: Proceedings of 14th International Conference on Advanced 61–7'1Technologies, Systems and Services in Telecommunications, TELSIKS 2019 (2019)
4. Gromova, E.A.: Digital economy development with an emphasis on automotive industry in Russia. Espacios (2019)
5. Rybakov, D.S.: A process model of a logistics system as a basis for optimisation programme implementation. Int. J. Logist. Res. App. **21**, 72–93 (2018)
6. The Six Stages of Digital Transformation. Altimer Prophet. https://www.prophet.com/download/six-stages-of-digital-transformation-2016/
7. Vital Digital Transformation Statistics: Spending, Adoption, Analysis & Data. Finances Online (2020). https://financesonline.com/digital-transformation-statistics
8. What is the digital transformation? Hewlett Packard Enterprise. https://www.hpe.com/ru/ru/what-is/digital-transformation.html
9. 20 facts about digital transformation: statistics, forecasts and surveys. RBC. https://trends.rbc.ru/trends/industry/5ece23569a79479c90f3377b
10. Key steps for a successful digital transformation. Eastern Peak. https://easternpeak.com/blog/key-steps-for-a-successful-digital-transformation/
11. Zaytsev, A., Rodionov, D., Dmitriev, N., Faisullin, R.: Bulding a model for managing the market value of an industrial enterprise based on regulating its innovation activity. Acad. Strateg. Manag. J. **19**, 1–13 (2020)
12. Digitalization: Gatner. https://www.gartner.com/en/information-technology/glossary/digitalization
13. Evans, N.D.: 6 steps for digital transformation. CIO US (2017)
14. Ready For Digital Transformation? Here Are 7 Steps To Get You Started - ArcherPoint RT. https://www.archerpoint.com/blog/Posts/7-steps-digital-transformation
15. Disadvantages of Digital Technology. Turbofuture. https://turbofuture.com/misc/Disadvantages-of-Digital-Technology
16. Soia, A. Konnikova, O. Konnikov, E.: The internet of things. In: Proceedings of the 33rd International Business Information Management Association Conference, IBIMA 2019: Education Excellence and Innovation Management through Vision 2020, pp. 8587–8591 (2019)
17. Demidenko, D.S., Dubolazova, Y.A.: Drawing up an optimal investment program for innovative development of an enterprise. In: Proceedings of the European Conference on Innovation and Entrepreneurship, ECIE (2019)
18. Kolmykova, O.N.: Business process management: the value of measuring the efficiency and effectiveness of business processes in the activities of organizations. Science and Business: Ways of Development (2019)
19. Zaborovskaia, O., Nadezhina, O., Avduevskaya, E.: The impact of digitalization on the formation of human capital at the regional level. J. Open Innov. Technol. Mark. Complex. **6**, 184 (2020)
20. Financial statements and financial analysis of Toyota Motor for 2011–2020. Audit-it.ru. https://www.audit-it.ru/buh_otchet/7710390358_ooo-toyota-motor
21. PWC Private Equity & Digital Transformation: PricewaterhouseCoopers Aktiengesellschaft Wirtschaftsprüfungsgesellschaft, p. 48 (2018)
22. 3D Coordinate Measuring Machine: Alibaba.com. https://www.alibaba.com/pla/Operate-By-Hand-Small-Travel_60652300699
23. Rotini, F.: Re–engineering of Products and Processes – How to Achieve Global Success in the Changing Marketplace. Industry and Innovation (2012)
24. Rihab Bellakhal Digitalisation and Firm Performance: Evidence from Tunisian SMEs. Industry and Innovation (2020)
25. Digital transformation: Workingmouse. https://workingmouse.com.au/innovation/digitisation-digitalisation-digital-transformation

26. Degtereva, V.A., Ivanov, M.V., Barabanov, A.A.: Issues of building a digital economy in modern Russia. In: Proceedings of the European Conference on Innovation and Entrepreneurship, ECIE, pp. 246–253 (2019)
27. Digital economy in Russia: Ministry of Digital Development, Communications and Mass Media of the Russian Federation. https://digital.gov.ru/ru/activity/directions/858/
28. Cassetta, E.: The relationship between digital technologies and internationalisation. Evidence from Italian SMEs. Industry and Innovation (2020)
29. Belov, V.B.: New paradigm of industrial development in Germany - "Industry 4.0" strategy. Modern Europe (2016)

Transformation of Software Project Management in Industry 4.0

Alexander Babkin[1] ⓘ, Anton Safiullin[2](✉) ⓘ, Vadim Tronin[2] ⓘ,
and Alexander Alexandrov[2] ⓘ

[1] Peter the Great St. Petersburg Polytechnic University, St. Petersburg, Russia
[2] Ulyanovsk State Technical University, Severnyj Venec Street, 32, 432027 Ulyanovsk, Russia
asaf79@mail.ru

Abstract. Digital technologies create not only new opportunities, but also form new business challenges caused by the integration of design, product development and business processes (from the moment an order is placed right through to outbound logistics), personalization and adaptive response on customer demands, real-time solving of tasks and problems, openness and access to resources for remote employees, accumulating big data for analytics and adaptive management with clouds. Modern software development in Industry 4.0 is complex process, both human-intensive, technology-intensive, knowledge- intensive and innovative-intensive. The modern software industry moves unrelentingly towards new methods for managing the ever-increasing complexity of software projects. The traditional project management methodology, which contains structured and standardized forms, and is focused on a greater certainty and planning horizon of several decades, no longer allows companies to fully adapt to the new opportunities, speeds and risks of Industry 4.0. The article systematizes new conceptual approaches and forms of projects management, including adaptive management methodologies. Agile-based digital project management creates new opportunities for business: accelerating decision-making and the rapid identification of incorrect approaches, effective cooperation between technical groups and business groups, creating a more attractive environment for collaboration and co-working, reducing the time to prepare documentation and others. The transformation of software project management is associated with dramatic changes, the risk of errors when updating products, diluting responsibility for product quality, and even problems with the companies reputation. Presently it seems to be more sustainable a combined or hybrid model of software projects management, combining traditional and Agile methodologies.

Keywords: Project management · Software · Agile methodologies · Industry 4.0 · Digital technologies

1 Introduction

The software industry moves unrelentingly towards new methods for managing the ever-increasing complexity of software projects.

© Springer Nature Switzerland AG 2022
D. Rodionov et al. (Eds.): SPBPU IDE 2021, CCIS 1619, pp. 159–170, 2022.
https://doi.org/10.1007/978-3-031-14985-6_11

The perception of the importance of software project management and consequently its development as a practical and research direction has continued to grow. Though general project management practice exists for a long time, however, the history of software project management is rather young. Most theories of software project management are taken from the historically established project management practices in other fields such as civil engineering, for example. In particular, Futrell et al. [1] describe software project management (SPM) as a specialization of general management studies that utilizes the typical management skills of planning, organizing, staffing, leading or directing, and controlling to achieve defined project objectives.

Futrell et al. suppose that the first public recognition of the importance of software project management was a discussion at a North Atlantic Treaty Organization (NATO) Science Committee conference in the late 1960s. Software engineers from different countries discussed not only technical aspects of design, production, implementation, distribution, and service of software, at this conference were also reports on «the difficulties of meeting schedules and specifications on large software projects» [1].

The growth of scientific interest led to the development of a software life cycle (SLC) in the 1970s to represent the sequence of events that occur in software development what also served to development of software project management. American computer scientist, director at Lockheed Software Technology Center in Austin Winston Walker Royce was a pioneer in the field of software development. Royce's 1970 paper «Managing the development of large software systems» [2] defined the stagewise «waterfall» model for software development, which demonstrated the steps to develop a large computer program for delivery to a customer from the top to the bottom, like a waterfall. Since the phases of «waterfall» model can be mapped to the project management process as groups of steps (initiating processes, planning processes, executing processes, and closing processes) therefore one may infer that the software project management was born in this period with the birth of software life cycle theory.

Research in software life cycles was intensified in the 1990s because of increasing software projects complexity and the low efficiency of their management and development. During this period researchers focused on the importance of planning and cost estimation within the project budget to meet planned performance or end-product goals [3, 4]; the implementation schedule for the successful completion of the project [5–7], improvement both the software product quality and development team productivity [8].

Development of software and software-intensive systems in early 21st century led to growth of new form, new models and methods in SPL. For example, proponents of agile software development founded «The Agile Alliance» [9] in 2001. The software industry in the face of increasing complexity of software projects are constantly moving to new management formms and methods. Software project management is one of the youngest and most dynamic fields among different management disciplines with its completely unresolved problems. As Frederick P. Brooks stated [10], that today's major problems with software development are «not technical problems, but management problems».

Software has become an integral part of human life in a digital world. Smartphones, mobile network, electronics, almost everything around us is controlled by software. Software development has become an integral part of modern technological changes. Moreover, new technologies are having an increasing impact on software project management as well as on any other project activities.

John McGrath and Jana Kostalova identified project management trends presented in the last three years such as impact of technological developments on project management, tailored hybrid approaches (traditional project management blended with agile), increasing demands on the role of the project manager, new requirements on team member skills and other trends [11]. New technologies such as Artificial Intelligence (AI), Machine Learning and Cloud Computing are driving a digital transformation of software project management approaches. AI technology helps managers to make accurate decisions. Moreover, according to Ankit Rastogi [12], AI and Machine Learning provide decision-making based on predictions, help to predict problems before they arise which will give project management team a big advantage. As AI technology and Machine Learning improves, the more relevant information and data will be able to project managers and the more accurate the project management decisions. Experts note more other AI impacts on project management [13]. Project management based on AI gains new benefits associated with identifying potential risks, resource leveling and intelligent scheduling, automating mundane and repetitive tasks and etc. The Cloud Computing ideology is to transfer the data processing and data storage from personal computers to the Internet that making data collection and analysis for project decision making more flexible.

2 Literature Review

Projects vary widely in size and type. All projects have the same characteristics. They are unique, specific, have desired completion dates.

Project Management Institute (PMI) defines «project» as «a temporary effort to create value through a unique product, service or result» [14]. Tameem Abdulbaset Abdulwahid ABDO Hezam [15] defines project through its characteristics: project has specific goal(s), has a definite start date and end date, is not group of routine tasks or daily activities rather involves planned activities unlike routine activities. comes to end when its goal(s) is achieved, requires enough resources in terms of time, skilled workforce, budget, material and other support. Samuel J. Mantel, Jr. et al. complete the PMI definition with an important characteristic – multidisciplinary, because projects composed of many interconnected elements and requiring input from groups «with different kinds of knowledge and expertise» [16].

Software development or creating software is a project. Software development refers to a «set of computer science activities dedicated to the process of creating, designing, deploying and supporting software» [17] or «any activity that involves the creation or customization of software» [18], for example, launching websites, installing a CRM (customer relationship management) tool, implementing a new accounting package, building a custom application for your business. Creating software is a process or «temporary endeavor with set of well-defined activities that leads achievement of a specific goal(s)» [15]. Therefore, software development is also a project activity. As other kind of projects, software development has specific goal, a definite start date and end date, requires enough resources (time, skilled workforce, budget and others), and comes to end when its goal is achieved.

Today, project management is the «application of knowledge, skills, tools and techniques to project activities to meet the project requirements» [14], which is accomplished through the application and integration of logically grouped project management processes divided into process groups: initiating, planning, executing, monitoring and controlling, and closing.

Features and specific character of software project management determined by the content of software as a product and the process of software development.

Software development has the same features as any other project as a «sequence of unique, complex, and connected activities that have one goal or purpose and that must be completed by a specific time, within budget, and according to specification» [19]. However, software development is a cognitive and more unpredictable process (as opposed to the more deterministic processes in traditional projects), and software is a result of innovative and intellectually intensive co-working of individuals engaged in a team. Software development as co-working in team is inseparable from communication and coordination among different team members with different skills, knowledge's levels, and ambitions.

Software projects and its management differentiate from other projects in a number of ways, some of the main differentiating features are the following (Jurison J. [20], Gunter Ruhe and Claes Wohlin [21]).

According to Jurison J. software projects are generally multifaceted; software development is also prone to changing business conditions and technologies and takes place in a dynamic setup, for example, such as users' lack of confidence in their needs and repeatedly changing requirements during the project.

Gunter Ruhe and Claes Wohlin defines software as an intangible product. The primary asset in its content is intellectual capital of software personal. Software project is a cognitive and human-based development process that requires sharing of documents and innovative problem-solving to create unique solutions. Software development is challenging because of the high complexity of product based on the enormous number of logical paths in program modules and all the combinations of interface details. This process often involves interactions of different vendor products and interfaces with other software and requires combining different elements consisting of diverse hardware, other software, and manual procedures. Organization of software development process includes communication and coordination within software teams and with project stakeholders (it often lacks clarity), it is challenging because initial planning and estimation of software projects depend on requirements that are often imprecise or based on lacking information. There is a degree of change of requirements in the course of the software development, may be a higher degree of uncertainty in the software project and product scope. Objective measurement and quantification of software quality is difficult. Learning and knowledge creation in software development is more difficult because processes, methods, and tools are constantly evolving. Software security is a large and growing challenge.

Thus, modern software development is complex process, both human-intensive, technology-intensive, knowledge-intensive and innovative-intensive. Quality of dealing with people and efficiency of team building, communication opportunity and conflict prevention, knowledge sharing and co-learning among team members, effective interactions inside software and software-intensive systems and outside environment (project stakeholders and other developers) will be determinants of good software project management.

3 Traditional Project Management Versus Agile Software Development Methodologies

Traditional project management (TPM, «waterfall» model or «cascade» model shown in Fig. 1) is a linear process all the phases of which occur in sequence: determination and analysis of requirements, design (general and detailed design or architecture), coding, testing, operations or implementation).

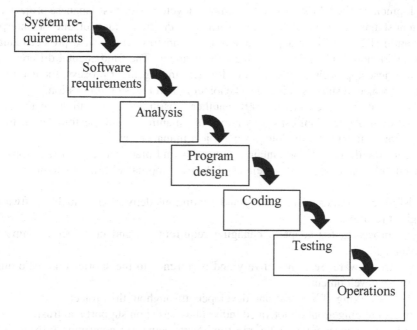

Fig. 1. «Waterfall» model as a sequence of steps to develop software for delivery to a customer.

Depending on the type of software, some more types or configuration of «waterfall» phases can be considered, for example, the integration of software can be considered separately between coding and testing [22]. Major deficiency of «waterfall» model is high costs of software correction because errors are detected only during testing. Besides developed software may not meet customer requirements if they changes during the project development. And finally, reports are the main source to trace the project progress and to assess risks. Barry W. Boehm [23] analyzed in details the software development costs. In particular, Barry W. Boehm stated that only 60% of errors can be detected by reading the code and software error correction at the end of the project is hundred times more expensive than immediate correction. So for every dollar spent on the software development two dollars are required for its management. The Traditional project management approach assumes that time and cost are variables and requirements are fixed. The TPM projects are plan-driven, process-heavy, and documentation-heavy and hence are very structured projects. So traditional project management faces budget and timeline issues.

The classical paradigm «Cost - Time - Content» based on traditional project management approach and prevailed in the second half of the 20th century, began to fail in the late 1990s [24]. Business tried to break the limits of classical project approach by increasing attention to risks, working with project stakeholders, building the project management up to the level of programs and project portfolios.

Japan, «outsider» of the classical management paradigm, after extensive research on the practices, standards and methodologies of project management in the USA and European countries, created the Committee for Innovative Project Management Model Development in 1999. In 2001, this Committee developed the first Japanese project management standard, The Guidebook for Project and Program Management for Enterprise Innovation (P2M). Unique Japanese approach transformed classical project management paradigm to «Complexity -Value - Resistance». The fundamental differences of new Japanese approach are focus on end-to-end management process, focus on value creation (project results as value to stakeholders), and focus on innovation.

Almost at the same time, in 2001, another «disruptive» innovation for the classical paradigm, Agile Manifesto, was born. The manifesto laid the foundation for the application of flexible methodologies in project management.

Agile Manifesto did not contain direct rules and practical recommendations, and declared only main ideas and principles of the new approach [25], for example:

- satisfy the customer through early and continuous delivery of valuable software as highest priority;
- Agile processes for adapt to changing requirements and customer's competitive advantage;
- working software frequent delivery and preference to the shorter timescale during software development;
- daily co-working of business and developers throughout the project;
- projects building around motivated individuals based on support and trust;
- face-to-face conversation as the most efficient method of conveying information to and within a development team;
- working software as the primary measure of progress;
- continuous attention to technical excellence and good design for agility and others principles.

Agile integrates various methodologies and project management approaches: focuses on goals and clients requirements, work in short cycles, product, service or result creation speed, customer feedback, high level of self-organization, humanistic approach. Agile-based project management means product creation by iterations (a timebox during which development takes place, usually between 1 and 4 weeks).

Agile methodologies and its management differentiate from other approaches («waterfall» model) in a number of ways, some of main differentiating features are the following (Table 1) [26, 27, 28].

Table 1. Compared features of «waterfall» development and Agile projects.

«Waterfall» development	Agile project
Tools and processes	People and human interactions
Documentation	Unique product
Contract-based approach to scope and requirements	Collaborative and interactive approach to requirements
Following a detailed plan	Flexible, interactive feedback
Detailed, long-term project plans	Shorter planning based on iterations
Requirements and a detailed plan for completing the project can be defined prior to implementing the project (plan-driven approach)	The requirements and plan for the project are expected to evolve as the project progresses (adaptive approach)
Costly changes if the product does not meet expectations	Lower costs as there is less risk of customer and product misalignment (lean type of software development)

Agile approach is effective for software development projects while traditional project management may not lead to success. Agile approach is more effective if the project requirements change frequently, customer sets short deadlines for the project and high uncertainty of project development is noted.

Agile approach has other advantages. Another advantage of Agile methodology is «time-to-market». Users have become better versed in IT products, can evaluate the product and give quick feedback. Therefore, development must proceed quickly and efficiently. In addition, the customer asks for a result that works right here and now («it should have been done yesterday»). Frequent demonstrations of the product current version to the customer allow testing the product and adjusting the software development process at any time. Daily team meetings and product demonstrations to the customer make software development process visual both for team members and for the customer. The customer can influence the result of development, and the team has the opportunity to change priorities, speed up and solve a problem.

Software development based on Agile methods creates new product that is really needed here and now. At the same time, it is possible to develop a quality product based on traditional project management exactly in accordance with the agreed requirements for a long time and then it will turns out that the requirements are no longer relevant.

Agile approach changes the project team structure. The levels of the management pyramid are delayering or debossing (reducing the number of management layers in project). Agile approach improves working life quality of all team members. Team members become interested in result and new skills and more creative, ready to work quickly, efficiently and with pleasure. A key tenet of agility is that practitioners be open to learning new skills – not just from project to project, but also as part of a lifelong learning process [29].

The most important priority of new paradigm based on Agile methods is speed of valuable results creation and providing first «minimum viable product» (MVP) to the customer, and then the competitive versions or individual modules of this product, modified during MVP testing. Agile projects are far more likely to deliver on time, on budget, and having met the customer's need.

After 2001, Agile went beyond software development and even beyond the IT industry, flexible methodologies (Scrum, Kanban, Lean Startup, etc.) began to be applied in the products development for other fields. 35% of companies use pure Agile, 30% use a hybrid approach, 24% use Agile or Waterfall depending on their product and 11% use Waterfall only [30].

Agile is not a single methodology, Agile is a complex of methods and approaches. Agile should not «simply equate to delivering software in sprints», rather, Agile is «a way of thinking that embraces change, regular feedback, value-driven delivery, full-team collaboration, learning through discovery, and continuous improvement» [31]. Today Agile is the main trend in the development of project management in large and small companies, in public and private sectors.

4   Fourth Industrial Revolution: New Demands on the Capabilities of Software Project Management

The digital economy has become more information intensive and even traditional industries, such as oil and gas or financial services, are becoming data driven. By 2023, forecasts Cisco, nearly two-thirds of the global population will have Internet access, the number of devices connected to IP networks will be more than three times the global population. Devices and connections are growing faster (10 percent CAGR) than both the population and the Internet users [32]. Digital 2022 Global Overview Report [33] named the main events of the past year in a digital world: growth of Internet users (+4.0% in 2021 and more than doubled in the past decade), double-digit growth in social media users (+10 .1% in 2021 and more than tripled in the past decade), the rise of social commerce, big gains for Youtube and etc.

OECD experts mentioned two technological pillars empowered by exponentially growing computing power, digitisation and interconnection, have been driving the digital, complemented by a growing ecosystem of inter-related technologies. Combined with constant mobile connectivity, a wide range of new products, applications and services has emerged over the past decade, forming a growing ecosystem of technologies and applications, which, through increasing use by individuals, firms and governments, is driving the digital transformation [34]. Key components of this ecosystem are new technologies of the fourth industrial revolution: the Internet of Things, Big Data analytics, Artificial intelligence, Blockchain and others.

Digital technologies of fourth industrial revolution create not only new opportunities, but also form new business challenges and new demands on the capabilities of software project management caused by;

- the integration of design, product development and business processes (from the moment an order is placed right through to outbound logistics),
- personalization and adaptive response to customer demands,
- real-time solving of tasks and problems, openness and access to resources for remote employees,
- accumulating big data for analytics and adaptive management with clouds.

On one hand, new digital technologies has changed project environments, empower project management approaches and impact on project management methods, tools and techniques through the full project life cycle: initiation, planning, execution, monitoring and controlling and project closeout. According to John McGrath and Jana Kostalova digitization empowers project teams to innovate in approaches to project work and organizations to harness data for data-driven strategic decision making by using other project management tools.

On the other hand, digitization creates new requirements on project management tools and project manager (team member) skills (hard skills, soft skills and skills in digital areas like AI, data analysis, design thinking, automation, robotics, machine learning, cybersecurity etc.). An important change associated with digital technologies and software development was the introduction of agile project management and its implementation in practice. Ben Aston [35] defined this characteristic of daily project management activity «stay flexible» (project change occurs daily, and sometimes even hourly or by-the-minute so it is necessary to use agile-based tools).

At first site, Agile methodology is more suitable for business using and developing technologies of fourth industrial revolution and new business environment. Agile has some benefits for the companies and the customers or stakeholders. Agile model is considered to bring in incremental changes, allowing a software development project to become more flexible in response to changing requirements. Today, most banks have switched to flexible methodologies. Companies in Silicon Valley, Facebook, Google, Uber work based on Agile methodology.

Agile works great in startups, small teams of developers, but large projects, as a rule, it may lead to different problems: delayed schedule for months or even complete failure. For example, in July 2015, trading on the New York Stock Exchange was stopped for four hours because was a bug problem during the next system update. After update of the Delta airline's software the information ceased to go to the dispatch system, and all flights had to be cancelled. So airline company had reputation problems. Start of Obama Care system is another example of Agile methodology failure.

Due to the above problems, the modern evolution of project management is characterized by the emergence of combined models. New versions of the «waterfall» model already include the features of Agile management.

5   Conclusion

As information and communication technologies are evolving, the need for newer innovations not only in of product development, but also in project management models is also becoming more dynamic and increasingly necessary. Customer preferences and needs change more rapidly than ever before, life cycles of software and other IT products are getting shorter, new versions or new products being needed to satisfy newer customer needs in digital and interconnected world.

The traditional project management methodology based on structured and standardized forms, and focused on a greater certainty and planning horizon of several decades, no longer allows companies to fully adapt to the new opportunities, speeds and risks of Industry 4.0 technologies. New approaches (Agile methodology and others) in project management solve some problems generated by accelerated digitalization. But Agile methodology has not only benefits (accelerating decision-making and the rapid identification of incorrect approaches, effective cooperation between technical groups and business groups, creating a more attractive environment for collaboration and co-working, reducing the time to prepare documentation and others) but failures (risk of errors when updating products, diluting responsibility for product quality, and even problems with the companies reputation) for the companies and the customers or stakeholders. Presently it seems to be more sustainable a combined or hybrid model of software projects management, combining traditional and Agile methodologies.

Acknowledgments. The research was partially funded by the Ministry of Science and Higher Education of the Russian Federation under the strategic academic leadership program 'Priority 2030' (agreement 075-15-2021-1333, dated 30 September 2021).

References

1. Futrell Robert, T., Shafer, L.I., Shafer, D.: Quality Software Project Management. Prentice Hall PTR, Hoboken (2001)
2. Royce, W.W.: Managing the development of large software systems. In: Proceedings of IEEE WESCON 26 (August) (1970). http://www-scf.usc.edu/~csci201/lectures/Lecture11/royce1 970.pdf
3. Lederer, A.L., Prasad, J.: Causes of inaccurate software development cost estimates. J. Syst. Softw. 31(2), 125–134 (1995)
4. Deephouse, C., Mukhopadhyay, T., Goldenson, D., Kellner, M.: Software processes and project performance. J. Manag. Inf. Syst. 12(3), 187–205 (1996)
5. Barki, H., Rivard, S., Talbot, J.: Towards an assessment of software development risk. J. Manag. Inf. Syst. 10(2), 203–225 (1993)
6. Johnson, D.M.: The system engineer and the software crisis. Softw. Eng. Notes. 21(2), 64–73 (1996)
7. Simmons, D.B., Ellis, N.C., Escamilla, T.D.: Manager associate. IEEE Trans. Knowl. Data Eng. 5(3), 426–438 (1993)
8. Möller, K.H., Paulish, D.J.: Software Metrics: A Practitioner's Guide to Improved Product Development. Chapman and Hall, London, New York (1993)
9. Agile Alliance. www.agilealliance.org

10. Brooks, F.P.: No Silver Bullet - Essence and Accident in Software Engineering (1987). http://worrydream.com/refs/Brooks-NoSilverBullet.pdf
11. McGrath, J., Kostalova, J.: Project Management Trends and New Challenges 2020+ (2020). https://www.researchgate.net/publication/340387660_Project_Management_Trends_and_New_Challenges_2020
12. Rastogi, A.: Project Management trends you need to look out for in the year (2019). https://www.greycampus.com/blog/project-management/top-project-management-trends-in-2019
13. Boogaard, K.: Project Management Trends and Predictions (2021). https://www.goskills.com/Project-Management/Resources/Project-management-trends-predictions-2021
14. What is Project Management I PMI. https://www.pmi.org/about/learn-about-pmi/what-is-project-management
15. ABDO Hezam, T.A.A.: Software project development and management, April 2021. https://www.researchgate.net/publication/350592250_Software_project_development_and_management
16. Mantel, S.J., Meredith, J.R., Shafer, S.M., Sutton, M.M.: Project Management in Practice. John Wiley & Sons, Hoboken (2011). https://faculty.ksu.edu.sa/sites/default/files/project_management_in_practice_-_samuel_j._mantel_jack_r._mer_1125.pdf
17. What is software development? IBM. https://www.ibm.com/topics/software-development
18. Murray, A.P.: The Complete Software Project Manager. Mastering Technology from Planning to Launch and Beyond, 230 p. Wiley, Canada (2016)
19. Wysocki, R.K.: Effective Project Management: Traditional, Agile, Extreme. 7th Edn. John Wiley & Sons, Inc., Hoboken (2014)
20. Jurison, J.: Software project management: the manager's view. Comm. AIS. **2**, 17 (1999)
21. Ruhe, G., Wohlin, C. (eds.): Software Project Management in a Changing World. Springer, Heidelberg (2014). https://doi.org/10.1007/978-3-642-55035-5
22. Peeter Normak Software Project Management (2014). http://www.tlu.ee/~pnormak/PM2015/Software_PM-Lecture-Notes-2014.pdf
23. Boehm, B.W.: Understanding and controlling software costs. IEEE Trans. Softw. Eng. **14**, 1462–1477 (1988). https://pdfs.semanticscholar.org/2147/c6218db2e35d40f4a7bdb87ed47e3814ef4b.pdf?_ga=2.260639374.288792651.1567350453-1589928215.1567350453
24. Paradigm Shift: Project Management 4.0. https://bpm-cg.ru/?page_id=5842
25. Principles behind the Agile Manifesto. http://agilemanifesto.org/principles.html
26. Fair, J.: Agile versus Waterfall: approach is right for my ERP project? In: PMI® Global Congress 2012-EMEA, Marsailles, Project Management Institute, Newtown Square, PA, France (2012). https://www.pmi.org/learning/library/agile-versus-waterfall-approach-erp-project-6300
27. Cobb, C.: What is the Truth About Agile versus Waterfall? https://managedagile.com/whats-the-truth-about-agile-versus-waterfall/
28. Eda Kavlakoglu Agile vs. Waterfall. https://www.ibm.com/cloud/blog/agile-vs-waterfall
29. Essential Skills for Agile Developers. Gartner (2022). https://www.gartner.com/en/articles/12-essential-skills-for-agile-developers
30. Agile, K.M.: Everything you need to know about Agile. Prod. Manag. J. (2019). https://www.productfocus.com/wp/wp-content/uploads/2019/10/Product_Focus_PMJ07_Agile.pdf
31. Agile Playbook. Booz Allen Hamilton (2017). https://www.agilealliance.org/wp-content/uploads/2018/12/08.031.17-Agile-Playbook-2.1-v12-One-Per-Student.pdf
32. Cisco Annual Internet Report, 2018–2023. https://www.cisco.com/c/en/us/solutions/collateral/executive-perspectives/annual-internet-report/white-paper-c11-741490.html?ysclid=l3namcx75t
33. Digital 2022 Global Overview Report (2022). https://datareportal.com/reports/digital-2022-global-overview-report

34. OECD: Digital Economy Outlook OECD Publishing, Paris, 321p. (2017)
35. Ben Aston 5 Emerging Project Management Trends (2020). https://thedigitalprojectmanager.com/project-management-trends/

Development of a Method for Assessing the Industrial Enterprise Digitalization Level

Ekaterina Abushova⬤, Ekaterina Burova$^{(\boxtimes)}$⬤, Andrei Stepanchuk⬤,
and Svetlana Suloeva⬤

Peter the Great St. Petersburg Polytechnic University,
29 Politechnicheskaya Ulitsa, St. Petersburg 195251, Russia
burova_ev@spbstu.ru

Abstract. The purpose of this study is to develop an express method for assessing the current level of the industrial enterprise digitalization. The relevance of the study is explained by the growing influence of digital technologies on the achievement of strategic goals and the efficiency of industrial enterprises. In this regard, there is a need to create a method for assessing the current level of digitalization of a company, which will reflect the real state of the enterprise in key aspects of digital production. The research results include (1) the author's definition of the concept of 'digitalization', (2) development of a method for assessing the level of digitalization of an industrial enterprise. The proposed method is based on the study of the digitalization level of each of 15 key aspects of a modern competitive industrial enterprise in various areas of its activity. Questionnaires and methods of expert assessments were used to determine the level of digitalization. The proposed method will allow assessing the current state of an enterprise, as well as identifying specific technologies, or systems in which an enterprise needs to make progress in order to achieve a higher level of digitalization, and which will contribute to the achievement of the strategic goals of the enterprise development. A feature of this technique is to assess the level of digitalization of each of key aspects of a modern competitive production enterprise and obtain a comprehensive indicator that allows further conclusions.

Keywords: Digital economy · Digitalization · Industrial enterprise · Level of digitalization · Expert assessments

1 Introduction

Digital technologies are universally and rapidly changing the everyday forms and methods of doing business [1]. Not only the business of individual companies is changing, but of industries, sectors of the economies of various regions and even entire countries. Digitalization goes far beyond the changes directly in technologies and business, as it becomes a significant macroeconomic and political factor [2].

Russia ranks among the lagging countries in the process of the current techno-economic wave, and the active process of digitalization of the national economy is a significant part of it [3]. The opportunity to take into account and use the leading

© Springer Nature Switzerland AG 2022
D. Rodionov et al. (Eds.): SPBPU IDE 2021, CCIS 1619, pp. 171–187, 2022.
https://doi.org/10.1007/978-3-031-14985-6_12

countries' experience in the formation and development of digital economy is a positive aspect of this situation. The introduction of digital technologies in various aspects of modern economic activity may be not as much expressed in the quantitative increase in labor productivity, as in effective qualitative changes in the existing business models of companies, ways of doing business, its manageability and flexibility. There will be a leapfrogging transition of the key indicators of cost-effectiveness, caused by introduction of digital technologies, to a new higher level as the scope of their application in various sectors of the economy expands. And the world economy is on the verge of such a leap right now.

The active process of the digital economy formation and development is inextricably linked with the concept of 'digitalization'. In these circumstances, it is very important for companies to determine their digital level [4]. It may also be necessary to determine the level of digitalization of certain aspects of their activities. This study focuses on the answers to these questions. An effective and universal method development for assessing the level of digitalization of an enterprise is an extremely urgent problem in the context of digital transformation and digitalization of enterprises [5–7]. To date, there is no single and generally accepted method for determining the level of digitalization of a single enterprise.

The goal of this study is to develop an express method for assessing the current level of digitalization of an industrial enterprise, as well as to clarify the very concept of digitalization. The developed method may be used both for the purpose of express assessment of the current digitalization level of an industrial enterprise, and for the purpose of forming goals and objectives related to the development of individual factors. A feature of this method is assessing the digitalization level of each of key aspects of a modern competitive manufacturing enterprise and obtaining a comprehensive indicator that contributes to further conclusions.

2   Literature Review

First of all, it makes sense to clarify the terminology of the complex and voluminous concept of digitalization while considering a phenomenon of digitalization in the economic sphere and society as a whole. Broadly, the 'digitalization' term commonly implies a socio-economic transformation that started together with the mass implementation and approbation of information and communication technologies, which are now called digital technologies, that is, technologies for creating, formatting, exchanging and providing information as such [8].

Determining which technologies should be considered or not considered digital seems a little more complicated. This also raises a dilemma as to what should be understood under the 'digital solutions' equivalent term. Active discussion and exchange of views on these issues currently take place in the research community [9, 10]. Disagreements in a single interpretation and a clear formalized definition of these terms are exacerbated by the fact that various world experts and analysts seem to have a fairly broad and fragmented interpretation of what stage of technical and economic development the world system is now at, as well as what breakthrough technologies (or groups of technologies) will most affect the economic structure of mankind in the near future

[10]. In this regard, it is difficult to determine the level of digital status of individual enterprises. Accordingly, the proposed methods vary in indicators, tools and factors that determine this level.

The concept of Industry 4.0 is inextricably linked with the concept of digitalization. Therefore, the task arises to form a definition of this term, as well as to explain why it is impossible to imagine the economy of the future without this process.

The 'digitalization' term can be used in both a narrow and a broad meaning these days. Narrowly, 'digitalization' means transformation of the information flow into the digital format, which entails a decrease in the overall level of costs, an increase in the speed of information transfer and processing, the emergence of new opportunities for its use, and so on. Multiple iterations of significant changes in information to digital format lead to positive results that stipulate the use of the concept of digitalization in a broad sense.

The process of digitalization has replaced such processes as informatization and computerization at a time when it was mainly about the use of computer technology, computers and supercomputers, as well as information and communication technologies to solve specific economic and technological problems. The possibility of obtaining information in digital format leads to the fact that digitalization processes form integral technological 'habitats' called ecosystems [11], within which users of these ecosystems can form the environments they need (technological, instrumental, documentary, etc.) in order to solve a class of tasks facing them.

Thus, the digital economy should be understood as an ecosystem in which the process of digitalization is the main factor of effective economic growth. Consequently, this makes the following distinctive feature of the digital economy: it is due to the process of digitalization that it is effectively developing [12].

If we consider interaction of the concepts of 'digitalization' and 'digital economy', it should be noted that digitalization is a fundamental aspect of the formation and development of the digital economy. This is the trend of global development that determines the process of evolution of the economy and society, and that forms the global digital economy. In other words, the process of digitalization is a fundamental trend in the development of the economy and society, based on the transformation of information and data into the digital format, which acts to increase the efficiency of the economy, quality and standard of living. The process of digitalization contributes to the consistent and gradual evolution (and even revolution in some cases) of all business processes of the economy and social spheres of society interacting with it, which (improvement) is based on an increase in the rate of exchange, the level of accessibility and degree of security of all information, as well as on the sharp growth of the role of automation as a fundamental process of digitalization.

Nowadays, it is necessary to be based on modern efficiently working digital production technologies in order to participate in the competition for the constant improvement of competitiveness in the new technological order. These digital technologies give a wide range of opportunities to manufacturing companies, namely, increasing productivity, efficient use of resources, energy intensity and energy efficiency, reducing various kinds of costs at all stages of the product life cycle, producing new types of products, and changing the business model of the enterprise.

The process of radical convergence of the digital and physical worlds has become extremely effective in the field of manufactured products and production tools. Moreover, this convergence is possible at all stages of the product life cycle. A 'smart model' of the manufactured product, the use of which significantly reduces the total cost of the product at all stages of production and reduces the time frame for this product to enter the market, is created using digital twin technology (see Fig. 1) [11].

A manufacturing company risks rapidly falling behind its competitors in the field of development and design in the conditions of the digital economy if it does not produce and deliver a new and improved model of its product to the market annually [12].

It is recommended to use various indicators in order to track other enterprises progress in developing their products and implementing digitalization. The only question is in the choice of a suitable method, a set of indicators and tools for assessing the level of digitalization.

A lot of different methods have recently been proposed to assess the level of digitalization. They may be divided according to the definition levels, among which are national, regional, sectoral and organizational levels [13]. It is the latter that this study is focused on.

Russian and foreign researchers have proposed many methods for assessing the level of digitalization for enterprises over the past 3 years. Additionally, methods have been developed to assess the level of digitalization of enterprises in various fields of activity. The difference between them is in the set of groups of indicators, in the form of assessment development as a sum of points or as an assessment level, as well as in the assessing methods [14–16].

As a rule, they are based on the statistical data analysis that are associated with the assessment of indicators such as the level of informatization, automation and digital maturity. The main challenge of these techniques is to obtain plausible data, which greatly complicates their use [17].

Analysis of the existing methods for determining the level of digitalization of enterprises showed that they may be divided into a number of groups with similar characteristics.

Among the existing methods, we can distinguish those that are based on the calculation of individual indicators that allow assessing the level of digitalization at the enterprise only as a whole. Such methods include, for example, Assessment of the level of digitalization of an industrial enterprise [18, 19], Assessment of digital transformation of the MIT Center for Digital Business and Capgemini Consulting [20]. The Babkin, A.V. and Pestova, A.Y. method includes indicators characterizing labor resources, material and technical support, digital infrastructure of the enterprise, software, financial resources, organizational and managerial indicators. A total of 19 indicators are proposed to be evaluated. The MIT Digital Business Center method includes 9 indicators of customer experience groups, operational processes, and business models.

Other methods suggest an excessive number of indicators, which may increase the accuracy of the assessing level of digitalization, but it is an expensive and time-consuming procedure. For example, the Deloitte Digital Maturity Model (179 indicators are used, including consumers, strategy, technology, production, structure, and culture of an organization).

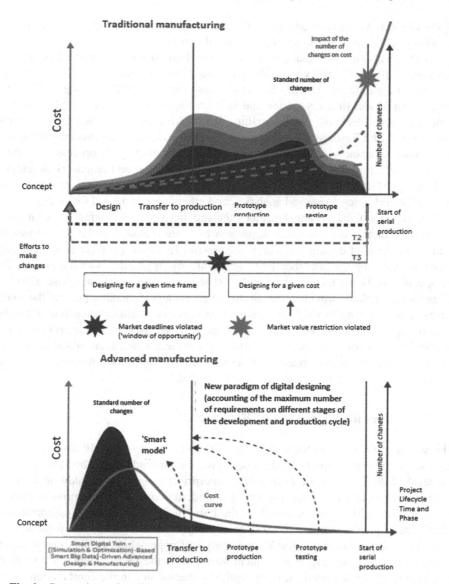

Fig. 1. Comparison of traditional and advanced manufacturing approaches. Source: [11].

A number of methods do not consider the specifics of the Russian economy, such as the Analytical Agency of Arthur D. Little Digital Transformation Index [21], the Acatech Industry 4.0 Maturity Index proposed by the German National Academy of Science and Engineering, and others [22]. The method of the Analytical Agency of Arthur D. Little considers 23 indicators, and strategy and leadership; products and services; customer management; operations and supply chains; corporate services and control; information technologies; workplace and culture are among them. The method of the German National Academy of Science and Engineering focuses on resources, information systems, culture and organizational structure.

There are also methods that assess the level of digitalization at industrial enterprises in various aspects of activity in combination. However, they also only give an idea of the level of digitalization for the enterprise. These include the KPMG Digital Maturity Assessment Model (it assess vision and strategy, digital talent, key digital processes, agile sources and technologies, leadership); Digitization Piano proposed by the Global Center for Digital Business Transformation (the method includes an overview of parameters related to business models, organizational structure, employees, processes, IT capabilities, interaction models, and others); Digital Transformation Framework developed by Ionology (factors as strategy and culture, personnel and customers, processes and innovation, technology, data and analytics, and others are considered for assessment).

The analysis of the presented methods showed that a different number of parameters and various factors are taken into account, which are included in the overall assessment of the level of digitalization at the enterprise. However, (1) there is no generally accepted single method, and therefore, each company choose the most suitable one for the specifics and certain conditions for the existence of a particular enterprise. Besides, (2) proposed methods provide no possibility of assessing individual aspects of the enterprises' activities, which would allow companies to assess measures taken to improve the level of digitalization on individual business projections, aspects, and areas of activity. In addition, (3) a consequence of this is that it is not clear which areas of activity should be developed in order to increase the level of digitalization of the enterprise to achieve and strengthen its competitive position in the market.

3   Resources and Methods of Research

The works of foreign and Russian researchers in the field of digitalization processes represent a theoretical and methodological basis for the study. A method for assessing the level of digitalization of an industrial enterprise, based on the study of the level of digitalization of each of key aspects of a modern competitive enterprise in various areas of its activities, was proposed on the basis of the analysis and systematization of existing approaches to assess the level of digitalization. Methods and tools such as drawing up a questionnaire, system and analytical approaches, the method of expert assessments, and group expert assessment were used in the development of the method. The feature of the development of the author's method lies in the combination of the classical fundamental methods of expert assessments considered in the works of A.L. Pavlevich, N.N. Staroverov, D.P. Khitrykh [23] and I.I. Blekhman, A.D. Myshkis, J.G. Panovko [24], with questionnaires and scoring.

4   Results

Various digitalization processes are an integral part of forming and developing the digital economy. These are very similar processes that are difficult to distinguish and very easy to confuse. The paper presents the author's definition, which distinguishes and differentiates this process from similar ones, such as digitization and digital transformation.

Digitalization is a process of active implementation and use of information and communication technologies (so-called digital technologies) in the existing business processes in order to increase their efficiency and reduce costs.

A method for assessing the level of digitalization at an enterprise developed by the authors of the study is proposed to assess the level of digitalization. It makes it possible to solve the following problems:

1. Assessment of an enterprise by means of comparative analysis with the leading companies by applying a system of assessing the best digital solutions of the manufacturing leaders in their industries.
2. Visualization of the stage of enterprise development in terms of implementing key aspects and systems of digital production to plan and implement a production program, as well as fulfill strategic goals of the organization.
3. Formation of ways of enterprise development to support it in achieving maximum results in terms of the key performance indicators.
4. Modeling the economic effect as a result of implementing the key production technologies.

The proposed method is based on the study of the level of digitalization of each of key aspects of a modern competitive industrial enterprise in various areas of its activities, such as design and technological pre-production, production processes, resource management and material supply, etc. A total of 15 key aspects were identified (see Fig. 2).

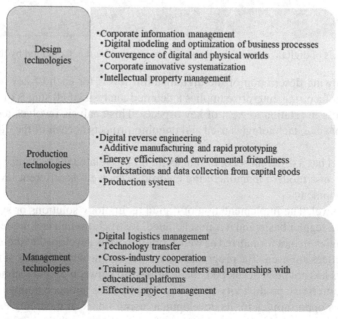

Fig. 2. List of key aspects of the modern enterprise. Source: compiled by the authors based on [11]

We recommend dividing the identified key aspects into three categories: (1) design technology, (2) production technology, (3) control technology. Such a classification of key aspects of industrial enterprises will determine the development degree of the main categories of technologies of a modern manufacturing enterprise, i.e. its design technologies, production technologies and management technologies, which are the most significant specifically for industrial enterprises [11].

It is proposed to highlight the following levels of digitalization to determine the level of digitalization of an industrial enterprise within the framework of this method (see Fig. 3). Each level has a different set of digital technologies related to the main categories of technologies of a modern manufacturing enterprise, as well as a different level of their digital development.

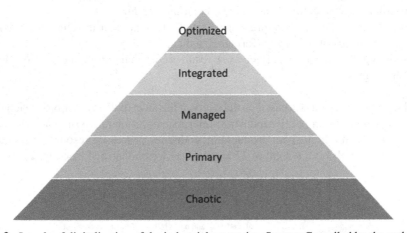

Fig. 3. Levels of digitalization of the industrial enterprise. Source: Compiled by the authors.

The following description of the digitalization levels for each of key aspects of a modern manufacturing enterprise implies a detailed analysis of all stages of the digitalization process in relation to each of key aspects. This analysis involves a description of the current state, technologies used and ongoing projects at each of the digitalization level.

Each level has a different set of digital technologies related to the main categories of technologies of a modern manufacturing enterprise, as well as different levels of their digital development:

Chaotic level. The implementation of digital technology solutions or systems does not occur on a regular basis, and it is unscheduled. Instructions and techniques for applying technologies are not formalized as well. Common tools developed without relying on the best practices are used. The program of activities for the development of technological initiatives has not been developed, the relationship between digital technologies and the level of enterprise productivity for its management has not been defined. The enterprise assesses opportunities for its development using financial modeling tools, market research and starts realizing the benefits of modernization through the implementation of digital technologies. The relationship between technologies, means of production, quality characteristics of a product and labor productivity is assessed. There is a low level of interest, understanding and confidence in the need for technological modernization in the organizational culture of the company and in the attitude of its management.

Primary level. The company has a formed common approach to implementation of various technologies at this level. The effectiveness of the technologies implemented to ensure the efficiency of the enterprise is determined. Separate technological modules are formed. The need for modernization is recognized by analyzing leading practices and reference visits to companies with a higher level of digitalization. A clear understanding of the effectiveness rate of digital technologies, systems and solutions in their activities is determined. The results of research and analytical reports on the use of digital technologies in the company are formed. Digital technologies are planned to be used, their impact on the company's results is determined and accepted by the management.

Managed level. Top management and other levels of the company's organizational structure are actively involved in the process of implementing digital technologies in all aspects of its activities. Leaders and members of various teams within the company have acquired the necessary digital competencies to work effectively with digital technologies. The company implements digital technologies through flexible project management. Digital systems and technologies operate in trial mode. The company forms and accumulates intellectual capital, best practices and gained experience.

Integrated level. The implementation of digital technologies is compared with the strategic goals and objectives of the organization at this level. The results of digital technologies implementation are synchronized with the results of other systems and are closely integrated into the business processes of the enterprise. A wide range of digital technologies and systems have already been introduced into the production process and other areas of the company's activities. The digital development of the enterprise is based on the documented results of the use of digital technologies and solutions in the past.

Optimized level. The enterprise has developed a certain number of standard procedures, quantitatively and qualitatively sufficient for replication as part of its global expansion. The best practices and the experience gained in managing projects for the development and application of digital technologies are systematized and stored in information banks of accumulated knowledge, intellectual capital of companies (Corporate books of knowledge). The company ensures replication of know-how, best practices, technological and production systems to new markets through the active development of a network of subsidiaries. Financial, time, qualitative and quantitative results obtained from the introduction and use of digital technologies and solutions are evaluated and described by the company.

Top management of each company makes the decision on which digitalization level and in which particular key aspects of activities is satisfactory for the company. They present the optimal balance between the necessary costs to achieve this level in this key aspect, and the benefits that will arise if this level is reached. Based on this decision, the company forms a matrix of target levels of digitalization for key aspects of the activities of a modern manufacturing enterprise.

One of key aspects of the effective functioning of an enterprise in the context of the fourth industrial revolution and the digital economy is a production system with efficiently functioning lean manufacturing technologies [25, 26]. We will show the application of individual stages of the developed method on it.

180   E. Abushova et al.

Currently, a large number of industrial premises in Russia are unkempt workshops that do not comply with environmental standards, with an ever-scattered working tools covered with a layer of metal shavings and dust. Manufacturing a truly competitive product is not possible under these conditions. It is essential to optimize the layout of the production workshop and individual work areas, standardize the production process, and improve the efficiency of production equipment. Digitalization levels will be characterized for this aspect as follows:

The chaotic level is characterized by the absence of a production system at the enterprise; lean manufacturing tools and techniques are not implemented.

The primary level is characterized by the development of the production system and a program for its implementation, as well as by formation of a calendar plan for introducing basic tools and methods of lean production into the production process. The production culture is at a high level.

The managed level involves introduction of key technologies and methods of lean production into the manufacturing system. The company's specialists and employees gain experience in organizing and using the lean manufacturing system.

A feature of the integrated level is functioning of the enterprise manufacturing system with adapted technologies and methods of lean production. Most of the methods and tools from the approved production program have been implemented. The enterprise develops and actively uses a bank of rationalization and innovative proposals. Value-added flows of manufactured products have already been formed and are applied in the process of company management.

The optimized level is characterized by effective functioning of visual management, 5S system, kaizen system, standardization of operational processes, Just In Time system [27]. Production control boards and communication centers are used in production halls. Value-added flows are analyzed and optimized.

The method proposed by the authors of the study implies determination of the current level of digitalization of an industrial enterprise through the sequential execution of the following stages presented in Fig. 4.

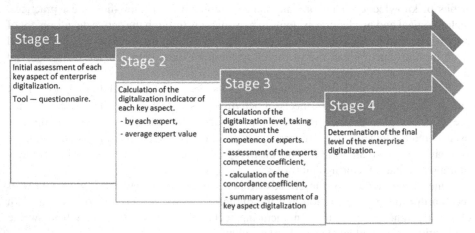

Fig. 4. Method for assessing the level of digitalization of the industrial enterprise. Source: Compiled by the authors.

The first stage involves an initial assessment of each key aspect of the enterprise digitalization using a questionnaire. A number of questions are presented in Table 1 (using the example of the 'production system' aspect). This list may and should be expanded by factors/issues that are most significant and related to the specifics and conditions of functioning of a particular enterprise. Each of the answer options has its own score, reflecting the value of digitalization of the subject of the question being asked and affecting the final level of digitalization of the enterprise as a whole.

Table 1. Questionnaire for assessing the level of digitalization of a manufacturing enterprise.

Factor/Criterion	Answer option	Number of points
Production system development	Lean production systems and tools comprehensively function on production sites	4
	Introduction of lean production components has started, first results has been obtained	3
	A production system project and an implementation project are in operation	2
	An analysis of the production systems of reference enterprises has been carried out	1
	Not available	0
Analysis of the products' value-added flow	An interactive and electronic analysis of the products value-added flow is carried out, which is used as a business development tool for the company	4
	An album of product value-added flow diagrams used in the planning of the production program has been created	3
	A project of the added-value flow of products is available	2
	The analysis of reference enterprises has been carried out	1
	Not available All workshops are equipped with control boards All workshops are equipped with control boards	0
Control boards for the execution of the production program of the enterprise	All workshops are equipped with control boards	4
	Pilot sites or workshops are equipped with control boards for the execution of the production program of the enterprise	3
	Project for developing and installing the appropriate tools is available	2
	The analysis of reference enterprises has been carried out	1
	Not available	0

(continued)

Table 1. (*continued*)

Factor/Criterion	Answer option	Number of points
Production flexibility, possibility of fast readjustment of production processes for new types of products	Flexible production cells, fast readjustment in most production areas	4
	Pilot sites gain experience in fast readjustment	3
	Site flexibility development project is available	2
	An analysis of the reference enterprises has been carried out, a report has been generated linking the effectiveness of the component and the results of the company	1
	Not available	0
Automated analysis of 3D models to select the optimal manufacturing process and capital goods (DFM, design-for-manufacturability)	DFM tools are used for most products in technological processes development	4
	DFM tools are used for some products in industrial operation, the connection between product design and manufacturing technology is supported by automation systems	3
	DFM tools are in trial operation, the work is proceeding in accordance with the implementation project	2
	The analysis of the systems use by reference enterprises has been carried out	1
	Not available	0
Etc.		

A group of experts is formed to fill out the questionnaire. It may include both employees of the assessed enterprise with sufficient competencies for the assessment, and external invited specialists-auditors.

At the second stage, an indicator of the digitalization level of each key aspect of an industrial enterprise is determined. Each expert determines the coefficient of significance of each question/criterion for this purpose. Their significance may vary for different enterprises depending on the industry, objective of activity, nature of production, and other factors.

The indicator of the digitalization level (DPa) of a specific aspect of the enterprise is determined for each expert assessor by the following formula (1):

$$DP_j^a = \sum_{i=1}^{n} (b_i \cdot p_i) \quad \sum_{1}^{n} p_i = 1 \tag{1}$$

where j is a sequential number of an expert assessor; a is a sequential number of the key aspect of an industrial enterprise; DPaj is a level of digitalization of the aspect a of an enterprise based on the results of an expert j assessment; i is a sequential number of the question; i = 1....n; bi is the score received for answering the question with sequential number i; pi is a coefficient of significance of the question i in the opinion of the expert.

Next, the average score among the experts is assessed. The sum of the scores of all the experts is divided by the number of expert assessors for this purpose:

$$DP_{cp}^a = \frac{\sum_{j=1}^{m} DP_j^a}{m} \tag{2}$$

where m is the number of experts.

At the third stage, the level of digitalization is estimated, using the method of group examination, and taking into account the experts' competence. Individual assessments are taken into account and the coefficients of competence of each expert are determined for this purpose [24]. The essence of this estimation lies in the assumption that the competence of experts should be assessed by the degree of consistency of their assessments with the objects' group assessment.

An expert's competence coefficient is assessed according to the formula (3):

$$K_j = \frac{DP_j^a * DP_{cp}^a}{\sum (DP_{cp}^a * DP_j^a)} \tag{3}$$

where Kj is the coefficient of competence of the j expert, Kj from 0 to 1, the sum of Kj = 1; DPacp is the average score of digitalization on aspect a.

The assessment of the examination quality is determined at the next step.

We propose to evaluate the examination quality using the coefficient of consistency of experts' opinions (Kendall's coefficient of concordance, or W-coefficient), which is assessed in this case according to the formula (4) [23]:

$$W = \frac{12S}{m^2} \tag{4}$$

where m is the number of experts; S is the sum of the squares of the deviations of the final assessments of each object from their average value:

$$S = \sum_{j=1}^{m} (DP_j^a - DP_{cp}^a)^2 \tag{5}$$

The coefficient of concordance varies from 0 to 1, with 0 indicating complete inconsistency and 1 indicating complete unanimity.

After that, we calculate the final assessment of the digitalization of a specific production aspect:

$$DP^a = \sum_{j=1}^{m} \left(DP_j^a \cdot K_j \right) \tag{6}$$

The DP^a indicator value is rounded to the nearest whole number.

At the fourth stage, the current general level of digitalization of an enterprise is determined:

$$DP = \frac{\sum DP^a}{a} \tag{7}$$

where DP is the level of digitalization of an industrial enterprise; $\sum DP^a$ is the sum of the digitalization levels of each of key aspects of a; a is a number of key aspects.

The indicator value is rounded to the nearest whole number.

The final level of digitalization of individual aspects and the enterprise is determined by the values of the DP^a and DP indicators (Table 2).

Table 2. The final level of digitalization of the manufacturing process.

DP value	Production digitalization level
0	Chaotic
1	Primary
2	Managed
3	Integrated
4	Optimized

Since any enterprise conducts a periodic rather than a single assessment, which is due to the processes of continuous improvement of certain key aspects, it is recommended to use the following economic and mathematical model for tracking the activities performed [28]. In this case, the improvement measures taken should lead to an increase in the level of digitalization of the manufacturing enterprise, and the calculated value is used as the DP indicator, and not the rounded one.

$$DP_t - DP_{t-1} \rightarrow max \qquad (8)$$

при $DP_t > DP_{t-1}$, $ЭDP > 1$,

where $ЭDP$ is the efficiency from implementing measures to improve key aspects of the enterprise. Relative indicators of the ratio of results and costs associated with the implementation of measures to increase the level of digitalization of an industrial enterprise may act as an indicator of efficiency. It is necessary to control that the results from the implementation of these measures exceed the costs of their implementation.

5 Discussion

The method proposed by the authors has a certain similarity with a number of the existing ones, such as Assessment of the level of digitalization of an industrial enterprise (by Babkin, A.V., Pestova, A.Yu.) [18, 19], Assessment of digital transformation by the MIT Center for Digital Business and Capgemini Consulting [20], which is aimed at assessing the level of digitalization of the enterprise. However, the authors' proposal is to improve and expand the possibilities of using the new technique.

The developed method for determining the level of digitalization of an industrial enterprise has significant advantages over the existing methods analyzed in the second section of the study. The main differences and advantages are as follows. The proposed method (1) is universal, since it allows one to determine the current level of digitalization for any manufacturing enterprise, regardless of the type of its activity, sector of the economy, nationality, company scale and other factors; (2) allows one to determine both an integral assessment of the current level of digitalization of the enterprise as a whole, and individual key aspects of its activity; (3) makes it possible to determine strategic goals and objectives for a more in-depth development of digital technologies at the enterprise, which consists in increasing the level of digitalization of certain key aspects and of the whole enterprise as a result. The tools used to apply this technique, such as questionnaires and group expertise, are simple and straightforward, which makes it easy to be used in practice.

6 Conclusion

The paper gives the author's definition of the 'digitalization' concept (1), which differentiates and distinguishes this process from similar ones, such as digitization and digital transformation. The method for determining the level of digitalization of an industrial enterprise developed and presented by the authors (2) makes it possible to determine the level of digital development for each of fifteen key aspects of a modern manufacturing enterprise, as well as to conduct a comprehensive assessment of the enterprise level of digitalization. Thus, the scientific novelty is that the proposed method is universal, that is, it can be used for enterprises in any sphere of production activity, as well as in complexity, that is, the possibility of determining both the level of digitalization of the enterprise as a whole and of its individual aspects. In turn, determining the location of an enterprise in the genesis of digital production makes it possible to determine the development goals of this enterprise, approve the program for achieving them and manage the company's development project using modern methods of effective project management, based on simple and measurable metrics. In conclusion, an economic and mathematical model (3) is proposed, which allows one to control the effectiveness of measures to improve key aspects of the enterprise's activities on the way to increasing the level of digitalization.

It should be noted that achieving the highest level of digitalization (optimized level) in all key aspects of the production enterprise and, as a result, achieving the highest level of digitalization at the enterprise, should not be the ultimate goal of the enterprise. The management of each company makes a managerial decision and determines its most effective level of digitalization of both the enterprise as a whole and of its individual key aspects depending on its strategic plan, mission, vision, established goals and objectives. In doing so, the management proceeds from a certain optimal balance between the necessary costs to achieve this level of digitalization and the benefits that will arise if this level is reached. Based on this, the company forms its own matrix of target levels of digitalization for key aspects of the activities of a modern manufacturing enterprise.

The authors see the prospects for further research of the problem (1) in the development and improvement of individual tools for assessing the level of digitalization of an industrial enterprise; (2) in the development of this method as one of the tools for assessing the current level of enterprise development.

Acknowledgments. The research was partially funded by the Ministry of Science and Higher Education of the Russian Federation under the strategic academic leadership program 'Priority 2030' (agreement 075-15-2021-1333, dated 30 September 2021).

References

1. Aturin, V.V., Moga, I.S., Smagulova, S.M.: Digital transformation management: Scientific approaches and economic policy. The Upravlenets (Manag. Sci. Anal. J.) **11**(2), 67–76 (2020). https://doi.org/10.29141/2218-5003-2020-11-2-6
2. Parviainen, P., Tihinen, M., Kääriäinen, J., Teppola, S.: Tackling the digitalization challenge: how to benefit from digitalization in practice. Int. J. Inf. Syst. Project Manag. **5**(1), 63–77 (2017). https://doi.org/10.12821/ijispm050104
3. Khalin, V.G., Chernova, G.V.: Digitalization and its impact on the Russian economy and society: advantages, challenges, threats and risks. Admin. Consult. **10**(10), 46–63 (2018). https://doi.org/10.22394/1726-1139-2018-10-46-63
4. Rachinger, M., Rauter, R., Müller, C., Vorraber, W., Schirgi, E.: Digitalization and its influence on business model innovation. J. Manuf. Technol. Manag. **30**(3), (2018). https://doi.org/10.1108/JMTM-01-2018-0020
5. Bickauske, D., Simanaviciene, Z., Jakubavicius, A., Vilys, M., Mykhalchyshyna, L.: Analysis and perspectives of the level of enterprises digitalization (Lithuanian manufacturing sector case). Indep. J. Manag. Prod. **11**(9), 2291–2307 (2020). https://doi.org/10.14807/ijmp.v11i9.1404
6. Limonova, E., Domnicheva, A., Manakhova, I.: Digitalization of companies–the basis of regions' competitive development. In: Proceedings of the International Scientific Conference "Competitive, Sustainable and Secure Development of the Regional Economy: Response to Global Challenges" (CSSDRE 2018), Advances in Economics, Business and Management Research (AEBMR), vol. 39. (2018). https://doi.org/10.2991/cssdre-18.2018.134
7. Fernández-Portillo, A., Hernández-Mogollón, R., Sánchez-Escobedo, M.C., Coca Pérez, J.L.: Does the performance of the company improve with the digitalization and the innovation? In: Gil-Lafuente, J., Marino, D., Morabito, F.C. (eds.) Economy, Business and Uncertainty: New Ideas for a Euro-Mediterranean Industrial Policy. SSDC, vol. 180, pp. 276–291. Springer, Cham (2019). https://doi.org/10.1007/978-3-030-00677-8_22
8. Foxconn replacing workers with robots. Hi-Tech (mass media) https://hightech.fm/2017/01/04/foxconn_automation. Accessed 21 Aug 2021
9. BarbierFive, F.: Trends for Manufacturing's Fourth Wave: Industry 4,0. Essentials for global operations leaders. Manufacturing outlook. https://www.themanufacturingoutlook.com/cxo insight/five-trends-for-manufacturing-s-fourth-wave-industry-40-essentials-for-global-ope rations-leaders-nwid-145.html. Accessed 18 Aug 2021
10. Dalenogare, L.S., Benitez, G.B., Ayala, N.F., Frank, A.G.: The expected contribution of Industry 4.0 technologies for industrial performance. Int. J. Prod. Econ. **204**, 383–394 (2018). https://doi.org/10.1016/j.ijpe.2018.08.019
11. Borovkov, A.I., Ryabov, Y.A., Kukushkin, K.V., Maruseva, V.M., Kulemin V.Y.: Digital duals and digital transformation of OPK enterprises. Vestnik Vostochno-Sibirskoj Otkrytoj Akademii. **32** (2019). https://vsoa.esrae.ru/206-1150
12. Rudskoy, A.I., Borovkov, A.I., Romanov, P.I.: Is the transfer of Russian engineering education to the American liberal arts system relevant? Vysshee Obrazovanie v Rossii (Higher Educ. Russia). **30**(6), 47–59 (2021). https://doi.org/10.31992/0869-3617-2021-30-6-47-59
13. Skolkovo Digital Russia Methodology (2019). https://finance.skolkovo.ru/. Accessed 25 July 2021
14. Buer, S.-V., Strandhagen, J.W., Semini, M., Strandhagen, J.O.: The digitalization of manufacturing: investigating the impact of production environment and company size. J. Manuf. Technol. Manag.2020https://doi.org/10.1108/jmtm-05-2019-0174
15. Kotarba, M.: Measuring digitalization: key metrics. Found. Manag. **9**(1), 123–138 (2017). https://doi.org/10.1515/fman-2017-0010

16. Schumacher, A., Schumacher, C., Sihn, W.: Industry 4.0 operationalization based on an integrated framework of industrial digitalization and automation. In: Durakbasa, N.M., Gençyılmaz, M.G. (eds.) ISPR -2019. LNME, pp. 301–310. Springer, Cham (2020). https://doi.org/10.1007/978-3-030-31343-2_26
17. Kupriyanova, M.V., Simikova, I.P.: Methodological approaches to digitalization assessment of the manufacturing industry. In: Proceedings of the All-Russian Scientific and Practical Conference with International Participation «Law, Economics, And Management: Relevant Issues», pp. 28–34 (2019). https://doi.org/10.31483/r-74149
18. Babkin, A.V., Pestova, A.Y.: Algorithm for the assessment of level of digitalization of the industrial enterprise. Digital transformation of economy and industry. In: Proceedings of the Scientific and Practical Conference with Foreign Participation, 20–22 June 2019, SPB, pp. 683–680. Polytech-Press (2019)
19. Babkin, A.V., Burkaltseva, D.D., Kosten, D.G., Vorobiev, Y.N.: Formation of digital economy in Russia: essence, features, technical normalization, development problems. St. Petersburg State Polytechn. Univ. J. Econ. 3, 9–25 (2017). https://doi.org/10.18721/JE.10301
20. The Digital Advantage: How digital leaders outperform their peers in every industry. https://www.capgemini.com/wp-con-tent/uploads/2017/07the_digital_advantage_how_digital_leaders_outperfom_their_peers_in_every_industry.pdf. Accessed 21 July 2021
21. Little, A.D.: Digital Transformation – How to Become Digital Leader. https://www.adlittle.com/sites/default/files/viewpoints/ADL_HowtoBecomeDigitalLeader_02.pdf. Accessed 21 July 2021
22. Industrie 4.0 Maturity Index. Managing the Digital Transformation of Companies. Acatech research. https://www.acatech.de/wp-content/uploads/2018/03/acatech_STUDIE_rus_Maturity_Index_WEB.Pdf. Accessed 3 Aug 2021
23. Pavlevich, A.L., Staroverov, N.N., Khitrykh. D.P.: Effective platform for applied research and comprehensive numerical modeling based on ANSYS solutions (in Russian). CADFEM Rev. 4 (2017)
24. Blekhman, I.I., Myshkis, A.D., Panovko, Y.G.: Applied Mathematics: Subject, Logic, Features of Approaches. Naukova Dumka, Kiev (1976)
25. Yadav, G., et al.: Development of a lean manufacturing framework to enhance its adoption within manufacturing companies in developing economies. J. Clean. Prod. 245, 118726 (2020). https://doi.org/10.1016/j.jclepro.2019.118726
26. Shibanov, K.S.: Lean manufacturing: continuous flow and pulling systems (in Russian) Colloq. J. 2–6(26), 41–42 (2019). https://cyberleninka.ru/article/n/berezhlivoe-proizvodstvo-neprerryvnyi-potok-i-sistemy-vytyagivaniya
27. Izmailova, A., Shapovalov, A.: Technological possibilities of reducing the production cost of metallurgical enterprises at the current stage. Trends Manag. (in Russian) (2017). https://cyberleninka.ru/article/n/tehnologicheskie-vozmozhnosti-sokrascheniya-sebestoimosti-produktsii-metallurgicheskih-predpriyatiy-na-sovremennom-etape, https://doi.org/10.7256/2454-0730.2017.2.2304
28. Abushova, E.E., Kuzmina, S.N., Leventsov, V.A., Chernikova, A.V.: Development of a methodology for assessing the level of the enterprise 'thrift' (in Russian). J. Econ. Entrepreneurs. 8(121), 993–997 (2020)

The Use of Neural Networks for Optimization of the Quality of Business Activity in the Digital Environment

Maksim Pasholikov[1] (ID), Leonid Vinogradov[2] (ID), Tatiana Leonova[2] (ID),
Vasily Burylov[3](✉) (ID), and Eitiram Mamedov[2] (ID)

[1] Peter the Great St. Petersburg Polytechnic University, Polytechnicheskaya, 29, St. Petersburg, Russia

[2] Saint-Petersburg State University of Economics, Sadovaya Street, 21, Saint-Petersburg 191023, Russia

[3] North-West Institute of Management, Branch of the Russian Presidential Academy of National Economy and Public Administration (RANEPA), Sredny Pr. V.O., 57/43, St. Petersburg 199178, Russia

vassily777@yandex.ru

Abstract. The article highlights the relevance of the study of optimization of the quality of business activities in the digitalization environment, in connection with the multi-dimensional nature of this category, which includes many single indicators of different nature. It presents an approach to the formation of the quality vector of entrepreneurial activity. The article lists prerequisites for the use of neural networks for optimization of the quality of the business activity. A sequence of measures to find the optimal quality vector has been compiled. The methods of multi-criteria optimization of the quality criteria in the field of business activity on water treatment have been tested. The neural networks have been trained for each of the single indicators of the quality vector, as well as for the entire quality vector. The optimal neural networks have been selected. As a result of the testing, the higher accuracy of models created with the help of neural networks in the field of water treatment forecasting in comparison with the previously constructed regression models has been confirmed. In the course of the study, the most important factors influencing the quality parameters have been identified. The trained neural network allows optimizing the water quality by selecting the optimal values of the controlled input parameters. The proposed approach can become the basis for the development of a common methodology for creating the optimal vector of business activity quality in any sector of the economy.

Keywords: Quality optimization · Neural networks · Business activity

1 Introduction

The business has changed quite a bit in the digital environment and continues to change, especially in some sectors of the economy, such as services, trade, and others.

© Springer Nature Switzerland AG 2022
D. Rodionov et al. (Eds.): SPBPU IDE 2021, CCIS 1619, pp. 188–198, 2022.
https://doi.org/10.1007/978-3-031-14985-6_13

Digitalization is driving growth in many areas of business. For example, entrepreneurs now have a vast new market, new consumers, and new services. With the development of the Internet and information technology, it is now possible to provide services and do business from any corner of the globe, such as remote administration. Consumers also have an opportunity to examine offers of various manufacturers, to gather information about prices and quality of goods and services. This information is obtained from various reviews, forums, social networks, and messenger channels. Consumers have more choice, which has resulted in higher requirements to the quality of products and services.

In general, digitalization, on the one hand, increases attention to the quality of business activities and, on the other hand, calls for the use of digital technologies to create and improve the quality. However, the achievement of optimal values of quality criteria due to the effective regulation of process control parameters becomes a challenging task, as a characteristic feature of the modern business processes is the existence of many parameters that affect the level of quality criteria. Moreover, in most cases, the input parameters are latent, i.e., the change of one parameter by the operator causes a stochastic change of some other parameters.

Thus, the complexity of defining the quality of objects lies in the multi-dimensional nature of this category [1, 2], which includes a large number of indicators of various spheres of activity: economic, technical, social, image-building and other, as well as in the stochastic nature of its formation.

The above raises the problem of applying information technologies to identify the complex level of quality and its further improvement.

In this respect, the science of qualimetry is widely recognized and developed, which traditionally uses the linear convolutions [3–5] through averaging, which leads to gross errors. In this regard, such approaches are already quite outdated. Therefore, it is recommended to use the vector representation of quality, as well as the modern means of mathematical modeling and analysis [6, 7], including the neural networks, to take into account a variety of indicators.

Some scholars have described the use of neural networks [8–12]. At the same time, the methodological recommendations for the practical application of neural networks for the optimization of the quality of business activities in the digital era are insufficient. There is a need for a new mathematical model to digitize the quality criterion, which would comply with the modern concepts of the surrounding reality. The study aims to optimize the quality of business activities through the use of neural networks on the example of business activities of water treatment organizations.

The study aims to optimize the quality of business activities through the use of neural networks on the example of business activities of water treatment organizations.

Objectives of the study:

– training the neural networks to predict the activities of the water treatment plant;
– selection of the optimal neural network;
– comparison of the optimal neural network with the earlier regression model constructed without the use of neural networks to prove the advantage of the optimal neural network;

– giving recommendations on the application of the constructed neural network for optimization of the quality of entrepreneurship activity.

2   Materials and Methods

Due to the fact that the number of parameters of the quality object is measured in dozens and sometimes even hundreds, it is reasonable to present the final quality vector in the form of a multidimensional space vector, the projections of which on the corresponding coordinate axes will represent the specific scalar values of the final vector in the appropriate direction (indicator).

Therefore, by analogy with the vector of quality of products and services we will introduce the concept of the summary vector of the level of quality of business activity (or just the vector of quality) Yk, which can be represented as the resulting vector for all levels of quality of individual indicators of business activity (Y1,...,Y2).

$$\vec{Y^k}\left(Y^1, Y^2, Y^3, \ldots, Y^n\right) \tag{1}$$

We proposed a method (see Fig. 1) [13] of optimization of the quality of enterprises' activity based on the theory of fuzzy sets, the classical mathematical statistics (dispersion and regression analysis), the multi-parameter analysis, the method of main components, the vector analysis of multidimensional spaces and a number of others. Part of this method is a sequence of measures to find the optimal vector of the quality of business activity.

According to this method, the quality vector can be represented as follows.

$$\vec{Y_i^k} = F\left(\vec{Z_j^k}, \vec{V_l^k}, \vec{U_m^k}\right) \tag{2}$$

Y - multidimensional vector of quality of business activity;
Z - vector of uncontrollable parameters of business processes;
V - vector of controlled parameters of business processes;
U - vector of controlled parameters of raw materials and materials;
i, j, l, m - parameters.

That is, a multidimensional quality vector can be represented by various parameters, both uncontrollable and controllable, which in turn are divided into process and raw material parameters.

At the output, we get a model that predicts the output parameters of the quality vector. By changing the controlled parameters and taking into account uncontrollable parameters, we can influence the quality vector, trying to achieve the required parameters.

To increase the accuracy of modelling, it was suggested to use the neural networks. The most well-developed method, which puts into practice the ideology of artificial intelligence, is the use of multilayered artificial neural networks, which connect the input and output parameters of the process.

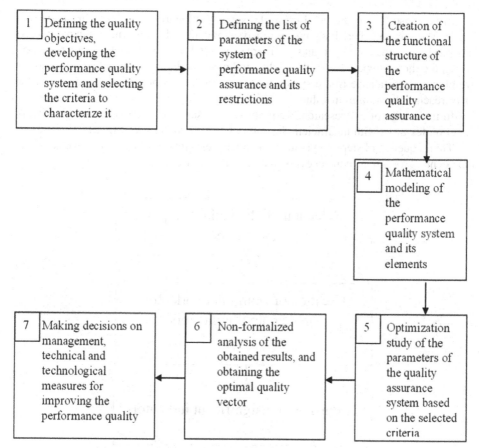

Fig. 1. A sequence of measures for finding the optimal quality vector of business activity.

The neural networks consist of the following main elements [14]:

- input layer neurons that receive signals;
- synapses that determine the weights of connections between the input and hidden neurons;
- hidden layer neurons that transform signals;
- axons that connect the hidden and output neurons;
- output layers neurons.

There are several basic approaches to teaching the neural networks - supervised learning [15], semi-supervised learning [16, 17], and unsupervised learning [18, 19].

In this case, we recommend using the supervised learning method. In the case of supervised learning, there is a predetermined set of data with input and output parameters of a particular process. The input signals are processed, and the output data are retrieved, which are then compared with those already known and an error is calculated, and the weights of significance in the synapses are adjusted. This process continues until the error reaches the minimum value.

In the course of our research, we proposed the stages of creating a neural network for complex tasks with insufficient data processing resources (see Fig. 2).

This sequence of steps can help independent researchers who do not have access to data centers (or when such access is impractical because of its cost).

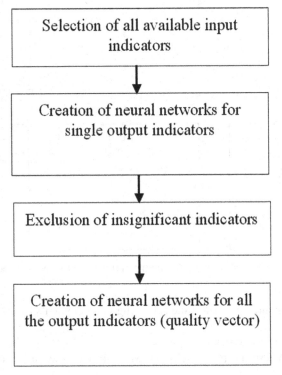

Fig. 2. Stages of creating a neural network with insufficient data processing resources.

The method has been used in various fields, including the optimization of St. Petersburg wastewater treatment [20], which is very critical for both people and the state [21].

Input indicators were taken based on the results of similar researches [22] and an array of indicators available at the wastewater treatment enterprise.

3   Results Obtained

In our case, water quality was seen as the resultant indicator of the quality of wastewater treatment business. For mathematical modeling, we have processed a set of statistical data linking the input and output variables of the study (it is possible to use applied programs such as "Statistics" and "Matlab"). Initially, the sequence of measures proposed by us was applied. A mathematical model was created in the form of regression equations describing dependencies of specific quality vector projections on the input parameters. However, the accuracy of such a model was not sufficient. That is why the neural networks were used to improve the accuracy of the model. The neural networks were constructed for single quality vector parameters. As a result, it was confirmed that some of the incoming parameters do not exert any serious influence on the quality vector and these parameters were excluded from the model. The following single parameters were used as the remaining input parameters:

X1 - turbidity;
X2 - chromaticity;
X3 - oxidation;
X4 - water consumption;
X5 - coagulant dosage;
X6 - flocculant dosage;
X7 - water temperature.

Turbidity and the content of various substances (suspended solids, nitrogen, phosphorus, and others) after water treatment were used as the single output parameters.

Python language or application package with a neural network module should be used for building neural networks.

For the turbidity index, we selected a network with configuration 7-22-1. Where 7 is the number of input parameters, 22 is the number of hidden neurons (parameters calculated based on input parameters), and 1 is the output parameter, in this case, "haziness."

The neural network has the following characteristics:

– training performance - 0.983536;
– test performance - 0.985082;
– validation performance - 0. 986970;
– hidden activation - exponential;
– output activation - logical.

The closer the first three values are to 1 and each other, the better the neural network has been trained. The last two indicators show the type of dependence.

To analyze the neural network, we also constructed an emission histogram, a scatter diagram, and analyzed the degree of impact of each parameter on the water quality. We analyzed the sensitivity of all the variables, which showed the importance of all the factors. The analysis showed that turbidity and temperature of the water supplied for treatment have a slightly higher impact on the quality of treated water.

The network architecture is shown in Fig. 3.

In the same way, we constructed neural networks for 7 more indicators.

The accuracy of these models turned out to be much higher than the accuracy of models created with other methods.

After that, we tried to construct a single neural network that would include all the output parameters.

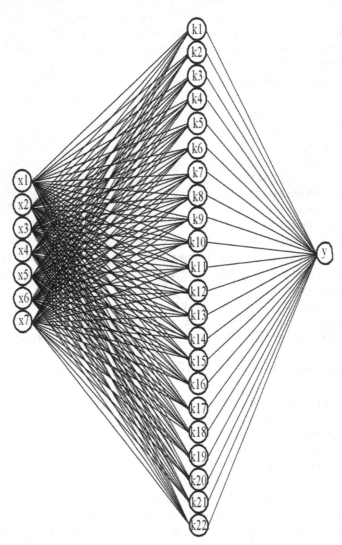

Fig. 3. Neural network architecture for configuration 7-22-1.

The following figure shows the architecture of the neural network with eight output parameters (Fig. 4).

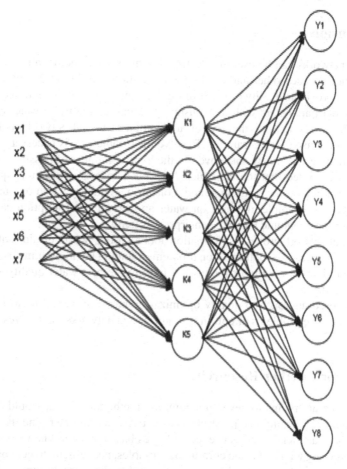

Fig. 4. Neural network architecture for configuration 7-5-8.

The accuracy of this neural network is already somewhat lower:

- training performance - 0.966460;
- test performance - 0.948329;
- validation performance - 0.933527;
- hidden activation - exponential;
- output activation - logical.

This model is simpler (not so cumbersome) for forecasting the results, but has less accuracy.

The creation of a more optimal network will require further research, which in addition to the 8 investigated indicators will include other indicators that are specified in the sanitary water treatment standards. The result can be a model that, in addition to predicting the water quality, will also provide the optimal parameters in terms of economic activity.

4 Conclusion

The neural networks can be used to identify the interrelated factors and the degree of their influence on each other and on the final result, which, in our example, makes it possible to improve the quality of water through the most optimal selection of values of controlled input parameters with the constantly changing quality of water coming for treatment. At the same time, the area of application of neural networks is limited by the range of data used for its training. To solve this problem, it is necessary to provide further training based on new data covering the highest number of possible situations.

It should be noted that the constructed neural networks of cleaning quality provide input information for building a model of business quality based on our proposed methodology. For example, the data on water and reagent consumption can serve as input data for the economic model of enterprise activity.

The neural network provides information about various possible values of input and output variables. Next, the optimization problem of finding the minimum costs to ensure a given level of water quality or the task of finding the best water quality at constant costs are solved.

The proposed approach to quality optimization based on neural networks is sufficiently unique. The problems of optimization of neural networks themselves are mainly covered [24, 25].

5 Areas for Further Research

Our further research aims to develop a common methodology that would allow us to build an optimized quality vector of business activity and to determine its parameters with the help of artificial intelligence technologies based on neural networks.

When working with latent and correlating variables, it is difficult to get unambiguous results. To improve the methodology, it is proposed to find a quality tensor [26] of the second rank. It takes into account not only the mutual influence of input variables, but also the components of the quality tensor themselves on each other, since a change in one input variable entails an avalanche-like change in all the others.

In the course of detailed elaboration of the method, it is necessary to test it in different spheres of business activity, using the solution of tasks not only of regression analysis but also of classification and clustering.

References

1. Okrepilov, V.: Quality and metrology Quality and Standards, vol. 5 pp. 47–-51 (2018)
2. Gorbashko, E.: Quality Management. Yurayt), Moscow (2016)
3. Kostin, A., Azgaldov, G.: Qualimetry - a way to quantify various intellectual products. http://www.treko.ru/show_article_2325. Accessed 10 May 2022

4. Azgaldov, G.: Theory and Practice of Goods Quality Assessment. Fundamentals of Qualimetry. http://www.labrate.ru/azgaldov/azgaldov_theory_and_practice_of_quality-assessment.pdf. Accessed 10 May 2022
5. Azgaldov, G, Kostin, A., Sadovov, V.: Qualimetry: Initial Information. https://ru.b-ok.cc/ire ader/2980486. Accessed 10 May 2022
6. Ginzburg, A.: Statistics. Piter, St. Petersburg (2013)
7. Orlov, A.: Non-Numeric Statistics, Press. M., Moscow (2004)
8. Konstantinov, M.: Brief course of machine learning or how to create a neural network to solve a scoring problem. https://habr.com/ru/post/340792/. Accessed 10 May 2022
9. Gavrilova, A.: Determination of optimal neural network parameters in the construction of mathematical models of technological processes. http://ispu.ru/files/str._87-90.pdf. Accessed 10 May 2022
10. Schaefferkoetter, J., et al.: Convolutional neural networks for improving image quality with noisy PET data. https://www.researchgate.net/publication/344343099_Convoluti onal_neural_networks_for_improving_image_quality_with_noisy_PET_data. Accessed 10 May 2022
11. De Filippo, M.: Training Neural Networks to Predict Rankings. https://towardsdatascience. com/training-neural-networks-to-predict-rankings-8a3308c472e6. Accessed 10 May 2022
12. Knocklein, O.: Classification Using Neural Networks (2019). https://towardsdatascience. com/classification-using-neural-networks-b8e98f3a904f. Accessed 10 May 2022
13. Vinogradov, L., Semyonov, V., Burylov, V.: Economic and Mathematical Methods of Quality Management. St. Petersburg State University of Engineering and Economics), St. Petersburg (2011)
14. Bunin, O.: Introduction to neural network architecture. https://habr.com/ru/company/oleg-bunin/blog/340184/. Accessed 10 May 2022
15. Belikova, K.: Supervised, semi-supervised & unsupervised learning of the neural network - what is the difference? Which algorithm is better? https://neurohive.io/ru/osnovy-data-sci ence/obuchenie-s-uchitelem-bez-uchitelja-s-podkrepleniem/. Accessed 10 May 2022
16. Kingma, D., Rezendey, D., Mohamedy, S., Welling, M.: 2014 Semi-supervised Learning with Generative Models (2014). http://papers.nips.cc/paper/5352-semi-supervised-learning-with-deep-generative-models.pdf. Accessed 10 May 2022
17. Wang, Y., Haffari, G., Wang, S., Mori, G.: A rate distortion approach for semi-supervised conditional random fields In: Advances in Neural Information Processing Systems (NIPS), pp. 2008–2016 (2009)
18. Clance, K., Graves, A.: Unsupervised learning: the curious pupil. https://deepmind.com/blog/ article/unsupervised-learning. Accessed 10 May 2022
19. Dosovitskiy, A., Springenberg, J., Riedmiller, M., Brox, T.: Discriminative Unsupervised Feature Learning with Convolutional Neural Networks. http://papers.nips.cc/paper/5548-discri minative-unsupervised-feature-learning-with-convolutional-neural-networks.pdf. Accessed 10 May 2022
20. Vinogradov, L., Gorbachev, V.: Increasing the efficiency of the wastewater treatment process in Saint-Petersburg by means of multi-criteria optimization of its parameters https://elibrary. ru/download/elibrary_29753395_74000527.pdf. Accessed 10 May 2022
21. Zaitseva, N., Sboev, A., Kleyn, S., Vekovshinina, S.: Drinking water quality: health risk factors and efficiency of control and surveillance activities by Rospotrebnadzor Health Risk Anal. **2**, 44–55 (2019)
22. Kalinin, A.: Optimization of wastewater treatment processes. https://aqua-therm.ru/articles/ articles_41.html. Accessed 10 May 2022

23. Walia, A.: Types of optimization algorithms used in neural networks and ways to optimize gradient descent. https://medium.com/nerd-for-tech/types-of-optimization-algorithms-used-in-neural-networks-and-ways-to-optimize-gradient-descent-1e32cdcbcf6c. Accessed 10 May 2022
24. Stewart, M.: Neural network optimization. https://towardsdatascience.com/neural-network-optimization-7ca72d4db3e0. Accessed 10 May 2022
25. Burylov, V., Vinogradov, L.: Process quality tensor optimization https://elibrary.ru/item.asp?id=43043704&ysclid=l3kkhoq6x1. Accessed 10 May 2022

Approach to Evaluating a Digital Company Activities Based on Intellectual Platform of Data Analysis

Igor Ilin⬤, Oksana Iliashenko⁽✉⁾ ⬤, Victoria Iliashenko⬤, and Sofia Kalyazina⬤

Peter the Great St. Petersburg Polytechnic University,
29 Polytechnicheskaya Street, St. Petersburg 195251, Russia
ioy120878@gmail.com

Abstract. During the digitalization period, each company strives to use modern technologies to improve the efficiency of its performance. Formation of a management system based on a data-driven approach is one of the priority tasks for a digital company. The introduction of appropriate digital solutions, taking into account business needs obtained from the analysis of data collected from various sources, will allow us to quickly solve the problems of providing digital services to the company's activities. Solving these problems requires a revision of the entire management system of digital company: from business services and business processes to the IT-architecture of a company. An approach has been developed for evaluating the digital company management effectiveness system based on the analysis of KPIs with using of an intelligent data analysis platform, which makes it possible to assess the effectiveness of the digital company management system according to the following parameters: to evaluate of KPI values that determine the digital company effectiveness; to evaluate of the intelligent data analysis platform implementation effectiveness. A method of integral assessment of the results of the implementation of an intelligent data analysis platform is proposed, taking into account: the effect and economic efficiency of the implementation; assessment of the quality of data processing results; technological assessment. The proposed approach to evaluating the management system of a digital company makes it possible to assess the feasibility of the goals set for the development of a digital company and to form goals for the further strategic development of the company.

Keywords: Intellectual platform · Data analysis · Digital company · Evaluating activities

1 Introduction

Modern digital companies strive to reduce time and financial costs by automating processes and implementation digital platform for management and increase business value of the company. The introduction of automated information solutions based on modern information technologies is an extremely expensive and time-consuming process, forcing the company to mobilize financial, human, and material resources [1, 2].

© Springer Nature Switzerland AG 2022
D. Rodionov et al. (Eds.): SPBPU IDE 2021, CCIS 1619, pp. 199–213, 2022.
https://doi.org/10.1007/978-3-031-14985-6_14

Modern management systems of digital companies are influenced by digital economy concept, on the one hand, and end-to-end digital technologies that ensure the implementation of digital economy concept (IoT, Big Data, blockchain, AI, etc.), with another. To achieve success in the integration of modern IT solutions, it is necessary to perform sequential actions, starting with the strategic vision of the organization's development and ending with the fundamental implementation tools [3].

The research object is digital companies, based their activities on data-driven approach.

The research subject is evaluating method of digital company management system. This method of evaluating the effectiveness of a digital company makes it possible to monitor the KPI system of a digital company using an intelligent data analysis platform integrated into the IT architecture of a medical organization. This makes it possible to assess the feasibility of the goals set for the development of a digital company [4, 5].

The paper presents several sections. First, the analysis of existing approaches to evaluating the company's activities is carried out. The features of calculating the economic effect for BI systems are described. At the next stage, the document proposes the process of forming a digital company management system based on an intelligent data analysis platform. All stages of this process are described in detail, as well as the components of instrumental support - an intelligent data analysis platform. The proposed method is then described in detail. A temporary and financial assessment of the expected effect from the implementation of this method is made.

2 Literature Review

2.1 Review of Approaches to Assessing the Effectiveness of the organization's Management Systems

The research of P. Drucker, R. Kaplan, D. Norton, I. Adizes, Taiichi Ohno, J. Collins, R.M. Yusupova [8] and others. An analysis of various interpretations and definitions of the concept of "organization management efficiency" is presenting in the works of G.N. Kalyanova, A.A. Ogarkov, P. Drucker, M.M. Panova and others.

A.A. Ogarkov in his work [9] understands the effectiveness of system management as "a relative characteristic of the performance of a particular control system, reflected in various indicators of both the object of management and the management activity itself (the subject of management), which have both quantitative and qualitative characteristics."

The issue of evaluating the effectiveness of the implementation of architectural models, information systems and information technologies currently remains debatable. This confirms the presence of a fairly large number of world-class standards and methods [9]. An analysis of various definitions of the concept of "efficiency" in relation to architectural models allows us to conclude that the formation of each architectural model based on a systematic approach. In the framework of our study, we will understand efficiency as "… a complex characteristic of a system, reflecting the degree of its compliance with the needs and interests of its customers, users, and other interested parties" [8].

The specificity of the architectural approach in the formation of an organization management system is that the goal of creating a system is presented in a formalized form through the needs of business customers, the interests of stakeholders, for example, the formation of requirements for services, for financial conditions, for the time of creating the system, for its performance, for the ability to scale, etc. This makes it possible to determine the effectiveness of the architectural model of organization management as the degree of compliance of the organization management system with the goals for which this system was created [10].

Such an understanding of the effectiveness of the architectural management model makes it possible to take into account a number of parameters: performance, economic efficiency of the system and other factors, the relevance and need to take into account which is individual, depending on the industry specifics of the organization. There are the following aspects of system efficiency [10]:

– the assessment of the effectiveness of the system is relevant in a given time period, sensitive to changes in the external and internal environment (for example, changes in the requirements of business customers, technologies used, etc.);
– assessment of the effectiveness of the system (information, communication, industry) in terms of assessing this system in achieving the stated goals of the organization.

The current international standards for the life cycle processes of IS and software products (ISO/IEC 12207) and systems of a more general nature (ISO/IEC 15288) describe an approach to understanding the effectiveness of information systems, similar to the approach presented above. In GOSTs GOST R 56875-2016 "Information technologies. complex and integrated security systems", GOST R ISO/IEC 12207-2010 "Information technology. System and software engineering. Software Life Cycle Processes" gives a similar semantic understanding of efficiency.

Consider the standards that describe approaches to evaluating the effectiveness of information systems.

In the Russian Federation, standards of several generations are currently in force. In this regard, the traditions in information systems design management that took place 20 years ago are to preserve, while these standards are gradually being replacing by a new idea of managing the life cycle of information systems based on modern standards.

Standards GOST 24.202:80 and GOST 34 describe a feasibility study (FS) as a method for evaluating efficiency. The feasibility study is one of the components of the system-wide technical documentation. At the same time, the work process described in these standards does not take into account the orientation of ongoing projects to modern standards and methods of project management and efficiency assessment methods, which leads to certain limitations in the use of these standards.

As result of the information systems development for e-government, socio-economic systems, regulatory and reference documents "Social and Economic Justification" (SEA), "Financial and Economic Justification" (FEO) appeared. This was due to the following factors:

– when implementing projects, initiatives for commercial and government organizations, it is advisable to use a combination of methods for determining the effectiveness and efficiency of the implementation of information systems that provide IT support for the organization's activities;

– the formation of goals and performance indicators, taking into account the specifics of socially-oriented organizations, which is expressed in the priorities of social effects (for example, medical and social effects for medical organizations) and in the limitations (but not exclusion) of economic effects, associated with profitability.

All of the above led to the formation of modern software and system engineering standards ISO/IEC 12207 and ISO/IEC 15288, ISO 9000. Many experts involved in the practical use of standards in the design and implementation of information systems express the opinion that it is advisable to integrate and gradually develop old and new standards.

In the ISO 9000 standard, "efficiency" was define as the relationship between the result achieved and the resources used.

Let us consider the features of evaluating the effectiveness of architectural models for managing organizations.

Modeling an organization management system based on the architectural approach involves taking into account the following aspects [11, 12]:

– complex engineering of the target state of the organization's architecture;
– application of architectural principles, methods and reference models and evaluation criteria, which makes it possible to select an architectural solution from the existing library of architectural solutions in accordance with the set goals;
– evaluation of the effectiveness of architectural models based on the models of information systems and technologies efficiency used in practice, allowing to apply the appropriate methodology for the formation of an investment portfolio in the organization's IT architecture: FEA PRM (IT efficiency/efficiency model for US government agencies), FOSTAS IT efficiency metamodel;
– a library of architectural models that provide the possibility of choosing a solution taking into account the specifics of the industry and the given restrictions and requirements;
– architectural modeling, which provides a formalization of the representation and verification of the complex architecture of the organization;
– calculation of the values of critical parameters of the proposed architectural models by detailing the architecture of the enterprise to justify the decision in favor of a particular model;
– formation of the transformation trajectory of the organization's architecture, taking into account the level of detail of various states depending on the time (when the implementation of the architectural model is planned).

The considered approaches make it possible to assess the effectiveness of information systems implementation, justify the feasibility of using architectural models for company management. However, they do not allow to fully take into account the specifics of the activities of a digital company that uses modern technologies for company management: digitalization of processes, monitoring of the organization's activities based on data analysis and predictive analysis with using machine learning technologies, innovative technologies for managing products and services.

2.2 The Business Value Evaluating of the Intelligent Data Analysis Platform Implementation

The main problem with evaluating the business value of IT systems is that they do not generate profit [13–15]. Additional value can only be to obtain if they are using correctly through the following effects:

- reducing of time spent on the implementation of actions;
- rejecting of part of the routine operations that require the involvement of human resources.

Not all results of the implementation of IT solutions can be digitalizing. Allocate intangible (immeasurable, qualitative) effects from the implementation of an IT solution, for example:

- improving the quality of management decisions by improving the quality of data, as a result of the analysis of which decisions are made;
- increasing employee satisfaction;
- improving the efficiency of decision-making processes through the transparency of automated processes.

Such effects are typical for all classes of systems, however, for business intelligence system (BI system), these effects are the main ones. This is due to the fact for BI systems the share of intangible benefits is significantly higher than for systems of other classes. The complexity of evaluating the effectiveness of business intelligence systems is due to the fact the effect of their use depends significantly on the "human factor", because the system only provides information, and the decision is making by the person himself based on the analyzed metrics.

Given the complexity of evaluating the effectiveness of analytical reporting systems, it is correct to speak only about the expected economic effect obtained through the information system using. To what extent this effect will be use fully depends on the users.

The problem of assessing the economic effect of the introduction of business intelligence has not been fully resolved to date [16, 17].

3 Methods

This section analyzes the activities of the company and the process of monitoring the technical condition of components.

The theoretical research basis is the architectural methodology of organization management, based on the TOGAF standard, approaches to the formation of digital business models of an organization based on the development and implementation of digital platforms, as well as the theoretical foundations of business process automation and data management.

The methodological research basis are general scientific methods, comparative analysis, the TOGAF architectural standard [6] and the data management body of knowledge (DAMA-DMBOK) [7].

3.1 The Process of Forming a Management System for a Digital Company Based on an Intelligent Data Analysis Platform

The intelligent data analysis platform of a digital company is focused on the use of modern data analytics technologies: technologies for the formation of primary analytics and data preparation, machine learning technologies used in the processing and research of big data, information visualization technologies using business intelligence systems. The platform is a tool that provides an opportunity to improve the management system of a digital company.

The process of forming a management system for a digital company based on an intelligent data analysis platform you can see in Fig. 1.

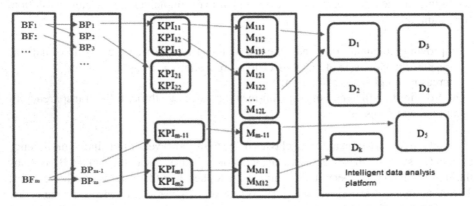

Fig. 1. The process of forming a management system for a digital company based on an intelligent data analysis platform: conceptual level. Source: compiled by the authors

Each business function BF_1, BF_2, BF_3,..., BF_n, implemented by a digital company, is carried out within the framework of one or more business processes BP_1, BP_2, BP_3,..., BP_m. For example, lets the business function BF_1 be implemented in the cancers of the business process BP1, which is characterized by three indicators KPI_{11}, KPI_{12}, KPI_{13}. Each indicator is describing by metrics, for example, KPI_{11} is described by metrics M_{111}, M_{112}, M_{113}. Visualization of metrics is carried out using data marts D_1, D_2, D_3,... D_k, developed using an intelligent data analysis platform. In one data mart, metrics describing different KPIs can be visualizing.

An intelligent data analysis platform integrated into the general management system of a digital company was chosen as a tool for implementing analytics of the KPI system. The data analysis platform assumes the availability of tools for collecting, transforming, integrating and loading data from various sources, data management tools, front-end services that ensure customer interaction with the platform.

The intelligent data analysis platform consist of the following modules:

– Data Lake of a digital company, which houses large amounts of heterogeneous data generated or collected by the company. The data is structured when a request is made to unload from the lake for analysis. At this moment, the user determines what data he needs and for what purposes. This technology allows you to operate with very large amounts of data and get access to them very quickly, which traditional data warehouses cannot provide;

– data management system that allows you to achieve "transparency" of receiving data in the final marts, the ability to form chains of data origin, receive and send data to external systems and consumers, subject to the data confidentiality policy defined in the medical organization;
– services like cloud applications, mobile applications for the personnel of the company and for clients, analytical reporting for personnel, and interfaces for integration into large digital platforms to form a community of a digital ecosystem.

The data management system integrates all the information about the data:

– data owners;
– methods for calculating analytics and indicators;
– registry of BI applications and their descriptions;
– a list of data sources connected to the data lake of a company, and their descriptions;
– the origin of data from the source system to the data lake showcase or BI application;
– a register of data quality metrics in the data lake of a company.

The data management system includes a set of interrelated components: enterprise data catalog, business glossary, analytics module, data quality module.

The workflow of an intelligent data analysis platform consist of the five stages. At the first stage, a variety of data (structured, semi-structured and unstructured) is obtained from various sources. Data sources can be accounting systems (ERP, CRM, MES, etc.), streaming data generated as a result of the operation of IoT devices, etc., data coming from internal and external (insurance companies, companies that supply and service equipment) partners, etc. The data flow to the Data Lake. The next step is to extract, transform and load data using ETL technologies. Further - the formation of layers of large data arrays (layers of processing, data consolidation, data storage layer) with the subsequent formation of data marts. At this stage, the tasks of metadata management, tracking the chain of origin of data, monitoring data quality are implementing. The final stage is the visualization stage, which includes the generation of reports, dashboards (web) or mobile dashboards that are using by end users (staff, clients).

The formed system of indicators of the activity of a medical organization is analyzing by means of an intellectual platform. The results of the analysis are providing to users as data showcases developed by means of the BI tool.

Developing a BI application layout involves the following steps [18]:

– definition of the list of metrics to be displayed in the BI system;
– choice of BI-system;
– aggregation of data from various sources;
– data model development;
– data marts development.

3.2 A Method for Assessing the Effectiveness of the Management System of a High-Tech Medical Organization Based on KPI Analysis by Means of an Intelligent Data Analysis Platform

The study proposes a method for evaluating the effectiveness of a digital company management system based on KPI analysis using an intelligent data analysis platform. The proposed method allows evaluating the effectiveness of the management system of a digital company in terms of the following parameters:

(1) assessment of KPI values that determine the effectiveness of the digital company;
(2) evaluation of the effectiveness of the intelligent data analysis platform implementation. A methodology for the integral assessment of the results of the intelligent data analysis platform implementation is proposed, taking into account:

   – effect and economic efficiency from implementation;
   – assessment of the quality of data processing results;
   – technology assessment.

4 Results

4.1 Assessment of KPI Target Values Level for Determine the Effectiveness of a Digital Company

We offer an approach to evaluating KPI indicators that evaluate the performance of a digital company. The assessment of KPI values achievement were carry out on the comparison of the values with the target and threshold values of the indicators. The KPI target is the percentage of the KPI level required to assess the scope of a process that has a particular KPI as usable ("good"). The KPI threshold represents the percentage level below which the KPI process requires serious attention and possibly adjustments. KPI values below the threshold value mean that this requirement is not met and provide for the search for causes, the adoption and implementation of management decisions. The proposed method for assessing KPI indicators has been practically testing in different companies (a state medical organization providing high-tech medical care, an oil company, logistic company, etc.) [19–22]. An example of a template and a report based on the results of the assessment of the KPI "Department staff load" you can see in Tables 1, 2.

Table 1. Table template for evaluating KPI values. Source: compiled by the authors

ID	Reporting period	Target value KPI	Threshold value KPI	Fact value KPI	Data transfer author	Departure date	Not matching the target value
118026	05-Oct-2021	95%	85%	97%	Ivanov I.I	05-Oct-2021	5

Table 1 presents a proposed option for evaluating KPI values with parameters: target, threshold, actual KPI value, reporting period, sample size, exclusions, author of information transfer, date of information submission. The sample size refers to the number of analyzed rows that contain data on process metric values. The "Does not match the target value" column indicates the number of sample rows containing data whose values do not correspond to the specified target values of the KPI metrics.

Table 2. Report on the results of the assessment of KPI "Department staff load". Source: compiled by the authors

ID	Reporting period	Target value KPI	Threshold value KPI	Fact value KPI	Data transfer author	Departure date	Not matching the target value
118026	05-Oct-2021	95%	85%	97%	Ivanov I.I	05-Oct-2021	5
118026	05-Oct-2021	95%	85%	97%	Ivanov I.I	05-Oct-2021	10
116006	28-Sep-2021	95%	85%	97%	Ivanov I.I	28-Sep-2021	10
113911	21-Sep-2021	95%	85%	97%	Ivanov I.I	21-Sep-2021	5
111756	14-Sep-2021	95%	85%	97%	Ivanov I.I	14-Sep-2021	5
109609	07-Sep-2021	95%	85%	97%	Ivanov I.I	07-Sep-2021	8
107485	31-Aug-2021	95%	85%	98%	Ivanov I.I	31-Aug-2021	0

Methodology for calculating actual KPI values
Let KPI1 was evaluating by metrics M1 and M2. The actual values of the M1 metric were obtaining based on the analysis of n records for the reporting period t. The values of the M2 metric were obtaining based on the analysis of m records for the reporting period t. The methodology for calculating the actual value of KPI1 is as follows:

1) to find the actual value of the metric M_1 for the reporting period t:

$$M_1\text{fact} = \frac{\sum_{j=1}^{n} m_{1j}}{n} \tag{1}$$

2) to find the actual value of the metric M_2 for the reporting period t:

$$M_2\text{fact} = \frac{\sum_{j=1}^{m} m_{2j}}{m} \tag{2}$$

3) to find the actual value of the KPI_1 for the reporting period t:

$$KPI_1 \text{ fact} = a_1 * M_1 \text{fact} + a_2 * M_2 \text{fact}, \tag{3}$$

where a1 and a2 are weights that allow taking into account the contribution of each metric to the formation of the actual value of KPI1:

$$a_1 = \frac{n}{n+m}, a_2 = \frac{m}{n+m}, \quad 0 < a_1 < 1, 0 < a_2 < 1, \tag{4}$$

Generalizing the proposed method, we obtain a formula for calculating the actual value of KPIk, determined by p metrics M1, M2,..., Mp.

$$KPI_k \text{fact} = \sum_{i=1}^{p} a_i * M_i \text{fact}, \tag{5}$$

$$M_i \text{fact} = \frac{\sum_{j=1}^{n} m_{ij}}{n}, \tag{6}$$

where n is the number of records mij that determine the value of the metric Mi.

$$a_i = \frac{n}{\sum_{n=1}^{p} n} 0 < a_i < 1, \tag{7}$$

where n is the number of records that determine the value of the metric Mi, p is the number of metrics that determine KPIk.

4.2 Evaluation of the Effectiveness of the Implementation of an Intelligent Data Analysis Platform

The proposed methodology for the integrated assessment of the results of implementation, taking into account:

1. The effect and cost-effectiveness of implementation

Difficulties in assessing the effectiveness of intelligent data analysis platforms and business intelligence systems (as a component of the platform) are associated with the fact that the effect of their use is highly dependent on the "human factor", since the system only provides information, and the decision is made by the person himself on the basis of the analyzed metrics. In this regard, it is correct to speak only about the expected economic effect obtained through the information system using. The effect of implementing business intelligence systems in digital companies can be quantitative or qualitative. Table 3 presents the main characteristics of the information analysis process when implementing a business intelligence system [22, 23].

Table 3. Comparison of key metrics of the processes of preparation and analysis of information before and after the implementation of a business intelligence system. Source: compiled by the authors

Description of characteristics	Time to complete the process	
	Before implementation	After implementation
ETL-process	1–2 months	1.5–3 h
Frequency of work with analytical applications	Once a week/once a month (depending on the department)	At least once a day
Time spent on document analysis	6–8 h	30 min–1.5 h (depending on the department and specialist) for 1 report

Table 4. Expected profit from the implementation of a business intelligence system. Source: compiled by the authors

Name of the source of expense, income	Income (rub/year)	Expense (rub/year)
Other sources	130 889 000	24 000 000
Implementation of a business intelligence system	35 279 000	16 514 000
Costs for other expenses	166 168 000	59 910 000

To calculate the ROI and PP indicators, it is necessary to find the values of the expected profit after the implementation of the business intelligence system in the company (Table 4) for a period of one year. When implementing a business intelligence system, the costs of the IT component of a medical organization increase by 16,514,000 rubles.

Thus, the expected income from investments in the development of a business intelligence system of the company (NP) is equal to [24]:

$$NP = 35279000 - 16514000(rub/year) \tag{8}$$

Based on the results, we calculate ROI and PP indicators:

$$ROI = \frac{35279000 - 16514000}{16514000} * 100\% = 110\% = 1,1\left(year^{-1}\right) \tag{9}$$

$$PP = \frac{16514000}{18765000} = 0,88(year) \approx 10,6(months) \tag{10}$$

This result suggests that in one planning interval (year), in the form of profit of a medical organization, 120% of investment costs will be reimbursing potentially. Those, project profitability indicator (ROI) = 110%, which indicates the economic feasibility of this project (project profitability should be >25%).

Thus, we can say that the costs of implementing a business intelligence system will potentially pay off in about 10.6 months. Based on the analysis of key indicators for assessing the effectiveness of the implementation of a business intelligence system, we can say that the implementation of a business intelligence system in a medical organization is an economical IT project with a payback period of less than one year.

2. Assessment of the data quality of processing results

Data is a strategic asset for a high-tech healthcare organization. Data quality is a characteristic of data that indicates how the data meets the established requirements of business users for indicators of their quality. Data quality metric - data properties reflecting their correctness and applicability for use by business users. The metric value is a value from 0 to 1 that reflects how much of the data from the considered dataset must obey a specific business rule.

Data health is a generalized indicator of the level of data quality of a digital company. It is expressed as the average value (formula (6)), of all data quality metrics (formula (12)), calculated based on the results of the implementation of technical rules on data quality (formula (11)).

$$Dc = \frac{Rc - Rm}{Rc},$$ (11)

where
Rc – records checked, pcs,
Rm – records with errors, pcs,
Dc – verified data, discrete indicator values in the range 0..1

$$Qd = \frac{\sum_{n=1}^{n} Dc_n}{n}$$ (12)

where
Qd – metric data quality,
n – number of checks related to the metric

$$DH = \frac{\sum_{k=1}^{k} Qd_k}{k}$$ (13)

where
DH – Data Health,
k – number of metrics involved.

3. Technological assessment.

The presence of an intelligent data analysis platform provides the possibility of further implementation of modern technologies (IoT, machine learning, etc.), which increases the value of a digital company and is one of the criteria for its assessment among other organizations.

From these calculations, it follows that the introduction of a predictive maintenance system is expedient in this company.

5   Conclusion

This paper discusses the approach to evaluate the effectiveness of the management system of a digital company based on KPI analysis by means of an intelligent data analysis platform. The proposed approach makes it possible to assess the effectiveness of the management system of a digital company according to the following parameters:

- assessment of the achievement of target KPI values, that determine the effectiveness of a high-tech medical organization;
- assessment the effectiveness of the implementation of an intelligent data analysis platform. The proposed methodology for the integrated assessment of the results of implementation, taking into account the effect and economic efficiency of the implementation, assessment of the quality of data processing results, technological assessment.

As a direction for further research, we can consider the formation of reference architectural models for managing digital company, taking into account the level of maturity of an intelligent data analysis platform in accordance with the Gartner analytics evolution model. Each level of maturity presupposes the use of appropriate methods and tools for data analysis, and, as a result, the development of an intelligent platform architecture. The level of maturity of an intelligent data analysis platform is one of the indicators of digitalization of a company and provides a further opportunity to improve the business value for the company.

The results of the presented study are unique, based on the studies presented in the DAMA-DMBOOK standard. These results confirm a number of achievements presented in the standard, which brings together the best practices for data management and implementation of data-driven approach in organizations.

References

1. Antonov, A., Iliashenko, V., Anselm, R.: Current state of MES systems development in the digital economy. In: ACM International Conference Proceeding Series (2020)
2. Iliashenko, V., Filippova, K., Overes, E., Iliashenko, O.: The modelling of intelligent transport system architecture based on big data technologies. In: Proceedings of the 33rd International Business Information Management Association Conference, IBIMA 2019: Education Excellence and Innovation Management through Vision 2020, pp. 8553–8561 (2019)
3. Pavlov, N., Kalyazina, S., Bagaeva, I., Iliashenko, V.: Key digital technologies for national business environment. In: Advances in Intelligent Systems and Computing, vol. 1259, pp. 143–157. AISC (2021)
4. Ilin, I.V., Levina, A.I., Lepekhin, A.A.: Reference model of service-oriented IT architecture of a healthcare organization. In: Arseniev, D.G., Overmeyer, L., Kälviäinen, H., Katalinić, B. (eds.) CPS&C 2019. LNNS, vol. 95, pp. 681–691. Springer, Cham (2020). https://doi.org/10.1007/978-3-030-34983-7_67
5. Barreto, L., Amaral, A., Pereira. T.: Industry 4.0 implications in logistics: an overview. Procedia Manuf. **13**, 1245–1252 (2017). https://doi.org/10.1016/j.promfg.2017.09.045
6. Lankhorst, M.M.: Enterprise architecture modelling – the issue of integration [Текст]. Adv. Eng. Inform. **18**(4), 205–216 (2004)

7. Henderson, D.: Data Management Body of Knowledge. 2nd edn. Bradley Beach, New Jersey (2020)
8. Yusupov, R.M., Musaev, A.A.: On the evaluation of the effectiveness of information systems: methodological aspects. Inf. Technol. **23**(5), 323–332 (2017)
9. Management efficiency: how to measure, evaluate and achieve it [Electronic resource]. http://www.elitarium.ru/ehffektivnost-upravleniya-sistema-organizaciya-deyatelnost-pok azatel-rabotnik-rabota-dostizhenie-rezultat-zatrata-navyk-umenie-ocenka-kachestvo-kri terij. Accessed 19 Mar 2022
10. Anisiforov, A.B.: Basic principles of formation, development and operation Information infrastructure of the enterprise in solving problems information management. Sci. J. NRU ITMO Ser. Econ. Environ. Manag. **3**(38). https://doi.org/10.17586/2310-1172-2019-12-3-128-136
11. Ilin, I.V., Iliashenko, O.Yu., Levina, A.I.: Application of service-oriented approach to business process reengineering. In: Proceedings of the 28th IBIMA, pp. 768–781 (2016)
12. Andreevsky, I.L., Sokolov, R.V., Tumarev, V.M.: Comparative analysis of the economic efficiency of traditional and cloud information systems. In: Proceedings of the St. Petersburg State University of Economics, vol. 3, No. 117, pp. 100–104 (2019)
13. Business Intelligence: Strengths, Weaknesses, and Opportunities. https://www.igi-global.com/chapter/business-intelligence/261940. Accessed 21 Mar 2022
14. Mogilko, D., Iliashenko, O., Ilin, I., Iliashenko, V.: The value creation chain: diagnostic restrictions and challenges. In: Journal of Physics: Conference Series. Сер. "International Scientific Conference Energy Management of Municipal Facilities and Sustainable Energy Technologies, p. 012029 (2020)
15. Iliashenko, O.Y., Iliashenko, V.M., Dubgorn, A.: IT-architecture development approach in implementing BI-systems in medicine. In: Arseniev, D.G., Overmeyer, L., Kälviäinen, H., Katalinić, B. (eds.) CPS&C 2019. LNNS, vol. 95, pp. 692–700. Springer, Cham (2020). https://doi.org/10.1007/978-3-030-34983-7_68
16. Business Intelligence: Challenges and Opportunities. https://egade.tec.mx/en/egade-ideas/opi nion/business-intelligence-challenges-and-opportunities. Accessed 11 Mar 2022
17. Bruskin, S.N.: Methods and tools of advanced business analytics for corporate information and analytical systems in the era of digital transformation. Sci. Anal. J. Sci. Pract. Russian Econ. Univ. G.V. Plekhanov. **10** (29) (2018)
18. Lars, B., Troyansky, O.: **Q**likview Your Business. An Expert Guide to Business Discovery with QlikView and Qlik Sense. John Wiley & Sons Limited (2015)
19. Mourtzis, D., Vlachou, E.: A cloud-based cyber-physical system for adaptive shop-floor scheduling and condition-based maintenance. J. Manuf. Syst. **47**, 179–198 (2018). https://doi.org/10.1016/j.jmsy.2018.05.008
20. Shlyakhto, E.V., et al.: Management of a Medical Organization: The Concept of Smart Hospital. Peter the Great St. Petersburg Polytechnic University, St. Petersburg (2020)
21. Iliashenko, V.M.: Digital platforms as an interface for sectoral interaction of enterprises. In: Ilyin, I.V., Iliashenko, V.M., Levina, A.I. (eds.) In the Collection: Digital Technologies in Logistics and Infrastructure. Materials of the International Conference. St. Petersburg, 315–321 (2021)
22. Problems Solved by Business Intelligence (BI) Solutions. https://addepto.com/8-problems-solved-by-business-intelligence-bi-solutions/. Accessed 10 Mar 2022
23. Ilin, I.V., Rostova, O.V.: Methods and models of investment management: a textbook for universities in the direction of training masters System analysis and management. In: Educational and educational-methodical literature (2017)

24. Iliashenko, V.M.: Evaluation of the effectiveness of the implementation of the analytical reporting system at the enterprise. In: In the Collection: Priority Areas of Innovation in Industry. Collection of Scientific Articles on the Results of an International Scientific Conference. - NPP Medpromdetal, pp. 269–272 (2021)
25. Gartner data analysis tools maturity model (2022) https://training.pwc.ru/upload/docs/F2_Gartner_Model.pdf. Accessed 10 Jan 2022

Reference Model of Digital Business-Architecture of Geographically Distributed Medical Organizations

Anastasia Levina, Alisa Dubgorn, Alexandra Borremans(✉),
and Evgenia Kseshinski

Peter the Great St. Petersburg Polytechnic University, Polytechnicheskaya 29,
195351 St. Petersburg, Russia
alexandra.borremans@mail.ru

Abstract. Currently, the healthcare sector is undergoing a digital transformation as one of the most important elements of society. Private and public medical companies have begun to actively develop and implement various digital technologies and solutions in their business processes. In such a situation, it is important to move away from the patchwork implementation of systems and take a step towards complex architectural structures, including a set of integrated solutions. The reference model of information technologies for geographically distributed medical organizations can help with this. The purpose of the study is to consider existing information technologies, their use abroad and in Russia within the framework of healthcare for integration into a single information system at the level of business architecture. This study considers information technologies such as Big Data, Artificial Intelligence, the Internet of Medical Things, Virtual and Augmented Reality, used both in Russian medical institutions and around the world. The article reveals a reference model for the use of information technology in terms of the need to simplify the management of geographically distributed organizations and improve the efficiency of medical services. When building the reference model, an architectural approach was used. This article discusses various ways in which modern healthcare information technologies can be used to improve the quality of direct care, increase benefits for commercial organizations, reduce costs for government enterprises, and improve user experience for patients.

Keywords: Digitalization · Healthcare · Information technologies · Medical information system

1 Introduction

Currently, the health sector is undergoing active changes. The situation of recent years related to the pandemic has shown how important it is to carry out a general digital transformation in the field of Russian healthcare. When a record number of cases of the new Covid-19 virus infection was registered across the country, the existing system experienced enormous strains, which became bottlenecks in the process of providing

© Springer Nature Switzerland AG 2022
D. Rodionov et al. (Eds.): SPBPU IDE 2021, CCIS 1619, pp. 214–223, 2022.
https://doi.org/10.1007/978-3-031-14985-6_15

timely medical care. However, the use of modern information technologies, such as the Gosuslugi portal and voice assistants based on the Unified State Health Information System, made it possible to cope with high patient traffic and showed significant results, allowing patients to be registered remotely, thereby balancing the resources of medical organizations.

In recent decades, the digital development of healthcare has been actively supported in Russia, the latest information technologies have been developed and implemented. These include: medical information systems (MIS), telemedicine, Artificial Intelligence, Internet of Medical Things, VR/AR. However, it should be noted that the number of medical organizations that have effectively implemented information technologies in their processes is not enough to talk about the general transformation of medicine at the moment. Nevertheless, MIS is currently the most common technology used in Russian healthcare.

The introduction of digital solutions, in general, makes it possible to simplify the decision-making process, optimize routine processes and reduce costs, which is relevant for both federal projects and private organizations. Therefore, it is important to consider the digitalization of healthcare from two sides: as an increase in the efficiency of patient care and the quality of medical services provided, as well as economic benefits for organizations. It should be noted that for medical information technologies, due to the peculiarity of existing business processes, more demanding development criteria are formed (the quality of life and the life of the patient depend on the adoption of medical decisions). In this regard, such systems are subject to more stringent requirements to ensure uninterrupted operation and data confidentiality.

The state healthcare system is a decentralized system of executive authorities and organizations providing medical services to the population, geographically distributed throughout the Russian Federation. There are also large private clinics that have branches and various departments throughout the country. Such network organizations are usually called geographically distributed, that is, their branches can be located in different territorial units, but all will be under a single management system [1]. For such institutions, the benefits and even the need to use modern IT platforms for making medical and managerial decisions to optimize work are especially obvious, since the management of decentralized companies is much more difficult than centralized ones due to geographical distance, which causes difficulties in communication and standardization of documentation, rules of work and services [2]. Among other things, the importance of integrating standard MIS is explained by the need to store, process, systematize and work with a large amount of data that is inevitable for medical practice [3]. Simplification of the workflow process will improve the quality and efficiency of medical care, as well as reduce economic costs [4]. It is also important to note that modern medicine is guided by such concepts as value-based medicine, personalized medicine and Health 4.0, which can be implemented, among other things, through the introduction of MIS integrated with other technologies [5].

At the moment, there are many products on the MIS market that are suitable for most medical organizations. MIS can be roughly divided into two broad groups: administrative and systems involved in clinical processes. Administrative systems are not much different from common ERP systems, therefore, in this study, only systems belonging to the second group are considered. Also, based on the architectural and functional features, the following levels of development of the MIS functionality can be distinguished: minimum functionality, basic functionality and extended functionality [6]. However, there are narrow-profile clinics that require special functionality in MIS, which is not supported by the most common and widely used MIS. This, in turn, makes it impossible for narrow-profile clinics or certain branches of network clinics to be in a single configuration with a large number of medical institutions throughout the country, which is very important for such a large territorial unit as Russia. This causes the problem of synchronizing data about patients who applied to different organizations. This problem resurrects the difficulties that information technologies had to solve within the framework of routine processes: multiple filling out applications, retelling the medical history from the patient's words, storing data on paper, and so on. Nevertheless, it is worth noting that the main item of expenditure of the federal budget in 2019–2024. is the development and implementation of various information systems for regional healthcare, provided for by the federal program "Creating a single digital contour in the field of healthcare based on the Unified State Health Information System", which means that this sector is extremely promising, and its tasks are relevant [7].

This study will review and analyze the work of medical organizations in Russia using information technology, as well as a comparison with countries with a high level of digitalization of medicine in order to develop and propose a reference digital business architecture for medical organizations to integrate into the digitalization process of the country as a whole.

2 Materials and Methods

In preparing this study, a systematic review of publications and sites on the Internet, as well as publications in bibliographic databases on the topic of modern information technologies and their application in domestic medical organizations and abroad was used.

Moreover, an important basis of the research is the concept of enterprise architecture in general and business architecture in particular. An enterprise architecture is a conceptual blueprint that defines the structure and operation of organizations. The goal of an enterprise architecture is to define how an organization can effectively achieve its current and future goals. Enterprise architecture includes the practice of analyzing, planning, designing, and ultimately analyzing an enterprise. Business architecture is a layer of enterprise architecture, which is an interconnected set of principles, methods and models that are used in the design and formation of organizational and role structures and business processes [8, 9]. Accordingly, business architecture is an essential component for modeling the efficient operation of modern organizations. Considering that healthcare is an important element of the social sphere and the economy, necessary for the functioning of society, as well as the unprecedented demand for these services among the population, the importance of having a reference model for medical organizations becomes obvious. The digital business architecture consists of IT solutions for organizations that need to modernize business processes. For medical organizations, certain stringent requirements are introduced to create a digital business architecture, since the activities of such organizations are directly related to human life and health [9].

This paper discusses various ways to use modern information technologies used in healthcare to improve the quality of direct treatment, increase benefits for commercial organizations, reduce costs for public enterprises and improve user experience for patients.

3 Results

Among the latest information technologies that are actively being introduced into medical organizations in this study, the following will be consistently considered: Big Data, Artificial Intelligence, Internet of Medical Things, Virtual and Augmented reality.

3.1 Big Data

Thanks to the active development of the science of Big Data, the knowledge gained is currently being applied in medicine. In Russia today, the active use of big data technology is mainly used to monitor people vaccinated against Covid-19, as well as to generate a heat map of the sick, which is published on the site stopcoronavirus.rf [10].

The world leader in the development and implementation of Big Data technologies in healthcare today is the United States. Organizations in health care are in no hurry to introduce this technology everywhere, despite the objective economic benefits and increased treatment efficiency. However, several companies in the US are already using Big Data. For example, Dignity Health, one of the largest medical organizations in the United States, is developing a cloud platform for processing big data obtained from the analysis of clinical, social, and behavioral characteristics of patients. Technologies developed by the company allow data to be collected and shared among nearly 40 hospitals and more than 9,000 healthcare providers [11]. Activities in the field of application of Big Data technology have a significant positive effect in preventive and predictive medical functions, which reduces the overall levels of morbidity, hospitalization and mortality.

Thus, despite the obvious financial benefits and improving the quality of treatment, Big Data technology is rarely used in healthcare. However, this technology is at the forefront of digitalization trends in healthcare around the world.

3.2 Artificial Intelligence

Along with Big Data technology, over the past decade, ways to use Artificial Intelligence (AI) in healthcare have been actively studied. The use of Artificial Intelligence is due to statistical data, according to which about a quarter of deaths are due to medical errors in the incorrect diagnosis [12, 13]. This is due to the impossibility of a person to know and remember all medical cases that have occurred in the history of mankind. However, Artificial Intelligence can do it: AI can study thousands of pages of medical publications all over the Internet per minute. In 2020, the development of Artificial Intelligence technology for diagnosing the level of health in order to create an individual rehabilitation program was introduced into the practice of medicine. The developer of the technology, the Institute of Automation and Control Processes of the Russian Academy of Sciences, used a method based on the principles of Artificial Intelligence, which allows diagnosing a person's physical and mental health. The use of this technology should increase the efficiency of medical care and preserve the health of citizens. To date, the following decision support systems for healthcare based on Artificial Intelligence methods have been created: diagnostics, analysis and selection of appropriate treatment, patient monitoring, accumulation of medical data and knowledge generation to optimize the decision-making process.

Abroad, thanks to more private investment and companies, modern technologies are now being used more widely. In the UK, a development from Deepmind Health is already being used. This development processes the patient's medical history, collects similar cases on the Internet and issues treatment recommendations to the attending physician. There are also programs designed not for doctors, but for patients, having a similar algorithm of work: the user enters his symptoms, and the program issues a preliminary analysis [14].

Summarizing the above, the Artificial Intelligence method can significantly improve the healthcare sector by reducing the human factor in the process of making a diagnosis and choosing a treatment method. But given the degree of responsibility placed on the tasks for AI, the full implementation of this technology requires a particularly precise and phased approach.

3.3 Internet of Medical Things

The Internet of Medical Things (IoMT) at this stage of development is most associated with telemedicine - IoMT is now mainly used in Russia for remote monitoring of patients. The main driver for the implementation of IoMT and telemedicine technologies is a pilot project from the Ministry of Health of the Russian Federation to introduce in a number of regions remote monitoring of patients with arterial hypertension, who have a very high risk of developing cardiovascular complications [15]. During the pilot, patients were given a telemedicine kit - a tonometer with a GSM connection, which itself transmitted data to the federal center for remote monitoring. In the event of a deterioration in the condition of the participants in the experiment, the staff of the center contacted the patient and urged him to call an ambulance or contact his doctor. As a result, for example, according to the Ministry of Health of the Belgorod Region, remote monitoring has reduced the number of requests for medical care by such patients in the region by 40%, and by another 17% the number of ambulance calls diagnosed with hypertension. In private practice, the most common use case for IoMT is smartwatches with health monitoring functions.

In Western practice, IoMT is used for the following purposes: remote health monitoring, medication tracking, medical asset monitoring, smart hospital space, personal health monitoring devices [16].

3.4 Virtual and Augmented Reality

Virtual and Augmented reality is a modern technology of a three-dimensional computer environment in which it is possible to model the world perceived by a person with the help of technical means. This technology allows to expand the horizons of therapeutic and surgical treatment, and is also used in the process of teaching medical students. In Russia, these technologies are used by specialists of branch No. 3 of the Moscow Scientific and Practical Center for Medical Rehabilitation, Restorative and Sports Medicine of the Moscow Department of Health for the rehabilitation of patients who have suffered a stroke. Also in the Pirogov Center, the Devirta-Delphi solution is used for the same purposes: with the help of sensors placed on the patient, a digital avatar is created, which then moves into virtual reality to perform exercises that restore motor functions, for example, swim in the sea with dolphins.

Abroad, VR/AR technologies are also successfully used in the most complex surgical operations. For example, the Surgical Theater virtual reality platform helps doctors in the US and Israel plan neurosurgery. With the help of this solution, in 2021, the Soroka Medical Center (Israel) performed the most difficult operation to separate twins fused at the head. Using the Surgical Theater, doctors created interactive 3D and VR models. This method helped to see and study the problem areas of organs through a special headset. It should be noted that the operation of separation of two twins fused with their heads is extremely rare and has been performed around 20 times worldwide. Therefore, these technologies are truly breakthrough for medicine [17].

Despite the high potential of these technologies, VR/AR solutions for patient care are not yet widely used in Russia. This is also due to the fact that in international practice the registration period for the latest technologies is much shorter, so innovative solutions are applied there somewhat faster. Moreover, aspects of Russian legislation also affect the application of international innovative solutions. While they are being formalized in Russia, such technologies may no longer be so innovative, or even obsolete [18].

3.5 MIS

Among other things, this study also explored the ways in which MIS are used and integrated in Russia.

As a rule, each MIS consists of blocks responsible for automating various components of the activities of a medical institution. These include: registry and electronic medical records of patients; medical research data; workplaces of a doctor and a nurse; distribution of resources of the institution, their schedule; financial management and accounting; administrative information and means of employee communication; medicinal prescriptions, prescription journal; standards of medical care and so on [19]. MIS allows solving the following tasks: big data management and process optimization, data fusion and reporting, information availability for analysis and processing.

As an example of the work of medical institutions with MIS in Russia, consider N3.Health, an integration platform created to integrate information systems of private clinics, laboratory services, and insurance companies [20]. This platform will allow user clinics to connect to various existing MIS. The N3.Health platform is a cloud service that brings together market participants across Russia to share a variety of health data.

With the platform, medical information system developers can offer commercial clinics additional opportunities in the field of digital services.

Initially, the main task of N3.Health was to simplify the process of registering patients in medical organizations by synchronizing the schedule data in the clinics. However, with the advent of updates, the platform has two new services that have expanded the functionality of the platform: the N3Health.Integrated electronic medical record service and the N3Health.Laboratory data exchange service. These services made it possible to create a centralized repository of medical records and organize the exchange of information between partner clinics, and also allows you to transfer patient information in electronic form to the Uniform State Health Information System of the Ministry of Health of the Russian Federation, which ensures compliance with the requirements of Decree of the Government of the Russian Federation No. 555.

At the moment, the platform has agreed on integration with several MIS: MIS MeDialog, MEDMIS, Element, MGERM, Renovatio. The platform also signed an agreement on integration in the field of artificial intelligence with the Webiomed platform. In addition, Netrika, the developer of the N3.Health platform, announced that it had carried out a pilot connection of the Onconet cloud service for remote monitoring of oncological patients. Information about the well-being of a patient undergoing chemotherapy on an outpatient basis will be included in his electronic medical record. Thus, the doctor will be able to timely and effectively adjust the treatment of patients outside the hospital.

Thus, this platform embodies most of the solutions required for modern medical centers, including cloud storage, artificial intelligence and machine learning, telemedicine and the Internet of medical things. However, this is only an intermediate solution on the way to creating a single digital space in healthcare in Russia, because the platform developers need time to connect new information systems and technologies for medical services, while this process needs to be optimized in order to increase the loyalty of clinics and developers information solutions for healthcare.

In Russia today, the main tool for storing and transmitting information are cloud services. Cloud services also help to optimize business processes. While in Western countries, in particular the US, researchers are working on the implementation of blockchain technology in healthcare, which will increase the speed of data transfer and confidentiality, which is incredibly important in the field of medicine.

For example, Change Healthcare develops software and network solutions based on innovative healthcare technologies [21]. The company's mission is to modernize the American healthcare system with the goal of increasing economic efficiency by using blockchain technology to process hundreds of medical transactions per second. To achieve this goal, a technology implementation project was implemented on the Hyperledger Fabric platform.

4 Discussion

The article discusses the ways of using modern technologies in the field of healthcare, which can be accumulated into a single platform, which will allow creating a single digital circuit of medical services in Russia. Speaking about the reference model of the digital architecture of geographically distributed medical organizations, it is worth focusing on the IT architecture and infrastructure of such medical organizations. This model is shown in Fig. 1.

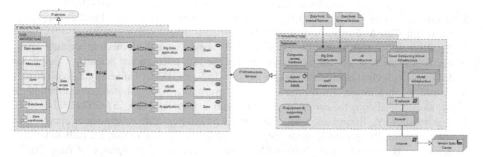

Fig. 1. Digital architecture of geographically distributed medical organizations.

To create a unified medical platform that would combine the modern IT solutions described above, future studies should consider the technical requirements for such solutions separately and submit such a task for development.

5 Conclusions

The Russian market of information technologies for use in medicine is actively developing, and it does not lag behind in comparison with Western countries. Every year there are many developments, studies and experiments that can significantly modernize the domestic healthcare system. All of the above technologies are gradually being introduced into the business processes of Russian medical organizations.

Creating a reference model of the digital business architecture of geographically distributed medical organizations is one of the key tasks in this area. The conducted benchmarking showed potential opportunities for the development of MIS, the introduction of technologies such as Big Data, Artificial Intelligence, Internet of Medical Things, Virtual and Augmented Reality and their integration with other platforms. Moreover, the measures taken by the government to digitalize healthcare also allow us to draw conclusions about the established vector for improving medical processes and the prospects of ongoing research.

In future studies, it is necessary to consider the technical requirements for integrating the above technologies into a single information system.

Acknowledgments. The reported study was funded by RFBR according to the research project № 20-010-00955.

References

1. Hick, J.L., Hanfling, D., Wynia, M.K., Pavia, A.T.: Duty to plan: health care, crisis standards of care, and novel coronavirus SARS-CoV-2. Nam Perspectives, vol. 2020 (2020)
2. Wager, K.A., Lee, F.W., Glaser, J.P.: Health Care Information Systems: A Practical Approach for Health Care Management. Wiley (2021)
3. Yelubayeva, M., Kabduyeva, G., Živitere, M.: Process-oriented approach in a quality management to medical services. In: Proceedings of the 15th International Scientific Conference Information Technologies and Management, pp. 162–163. ISMA University, Latvia (2017)
4. Kraus, S., Schiavone, F., Pluzhnikova, A., Invernizzi, A.C.: Digital transformation in healthcare: analyzing the current state-of-research. J. Bus. Res. **123**, 557–567 (2021)
5. Iliashenko, O.Y., Iliashenko, V.M., Dubgorn, A.: IT-architecture development approach in implementing BI-systems in medicine. In: Arseniev, D.G., Overmeyer, L., Kälviäinen, H., Katalinić, B. (eds.) CPS&C 2019. LNNS, vol. 95, pp. 692–700. Springer, Cham (2020). https://doi.org/10.1007/978-3-030-34983-7_68
6. Cáceres, C., Rosário, J.M., Amaya, D.: Towards health 4.0: e-hospital proposal based industry 4.0 and artificial intelligence concepts. In: Riaño, D., Wilk, S., ten Teije, A. (eds.) AIME 2019. LNCS (LNAI), vol. 11526, pp. 84–89. Springer, Cham (2019). https://doi.org/10.1007/978-3-030-21642-9_12
7. Maydanova, S., Ilin, I.V.: Strategic approach to global company digital transformation. In: Proceedings of the 33rd International Business Information Management Association Conference, pp. 8818–8833. Granada, Spain (2019)
8. Anisiforov, A., Dubgorn, A., Lepekhin, A.: Organizational and economic changes in the development of enterprise architecture. In: E3S Web of Conferences, p. 02051. EDP Sciences (2019). https://doi.org/10.1051/e3sconf/201911002051
9. Ilin, I., Levina, A., Lepekhin, A., Kalyazina, S.: Business requirements to the IT architecture: a case of a healthcare organization. In: Murgul, V., Pasetti, M. (eds.) EMMFT-2018 2018. AISC, vol. 983, pp. 287–294. Springer, Cham (2019). https://doi.org/10.1007/978-3-030-19868-8_29
10. Gavrilov, D.V., Abramov, R.V., Kirilkina, A.V., Ivshin, A.A., Novitskiy, R.E.: COVID-19 pandemic prediction model based on machine learning in selected regions of the Russian Federation FARMAKOEKONOMIKA. Mod. Pharmacoecon. Pharmacoepidemiol. **14**, 342–356 (2021)
11. Andreu-Perez, J., Poon, C.C., Merrifield, R.D., Wong, S.T., Yang, G.-Z.: Big data for health. IEEE J. Biomed. Health Inform. **19**, 1193–1208 (2015)
12. Dwivedi, Y.K., et al.: Artificial Intelligence (AI): multidisciplinary perspectives on emerging challenges, opportunities, and agenda for research, practice and policy. Int. J. Inform. Manage. 101994 (2019). https://doi.org/10.1007/978-3-030-19868-8_29
13. Ilin, I.V., Levina, A.I., Ershova, A.S., Efremova, M.A.: Methodology for the transition to a digital enterprise. Econ. Entrepreneurship (2021). https://doi.org/10.34925/EIP.2021.131.6.229
14. Morley, J., Taddeo, M., Floridi, L.: Google Health and the NHS: overcoming the trust deficit. Lancet Dig. Health **1**, e389 (2019)
15. Lepekhin, A., Borremans, A., Ilin, I., Jantunen, S.: A systematic mapping study on internet of things challenges. In: 2019 IEEE/ACM 1st International Workshop on Software Engineering Research & Practices for the Internet of Things (SERP4IoT), pp. 9–16. IEEE (2019)
16. Levina, A., Kalyazina, S., Ershova, A., Schuur, P.C.: IIOT within the architecture of the manufacturing company. In: Proceedings of the International Scientific Conference-Digital Transformation on Manufacturing, Infrastructure and Service, pp. 1–6 (2020)

17. Pillai, A.S., Mathew, P.S.: Impact of virtual reality in healthcare: a review. Virtual and Augmented Reality in Mental Health Treatment, pp. 17–31 (2019)
18. Ferrari, V., Klinker, G., Cutolo, F.: Augmented reality in healthcare (2019)
19. Blagodatsky, G., Ponomarev, D., Gorokhov, M., Ponomarev, S., Vologdin, S.: Informatization of the quality of medical care in the management of the medical service of the Federal penitentiary service of Russia. In: IV International research conference Information technologies in Science, Management, Social sphere and Medicine (ITSMSSM 2017), pp. 481–484. Atlantis Press (2017)
20. Gavrilov, D., Gusev, A., Korsakov, I., Novitsky, R., Serova, L.: Feature extraction method from electronic health records in Russia. In: Conference of Open Innovations Association, FRUCT, pp. 497–500. FRUCT Oy (2020)
21. Mahnev, D.A., Korzhavchikova, N.M.: The medical information system as a universal tool to improve the efficiency of commercial activities of modern hospital. Med. Herald South Russia **8**, 75–80 (2017)

Information Trends and Digital Management Tools of the "New Industrialization"

Galina Silkina[1] (ID), Natalia Alekseeva[1(✉)] (ID), Svetlana Shevchenko[2] (ID),
and Lyudmila Pshebel'skaya[3] (ID)

[1] Peter the Great St. Petersburg Polytechnic University, Polytechnicheskaya. 29,
195251 St. Petersburg, Russia
alekseeva_ns@spbstu.ru
[2] St. Petersburg State University of Economics, Griboedov Canal Emb., 30-32,
191023 St. Petersburg, Russia
[3] Belarusian State Technological University, Sverdlova Street 13A, 220006 Minsk, Belarus

Abstract. The keystone of New Industrialization is the organization of highly effective and efficient production activities; it closely correlates with the Industry 4.0 Concept and is implemented through the large-scale spreading and practical application of information digital technologies. This justifies the relevance of this research, the purpose of which is to study, systematize and analyze modern technological and business trends, justify the choice of tools for managing the process of New Industrialization. The paper presents the results of conceptual framework study and practical tools of the New Industrialization, the priority of management technologies is proved, the role of the Industrial Internet of Things is substantiated. The tools of the New Industrialization are defined: technologies enabling communication networks; protocols and standards for data transmission; equipment for ensuring interaction; terminal devices; platforms. The use of industrial knowledge graphs as a semantic basis for decision-making is substantiated. The prospects for the further development of new industrialization are outlined. The authors see the further development of the study in the analysis of modern technological trends, the identification of their potential in business development, and the formation of tools for managing development processes, consistent with evolving production concepts, in particular, Industry 5.0. The presented material can be useful for both scientific and business communities, as it develops the theoretical foundations of the New Industrialization, determines its prospects and tools, and systematizes the scientific background and best practices necessary to select the digital tools for managing the New Industrialization.

Keywords: New industrialization · Robotization · Control technologies · Industrial Internet of Things · Digital tools

1 Introduction

The current stage of economic development is associated with the formation of a post-industrial society [1]. A society is called post-industrial if its economy is dominated by an

© Springer Nature Switzerland AG 2022
D. Rodionov et al. (Eds.): SPBPU IDE 2021, CCIS 1619, pp. 224–238, 2022.
https://doi.org/10.1007/978-3-031-14985-6_16

innovative sector with a highly productive industry, a knowledge industry, and a high rate of innovative development [2]. It is the industry that most analytical agencies, experts, and practitioners recognize as the foundation of the economy of each country - its development is accompanied by an increase in scientific and research activities, contributes to the formation of a new knowledge basis and new industries, the implementation of innovations [3]. The transition to new economic realities does not negate the dominant role of industry; only its technological and instrumental equipment is changing. And in this sense, the term "New Industrialization" is seen as more adequate to modernity, in the most appropriate to the ongoing processes and observed phenomena.

The central component of the New Industrialization is new industrial technologies that have high potential, demonstrate rapid development but have received relatively little distribution compared to traditional technologies so far. This is a totality of new approaches, materials, methods, and processes that are used to design and manufacture globally competitive products or goods that are in demand on the world market, the most advanced technical means and methods of work that are used not only in industrial production but also in all spheres of human activities [4]. Industrial technologies that form the basis of New Industrialization are, first of all, information and communication technologies in their modern, digital format [5]. The New Industrialization in this context closely correlates with the concept of Industry 4.0, in which the economy has existed for the past 10 years [6].

In a broad sense, Industry 4.0 characterizes the current trend in the development of automation; it represents a new level of production organization and management of the value chain throughout the entire life cycle of manufactured products [7]. The concept of the Fourth Industrial Revolution was first heard in 2011 at an industrial exhibition in Hannover, where the German government set the task of expanding the use of information technology in the industry. It was recorded in the documents of the International Economic Forum and reflected the current level of automation and data exchange at that time [8, 9].

Industry 4.0 components are cloud technologies, the Internet of Things, additive manufacturing, cyber-physical systems, artificial intelligence and robotics, digital modeling and design, augmented and virtual reality [10]. Many of these components have already become a reality and are successfully applied in practice, but it is their combination into one integrated system that will allow us to develop the concept of Industry 4.0 and provide a new level of production efficiency and additional income due to the use of digital technologies, the formation of networking coordination between suppliers and partners, as well as implementation of innovative business models [11–13].

At the same time, we have to state that the theoretical foundations of the New Industrialization have not been studied fully enough. The ambiguous vision of prospects and tools of the New Industrialization determines the relevance of the scientific study of its basic trends and tools, determines the vitality of this research, the purpose of which is to systematize existing scientific groundwork and best practices, to form on this basis a reasonable choice of tools for managing the New Industrialization.

The goal of the study could be achieved by setting and solving the following tasks:

- to review the available literature based on the definition and vision of the prospects for the New Industrialization;

- to identify the most relevant blocks of technology for the New Industrialization;
- to justify the priority of management technologies, the choice of management tools for the New Industrialization;
- to outline the prospects for the process of the New Industrialization.

2 Materials and Methods

The methodological basis of the study was formed by regulatory documents, bibliographic analysis, scientific and specialized publications, and statistical data. An additional empirical basis was made up of information, reference, and analytical materials belonging to consulting companies, materials of scientific and practical conferences, a study of the experience of Russian and foreign enterprises, taking into account global technological trends and predictive estimates (see Fig. 1).

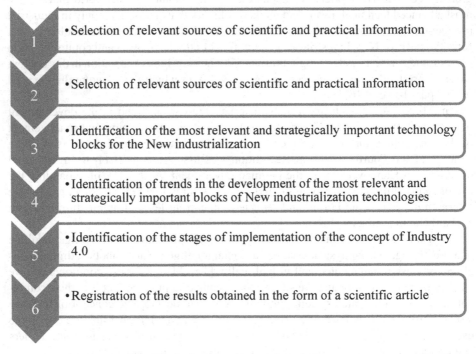

1 • Selection of relevant sources of scientific and practical information

2 • Selection of relevant sources of scientific and practical information

3 • Identification of the most relevant and strategically important technology blocks for the New industrialization

4 • Identification of trends in the development of the most relevant and strategically important blocks of New industrialization technologies

5 • Identification of the stages of implementation of the concept of Industry 4.0

6 • Registration of the results obtained in the form of a scientific article

Fig. 1. Logic and research methods.

During the study, based on the analysis of literary sources, the most relevant and strategically important blocks of technologies for the New Industrialization were identified. Cloud technologies are currently the most in-demand, and there are a lot of examples of their application in various spheres. According to analysts at Gartner, in 2021, companies' spending on public cloud services worldwide reached 451 billion USD; an increase of 22% with respect to 2020. An important area of growth in the use of cloud technologies is the real sector, primarily industry (mining, manufacturing), which requires not just automation, but the construction of a digital business platform [14].

The Internet of Things is an integrating technology that is closely related to most other technologies [15]. The concept of the Internet of Things as a unified communication environment and a new stage in the development of the Internet was formulated at the end of the 20th century, but the prerequisites for its full implementation were formed only in the 2010s: miniaturization of the element base, large-scale distribution of 4G networks, development of cloud services.

Industry 4.0, in addition to these areas of accelerated development, also includes the widespread introduction of additive manufacturing, printed electronics, the use of distributed registries, the use of augmented and virtual reality, the development of autonomous robots that will not be components of automated lines, as they are now, but completely mobile highly intelligent devices, able to work with people. According to WEF (World Economic Forum) forecasts, most of these technologies will become an everyday reality in 2027 [16].

The additive manufacturing technology is one of the most popular, which is constantly developing; as the industry discovers new applications, new materials, and new 3D printers, new concepts are emerging – 4D and 5D printing. 4D printing technologies assume that a fourth one is added to three-dimensional coordinates - time, that is, printed three-dimensional products in the future can change in a special way under the influence of external factors. An object is generated on a platform that can swing along two axes in 5D printing technology. It became possible to manufacture objects with a completely new internal structure by adding two more axes to the 3D printer. 5D printing technology is already showing high commercial viability; in addition, it is "cross-cutting", that is, it can be applied in completely different industries, from aviation to medical prosthesis.

Due to its rather complex character, the concept of Industry 4.0 is being implemented in several stages, the first of which is automation; it is the digitization of processes and the transfer of their management to information systems. Digitization is the next level of change; here, digitized data and processes can already be used to simplify and streamline operations [17].

The transition to Industry 4.0 is not an end in itself, it should lead to greater resource efficiency, faster time to appear in the market, lower end product costs, and new services [18, 19].

For Russia, it is especially important to accelerate the process of New Industrialization, first of all, the restoration and further development of mechanical engineering, electronics, and manufacturing industries. The analysis of advanced Russian and foreign practices shows that the initial stages of implementing the Industry 4.0 concept - automation and digitalization - have already been completed. The main achievement of these stages is the creation of digital industries, the main task of which is the development of manufactured product models using digital design and simulation tools.

3 Results

The most vital tasks of a general nature, for the solution of which industrial enterprises are now implementing digital technologies, are:

- improving operational efficiency: reducing costs, optimizing business processes, increasing the speed of bringing new products to market;

- increasing production safety, stability, and continuity, reducing the risk of shutdown;
- exclusion of manual operations from the production and automation of routine ones;
- a new level of interaction with contractors;
- the use of augmented and virtual reality and robotics for complex, dangerous, and highly loaded processes;
- building a data-driven company;
- creation of a digital model of the enterprise, from the receipt of raw materials to the delivery of products to the consumer;
- compliance with the principles of responsible business conduct (ESG agenda);
- creation of a product that works without human intervention.

The need to solve these problems by enterprises stimulates both their own development of information technologies and their application in the industry (see Fig. 2).

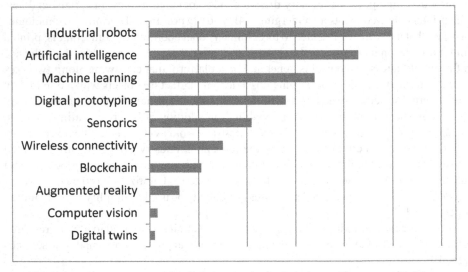

Fig. 2. The level of demand for digital technologies in industry. The source: Tadviser.

Many scientists and engineers directly involved in the new industrial revolution often follow predominantly technocratic beliefs. They believe that the revolution comes down to the sum of new, but already well-known technologies. There are industrial robots, artificial intelligence, machine learning, and digital prototyping in large industrial companies at the peak of the introduction of information technology [20].

Nowadays, robots are exponentially included in the industrial environment [21]. They introduce incredible precision, performance, and flexibility. In addition, enterprises see prospects for the joint work of automatic robotic systems and human resources. According to Research and Markets, the global market for industrial robots in 2018 amounted to $48.7 billion; in 2024 the volume will increase to $75.6 billion at a combined annual growth rate of 9.2%. At the same time, the scale of the introduction of robotics is significantly differentiated by region and country (see Fig. 2).

According to the Association for the Advancement of Automation, 2021 set a new record for the number of robots sold in the US with 39,708 units, which is 28% higher than in a year earlier; in monetary terms, sales were estimated at $2 billion. 58% of these orders were made by the automotive industry, the traditional backbone of the US robotics industry. The largest growth in sales of robots in the non-automotive sector was observed in metallurgy - here the rise was 91%; 29% growth in food and consumer goods production.

1007 industrial robots were installed in 2018 in the Russian Federation; according to the National Association of Robotics Market Participants - shipments increased by 43% compared to 2017. At the same time, the density indicator of robotic application is quite low - 5 robots per 10 thousand employees of enterprises in Russia, which is 20 times less than the average indicator in the world, and only 5% of the installed robots were produced in the country (Fig. 3).

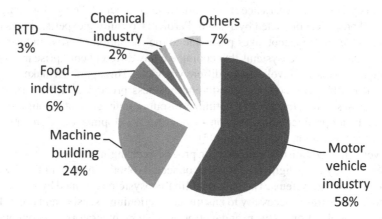

Fig. 3. Industry distribution of robotics in Russia. The source: Tadviser.

The main trends in the development of industrial robots are the introduction of machine vision, artificial intelligence, the creation of service robots, and collaborative robots (cobots). A collaborative robot is a new direction in the development of industrial robotics; it is a robot designed to interact directly with a human within a defined collaborative workspace. Robots are becoming more versatile, flexible, and accurate in the implementation of the next stage of the New Industrialization - the Fifth Industrial Revolution (Industry 5.0), which changes the meaning of the very concept of "robot". Robots are no longer perceived solely as programmable machines that can perform routine tasks; they are turning into an ideal human companion to perform tasks in some scenarios. The Fifth Industrial Revolution is expected to bring together human intelligence, creativity, and machine capabilities to improve process efficiency. While the main challenge in Industry 4.0 is intelligent automation, Industry 5.0 involves synergy between humans and autonomous machines.

Drivers of the New Industrialization are several technological and business trends. The first of them manifests itself on a global scale - universal digitalization, which is not limited to production technologies only. The technological factor that has been noted by management for several years as having the greatest impact on the change of enterprises is the management technologies modification, and not only technologies incorporated in the production. It is the junction of automation and control technologies, unlike previous industrial revolutions, that determines the transition to new qualitative growth.

The largest segment of the Internet of Things is the Industrial Internet of Things (IIoT) - a virtual environment that provides control of the technological cycle as a whole and each piece of production equipment separately using various actuators, as well as detectors, sensors, and software. The IIoT technology transforms the automation of production processes by integrating various automation units through unified cyber-physical systems into a single control system - from product development and design to automated quality control throughout the value chain [22]. Cyber-physical systems create virtual copies of objects in the physical world, control physical processes, and make decentralized decisions. They can form jointly a single network, interact in real-time, self-adjust and self-learn.

The analysis of the experience of the Industrial Internet of Things implementation in the world practice, conducted by J'son & Partners Consulting experts, shows that the transition to the IIoT concept takes place due to the formation of cross-industrial open production and service ecosystems that combine many different enterprise management information systems and involve many different devices. This approach makes it possible to implement arbitrarily complex end-to-end business processes in the virtual space. These processes can automatically optimize resource management through the entire supply chain and product value creation - from idea development, design, engineering to production, operation, and disposal [23].

The very organization of the production process is changing radically. Today's industry leaders already have digitized, Internet-connected robotic equipment fitted with sensors and information systems. The industrial IIoT ecosystem is formed by all the components and manufacturers necessary to ensure its functioning - sensors and other devices, developers of application software and platforms, system integrators, telecom operators, and customers (consumers) of solutions.

Market researchers and practitioners have found that the basic tools for the IIoT are: technologies for building communication networks, protocols and standards for data transmission, equipment for ensuring interaction, terminal devices, platforms [24].

The main trend in the development of the Industrial Internet of Things is the mass application of its technologies. According to Microsoft, 85% of the largest enterprises in developed countries have developed at least one project using the IIoT in production. By the end of 2019, there were 7.6 billion devices connected to the Industrial Internet in the world, and by 2030 the number of these devices will increase to 24.1 billion.

Quantum sensors - highly sensitive devices based on the registration of individual quantum effects relating to individual quantum systems are called a new tool that provides obtaining relevant and reliable data. It is expected that the potential of the new tool is implemented in many areas: navigation (space industry, unmanned vehicles), defense and security, geological exploration, oil production and construction. An interesting development was created by scientists from the USA, Canada, and Germany. Researchers have implemented a quantum gravimeter that will help in the exploration of oil and other minerals. Devices equipped with it will be able to detect air voids underground, which will make working in mines safer.

The Company SAS, a software developer for class BI systems, cites networks that are already evolving towards 5G, as well as easy-to-use platforms for accessing the IIoT data in dataflow form as factors driving progress in the use of the IIoT. 5G networks significantly expand the limited functionality of previous-generation mobile networks and should bring the highest data transfer rates with minimal delay to IIoT interconnection. The main functional features of 5G networks are as follows: improved mobile broadband access, eMBB (enhanced MBB); ultra-reliable communications with low latency, ULLRC (Ultra Low Latency Reliable Communication); massive machine-to-machine communications Massive IoT/IIoT, mMTC (massive Machine Type Communication). Based on these three generalized types of functionalities, the whole variety of services and capabilities of 5G networks is maintained.

For the past two years, we have been talking about 6G networks. On July 14, 2020, Samsung Electronics released a report titled "Next Generation Hyperconnectivity Technology for All" in which it outlined its vision for a sixth generation (6G) communications system. The project document includes technical and social trends, new services, requirements, potential technologies, and the expected timeline for network standardization. According to the report, the completion of the 6G standard development and the beginning of its commercialization may occur as early as 2028, and the mass commercial launch around 2030. The main users of 6G will be both people and machines. 6G will enable services such as immersive augmented reality, high-quality mobile holograms, and digital replication.

Experts see significant prospects in the integration of IIoT systems and artificial intelligence. The merging of the two high-tech developments, called AIoT (AI + Iot). Research and Markets analysts predict that by 2024 the global market for ALoT devices will be $4.6 billion. At the same time, about 10% of this amount will fall on industrial solutions, including collaborative robots working together with personnel.

The IIoT projects are being implemented or planned for implementation by almost all the world's leading companies in a wide range of industries. The project of the company for the production of motorbikes Harley Davidson has become encyclopedic.

The peculiarity of the Industrial Internet of Things is that, by connecting to it, industrial enterprises get the opportunity not only to increase the efficiency of their technological and business processes but also to bring relationships with partners and customers to a new level. Due to the implementation of the IIoT solutions, they can provide monitoring services for equipment installed at the client's site and, if necessary, to carry out preventive repairs. Thus, industrial enterprises can begin a gradual transition to a new, service business model of interaction with the consumer and with partners, allowing the latter to shift the focus from capital expenditures to operating costs.

According to the survey of 1,400 business leaders worldwide performed by analytic agency Accenture, the IIoT will contribute more than $14 trillion to the global economy by 2030. At the same time, the introduction of such technologies over the same period can bring up to 6 trillion dollars to US GDP and more than 70 billion dollars to the German economy. However, Accenture's research also shows that the prospects for returns and effects from the IIoT are not yet obvious to large businesses. The lack of plans to use such technologies is largely due to their complexity and lack of understanding of the possible income.

For Russian enterprises, the adaptation and implementation of the most successful world practices in the IIoT are of particular importance as one of the important conditions for achieving competitiveness in the domestic and foreign markets (see Fig. 4).

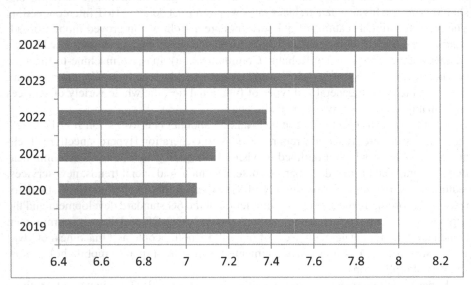

Fig. 4. Assessment and forecast of the development of the IIoT market in Russia, billion rubles (2021–2024 - forecast values). The source: iKS-Consulting.

There are already quite a lot of areas for the application of IIoT technologies in Russian enterprises. However, projects usually require an individual approach, considering the specifics of a particular enterprise, which is also confirmed by real cases.

The most striking project was implemented by ATB Electronics Company at a metallurgical enterprise. A sensor-based software and hardware system was introduced there to optimize the output of the rolling mill. A solution worth thousands of rubles provided an annual effect of millions of rubles. It took 4 months from the moment of signing the terms of reference to the commissioning of the software and hardware complex for trial operation, which is unique for the industrial sector.

The Proteus Science and Technology Center has developed a Private LTE/5G integrated solution that can be used to digitalize production within the Industry 4.0 concept, for example, provide data exchange with wireless robots and support the movement of wireless vehicles. Also, based on a private LTE/5G network, MCPTT services can operate in case of critical scenarios and for monitoring remote industrial facilities and facilities with a massive presence of people.

For a long time, the lack of technology standards has been a factor holding back the use of the IIoT. A significant milestone in filling this gap was the internationally approved first standard of the Industrial Internet of Things created by Russia; this was reported on February 14, 2022. Adopted by the International Organization for Standardization and the International Electrotechnical Commission (ISO/IEC), the standard establishes uniform requirements for the compatibility of various IIoT devices and systems. It is intended to become the basis for the practical implementation of the concept of smart production and provide opportunities for the promotion of Russian technologies. The introduction of uniform requirements for the compatibility of the IIoT devices, networks, and systems in enterprises will allow the implementation of a heterogeneous system consisting of equipment from different suppliers for each specific enterprise and, thus, will reduce the cost and speed up the implementation of the IIoT technologies.

Even though the IIoT is almost universally recognized as the basic technology of the New Industrialization, there are certain barriers to its wide distribution, the most critical of which is the lack of a common architectural approach to creating digital production management platforms, on the one hand, the variety of formats and standards for working with data and interpretation of the results, on the other hand.

A promising direction for solving the problem of unification of data processing operations and the formation of practical recommendations for production management is the use of semantic technologies, primarily ontologies. The task of ontological modeling is to create formalized electronic knowledge models. The purposes of these models application are determined by the business area, and may include: performing simulation modeling of processes to optimize them; quick derivation of logical conclusions based on a large amount of information to support decision-making; ensuring accessibility for the perception of users of large volumes of complexly structured information, knowledge sharing; solution of several technical problems, primarily in the field of information systems integration.

Tools for solving the above problems already exist - these are Industrial Knowledge Graphs. They demonstrate the advantages of an ontological approach that provides flexible modeling and data interoperability, a stack of semantic technologies that allows you to analyze unstructured information and intelligent data search in a variety of heterogeneous sources, as well as machine learning for data analysis and classification, including in conditions of incomplete information. Industrial Knowledge Graphs allow solving intellectual problems that are difficult to formalize, shifting the focus from the problem of data storage towards linking, reusing, and coherent circulation of data and knowledge. Industrial Knowledge Graphs can not only combine various data sources into a common repository but also solve the problem of information compatibility and formalization of industrial knowledge.

The typical tasks for industrial knowledge graphs are:

- Generation of digital twins [25]. Knowledge graphs allow you to integrate a variety of information about the company's equipment and infrastructure in the form of a virtual copy of real objects. Joint analysis of dynamic readings of sensors and data on the design of objects reduces the time for making management decisions;
- Management of risks. The combination of information on financial, legal, and other parameters of the company's work in the knowledge graphs makes it possible to increase the efficiency of identifying risks and possible conflicts of interest when planning and monitoring production situations;
- Process monitoring. Numerous production and technological processes at the enterprise are associated with the acquisition and analysis of data from various sensors

and information systems. Such information is usually presented at different levels of abstraction and detailing of data, and work with it is carried out by different departments and specialists. The combination of these levels in a common knowledge graph allows for comprehensive observation and monitoring of processes, bringing together different points of view and contexts;

- Operational services for complex equipment. Knowledge graphs allow you to combine technical documentation, regulations, and equipment specifications with operational data, which greatly simplifies decision-making.

The creation of industrial automated solutions based on semantic technologies, controlled by formalized knowledge, is a necessary and, perhaps, the most important step towards the New Economic Order.

The drivers and trends of the New Industrialization are summarized in Table 1.

Table 1. Drivers and trends of the New Industrialization

	Trends of New Industrialization	Composition of new industrial technologies	Results of application of new industrial technologies
Drivers of New Industrialization	Production technologies	Additive manufacturing Robotics Augmented Reality Virtual reality Sensorics	- optimization of business processes, - cost reduction, - automation of the process of monitoring and life cycle management of equipment, - improvement of production safety, - ensuring stability and continuity, - reducing risks, dangerous and highly loaded processes, - creating intelligent production that works without human participation
	Management technologies	Industrial Internet of Things Artificial intelligence Ontological modeling Semantic technologies	- a new level of interaction with counterparties, - building a data-driven company; - creation of a digital model of the enterprise, - transfer of management and decision-making functions to intelligent systems, - virtualization of production functions and transition to models of the sharing economy, - compliance with the principles of responsible business conduct

The tools of the new industrialization are shown in Fig. 5.

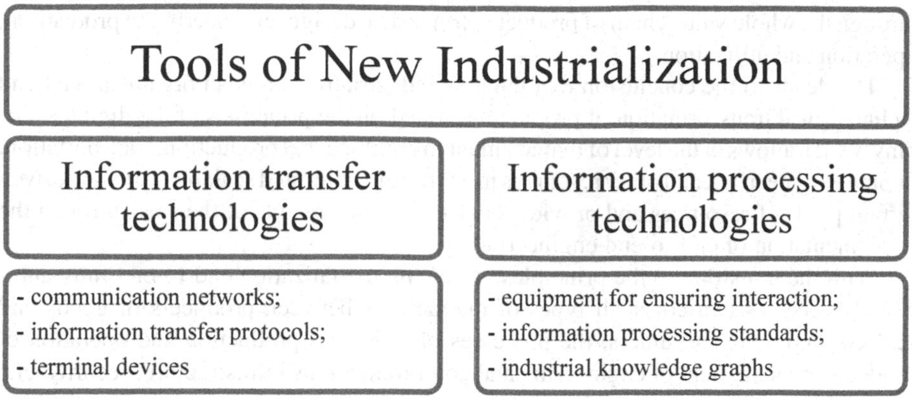

Fig. 5. Tools of New Industrialization

4 Discussion

The current stage of economic development is associated with high-tech technologies, which is also reflected in the works (Huggins et al. 2021; Vu, Haraguchi, and Amann 2021; Kobzev et al. 2020). The core of the New Industrialization is industrial technologies, which is also indicated in the works of foreign authors (Ivaldi, Scaratti, and Fregnan 2022; Berges, Ramírez-Durán, and Illarramendi 2021; Philbeck and Davis 2018). The idea that the transition to Industry 4.0 is not an end in itself often eludes modern researchers (Alfonso et al. 2021; Soomro et al. 2021), which we are trying to make up for with the presented research.

This article presents that Industry 4.0 components are: cloud technologies; Internet of Things; additive manufacturing; cyber-physical systems; artificial intelligence and robotics; digital modeling and design; augmented and virtual reality. These provisions are consistent with the research of other authors. At the same time, we have to state that the theoretical foundations of the New Industrialization have not been studied fully enough. The analyzed sources ambiguously define the vision of the prospects and tools of the new industrialization. In the presented article, we systemized the existing scientific foundations and best practices, which distinguishes the presented study from the available ones.

The conducted research proves: technologies and tools of new industrialization radically change the models of production and organization of interaction of economic entities, bring irreversible transformation in the organization of modern production and business processes, generate new business models.

The analysis of experience in implementing technologies and tools shows that the transition to the concept of new industrialization is due to the formation of cross-industrial open industrial-service ecosystems, combining many different information management systems of different enterprises and many different devices. This approach allows you to implement in virtual space however complex end-to-end business processes, which can automatically perform optimization management of various resources through the whole value chain of products - from idea, design, engineering to production, operation and utilization.

This leads to the conclusion that the new industrialization is an organizational and technological transformation of production, based on the principles of the digital economy, which allows at the level of management to combine real production, transportation, human, engineering, and other resources in a virtually unlimited scalable software-driven virtual pools of resources and provide the user with the results of their use through the implementation of end-to-end engineering.

With the transition to the principles of new industrialization end-to-end fully automated processes can cover all types of interactions between producers of goods and services and their consumers: the processes of industrial production and operation of products, management of engineering and communications infrastructure, security, etc.

5   Conclusion

The study substantiates the place of the New Industrialization in modern economic development. The discovered correlation of the processes of the New Industrialization of the ideology of Industry 4.0 made it possible to apply the analysis of the conceptual foundations and best practices of Industry 4.0 to the definition of the technological foundations of the New Industrialization. It is proven that the drivers of new industrialization are several technological and business trends. The first of them manifests itself on a global scale - universal digitalization, which is not limited to production technologies only. The technological factor that has been noted by management for several years as having the greatest impact on the change of enterprises is the change in management technologies, and not only in production technologies. It is the junction of automation and control technologies, unlike previous industrial revolutions, that determines the transition to new qualitative growth.

The authors see the further development of the study in the analysis of modern technological trends, the identification of their potential in business development, and the formation of tools for managing development processes consistent with evolving production concepts, in particular, Industry 5.0.

Acknowledgments. The research is partially funded by the Ministry of Science and Higher Education of the Russian Federation under the strategic academic leadership program 'Priority 2030' (Agreement 075-15-2021-1333 dated 30.09.2021).

References

1. Huggins, R., Stuetzer, M., Obschonka, M., Thompson, P.: Historical industrialisation, path dependence and contemporary culture: the lasting imprint of economic heritage on local communities. J. Econ. Geograp. **21**, 841–867 (2021). https://doi.org/10.1093/jeg/lbab010
2. Vu, K., Haraguchi, N., Amann, J.: Deindustrialization in developed countries amid accelerated globalization: patterns, influencers, and policy insights. Struct. Chang. Econ. Dyn. **59**, 454–469 (2021). https://doi.org/10.1016/j.strueco.2021.09.013

3. Kobzev, V., Izmaylov, M., Skvortsov, S., Capo, D.: Digital transformation in the Russian industry: key aspects, prospects and trends. In: Proceedings of the International Scientific Conference - Digital Transformation on Manufacturing, Infrastructure and Service, pp. 1–8. ACM, Saint Petersburg Russian Federation (2020). https://doi.org/10.1145/3446434.344 6451

4. Ivaldi, S., Scaratti, G., Fregnan, E.: Dwelling within the fourth industrial revolution: organizational learning for new competences, processes and work cultures. JWL. **34**, 1–26 (2022). https://doi.org/10.1108/JWL-07-2020-0127

5. Berges, I., Ramírez-Durán, V.J., Illarramendi, A.: A semantic approach for big data exploration in industry 4.0. Big Data Res. **25**, 100222 (2021). https://doi.org/10.1016/j.bdr.2021.100222

6. Philbeck, T., Davis, N.: The fourth industrial revolution: shaping a new era. J. Int. Affairs **72** (2018)

7. Soomro, M.A., Hizam-Hanafiah, M., Abdullah, N.L., Ali, M.H., Jusoh, M.S.: Industry 4.0 readiness of technology companies: a pilot study from Malaysia. Admin. Sci. **11**, 56 (2021). https://doi.org/10.3390/admsci11020056

8. Schwab, K.: The Fourth Industrial Revolution - Klaus Schwab - Google Books (2016)

9. Schwab, K., Davis, N.: Shaping the future of the fourth industrial revolution. J. Chem. Inform. Model. (2018)

10. Babkin, I., Alekseeva, N., Barabaner, H., Antoshkova, N.: Forecasting digital economy development trends based on scientometric data monitoring. In: Beskopylny, A., Shamtsyan, M. (eds.) XIV International Scientific Conference "INTERAGROMASH 2021." LNNS, vol. 246, pp. 771–779. Springer, Cham (2022). https://doi.org/10.1007/978-3-030-81619-3_86

11. Didenko, N., Skripnuk, D., Kikkas, K., Kalinina, O., Kosinski, E.: The impact of digital transformation on the micrologistic system, and the open innovation in logistics. J. Open Innov. Technol. Market Complex. **7**, 115 (2021). https://doi.org/10.3390/joitmc7020115

12. Dubolazov, V., Simakova, Z., Leicht, O., Shchelkonogov, A.: The impact of digitalization on a production structures and management in industrial enterprises and complexes. In: Schaumburg, H., Korablev, V., Ungvari, L. (eds.) TT 2020. LNNS, vol. 157, pp. 39–47. Springer, Cham (2021). https://doi.org/10.1007/978-3-030-64430-7_4

13. Silkina, G.Y., Shevchenko, S., Sharapaev, P.: Digital innovation in process management. Acad. Strateg. Manag. J. **20**, 1–25 (2021)

14. Silkina, G.: From analogue to digital tools of business control: succession and transformation. IOP Conf. Ser. Mater. Sci. Eng. **497**, 012018 (2019). https://doi.org/10.1088/1757-899X/497/1/012018

15. Alfonso, I., Garcés, K., Castro, H., Cabot, J.: Self-adaptive architectures in IoT systems: a systematic literature review. J. Internet Serv. Appl. **12**(1), 1–28 (2021). https://doi.org/10.1186/s13174-021-00145-8

16. Schwab, K.: The fourth industrial revolution. In: World Economic Forum (2017)

17. Zhang, Y., Zhang, C., Yan, J., Yang, C., Liu, Z.: Rapid construction method of equipment model for discrete manufacturing digital twin workshop system. Robot. Comput. Integrat. Manuf. **75**, 102309 (2022). https://doi.org/10.1016/j.rcim.2021.102309

18. Zoubek, M., Poor, P., Broum, T., Basl, J., Simon, M.: Industry 4.0 maturity model assessing environmental attributes of manufacturing company. Appl. Sci. **11**, 5151 (2021). https://doi.org/10.3390/app11115151

19. Habib, L., Pacaux-Lemoine, M.-P., Berdal, Q., Trentesaux, D.: From human-human to human-machine cooperation in manufacturing 4.0. Processes **9**, 1910 (2021). https://doi.org/10.3390/pr9111910

20. Chalmers, D., MacKenzie, N.G., Carter, S.: Artificial Intelligence and entrepreneurship: implications for venture creation in the fourth industrial revolution. Entrep. Theory Pract. **45**, 1028–1053 (2021). https://doi.org/10.1177/1042258720934581

21. Soares, I., Petry, M., Moreira, A.P.: Programming robots by demonstration using augmented reality. Sensors **21**, 5976 (2021). https://doi.org/10.3390/s21175976
22. Bahga, A., Madisetti, V.K.: Blockchain platform for industrial Internet of Things. JSEA **09**, 533–546 (2016). https://doi.org/10.4236/jsea.2016.910036
23. Jahani, N., Sepehri, A., Vandchali, H.R., Tirkolaee, E.B.: Application of Industry 4.0 in the procurement processes of supply chains: a systematic literature review. Sustainability **13**, 7520 (2021). https://doi.org/10.3390/su13147520
24. Bartlett, D.: Industrial Internet. In: Geng, H. (ed.) Internet of Things and Data Analytics Handbook, pp. 447–455. Wiley, Hoboken, NJ, USA (2016). https://doi.org/10.1002/978111 9173601.ch26
25. Warke, V., Kumar, S., Bongale, A., Kotecha, K.: Sustainable development of smart manufacturing driven by the digital twin framework: a statistical analysis. Sustainability **13**, 10139 (2021). https://doi.org/10.3390/su131810139

Response of an Educational System and Labor Market to the Digital-Driven Changes in the Economic System

Features of the Russian National Qualifications System Under the Influence of Digitalization

Viktoriya Degtyareva[1]([✉]) [iD], Svetlana Lyapina[2] [iD], and Valentina Tarasova[3] [iD]

[1] State University of Management, 99 Ryazansky Prospekt, Moscow 109542, Russian Federation
iump@mail.ru
[2] National Research University Higher School of Economics, 20, Myasnitskaya, Moscow 101000, Russian Federation
[3] Russian University of Transport, 9 Obraztsova, Moscow 127994, Russian Federation

Abstract. The article discusses the problems of developing new educational programs for universities and issues that need to be addressed by coordinating with various institutions of the system in the context of the spread of digitalization. The methods of analysis, generalization of the regulatory and methodological framework, external expertise with active interaction with employers and the results of activities were used. The scheme of interaction of elements of the national qualifications system in the development of an educational program is proposed. The hypothesis about the inclusion of the considered elements for the development of relevant educational programs is confirmed. Correlation dependence and percentage approximation proved the need to use all components in the development of modern educational programs. A number of issues related to the development of educational programs by universities and requiring further clarification are highlighted, including issues of harmonization of professional and educational standards under the influence of digitalization. The results of the work determine the following directions for the further development of educational programs: normative and methodological development, the use of external expertise and the expansion of cooperation with employers.

Keywords: Digital education · Educational programs · Universities · Examination of educational programs · National Qualifications System · Digitalization · Industry 4.0

1 Introduction

The influence of digitalization penetrates into all spheres of activity. In the Russian Federation, approaches to formalization and consolidation of updated elements in the education system are changing qualitatively. In the period from 2014 to the present, there has been the development of individual elements of the National Qualifications System (NSC) and the development of their synergy.

According to Russian legislation, "The National Qualifications System (NCS) is a set of legal, organizational and institutional mechanisms that ensure the coordination

© Springer Nature Switzerland AG 2022
D. Rodionov et al. (Eds.): SPBPU IDE 2021, CCIS 1619, pp. 241–252, 2022.
https://doi.org/10.1007/978-3-031-14985-6_17

of supply and demand for qualifications, the interaction of vocational education and labor, the creation of conditions for professional growth and improving the quality of labor resources that meet national and international requirements" (Consultant.ru 2021; Kremlin.ru 2020).

The labor market must be provided with candidates of the required level, taking into account Russian as well as international requirements. The development of elements of the qualification system is aimed at the formation of mechanisms for the training of competitive specialists by educational institutions.

The development of the national qualifications system puts before universities the task of training specialists to solve strategically important tasks for the labor market in various sectors of the economy. As world practice and successful experience in the implementation of Russian educational programs show, it is possible thanks to the mechanisms of active interaction of various elements of the qualification and education system (Consultant.ru 2021; Kremlin.ru 2020).

The purpose of the article is to compare the elements of the national qualifications system in the process of developing educational programs and the impact of digitalization. To achieve this goal, the authors propose the development of educational programs of higher education in the context of the evolution of NQS. The experience of developing an educational program in the direction of "Innovation" allowed us to draw a number of conclusions and offer options for active interaction of elements of the national qualifications system, the educational community and the inclusion of digital aspects.

2 Literature Review

A number of authors support the point of view, including the one concerning the training of specialists for the transport industry (Degtyareva et al. 2021). The authors have previously assessed the development of digital universities in the Russian Federation (Degtyareva et al. 2020). In their work, it is determined that digital universities become a link between the applicant and the employer. A number of authors touch upon the issues of improving the processes of using university infrastructure through digital technologies (Gafurov et al. 2020). Dualism and changes in higher education are studied by the authors (Bygstad et al. 2022).

Many researchers take upon the subject of Industry 4.0 impact on the labour market in their works. For example, in their work Grodek-Szostak, Z., Siguencia, L. O., Szelag-Sikora, A., & Marzano, G. highlight the potential opportunities and problems arising with employees as well as with employers in the context of Industry 4.0 (Grodek-Szostak et al. 2020). This approach is being developed in the work devoted to the training of IT specialists (Szafrański et al. 2022). Researchers Chala, N., Poplavska, O., Danylevych, N., & Maksma, M. analyse the models of the employees' competencies under the condition of Industry 4.0 (Chala et al. 2021). The process of the labour market transformation and the study of the main trends of intelligent technologies impact on it is reflected in the work by Mizintseva, M. F., Gerbina, T. V., Sardaryan, A. R., & Chugrina, M. A. (Mizintseva et al. 2021).

A particular impact on the labour market which previously was influenced majorly by the factors and products of the technological process was produced by pandemic as a result of manifestation of crisis phenomena. The researchers Smolina, E. S., Greshnova, M. V., & Ryzhova, A. S. concerns this problem in their work (Smolina et al. 2021). The pandemic has had its impact on the geography of the labor market (Herod et al. 2022).

Axiological or value-based approach to the analysis of various aspects due to the global digitalization and identification of the most relevant competencies for existing professions present one more subject for discussion. The paper by Mantulenko, V. V., Zotova, A. S., & Makhovikov, A. E. analyses the influence of digitalization on the creation of new professions and the destruction or transformation of the old ones, as well as the competencies required in future (Mantulenko et al. 2021). There is a need for professional competencies related to the needs of enterprises in the era of the Fourth Industrial Revolution (Szafrański, Higher education institutions also need to change and there is a need to train people with digital skills (Teixeira et al. 2021). Also, changes in higher education institutions have occurred due to the impact of the pandemic (Dereso et al. 2022). The classification of challenges of economy digital transformation and their influence on the labour market is defined by the real set of new competencies (Vladimirov et al. 2021) due to the realization of the main provisions of digital changes. This topic is highlighted in the work by Guseva, M. S. on the example of a particular region (Guseva 2021).

The analysis of the impact of the digital transformation on the labour market and the justification of the necessity of training and retraining of the employees in the context of the digital education are reflected in the research by Gromova, T. V. (Gromova 2021).

The current state of the human capital and the educational environment as an important factor of its transformation may have a particular connection with deep social-economic changes which influence the labour market. In his work Popov, D. S. treats these issues (Popov 2020).

The classification of challenges of digital transformation of global, national and regional economies, structured causal relationship of unstable state of economy with structural shifts and cyclical recession, the possibility to eliminate the causes of the unstable state of the labor market by using digital technologies are analysed by Golovetsky, N. Y., Grebenik, V. V., & Khamalinskaya, V. V. on the example of a particular region (Golovetsky et al. 2021).

In the work of Degtyareva V.V., practical skills and tools that specialists who have received education should possess in order to actively apply them in practice are considered (Degtyareva 2021).

The next important problem that influences the choice of the profession and the branch of labour is labour mobility. The main trend of the labour mobility of the population are treated by Tikhonov, A., Novikov, S., Kalachanov, V., & Solimene, U. (Tikhonov et al. 2020).

Thus, the problem under study is currently relevant. The authors reveal various aspects of this problem. The paper will clarify some aspects stated in the literature review.

After analyzing the literature of various aspects of the development of educational programs, we can conclude that the problem under study is currently relevant. The authors will partially reveal aspects of this problem. The article will reveal and clarify some aspects outlined in the literature review.

3 Methods

The study was conducted using methods of analysis, generalization and study of the results of the activities of universities in the development of educational programs. The study was conducted using methods of analysis, generalization and study of the results of activities. The normative and methodological support, the possibilities of external expertise, evaluation and expansion of opportunities for further development of unique educational programs with active cooperation with employers were analyzed and summarized. The results of the authors' activity in the preparation of the educational program are studied.

Within the framework of regulatory and methodological support, decrees, strategies, federal laws, labor legislation that are related to education and obtaining the necessary skills laid down in the main documents of the country to achieve professional development are analyzed.

Within the framework of the study, the roles of the elements of the NQS in relation to the goals of education development and strengthening interaction with the labor market are determined:

– National Agency for Qualifications Development (NAQD).
– Professional qualifications councils in various fields (PQC).
– Ministry of Science and Higher Education.
– Enterprises, organizations, industry communities and etc.
– Educational organizations.
– Expert and consulting organizations.

The above approach is consistent with the well-known concept of the "triple helix" by Henry Etzkowitz (Etzkowitz and Leydesdorff 2000; Etzkowitz 2003). The essence of the approach is that the most successful and universally recognized form of university participation in the development of an innovative economy is a model of close interaction between business and universities with an integral role of the state, whose influence is noticeable in any sphere, especially in Russia. This point of view is supported by other foreign authors (Liu et al. 2021; Ribeiro and Nagano 2021).

To date, some experience in the interaction of elements of the education system and qualifications has already been accumulated, but developing a specific educational program demands a unique complex of solving interaction problems (Degtyareva et al. 2021; Lyapina et al. 2020; Mantulenko et al. 2021; Jüttler et al. 2021).

To test the hypothesis of the need to include all elements in the process of creating modern educational programs, their analysis was carried out. To do this, we worked with a sample of 14 training areas and more than 44 educational programs in 3 higher educational institutions. The results using correlation of dependence and percentage of approximation will help to realize the need to include all components in the development of modern educational programs and the degree of their influence on this model. This may affect the quality of educational services and student satisfaction (Abbas 2020), as well as the development of professional skills that modern graduates should possess (Yu 2017).

Further development of the NQS from the perspective of the tasks of developing successful educational programs is possible only if there are clear and understandable rules of interaction with the relevant institutions of the system, methodological tools, as well as implementing the conditions for close cooperation between educational organizations and employers and their motivation for partnership. All this determined the essence and results of the study.

4   Conducting Research and Results

4.1   The Main Elements of NQS in the Development of an Educational Program

Let's consider the main processes of developing an educational program on major "Innovations" taking into account the specifics of the transport industry through interaction with various elements of the national qualifications system (Fig. 1).

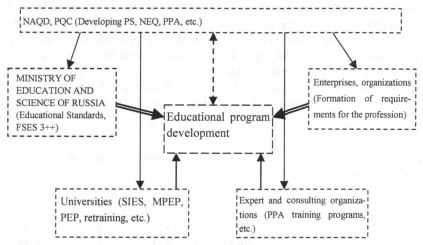

Fig. 1. Interaction of elements of the national qualifications system in the process of developing an educational program.

1. Ministry of Science and Higher Education of the Russian Federation. When developing an educational program, an educational organization solves the following questions: on the basis of what standard and on what major (for example, the Federal State Educational Standard), the program will be implemented, what level of training is required (for example, bachelor's degree/master's degree/specialty), areas of professional activity, etc.
2. Professional qualifications councils in various fields (PQC). Tasks: to determine on the basis of which professional standards the educational program will be developed, to check the compliance of the level of education, to consider the possibilities of coordinating professional competencies and indicators of their achievement with the appropriate working group within the corresponding PQC.

3. Enterprises, organizations, industry communities, etc. Tasks: coordination/formation of requirements for the educational program, participation in the development and public discussion of educational programs, reviewing.
4. Educational organizations. Tasks: consideration of the feasibility of developing joint educational programs on the major, work experience analysis, receiving feedback, etc.
5. Expert and consulting organizations. Tasks: making decisions on attracting representatives of the organization to the examination and review of individual tasks; conducting an examination of the implemented educational programs as a whole.

As for the experience of conducting professional and public accreditation of higher education programs, it is worth paying attention to two aspects - the expediency of obtaining a PPA certificate and the choice of an organization for this purpose. The loss of accreditation leads to a decrease in the level of perception of the organization (Castro et al. 2021). In this regard, with the approval in 2020 of the Federal State Educational Standard for Higher Education (for the major «Innovations» as well), which includes direct requirements for taking into account professional standards when developing educational programs, obtaining a PPA certificate is an external confirmation of the program's compliance with the requirements of professional standards and employers (at least in terms of professional competencies).

The hypothesis of the need to include all elements in the development of educational programs will be tested when determining the correlation between dependent indicators (Table 1).

Table 1. Data on the assessment of correlation between dependent indicators in the process of creating an educational program

	Y	X1	X2	X3	X4	X5
Y	1	0,62	0,18	0,53	−0,02	0,31
X1	0,62	1	0,14	0,81	−0,06	0,35
X2	0,18	0,14	1	0,20	−0,09	0,03
X3	0,53	0,81	0,20	1	0,02	0,19
X4	−0,02	−0,06	−0,09	0,02	1	0,18
X5	0,31	0,35	0,03	0,19	0,18	1

When calculating, the following indicators showed the greatest dependence on the variable Y − the effectiveness of the educational program from the dependent ones in descending order:

X1 - Ministry of Education and Science, regulatory documentation;
X3 - Expertise of enterprises, industry communities;
X5 - Expertise of consulting organizations;
X2 - Tips on professional qualifications;
X4 - Experience of educational organizations;

The approximation of the model was 6.5%, which proves the need to include all components in the development of modern educational programs.

Examples of solutions for the development of educational programs in cooperation with various elements of the NQS are presented in Table 2.

In general, in the development of the NQF it is possible to note tendencies towards strengthening the interaction between various components of the system. At this stage of development, we are observing the coordination of the requirements of the PS and the Federal State Educational Standard, which is directly reflected in the approved Federal State Educational Standard and in the major "Innovations".

4.2 Directions for Further Development of Educational Programs

In the course of considering interaction tasks in the development of educational programs with various institutes of the NQS some directions were identified for further development and clarification of options and forms of work:

1. Taking into account the requirements of the Federal State Educational Standard and the requests of employers in the development of the program. Current situation: programs of higher education in the field of "Innovations" are designed in accordance with the requirements of the current Federal State Educational Standard and, as a rule, taking into account the past experience of implementing programs. The needs of employers are taken into account in terms of professional programs (the development of professional competencies, indicators, disciplines).
2. The base of professional standards, used in the development of educational programs. Current situation: according to higher education programs, universities independently implement a scheme for choosing professional standards and form professional competencies on the basis of them (as a rule, on the basis of those recommended by the Federal State Educational Standard). One of the methods of solution: the development of recommendations for the formation of professional competencies of the corresponding PQC (by levels of education), due to this additional strengthening of the elements of the NQF. In a situation where it is necessary to develop an industry-specific program, there should be additional justification of professional competencies with links to relevant research and peer review of programs by professionals.
3. Development of teaching materials and assessment tools. This task is essential in the development of the content of the program (disciplines, teaching materials, assessment tools, etc.). Current situation: universities and developers of programs as a rule develop training materials using the capabilities of employers, other educational programs of universities, etc. Another debatable issue related to the use of assessment tools developed by the Councils for the relevant PS is the expediency of a joint assessment of qualifications with the state final certification procedure. Such tasks are implemented in the SVE system, but not solved in the higher education system.
4. Taking into account the development of the industry in the formation of educational programs. Current situation: the designation of the circumstances of the industry begins with the choice of the field of professional activity in the formation of the program. According to past experience, it was confirmed by comments/reviews

Table 2. Examples of solving the problems of developing educational programs in the framework of interaction with various elements of the NQS

№ Tasks to be solved when developing an educational program and interacting with various institutions	Educational program «Innovations in transport» (Bachelor's degree level)	Educational program «Research and analytics in the transport industry» (Master's degree level)
1 The task of substantiating the FSES to develop the program	The choice of the FSES for bachelor's degree programs is almost immediately connected with the orientation of the program.	Development on the basis of the FSES for Innovations. Master's degree programs with contents in innovation can also be developed on the basis of other FSESs, for example, "Economics", which may be associated with the development of competencies at the intersection of several areas.
2 Areas and spheres of professional activity	Initially, the choice is based on the FSES specified list, then it can be from other areas. An important issue here is understanding how multi-sectoral (or not) the activity is.	
3 Selection and justification of the professional standard(s) for professional competence development	At first the choice is based on the FSES specified list, but, as a rule, in relation to the field of professional activity.	
4 Choosing the tasks of professional activity	It can be recommended in consultation with representatives of the main employers, leading companies in the industry. Focus on the goals of the type of professional activity specified in the professional standard, as well as the group of occupations (All-Russian Classifier of Occupations) and types of economic activity (All-Russian Classifier of Economic Activities) specified in the selected professional standard. Use Russian classifiers in general: All-Russian Classifier of Occupations, All-Russian Classifier of Economic Activities, etc.	
5 Tasks of interaction with employers, industry/professional communities, etc.	Work with representatives of employers during the development and implementation of programs (questioning employers to understand the needs for training specialists, developing programs on request, a practical training base, etc.).	Interaction is complemented by work with research structures, research institutes, etc. For example: analytical associations, the industry analytical center of the Russian Open Academy of Transport, JSC «Russian Railways» (research and analytical divisions), State Corporation «Roscosmos», Specialized Research Institutes and structures of the transport industry (JSC «VNIIZhT», JSC «NIIAS», FSUE «Agat» Organization», etc.).
6 Tasks of interaction with the Professional Qualifications Councils	Coordination of professional competencies and indicators of their achievement with recommendations from the PQC (for the 6th level of qualifications), participation in round tables and public discussions, etc.	Coordination of professional competencies and indicators of their achievement with recommendations from the PQC (for the 7th level qualifications), participation in round tables and public discussions, etc.

of the educational program and its components. The impact of digitalization must necessarily be reflected in the development of educational programs.

A significant debatable issue in the formation of an educational program is accounting for specific objects of the industry, region, etc. in its contents. So, for example, taking into account the internal characteristics and technologies of the industry, how global trends affect its development, is relevant, for example, for educational programs in the field of "innovations in the transport industry". The contents of such programs should reflect the following aspects of training: taking into account global trends that are changing the world economy as a whole, the tasks of digital transformation (associated with management issues and new relationships when working with a client), a new approach to innovation, associated not just with technological innovation, but with the development of the "product and business process" approach, etc.

5. Information and communication opportunities used by universities in the learning process. Current situation: universities actively use information resources to post educational materials and conduct online classes, test the development of educational materials, for this they actively use various public platforms (for example, Skype, Zoom, etc.).

The influence of all the elements discussed above in the creation of relevant educational programs in a rapidly changing digital environment is traced.

5 Conclusion

During the considered period of development of the NQS, there is an increase in interaction between the participants in the formation of the system. Today, this can be found in the legislative sphere, for example, and in the sphere of higher education we see requirements for the consistency of educational and professional standards.

Consistency requirements can also be found in the structure of the educational programs being formed, for example, if the educational program has a specific specialization profile or industry affiliation, then the professional part should be developed taking into account the industry affiliation of the field of activity and the corresponding professional standards (individual labor functions).

Further development of higher education programs within the framework of the NQS development fields poses questions for universities related to understanding the ratio of the formation of universal and special/professional competencies, since in a rapidly changing world with modern digitalization opportunities, it is necessary to understand and forecast the need for the formation of «soft» and «infrastructural» management skills related to the restructuring and flexible management of various systems, which is very relevant for the transport industry, considered in the example of the article. Engineering specialties require a special approach to the formation of competencies (Chan and Luk 2022). This will allow universities to choose a learning-oriented approach (Combey and López 2022).

The importance of interaction between universities and employers continues to grow, the practice of corporate structures shows that the search for "talents" is moving to the beginning of the educational chain (preschool and school education) and it is necessary to build educational programs in universities taking into account such features.

Another peculiarity is the situation when universities understand that it is impossible to study individual modules and topics without inviting a practicing teacher from a specific company.

Another direction in the development of university programs is the formation of private unique programs. Moreover, the uniqueness, on the one hand, manifests itself in the implementation of single educational programs at the request of the employer-customer, the possibility of quickly making changes to the current program, and, on the other hand, in the need to take into account the individual characteristics of the audience (personal perception, the need to combine the possibilities of on- and offline learning listeners in one group, etc.). Such issues are still poorly regulated by the current standards.

All of the above allows us to outline further tasks for the development of higher education programs by searching for new options for the interaction of various institutions of the NQS, which make it possible to develop educational programs that meet the needs of the labor market, ensuring the continuity of educational trajectories with the formation of a specialist's qualifications. This approach is quite appropriate for training specialists in the field of innovation.

This approach is quite appropriate for training specialists in the field of innovation and the impact of digitalization.

References

Abbas, J.: HEISQUAL: a modern approach to measure service quality in higher education institutions. Stud. Educ. Eval. **67**, 1–11 (2020). https://doi.org/10.1016/j.stueduc.2020.100933

Bygstad, B., Øvrelid, E., Ludvigsen, S., Dæhlen, M.: From dual digitalization to digital learning space: exploring the digital transformation of higher education. Comput. Educ. **182** (2022). https://doi.org/10.1016/j.compedu.2022.104463

Castro, C.A., Pavez, C.A., Contreras, F.J.: Loss of institutional accreditation and its effects on first-year retention: Universidad de las américas 2010–2014, chile. [Pérdida de acreditación institucional y sus efectos sobre la retención de primer año: Universidad de Las Américas 2010–2014, Chile] Formacion Universitaria **14**(5), 39–50 (2021). https://doi.org/10.4067/S0718-500 62021000500039

Chala, N., Poplavska, O., Danylevych, N., Maksma, M.: Competencies of personnel in economy 4.0: challenges and solutions. J. Optim. Indust. Eng. **14**(1), 71–77 (2021). https://doi.org/10. 22094/JOIE.2020.677818

Chan, C.K.Y., Luk, L.Y.Y.: Academics' beliefs towards holistic competency development and assessment: a case study in engineering education. Stud. Educ. Eval. **72** (2022). https://doi.org/ 10.1016/j.stueduc.2021.101102

Combey, L.B., López, B.G.: Student-centred methods. Their effects on university students' strategies and learning approaches. Teoria De La Educacion **34**(1), 215–237 (2022). doi:https://doi. org/10.14201/TERI.25600

Consultant.ru: Strategy for the development of the national qualifications system of the Russian Federation for the period up to 2030 (2021). http://www.consultant.ru/document/cons_doc_ LAW_384038/. (in Russ.)

Degtyareva, V.V.: Digital HR tools and their role in improving the competitiveness of companies. Management **9**(2), 90–102 (2021). https://doi.org/10.26425/2309-3633-2021-9-2-90-102. (In Russ.)

Degtyareva, V.V., Lyapina, S.Y., Tarasova, V.N.: Forming analyst's competencies of specialists for modern transport companies. In: Popkova, E.G., Sergi, B.S. (eds.) ISC 2020. LNNS, vol. 155, pp. 538–547. Springer, Cham (2021). https://doi.org/10.1007/978-3-030-59126-7_61

Degtyareva, V.V., Tarasova, V.N., Fedotova, M.A., Ziroyan, M.A.: Creation of digital universities through interaction of higher education institutions and analysis of readiness for digitalization: an example of Russia. Revista Turismo Estudos Práticas, no S4, 14 (2020)

Dereso, C.W., Meher, K.C., Shobe, A.A.: COVID-19 pandemic and strategizing the higher education policies of public universities of ethiopia. Int. J. Sociotechnol. Knowl. Develop. 14(2), 1–16 (2022). https://doi.org/10.4018/IJSKD.2022040101

Etzkowitz, H., Leydesdorff, L.: The dynamics of innovation: from national systems and "mode 2" to a triple helix of university-industry-government relations. Res. Policy 29(2), 109–123 (2000). https://doi.org/10.1016/S0048-7333(99)00055-4

Etzkowitz, H.: Innovation in innovation: the triple helix of university-industry-government relations. Soc. Sci. Inf. 42(3), 293–337 (2003). https://doi.org/10.1177/05390184030423002

Gafurov, I.R., Safiullin, M.R., Akhmetshin, E.M., Gapsalamov, A.R., Vasilev, V.L.: Change of the higher education paradigm in the context of digital transformation: from resource management to access control. Int. J. High. Educ. 9(3), 71–85 (2020). https://doi.org/10.5430/ijhe.v9n3p71

Golovetsky, N.Y., Grebenik, V.V., Khamalinskaya, V.V.: Factors of development of the Region's labour market in the conditions of the digital economy and the tools of their management. In: Buchaev, Y.G., Abdulmanapov, S.G., Abdulkadyrov, A.S., Khachaturyan, A.A. (eds.) State and Corporate Management of Region's Development in the Conditions of the Digital Economy. ASTI, pp. 7–11. Springer, Cham (2021). https://doi.org/10.1007/978-3-030-46394-6_2

Grodek-Szostak, Z., Siguencia, L.O., Szelag-Sikora, A., Marzano, G.: The impact of industry 4.0 on the labor market. Paper presented at the 2020 61st International Scientific Conference on Information Technology and Management Science of Riga Technical University, ITMS 2020 – Proceedings (2020). https://doi.org/10.1109/ITMS51158.2020.9259295

Gromova, T.V.: Features of personnel Training/Retraining in the conditions of digital transformation. In: Ashmarina, S.I., Mantulenko, V.V. (eds.) IPM 2020. LNNS, vol. 161, pp. 162–169. Springer, Cham (2021). https://doi.org/10.1007/978-3-030-60926-9_22

Guseva, M.S.: Regional market adaptation to the demands of digital economy. In: Ashmarina, S.I., Mantulenko, V.V., Vochozka, M. (eds.) ENGINEERING ECONOMICS WEEK 2020. LNNS, vol. 139, pp. 354–363. Springer, Cham (2021). https://doi.org/10.1007/978-3-030-53277-2_43

Herod, A., Gialis, S., Psifis, S., Gourzis, K., Mavroudeas, S.: The impact of the COVID-19 pandemic upon employment and inequality in the mediterranean EU: an early look from a labour geography perspective. Europ. Urban Reg. Stud. 29(1), 3–20 (2022). https://doi.org/10.1177/09697764211037126

Jüttler, A., Schumann, S., Neuenschwander, M.P., Hofmann, J.: General or vocational education? The role of vocational interests in educational decisions at the end of compulsory school in Switzerland. Vocat. Learn. 14(1), 115–145 (2020). https://doi.org/10.1007/s12186-020-09256-y

Kremlin.ru: Decree of the President of the Russian Federation # 474 of July 21, 2020 "On the National Development Goals of the Russian Federation for the period up to 2030 (2020). http://www.kremlin.ru/events/president/news/63728. (in Russ.)

Liu, S., Zhang, X., Chen, W., Zhang, W.: The path of university collaborative innovation mechanism based on the triple-helix model. Paper presented at the 2021 10th International Conference on Educational and Information Technology, ICEIT 2021, pp. 185–189 (2021). https://doi.org/10.1109/ICEIT51700.2021.9375561

Lyapina, S., Tarasova, V., Fedotova, M.: Problems of analyst competency formation for modern transport systems. Transp. Prob. 15(2), 71–82 (2020). https://doi.org/10.21307/tp-2020-021

Mantulenko, V.V., Zotova, A.S., Makhovikov, A.E.: Digital transformation of the labor market: values and competences. In: Ashmarina, S.I., Mantulenko, V.V. (eds.) IPM 2020. LNNS, vol. 161, pp. 321–328. Springer, Cham (2021). https://doi.org/10.1007/978-3-030-60926-9_41

Mizintseva, M.F., Gerbina, T.V., Sardaryan, A.R., Chugrina, M.A.: The role of smart technologies in the process of the labor market transformation: Tendencies and problems. In: Popkova, E.G., Sergi, B.S. (eds.) ISC 2020. LNNS, vol. 155, pp. 483–489. Springer, Cham (2021). https://doi.org/10.1007/978-3-030-59126-7_54

Popov, D.S.: Human capital in Russia: measurement accuracy and limitations of the method. Sotsiologicheskie Issledovaniya **2020**(11), 27–38 (2020). https://doi.org/10.31857/S013216250010466-5

Ribeiro, S.X., Nagano, M.S.: On the relation between knowledge management and university-industry-government collaboration in brazilian national institutes of science and technology. VINE J. Inform. Knowl. Manage. Syst. (2021). https://doi.org/10.1108/VJIKMS-01-2020-0002

Smolina, E.S., Greshnova, M.V., Ryzhova, A.S.: Current trends in the labor market transformation under the influence of environmental factors. In: Ashmarina, S.I., Mantulenko, V. V. (eds.) IPM 2020. LNNS, vol. 161, pp. 71–76. Springer, Cham (2021). https://doi.org/10.1007/978-3-030-60926-9_10

Szafrański, M., Gütmen, S., Graczyk-Kucharska, M., Weber, G.W.: Modelling IT specialists competency in the era of industry 4.0. In: Machado, J., Soares, F., Trojanowska, J., Yildirim, S. (eds.) icieng 2021. LNME, pp. 257–269. Springer, Cham (2022). https://doi.org/10.1007/978-3-030-79168-1_24

Teixeira, A.F., Gonçalves, M.J.A., Taylor, M.L.M.: How higher education institutions are driving to digital transformation: a case study. Educ. Sci. **11**(10) (2021). https://doi.org/10.3390/educsci11100636

Tikhonov, A., Novikov, S., Kalachanov, V., Solimene, U.: Influence of the profession and industry of work on the labor mobility of the applicant. Soc. Sci. **9**(11), 1–14 (2020). https://doi.org/10.3390/socsci9110213

Vladimirov, I.S., Kamchatova, E.Y., Burlakov, V.V.: Digitalization of the labor market in the fourth industrial revolution. In: Ashmarina, S.I., Mantulenko, V.V. (eds.) IPM 2020. LNNS, vol. 161, pp. 275–282. Springer, Cham (2021). https://doi.org/10.1007/978-3-030-60926-9_35

Yu, P.-L.: Innovative culture and professional skills. Int. J. Manpow. **38**(2), 198–214 (2017). https://doi.org/10.1108/ijm-10-2014-0214

Employee Development and Digitalization in BANI World

Svetlana Evseeva[1]([✉]) [iD], Oksana Evseeva[1] [iD], and Preeti Rawat[2] [iD]

[1] Peter the Great St. Petersburg Polytechnic University, Saint-Petersburg 195251, Russia
evseeva_sa@spbstu.ru
[2] K J Somaiya Institute of Management, Somaiya Vidyavihar University, Mumbai 400077, India

Abstract. The modern environment is rapidly changing. Decision-making in an organization significantly depends on the effectiveness of personnel management. It influences a lot on employee development as one of the milestones of the organization development. The aim is to study the modern features of the external environment of the organization and its impact on the employee development. A literature review based on analysis, synthesis, comparison was chosen as a method. The environment changes from VUCA (volatility, uncertainty, complexity, and ambiguity) to BANI (brittle, anxious, nonlinear, and incomprehenwsible) world. BANI world sets completely new needs for the application of digital technologies. Modern decision-making systems for personnel management are based on a complex of digital solutions that actively use advanced information technologies. Skills like remote team management, digital tools skills, leadership and decision-making during a crisis should be presented in the training programs of organizations. The research results shew that the features of BANI world should be taken into account in the development of the organization's personnel. Organizations, faced with the challenges of BANI world, are forced to make decisions in a situation of uncertainty, and digital tools that respond to the challenges of BANI world are offered to make informed decisions on the employee development. Our results allow companies to design employee development programs based on BANI world characteristics. The use of digital technologies in employee development programs allow to receive specialists with the necessary qualifications faster and at lower costs.

Keywords: Employee development · Digitalization · BANI · Reskilling and Training · Digital tools · Communication

1 Introduction

The modern world is constantly changing. The rate of change increases from year to year in all spheres of society and the economy. Digitalization has become one of the most important trends in recent years in many countries [1–3]. Digitalization of the economy should ensure a qualitative change in its structure and long-term opportunities and ultimately lead to its growth. The technology development has changed many areas of activity, such concepts as digital factories, digital competencies, etc. have appeared.

© Springer Nature Switzerland AG 2022
D. Rodionov et al. (Eds.): SPBPU IDE 2021, CCIS 1619, pp. 253–264, 2022.
https://doi.org/10.1007/978-3-031-14985-6_18

The environment in which companies operate is changing. The modern world was described using the VUCA (volatility, uncertainty, complexity, and ambiguity) concept of the world. Nathan Bennett and James Lemoine described main features of VUCA [4]. Volatility is characterized as relatively unstable, frequent, and sometimes unpredictable changes. Uncertainty is considered from the point of view that it is unknown whether the event will lead to significant changes. The complexity is because of the presence of many interconnected parts. A lack of knowledge about the object and interdependencies causes ambiguity; there is no basis for making forecasts of the future. The environment becomes extremely difficult for planning the organization's activities and making management decisions. However, we see rapid pace of changes in many areas of life, acceleration of uncertainty, unpredictability, inability to provide long-term solutions to problems. A striking example is the COVID pandemic, in which companies had to change quickly to remain viable in the market. The world has changed and the concept of describing the world has changed too. A new concept that describes the modern world is BANI (brittle, anxious, nonlinear, and incomprehensible) world. The concept of BANI world was proposed by Jamais Cascio in 2020. Moacir Fernandes de Godoy and Durval Ribas Filho support the idea of importance to research different aspects of a new vision [5]. A.A. Fedchenko, I.V. Filimonova, and V.N. Yaryshina consider the appraisal and recruitment process in the context of the transformation of social and labor relations and BANI world influence on the requirements for professional and over-professional (soft) skills of employees [6]. Gonzalo Casaravilla, Ruben Chaer, and Ximena Caporale investigated generation investment planning and risk management in BANI context [7]. In general, we can conclude that the topic of research is just emerging, and scientists see the importance of studying these features.

All organizations understand the need for constant changes. Organizations must make changes and adapt to the ongoing processes in implementing all their activities, including human capital management. The ongoing changes in the external environment: the quality of labor in the market, changes in the content of labor functions and a decrease in the share of routine operations, demographic changes, including an increase in life expectancy and an aging population, the possibility of training personnel outside the organization, etc. [8] affect its ability to achieve goals. A striking example of the influence of the external environment on the company's human resource management is the COVID pandemic [9]. Many companies had to restructure business processes in the company and revise approaches to the management of personnel under modern trends: remote work opportunities, online education, etc.

Companies that aim to compete globally have to invest in knowledge and have to use knowledge returns in training and skills to increase their competitive advantage [10, 11]. Human capital is defined through the knowledge, skills, abilities and others (KSAO) concept [12, 13]. The development of personnel directly affects the human capital of the organization [14, 15]. In the process of personnel development, employees gain new knowledge, skills, and abilities, which ultimately leads to an increase in the quality of human capital and the occupation of leading positions in the market.

Scientists consider many aspects of the employee development: training and innovation [16], benefits of training and development [17], investment in training and skills [10, 11, 18]. A few studies are devoted to the analysis of the environment [11, 19]. However, the modern environment has undergone several changes that affect personnel management and the employee development in particular. Hence, the research gap concerns the lack of knowledge about the peculiarities of personnel development in the modern environment. Therefore, we aimed to study the modern features of the external environment of the organization and its impact on the employee development.

2   Materials and Methods

2.1   Research Methodology

We found that employee development needs to be studied deeply in the modern environment. Digitalization changes training sphere and technology development changes skills in organization. Based on the human capital concept, skills are a very important component. So, we need to investigate modern features of environment and then rethink the role of employee development. Also, it is important to identify major factors that effect on changing approaches to employee development. The process of analysis has 3 steps (Fig. 1).

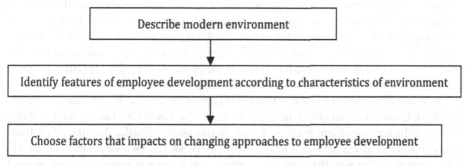

Fig. 1. Process of analysis employee development approaches in BANI world

We used methods of analysis, synthesis, comparison in the work. We conducted a literature review. Open sources data were used. The data were collected from scientific articles and consulting company McKinsey report 2020 "Beyond hiring: How companies are reskilling to address talent gaps".

The logic of the study is constructed as follows. First, we described the environment using modern concepts about the world. Since the world has become very changeable, new concepts that characterize it have begun to appear. Having identified the concept of the world, i.e., the description of the environment in which companies operate, we determined how each of the characteristics is implemented in employee development. Further describing the challenges, we analyzed the features of employee development taking into account digitalization processes. After that, we offered digital technologies that can neutralize the challenges of BANI world in employee development.

2.2 Theoretical Fundamentals

Employee development is concerned with the employee's personal growth in ways that can help the organization [20]. Development activities include formal education, job experiences, professional relationships, and assessment of personality, skills and abilities that help employees grow professionally [21]. At the beginning of the employee development study, it was assumed that development is an episodic intervention of the organization aimed at facilitating or directly developing the knowledge and skills necessary for work [22]. In the 21st century, there has been a greater interest in understanding how to promote and improve voluntary employee development through easier access to such opportunities. Several studies examine how employees learn from work experience [23], mentoring and coaching [1]. Development studies have recognized the active role of the learner in creating an effective learning environment. However, it is noted that modern theories and concepts of development are far from positioning employees as active investors who should actively manage their personal human resources [24].

3 Results

Previously, researchers described the modern world as a VUCA world: volatility, uncertainty, complexity, and ambiguity [4]. VUCA has significantly shaped by the results of the Cold War. Afterwards it served as a great point of orientation in terms of agile and self-oriented approaches to working, thinking, and making sense of the world in general. The situation has substantially changed since the term was coined in the 1980s, and complexity for instance seems to have evolved into chaos. Managing companies in such a world required a revision of many approaches to doing business, which were described in the book Mack, O., Khare, A., Krämer, A., & Burgartz, T. [20]. The chaos faced today is larger than VUCA – in politics, global warming, and the current pandemic, and in many other spheres of life. A new concept of describing the modern world has appeared. Chaotic conditions, completely unpredictable results, and incomprehensibility of what is happening characterize it. This is BANI world (Brittle, Anxious, Nonlinear, and Incomprehensible) [25]. Brittle arises from dependence on a single critical point of failure and from the unwillingness - or inability - to leave any excess capacity or slack in the system. "A" means disturbing. Anxiety brings with it a feeling of helplessness, a fear that no matter what we do, it will always be wrong. In a Nonlinear world, cause and effect are disconnected or disproportionate. Incomprehensible - we try to find answers, but the answers make little sense. New environmental characteristics are changing the emphasis on the content of the employee development function (Table 1).

Changes in personnel development are determined by the influence of many factors. It is necessary to revise approaches to personnel development in the company.

Consider the impact on the development of personnel in the organization. In modern conditions, there are changes in the career of employees. Traditionally, a career has been associated with inter-organizational mobility and a combination of unique work experience [26, 27]. Basically, vertical career development was considered. Continuity is one of the key principles of career management, which reduces the risk of a shortage of human capital within the organization [28]. More recent studies study career capital from the perspective of the possibility of managing the professional development of employees

Table 1. Personnel development in BANI world.

BANI	Description
Brittle	The critical point of failure in the personnel development system may be the variety of training methods and programs because of the limited budget of companies. The decision to attract employees from outside or to train within the organization is critically important. A change in the trend of industry development may occur faster than the company's ability to consider new requirements for personnel competencies
Anxious	Employees feel helpless to decide. They become passive to avoid potentially incorrect decisions altogether. They feel despair and desperation about missed opportunities. It becomes important to include in the personnel development program areas that help to cope productively with anxiety and start making rational decisions, keeping clarity in mind. For example, programs in psychology can help in this direction
Nonlinear	Small decisions have disproportionate consequences that can be both beneficial and destructive. The results of training program and other methods of personnel development are new knowledge and skills. However, after receiving them, they can become obsolete quickly and investment and time costs for personnel will be required again. Also, employees often leave the company, which makes the personnel development process less effective for the business and increases its risks. At the same time, other training programs (aimed at developing skills more than soft skills) can give significant results not immediately, but after a long amount of time and will increase the efficiency of the company's work once
Incomprehensible	Having more information and data makes it difficult to find the answer. The ability to comprehend the world remains the same in humans. Therefore, additional information can only overload our thinking abilities. Professional development programs will help to overcome this barrier. At the same time, the development of such programs becomes a hard task

[a]Compiled by authors.

[29], created a certain value [30], which determines the possibilities of building an employee's career much more broadly. Different tasks in the organization become the basis for differentiating career scenarios for different categories of employees. Putting these opportunities into personnel (talent) development programs [31] companies get more motivated employees.

People are actively rethinking their career path. Commitment to continuous work experience or specialization in a particular field is becoming less common. More and more people are thinking about alternative development trajectories. Digitalization, automation, and downsizing risks speed up the decision to upgrade skills or even change careers. From 75 million to 375 million people may need to change professional categories and learn new skills [32].

Attracting new staff and freelancers is one of the primary tools for closing the gap in competencies. The experience of using new formats is interesting, for example, urgent exchange programs for Staff Exchange and VDele have been launched in Russia to carry out certain projects or strengthen the company's capacities during periods of seasonal load increase. Digitalization also expands the capabilities of organizations in this direction [33]. Therefore, the recruitment of personnel is closely related to the development and recruitment policy. Some companies shift responsibility for developing employee skills to the employees themselves. And it is important for the company to hire those who are capable of self-study.

Large-scale changes in many areas of life lead to the fact that some segments of labor become obsolete and are abolished, and emerging professions in which the labor market is in need are instantly in short supply. New emerging job titles on the market complicate the recruitment process to a certain extent. Companies use different job titles to perform a similar set of functions, and narrowly specialized positions appear. This is most clearly represented in small and medium-sized businesses, where regulation is not very high. All this leads to the fact that it is already becoming difficult to navigate the market based on positions, to a large extent, it is necessary to consider experience: competencies, projects of the applicant.

Many employees may lose their jobs, or they will need to change their career trajectory. For organizations, there is a problem of retraining specialists. Classical approaches to personnel training and development still prevail in the practice of companies, and the acceleration of automation and the growth of staff shortages requires a revision of existing approaches.

Every year, the need of organizations for specialists with digital skills is growing. Organizations are actively using a wide range of tools to attract technology specialists, but this is not enough to solve the problem of personnel shortage. It is necessary to develop retraining of employees. One of the most common types of retraining programs in the IT field is intensive and short-term training solutions. Online learning practices, especially rapidly developing in a pandemic and the need for remote work, have gained powerful positions. In addition, in the pandemic, self-learning has given way to corporate training.

Remote team management, digital tools skills, leadership and decision-making during a crisis are becoming increasingly important. These skills should also be present in the training programs of organizations. According to research by McKinsey and others, reskilling programs are most often aimed at developing employees' skills of critical thinking and decision-making, leadership and management [34]. Personnel development departments are successfully adapting to new learning conditions, and more educational programs are being developed. However, the system is limited by the company's capabilities. The most common steps that training and development departments used to provide more effective training during the crisis were:

- reducing the duration of training sessions;
- methodological recommendations for best practices;
- increasing the frequency of communications;
- increasing the use of training platforms.

Retraining initiatives will not be successful without the formation of a special climate in the organization - its transformation into a learning one. The tools of such transformation will create an environment in which employees themselves can keep up with the pace of change, produce new solutions faster than competitors, increase their expertise and grow their reputation. Employee development involves the active and positive participation: without motivational efforts, the most perfect program can end in failure.

According to scientists and practitioners, the most valuable today is the so-called "T-shaped" (T-shaped) specialists [13] - these are specialists with deep fundamental knowledge in a particular subject and broad knowledge and motivation useful for their core activities. They have the three most important competencies: they synthesize ideas easily, learn quickly and adapt easily to new things. T-shaped employees expect the further development of their field and create novel approaches to perform tasks. They optimize their own workflow and reform the business processes of the entire company. For the training and development of such professionals, appropriate personnel development programs are needed.

Employers today prefer versatile multifunctional employees who can work in a multitasking environment. According to most experts, there is a rapid obsolescence of knowledge and accumulated theoretical knowledge all over the world, a decline in the importance of formal education, and "soft skills", the ability to learn and enter a new subject area on their own, come to the fore. The development of cross-functional teams reinforces this trend. In such teams, it is not the positions that are important, but the roles (skills) of employees. Employees can change companies, positions, or they can stay in the same company, but change roles or areas of activity (functions). The characteristics of the generations to which employees belong may reinforce this trend. Representatives of generation Z are more often ready to change jobs [3]. Teaching the fundamentals of the subject becomes unprofitable for the employer, it makes sense to revise the composition of development programs in favor of short-term courses. The fundamental ones are the responsibility of the employees themselves. This raises the problem of planning personnel development programs and evaluating their economic efficiency. In crisis conditions, multifunctional people are more important: who can quickly switch from task to task, learn, take responsibility for themselves, are very independent, communicate effectively. It is on these abilities that development programs should be directed in hard conditions.

Digital technologies, automatization, artificial intelligence technologies [35], robotization - all this will lead to the release of personal in the future, but robots will not be able to replace people. Modern technologies are changing the requirements for employees: to complement robots (and not compete with them), people need to develop qualities such as creativity, emotional intelligence, and cognitive flexibility. Many companies will follow the path of merging human and artificial intelligence, combining the efforts of humans and robots, so the environment will become more complex. The ability to work with people, especially considering that many of them will be even more highly developed than today, will continue to be an important task. There will be more opportunities for career and personal growth. Career paths will become more complicated. The rapid obsolescence of knowledge and skills will speed up, as will the departure from a narrow specialization. Retraining will also have to undergo changes, with the strengthening of the role of soft skills. In addition, professions, positions, and competencies that currently do not exist will appear.

Taking into account the analysis of the literature and the above, we highlight the following digital technologies in the development of personnel in BANI world (Table 2).

Table 2. Digital technologies for employee development in BANI world.

BANI	Digital technologies
Brittle	The possibility of making a decision on hiring a new employee or training an existing one based on an internal digital competence assessment platforms
Anxious	Using the ecosystem of talent development, online coaching platforms, well-being programs in the organization
Nonlinear	The use of artificial intelligence-based personnel monitoring systems to accumulate a relevant database of employees. Based on the data, decisions are made on timely response to improve the skills and motivation of personnel so that they remain in the organization
Incomprehensible	The use of e-learning, learning management systems, the formation of individual learning trajectories, the inclusion of topics related to the peculiarities of decision-making in conditions of extremely high variability

[a]Compiled by authors.

Every feature of BANI world is a challenge to build an employee development system. Digital technologies, which are actively developing now, can help overcome the challenges.

Modern conditions of organizations have changed a lot and such an environment is characterized as a BANI world. In accordance with the new characteristics, we have studied how this manifests itself in the employee development system, how it changes. The features of the environment and what managers need to pay attention to were described. We also proposed digital technologies for every feature of the BANI world which will be able to facilitate the decision-making process in order to overcome the challenges of the BANI world.

4 Discussion

In modern realities, it is necessary to ensure the possibility of continuous training and development of personnel [36]. Implementing development programs is a strategic response to the two key challenges of our time: to provide a pool of specialists in new professions and to help specialists in vulnerable areas to remain in demand in the labor market. No matter how events develop, companies and their employees should be ready for changes.

Companies have several ways to fill in the missing competencies: the search for talented employees in the labor market and the use of new employment forms or retraining.

If the second path is chosen, they will invest more in training or retraining of employees [36]. In general, the flexibility of approaches plays a crucial role: the complex management hierarchy is changing to work in teams that can decide independently. The importance of career development remains high [31], but the very form of a career is undergoing some changes. Its interests to focus on issues of career transitions, evaluation systems, remuneration, types of employment contracts under various types of careers. The approaches to personnel development should be based on the dynamics and continuous training of employees. This is critically important for successful business development in the digital age. This idea is supported in the works of scientists: Herman Aguinis and Kurt Kraiger [36], Alison M. Dachner, Jill E. Ellingson, Raymond A. Noe, and Brian M. Saxton [30], etc.

The results obtained coincide with the results of the authors who studied the environment and concluded that it is necessary to take into account the new features of the environment in the management of the organization. Asmolov A. considered the context of transition from steady, predictable, ordinary, definite environment (SPOD) to VUCA world [37]. Mack O., Khare A., Krämer A. and Burgartz T. studied organization management in a VUCA world. Bennett N. and Lemoine, G.J. considered threats to performance in a VUCA world. Researchers [5] now confirm the need to study the BANI world.

A.A. Fedchenko, I.V. Filimonova, and V.N. Yaryshina also emphasize the need to study personnel management in the BANI world. They offered tools for evaluating and hiring employees in the world of BANI, based on the requirements for professional and over professional (soft) skills of employees.

Casaravilla G., Chaer R., Caporale X. investigated another aspect of risk management in the BANI contexts [7]. They noted that it is very important to take into account the stochastic nature of all factors, as well as to be able to model and plan without losing statistical accuracy and, thus, be able to adequately manage risks.

The results obtained fit into the concept of employee development, characterized by a partnership between employer and employee, proposed by Dachner Alison M., Ellingson Jill E., Noe Raymond A., Saxton Brian M. [30].

The conducted research has shown that the features of BANI world should be taken into account in the development of the organization's personnel. Organizations, faced with the challenges of BANI world, are forced to make decisions in a situation of uncertainty, and digital tools that respond to the challenges of BANI world are offered to make informed decisions on the employee development.

5 Conclusion

It becomes extremely difficult to carry out planning in such conditions. Today we need employees with some competencies, and tomorrow with others. Of particular importance are temporary recruitment of personnel, remote work, digitalization, etc. Choosing an approach to how to develop personnel becomes a very important task. It is necessary to expand the view of professional development and possible career paths. It requires quick training and adaptation to new conditions, up to a change in industry or profession. The ability to adapt quickly and introduce alternative forms of training is becoming an important element of human resources and training departments.

Changes are occurring in the development of personnel in the BANI world. The analysis of the identified factors influencing the choice of approach to employee development management showed the need to change approaches to the development of personnel. The identified features should be considered when developing new programs for the development of the company's personnel.

Limitations of this research are analysis of a limited number of scientific publications on the topic of employee development. The fields of future research are:

- employee development methods in BANI world;
- the influence of use digital tools in employee development concerning BANI world concept;
- features of employee development in different industries;
- effectiveness of digitalization processes in employee development.

Decision-making on the development (training) of personnel takes place in an extremely uncertain environment, and changes must be implemented quickly. Therefore, it is also of interest to study the use of programs aimed at developing fundamental knowledge on the subject and short-term, applied programs aimed primarily at accomplishing specific tasks.

Our results allow companies to design employee development programs based on BANI world characteristics. The use of digital technologies in employee development programs allow to receive specialists with the necessary qualifications faster and at lower costs. Implementation of digital tools will also contribute to creating a more comfortable environment in the company and increase employee loyalty. Maintaining a database for the dynamics of changes in personnel development enables the company to be more flexible and quickly restructure when external conditions change.

Acknowledgments. The research partially funded by the Ministry of Science and Higher Education of the Russian Federation under the strategic academic leadership 'Priority 2030' (Agreement 075-15-2021-1333 dated 30.09.2021).

References

1. Pirogova, O., Makarevich, M.: The formation of the enterprises human capital in the context of digitalization. E3S Web Conf. **164** (2020). https://doi.org/10.1051/E3SCONF/202016409011
2. Lamb, M., Sutherland, M.: The components of career capital for knowledge workers in the global economy. Int. J. Hum. Resour. Manag. **21**, 295–312 (2010). https://doi.org/10.1080/09585190903546839
3. Evseeva, S., Rasskazova, O., Kalchenko, O., Evseeva, O.: Training generations X y Z in human resource management. ACM Int. Conf. Proc. Ser. (2020). https://doi.org/10.1145/3446434.3446513
4. Bennett, N., Lemoine, G.J.: What a difference a word makes: understanding threats to performance in a VUCA world. Bus. Horiz. **57**, 311–317 (2014). https://doi.org/10.1016/J.BUSHOR.2014.01.001
5. de Godoy, M.F., Filho, D.R.: Facing the BANI world. Int. J. Nutrology. **14**, e33–e33 (2021). https://doi.org/10.1055/s-0041-1735848

6. Fedchenko, A.A., Filimonova, I.V., Yaryshina, V.N.: Tools for evaluating and selecting employees in the conditions of the BANI-world. Soc. labor Res. **47**(2), 98–105 (2022). https://doi.org/10.34022/2658-3712-2022-47-2-98-105

7. Casaravilla, G., Chaer, R., Caporale, X.: Generation Investment Planning and Risk Management in BANI context. In: 2021 IEEE URUCON, pp. 355–359 (2021)

8. McKinsey: Beyond hiring: how companies are reskilling to address talent gaps (2020)

9. Evseeva, S., Evseeva, O., Burmistrov, A., Siniavina, M.: Application of artificial intelligence in human resource management in the agricultural sector. E3S Web Conf. **258** (2021). https://doi.org/10.1051/e3sconf/202125801010

10. Schislyaeva, E.R., Plis, K.S.: Personnel management innovations in the digital era: case of Russia in covid-19 pandemic. Acad. Strateg. Manag. J. **20**, 1–16 (2021)

11. Acemoglu, D.: Training and innovation in an imperfect labour market. Rev. Econ. Stud. **64**, 445–464 (1997). https://doi.org/10.2307/2971723

12. Kichigin, O., Gonin, D., Degtereva, V.: Specifics of formation of the mechanism for increasing regional competitiveness via development of civil servant human capital. ACM Int. Conf. Proc. Ser. (2020). https://doi.org/10.1145/3446434.3446466

13. Chan, K., Ho, M.R., Ramaya, R.: A " T-shaped " Metaphor for Holistic Development: Entrepreneurial, Professional and Leadership (EPL) Efficacies Predict Self-perceived Employability. Springer Singapore (2020)

14. Dickmann, M., Cerdin, J.L.: Exploring the development and transfer of career capital in an international governmental organization. Int. J. Hum. Res. Manage. **29**, 2253–2283 (2016). https://doi.org/10.1080/09585192.2016.1239217

15. Ployhart, R.E., Nyberg, A.J., Reilly, G., Maltarich, M.A.: Human capital is dead; long live human capital resources! J. Manage. **40**, 371–398 (2014). https://doi.org/10.1177/0149206313512152

16. Barykin, S.Y., Kapustina, I.V., Kirillova, T.V., Yadykin, V.K., Konnikov, Y.A.: Economics of digital ecosystems. J. Open Innov. Technol. Mark. Complex. **6**, 1–16 (2020). https://doi.org/10.3390/joitmc6040124

17. Li, R., Gospodarik, C.G.: The impact of digital economy on economic growth based on pearson correlation test analysis. Lect. Notes Data Eng. Commun. Technol. **85**, 19–27 (2022). https://doi.org/10.1007/978-981-16-5854-9_3

18. Belitski, M., Caiazza, R., Rodionova, Y.: Investment in training and skills for innovation in entrepreneurial start-ups and incumbents: evidence from the United Kingdom. Int. Entrep. Manage. J. **16**(2), 617–640 (2019). https://doi.org/10.1007/s11365-019-00606-4

19. Sutherland, M., Naidu, G., Seabela, S., Crosson, S., Nyembe, E.: The components of career capital and how they are acquired by knowledge workers across different industries. South African J. Bus. Manag. **46**, 1 (2015). https://doi.org/10.4102/sajbm.v46i4.104

20. Mack, O., Khare, A., Krämer, A., Burgartz, T.: Managing in a VUCA world (2015)

21. Evseeva, S., Evseeva, O., Kalinina, O.: HR staff leasing: Opportunities in the digital economy environment (case of Russia). E3S Web Conf. **175** (2020). https://doi.org/10.1051/e3sconf/202017513041

22. Defillippi, R.J., Arthur, M.B.: The boundaryless career: a competency-based perspective. J. Organ. Behav. **15**, 307–324 (1994). https://doi.org/10.1002/JOB.4030150403

23. Hurtz, G.M., Williams, K.J.: Attitudinal and motivational antecedents of participation in voluntary employee development activities. J. Appl. Psychol. **94**, 635–653 (2009). https://doi.org/10.1037/A0014580

24. Rodionov, D., Rudskaia, I.: Problems of infrastructural development of "industry 4.0" in Russia on sibur experience. Proceedings of the 32nd International Business Information Management Association Conference, IBIMA 2018 - Vision 2020: Sustainable Economic Development and Application of Innovation Management from Regional expansion to Global Growth, pp. 3534–3544 (2018)

25. Cascio, J.: Facing the Age of Chaos. We are in an age of chaos, an era that…. https://med ium.com/@cascio/facing-the-age-of-chaos-b00687b1f51d

26. DeCenzo, D.A., Robbins, S.P., Verhulst, S.L.: Fundamentals of Human Resource Management, 12th edn. (2016)

27. Noe, R.A., Clarke, A.D.M., Klein, H.J.: Learning in the Twenty-First-Century Workplace, vol. 1, pp. 245–275 (2014). http://dx.doi.org/https://doi.org/10.1146/annurev-orgpsych-031 413-091321

28. Gegenfurtner, A., Schmidt-Hertha, B., Lewis, P.: Digital technologies in training and adult education. Int. J. Train. Dev. **24**, 1–4 (2020). https://doi.org/10.1111/ijtd.12172

29. De Vos, A., Dries, N.: Applying a talent management lens to career management: the role of human capital composition and continuity. Int. J. Hum. Resour. Manag. **24**, 1816–1831 (2013). https://doi.org/10.1080/09585192.2013.777537

30. Dachner, A.M., Ellingson, J.E., Noe, R.A., Saxton, B.M.: The future of employee development. Hum. Resour. Manag. Rev. **31**, 100732 (2021). https://doi.org/10.1016/J.HRMR.2019. 100732

31. Curado, C., Bernardino, G.: Training programs' return on investment in the Portuguese railway company: a fuzzy-set Qualitative Comparative Analysis. Int. J. Train. Dev. **22**, 239–255 (2018). https://doi.org/10.1111/ijtd.12136

32. Brown, C., Hooley, T., Wond, T.: Building career capital: developing business leaders' career mobility. Career Dev. Int. **25**, 445–459 (2020). https://doi.org/10.1108/CDI-07-2019-0186/ FULL/XML

33. Allen, T.D., Eby, L.T., Chao, G.T., Bauer, T.N.: Taking stock of two relational aspects of organizational life: tracing the history and shaping the future of socialization and mentoring research. J. Appl. Psychol. **102**, 324–337 (2017). https://doi.org/10.1037/APL0000086

34. Manyika, J.C.M., Lund, S., Bughin, J., Woetzel, J., Batra, P., Ko, R.: Jobs lost, jobs gained: workforce transitions in a time of automation, vol. 150 (2017)

35. Eby, L.T., Butts, M.M., Hoffman, B.J., Sauer, J.B.: Cross-lagged relations between mentoring received from supervisors and employee OCBs: disentangling causal direction and identifying boundary conditions. J. Appl. Psychol. **100**, 1275–1285 (2015). https://doi.org/10.1037/A00 38628

36. Aguinis, H., Kraiger, K.: Benefits of training and development for individuals and teams, organizations, and society. Annu. Rev. Psychol. **60**, 451–474 (2009). https://doi.org/10.1146/ annurev.psych.60.110707.163505

37. Asmolov, A.G.: Race for the future. Russ. Soc. Sci. Rev. **59**, 484–492 (2018). https://doi.org/ 10.1080/10611428.2018.1547054

Study of Labour Digital Potential Usage by Organizations of Ural Federal District

Aleksandr Kozlov(iD), Alina Kankovskaya(iD), Anna Teslya(iD),
and Artem Ivashchenko(⊠) (iD)

Peter the Great St. Petersburg Polytechnic University, St. Petersburg 195251, Russian Federation
orrivashchenkoartyom@yandex.ru

Abstract. Nowadays the role of information and communication technologies widen gradually covering all business functions and activities. Nevertheless, the role of human resources is still essential since the digital transformation capability depends largely on the organizational capability of using local employees in the formation of internal business processes based on digital technologies. The foregoing defined the objective as the study of labor digital potential of regions of Ural Federal District and the analysis of using it by local organizations. The literature review depicted that the indicator defining labour digital potential of regions was never used in both Russian and foreign literature. The indicators allowing to measure the labour digital potential of a region are determined. The statistical series for chosen indicators is constructed. The authors focused on open-source data while selecting indicators. Such an approach makes the analysis of labour digital potential in a region possible for all economic agents. The comparison of labour digital potential of Ural Federal district regions is made based on the specified indicators. The correlation between the value and activity of employers in the use of digital skills of the population is revealed. The trajectory of further research is determined particularly in the comparison of the labour digital potential of regions and the digital potentials of regions. The upward trend of digital skills of the population is revealed. The differentiation of regions in terms of the intensity of the use of digital skills of the population by employers is identified.

Keywords: Labour digital potential of a region · Labour force · Digital transformation · Information and communication technologies

1 Introduction

Although information and communication technologies (ICT) are spreading in modern organisations covering all business functions and activities, the role of human resources is steadily increasing since the labour force is still responsible for monitoring, control, maintenance, and decision making [1]. That's why the success of innovative processes including digital transformation depends on the capability of organisations to use the digital potential of local human resources, to embed the labour force into internal processes based on modern ICT [2]. Every organization is operating in a definite environment provided by the regional infrastructure and available human resources. The local labour

© Springer Nature Switzerland AG 2022
D. Rodionov et al. (Eds.): SPBPU IDE 2021, CCIS 1619, pp. 265–276, 2022.
https://doi.org/10.1007/978-3-031-14985-6_19

force in every region is characterized by a specific level of digital skills and competencies which could be employed by organisations. That arouses the question: To what extent are regional organizations employing existing digital labour potential and what are indicators characterizing the level of usage of regional labour potential?

In the context of this study, the authors explore the Ural Federal district of the Russian Federation playing a really important role in the national economy, contributing to Russian GDP by 13.9% (calculated on official data of the Russian statistical service (https://rosstat.gov.ru/storage/mediabank/Region_Pokaz_2021.pdf).

The leading role in the economy of the Ural Federal district is taken by the fuel and energy corporations, metallurgical enterprises together with the raw materials base, heavy machine building, mechanical engineering and high-tech enterprises, nuclear industry, agriculture, and transport (railways and pipelines). The sectoral structure of the economy of the Ural Federal district is like the pattern of the Russian economy.

Thus, the goal of the article is to study the labour digital potential in regions of the Ural Federal district and investigate the extent the local organizations are employing it.

Tasks to perform to achieve the goal:

- Define the concept of regional labour digital potential.
- Identify the indicators referring to labour digital potential usage in regions.
- Calculate the dynamics of the labour digital potential usage by organizations of the Ural Federal district of Russian Federation.
- Conduct a comparative analysis of the indicators for organizations of the Ural Federal district.
- Formulate inferences and recommendations for the situation's enhancement.

Subsequent paragraphs, however, are indented.

2 Theoretical Fundamentals

The subject of research in this article is the digital competencies of the workforce, which can potentially be used by enterprises in the region. We can call it the labor digital potential of the region. Note that the term "labour potential" is very popular in Russian science [3, 4] and wider, post-Soviet science. Some authors interpret it as an analogue of the concept of human resources [5], but, in our opinion, the fundamental difference between these terms is that the potential includes opportunities [6] and the resources are the actual presence of the characteristics and competencies of the workforce.

Therefore, interpreting the labour potential as a set of labour opportunities formed under certain production relations and conditions of reproduction, which can be effectively used in production activities, we will focus on the existing and potential competencies and characteristics of the labour force.

Let's focus on the resources of the region that form digital competencies.

R. Wahyuningtyas et al. [7] show that digital orientation, government support, and digital opportunities are the most important factors that have a positive and significant impact on competitiveness. As one of the factors, the authors consider employee resistance, finding the absence of a significant effect of this factor. Employee resistance to digitalization has long been studied by scientists [8–10], but in our opinion, we can talk about the presence of the digital employee potential and the individual competencies they have accumulated that can be used by employers. The process of digitalization is not only the process of introducing digital tools into business with some employee resistance but also the process of acquiring digital competencies by the population. Thus, the population acquires new knowledge and skills that can be used by employers.

Pedersen, T., Scedrova, A., and Grecu, A. [11] have proven that investment in IT and a skilled workforce add value to companies but these factors act through different channels. The authors think that investments in skilled labour force work by raising the production frontier itself.

Zaborovskaya O. et al. [12] The authors explore and substantiate in detail the impact of digitalization factors on the growth of human capital, however, their study does not aim to determine the impact of the growth of human capital and individual competencies, including digital ones, on business growth in the region.

Mirolyubova T. and Voronchikhina E. [13] identified the impact of digitalization on the gross regional product and sustainable development revealing the superiority of industrial regions. The results obtained are undoubtedly important for regional policy, however, in our opinion, they should be supplemented by a study of the factors that form the digital potential of the region and the digital labor potential.

Aleksandrov I. N. and Fedorova M. Y. [14] show that the development of digital resources and competencies of the population creates an opportunity for the economic growth of rural areas, which make up a significant part of the Russian economy. We agree with this point of view and propose to study in detail the opportunities for business created by the presence of digital competencies in the population, formed not only in the process of education but also in private life.

In this context, we consider important the results obtained in the study of the impact of an innovative digital economy on total factor productivity in China [15]. This study shows a positively non-linear relationship between these indicators, and also revealed regional differences in the nature and pace of the relationship.

The problem of the influence of digital competencies of the population on the level of business digitalization is relevant and is considered by researchers from different countries [16–18], however, we highlight some of the most actual areas of research. The article [19] presents the possibilities of using the digital resources of the region for the formation of digital skills of the population and their maintenance during all stages of the life cycle of an employee. When studying the relationship between digital labour potential and the level of digitalization in the region, it is necessary to take into account the results of a study [20] that revealed the digital divide in Austria and showed the vulnerability of low-income segments of the population and women. These results correlate well with the results of the study, which shows the differences in the digital capabilities of enterprises in various industries in urban and rural areas [21].

The article [22] shows the need to study and reduce the gap between the digital competencies of employees, and consequently the digital level of their service, the level of digital literacy, and the needs of the population of the region.

In this area, a very interesting study [23] shows the multiplicity of goals in a case study of Apotti, a Finnish social services and healthcare information system renewal project, where several goals and objectives are of an advertising nature and are not aimed at implementation. However, the existence of such a project encourages the population to improve their digital skills in obtaining public services. This area of research is of the greatest relevance for developing countries and regions where the low level of digital literacy of the population hinders the development of digital business and, more broadly, the digital sector of the economy. Thus, the study uses multiple linear regression models and found that digital literacy and digital media usage enablers influence digital sales and transactions in Pakistan [24].

We agree with the authors [25] that the use of the Network Readiness Index (NRI) gives only a general assessment of the country's digitalization, but does not take into account the level of influence of each subfactor and the mutual influence of factors and subfactors. Therefore, it seems necessary to narrow the model and explore the impact of the level of digital skills of the population on the process of digital business development in the region.

The literature review depicted that even as different aspects describing the level of acquisition of digital skills and digital literacy of residents of different regions are analyzed, the indicator defining labour digital potential of regions was never used in both Russian and foreign literature.

Therefore, it is suggested to introduce the concept of labour digital potential of a region. The concept could be defined as the quotient of the labour force of a region by the appliance in the professional engagement of information and communication technologies based on global network usage. As a form of such an indicator, it is suggested to take the share of the population using the Internet regularly (Rosstat indicator - share of the population using the Internet every day or almost every day). It is quite likely that such a population category consists of confident Internet users who could be considered as the component element of labour digital potential of the region. The part Discussion describes the restraints and possible inaccuracy connected to the indicator usage.

3   Materials and Methods

The following methods were used within the framework of the study: content analysis, comparative analysis, analog approach, and quantitative methods of statistical data processing.

To determine the extent of labour potential usage by local organizations it is proposed to use the indicator of provision of workplaces with personal computers with access to the Internet. This indicator is presented in Rosstat statistical database (Number of personal computers including personal computers with access to the Internet per 100 employees).

This indicator determines the extent of digitalization of workplaces, which function and maintenance can provide employees' digital potential realization.

Thus, the following steps need to be taken to accomplish the research objective:

1. To construct statistical series of two Rosstat indexes: firstly, the share of the population using the Internet every day or almost every day by UFD, and secondly, the number of personal computers including personal computers with access to the Internet per 100 employees.

2. To analyze the extent of labour digital potential usage by organizations of Ural Federal district regions.
3. To perform a comparative analysis of statistical series and determine differ-rences in the extent of labour digital potential usage by organizations in the Ural Federal District region.
4. To identify the causes of differences in labour digital potential usage by organizations of Ural Federal district regions including the comparison with the Northwestern Federal district.
5. To develop the recommendations to increase digital potential usage by orga-nizations in the Ural Federal district.

4 Results

The usage of the Internet by residents should be the simplest and most self-explanatory index, which allows for measuring labour's digital potential. The index is calculated as a percentage of sampling survey of the population in the age window from about 15 to 75 years. Until 2017 people aged less than 72 years were surveyed. The data is demonstrated in Table 1.

Table 1. Internet usage by residents (compiled by the authors based on statistical data).

Region	Internet usage by residents						Residents using Internet every day or almost every day					
	2015	2016	2017	2018	2019	2020	2015	2016	2017	2018	2019	2020
Northwestern Federal District	78.6	80.8	81.5	84.1	86.3	87.0	61.7	60.9	62.8	70.2	74.9	77.0
Ural Federal District	75.5	79.5	79.9	84.2	85.6	87.8	58.5	64.3	64.6	73.0	74.4	80.0
Kurgan Region	69.4	70.8	73.2	76.9	82.1	80.0	53.4	55.7	58.6	65.8	66.6	73.0
Sverdlovsk Region	73.9	79.5	77.9	82.8	84.3	87.8	56.6	63.6	65.4	71.4	75.5	80.7
Tyumen Region	80.8	83.1	86.3	91.3	89.9	90.7	65.9	70.9	69.3	82.0	78.0	84.7
Chelyabinsk Region	73.7	77.7	77.5	80.1	83.5	86.5	54.5	60.5	60.1	67.4	71.1	76.0

Table 1 shows the sustainable growth of the share of the population both using the Internet and using the Internet every day. Moreover, the share of the Northwestern Federal District in 2015 was slightly higher (3.1 and 2.8 p.p. correspondingly) and by the year 2019 the situation flattened out, and by the year 2020 the share of the population using the Internet every day in the Ural Federal District was 3 p.p. higher. The variation of Internet usage by regions was significant in 2015 and by the year 2020 it became insignificantly smoother (11.4 p.p. and 12.5 p.p. in 2015 and 7.8 p.p. 11.6 p.p. in 2020).

It is interesting to study the index describing the rate of active Internet users. There are high chances that Internet usage on a day-to-day basis means that the resource is used during the work or studying processes. In other words, it can describe the labour digital potential of a region. Let us consider the data in more detail (Table 2).

It is obvious from an analysis of Table 2 that the rate of increase of Internet users grows sustainably year after year. Concurrently, the frequency of Internet usage grows with the fastest rate of increase, according to the data in Table 3.

Table 2. Expansion rate of the Internet usage by residents (compiled by the authors based on statistical data).

Region	Internet usage by residents						Residents using the Internet every day or almost every day					
	2015	2016	2017	2018	2019	2020	2015	2016	2017	2018	2019	2020
Northwestern Federal District	-	1.03	1.04	1.07	1.10	1.11	-	0.99	1.02	1.14	1.21	1.25
Ural Federal District	-	1.05	1.06	1.12	1.13	1.16	-	1.10	1.10	1.25	1.27	1.37
Kurgan Region	-	1.02	1.05	1.11	1.18	1.15	-	1.04	1.10	1.23	1.25	1.37
Sverdlovsk Region	-	1.08	1.05	1.12	1.14	1.19	-	1.12	1.16	1.26	1.33	1.43
Tyumen Region	-	1.03	1.07	1.13	1.11	1.12	-	1.08	1.05	1.24	1.18	1.29
Chelyabinsk Region	-	1.05	1.05	1.09	1.13	1.17	-	1.11	1.10	1.24	1.30	1.39

Table 3. Share of population using the Internet every day or almost every day (compiled by the authors based on statistical data).

Region	Share of population using the Internet every day or almost every day					
	2015	2016	2017	2018	2019	2020
Northwestern Federal District	0.78	0.75	0.77	0.83	0.87	0.89
Ural Federal District	0.77	0.81	0.81	0.87	0.87	0.91
Kurgan Region	0.77	0.79	0.80	0.86	0.81	0.91
Sverdlovsk Region	0.77	0.80	0.84	0.86	0.90	0.92
Tyumen Region	0.82	0.85	0.80	0.90	0.87	0.93
Chelyabinsk Region	0.74	0.78	0.78	0.84	0.85	0.88

It follows from an analysis of Table 3 that the share of the Internet users on a day-to-day basis in the total amount of users increased by 10–14%. By 2020 the share of active users of the Internet is more than 90% of the total amount of users.

This index is differentiated by districts and regions (5 p.p. between Tyumen Region and Chelyabinsk Region). It represents the growth of the population's digital skills. While that index is minimal in Chelyabinsk Region (0.88), the rate of active users' increase is one of the highest (1.39).

The only index that could circumstantially show digital skills usage in the working process is the number of personal computers used by employers (Table 4).

Table 4. Number of personal computers including personal computers with access to the Internet per 100 employees (compiled by the authors based on statistical data).

Region	Number of personal computers						Number of personal computers with access to the Internet					
	2015	2016	2017	2018	2019	2020	2015	2016	2017	2018	2019	2020
Northwestern Federal District	52	52	53	55	53	60	32	34	36	37	38	42
Ural Federal District	44	45	46	47	47	51	26	28	29	30	32	35
Kurgan Region	42	44	43	45	46	50	26	28	28	29	31	34
Sverdlovsk Region	46	48	49	50	51	55	28	30	31	33	35	38
Tyumen Region	44	43	43	44	44	47	27	27	28	30	30	33
Chelyabinsk Region	43	44	46	47	48	51	24	26	27	28	31	34

Table 4 shows the difference between the Northwestern and the Ural Federal Districts. The provision of computers rate is 85% for the Ural Federal District to the Northwestern Federal District. The index did not change from 2015 to 2020. The share of computers connected to the global network in the Ural Federal District was 81% of the total number of computers connected to the global network in the Northwestern Federal District. By 2020 that index increased by 2 p.p. Let us consider the dynamics of the indexes to 2015 (Table 5).

There are heady growth rates of computers connected to the Internet compared to the general number of computers for all regions and districts. By analyzing the data for the Ural Federal District, we can see significant scatter for regions including the Internet connection expansion rate which was 20 p.p. by 2020 between Tyumen and Chelyabinsk Regions. In Tyumen Region by 2020 there are minimal absolute values for personal computers with access to the Internet per 100 employees. By comparison, in 2015 the same index was aligned with the general trend.

The next step is to align indexes in Fig. 1. On the X-axis, there is a share of active users for 2015 and 2020 years. On the Y-axis, there is the number of computers with access to the Internet per 100 employees. The size of the circle for 2015 is accepted as 1, the diametric line of the circle for 2020 also includes the increase of computers connected to the Internet compared to 2015.

Table 5. Expansion rate of the number of personal computers including personal computers with access to the Internet per 100 employees (compiled by the authors based on statistical data).

Region	Number of personal computers						Number of personal computers with access to the Internet					
	2015	2016	2017	2018	2019	2020	2015	2016	2017	2018	2019	2020
Northwestern Federal District	1	1.00	1.02	1.06	1,02	1.15	1	1.06	1.13	1.16	1.19	1.31
Ural Federal District	1	1.02	1.05	1.07	1.07	1.16	1	1.08	1.12	1.15	1.23	1.35
Kurgan Region	1	1.05	1.02	1.07	1.10	1.19	1	1.08	1.08	1.12	1.19	1.31
Sverdlovsk Region	1	1.04	1.07	1.09	1.11	1.20	1	1.07	1.11	1.18	1.25	1.36
Tyumen Region	1	0.98	0.98	1.00	1.00	1.07	1	1.00	1.04	1.11	1.11	1.22
Chelyabinsk Region	1	1.02	1.07	1.09	1.12	1.19	1	1.08	1.13	1.17	1.29	1.42

Table 6. Indicators of telematics services and data communication network usage 2020 (compiled by the authors based on statistical data)

Region	Gross regional product, 2020	Number of active users of broadband access, this		Share of population using the mobile web, %	Data transferred through the Internet, petabyte	
		All	Entities		Individuals	Entities
Northwestern Federal District	10,522,568.9	3,454.7	196.8	115	9,465.4	2,277.0
Ural Federal District	13,227,689.2	3,151.8	170.9	103	5,166.4	2,022.4
Kurgan Region	233,468.6	174.5	10.7	103	240.5	138.6
Sverdlovsk Region	2,529,549.3	1,139.0	64.0	99	1,951.5	629.1
Tyumen Region	8,919,088.8	961.4	55.4	115	1,507.1	768.6
Chelyabinsk Region	1,545,582.5	876.9	40.8	96	1,467.3	486.0

It follows from the analysis of Fig. 1 that the dynamics is positive due to the fact that the employers actively used the population's digital skills. It is also noticeable that

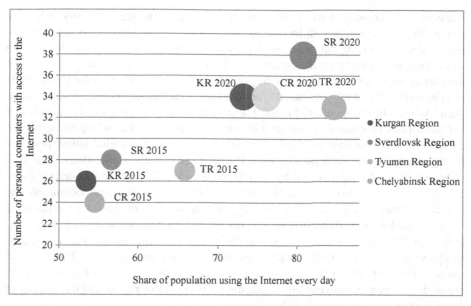

Fig. 1. Dynamics of the digital potential of population (compiled by the authors).

Chelyabinsk Region' recession was compensated by 2015. That happened due to the increase of opportunities provided by employers, and namely heady growth rate of the Internet access at the workplaces. The gap between indexes of Chelyabinsk and Kurgan Regions was reduced.

By contrast, let us notice that the population of the Tyumen Region actively uses the Internet while the provision of computers by employers is insufficient. The digital potential of the Tyumen Region's population is incomplete. The data shown in Table 6 could be considered as indirect proof of the high digital potential of the Tyumen Region.

The share of the population using the Mobile web matches (99–103%) or exceeds (115%) the population in the region or district. It partially means that some people have more than one SIM card in a single mobile phone or different mobile phones (personal and corporate as an example). Significantly, the share of the mobile web usage is higher for Tyumen Region. This indicates the extensive use of different access channels of the Mobile web and indirectly supports the high level of the population's digital skills. But along with this, it becomes harder to make a distinction between personal and operational traffic load.

5 Discussion

In our study, we focused on widely available data. This, according to the authors, will allow any interested person to assess the digital potential of the region's labour resources without additional research. The availability of indexes for analysis forced us to choose two indexes as indicators: the proportion of the population that regularly uses the Internet, as this allows us to identify them as confident Internet users, and therefore they can be considered as an integral part of the digital potential of the region's workforce. The availability of computers with Internet access makes it possible to assess the ability of employers to use the digital potential of the labour resources of the region. On the other hand, this indicator reflects the demand for digital competencies of the population on the part of employers and stimulates the population to improve their digital skills. There is a lag in official statistics in time, it is on average 2 years. However, the trends are quite clear. As was already mentioned in the Theoretical Fundamentals part, when analyzing various aspects characterizing the level of mastering digital skills and digital literacy of residents of different regions, the indicator that determines the digital labour potential of regions has never been used in both Russian and foreign publications. The level of use of labour digital potential by organizations of the Ural Federal District regions, alongside the comparison with the Northwestern Federal District, is commeasurable and reflects common trends caused by the economic advance of the regions. Certain time lag associated with the delay in obtaining statistical data does not allow us to assess the trends for 2021–2022. Meanwhile, the analysis of data for the last two years should be analyzed in the context of studies [26] that used Digital Impact concept. This is one of the directions for further research since this approach fully confirms our conclusions about the correlation between the labour digital potential of region and the activity of employers in using the digital skills of the population.

6 Conclusions

We note the following trends among the results of the study:

1. There is a slight differentiation in the level of digital potential of the region's resources, both for individual federal districts and for regions within the federal district.
2. There is a definite growth trend, both in the digital skills of the population and in the willingness of employers to use the digital competencies of the workforce.
3. Regions are characterized by the different intensity of use of digital skills of the population. There are leading ones among them, such as the Chelyabinsk region. A backlog in the Chelyabinsk region was compensated by 2015, inclusive of the increase in opportunities provided by employers. There are also regions with insufficient use of digital potential (Tyumen region), where, with a high level of digital potential of the population, it is not fully used by employers.

The results of the study of the processes of formation of the digital potential of the labour resources of the region can be used by regional and municipal authorities in selection options for the digitalization of the region's economy. Depending on the situation, a set of measures can be aimed at the formation and development of digital skills of the population following business needs or at stimulating and training entrepreneurs to fully use the digital competencies that the labour resources of the region possess.

The authors plan to compare the dynamics of the labour digital potential of region and the digital potential of region in calculated according to the methodology [27] to analyze if there is a correlation between these potentials on the example of a pool of regions. Consideration and data acquisition for regions with a further correlation detection between the indicators of regional development and indicators of the quality of life of the population of region will determine the directions for further research.

Acknowledgments. The research is partially funded by the Ministry of Science and Higher Education of the Russian Federation under the strategic academic leadership program 'Priority 2030' (Agreement No. 075–15-2021–1333 dd 09/30/2021).

References

1. Wang, L., Zhou, Y., Zheng, G.: Linking digital HRM practices with HRM effectiveness: the moderate role of HRM capability maturity from the adaptive structuration perspective. Sustain. **14**, 1003 (2022). https://doi.org/10.3390/su14021003
2. Zhilenkova, E., Budanova, M., Bulkhov, N., Rodionov, D.: Reproduction of intellectual capital in innovative-digital economy environment. IOP Conf. Ser. Mater. Sci. Eng. **497**, 012065 (2019). https://doi.org/10.1088/1757-899X/497/1/012065
3. Antonov, E.V.: Urban agglomerations: approaches to the allocation and delimitation. outlines Glob. Transform. Polit. Econ. Law **13**, 180–202 (2020). https://doi.org/10.23932/2542-0240-2020-13-1-10
4. Didenko, N., Skripnuk, D., Kikkas, K., Kalinina, O., Kosinski, E.: The impact of digital transformation on the micrologistic system, and the open innovation in logistics. J. Open Innov. Technol. Mark. Complex. **7**, 115 (2021). https://doi.org/10.3390/joitmc7020115
5. Maratovich, G.N., Nailevich, K.B., Alexandrovich, K.I.: Cluster analysis of the Russian regions by the human capital development and digital resources factors. Int. J. Emerg. Technol. **10**, 225–231 (2019)
6. Simonova, M., Kolesnikov, S., Karakova, T.: Assessment of labor potential on the regional level by the index method. MATEC Web Conf. **170**, 01069 (2018). https://doi.org/10.1051/matecconf/201817001069
7. Wahyuningtyas, R., Disastra, G., Rismayani, R.: Toward cooperative competitiveness for community development in Economic Society 5.0. J. Enterpr. Commun. (2022). https://doi.org/10.1108/JEC-10-2021-0149
8. Christ-Brendemühl, S., Schaarschmidt, M.: Frontline backlash: service employees' deviance from digital processes. J. Serv. Mark. **33**, 936–945 (2019). https://doi.org/10.1108/JSM-03-2019-0125
9. Langstrand, J., Elg, M.: Non-human resistance in changes towards lean. J. Organ. Chang. Manag. **25**, 853–866 (2012). https://doi.org/10.1108/09534811211280609
10. Nel, J., Boshoff, C.: Traditional-bank customers' digital-only bank resistance: evidence from South Africa. Int. J. Bank Mark. **39**, 429–454 (2020). https://doi.org/10.1108/IJBM-07-2020-0380
11. Pedersen, T., Scedrova, A., Grecu, A.: The effects of IT investments and skilled labor on firms' value added. Technovation **116**, 102479 (2022). https://doi.org/10.1016/j.technovation.2022.102479
12. Zaborovskaia, O., Nadezhina, O., Avduevskaya, E.: The impact of digitalization on the formation of human capital at the regional level. J. Open Innov. Technol. Mark. Complex. **6**, 1–24 (2020). https://doi.org/10.3390/joitmc6040184
13. Mirolyubova, T., Voronchikhina, E.: Assessment of the digital transformation impact on regional sustainable development: the case study in Russia. Int. J. Sustain. Econ. **14**, 24–54 (2022). https://doi.org/10.1504/IJSE.2022.119723

14. Aleksandrov, I.N., Fedorova, M.Y.: Digital economy and green economy: rural unemployment and territorial self-development in Russia. E3S Web Conf. **110**, 02019 (2019). https://doi.org/10.1051/e3sconf/201911002019
15. Pan, W., Xie, T., Wang, Z., Ma, L.: Digital economy: an innovation driver for total factor productivity. J. Bus. Res. **139**, 303–311 (2022). https://doi.org/10.1016/j.jbusres.2021.09.061
16. Bai, H.: Role of digital technology in transforming organizational competencies influencing green economy: moderating role of product knowledge hiding. Front. Psychol. **12** (2021). https://doi.org/10.3389/fpsyg.2021.792550
17. Riveros, C., Arenas, Á., Castro, M., Olivares, M.: Public policies, gaps and digital literacy of the elderly people: The Chilean reality observed from the communes of talca and San Joaquín. Rev. Direito, Estado e Telecomunicacoes. **12**, 137–158 (2020). https://doi.org/10.26512/lstr.v12i1.31180
18. Sirotkina, N., Mishchenko, V., Greshonkov, A., Kaminskiy, S., Kazartseva, A.: Challenges and opportunities of human potential in the conditions of technological breakthrough. In: Proceedings of the 33rd International Business Information Management Association Conference, IBIMA 2019 Education Excellence and Innovation Management Through Vision, 2020, pp. 7910–7918 (2019)
19. Abrahamyan, G., Atayan, A., Sharabaeva, L., Gureva, T.: The model of an online digital competencies development system for the management personnel of the Arctic region. IOP Conf. Ser. Earth Environ. Sci. **678**, 012027 (2021). https://doi.org/10.1088/1755-1315/678/1/012027
20. Zilian, S.S., Zilian, L.S.: Digital inequality in Austria: Empirical evidence from the survey of the OECD "Programme for the International Assessment of Adult Competencies." Technol. Soc. **63**, 101397 (2020). https://doi.org/10.1016/j.techsoc.2020.101397
21. Reynolds, L., Henderson, D., Xu, C., Norris, L.: Digitalisation and the foundational economy: a digital opportunity or a digital divide for less-developed regions? Local Econ. **36**, 451–467 (2021). https://doi.org/10.1177/02690942211072239
22. Jiménez-Pitre, I.A., Martelo, R.J., Jaimes, J.D.C.: Government school based on ICT: a key strategy for achieving digital empowerment, accessibility, and integrality. Inf. Tecnol. **28**, 75–86 (2017). https://doi.org/10.4067/s0718-07642017000500010
23. Grön, K.: Common good in the era of data-intensive healthcare. Humanit. Soc. Sci. Commun. **8**, 230 (2021). https://doi.org/10.1057/s41599-021-00911-w
24. Irfan, E., Ali, Y., Sabir, M.: Analysing role of businesses' investment in digital literacy: a case of Pakistan. Technol. Forecast. Soc. Change. **176**, 121484 (2022). https://doi.org/10.1016/j.techfore.2022.121484
25. Silva, D.S., Yamashita, G.H., Cortimiglia, M.N., Brust-Renck, P.G., ten Caten, C.S.: Are we ready to assess digital readiness? Exploring digital implications for social progress from the Network Readiness Index. Technol. Soc. **68**, 101875 (2022). https://doi.org/10.1016/j.techsoc.2022.101875
26. Nakhusheva, Z.A. Ashinova, I.V. Alikaeva, M.V.: Construction of function of influence of digital impact on socio-economic ecosystem of the region. News Kabard. Sci. Cent. RAS. **6**, 214–221 (2021). https://doi.org/10.35330/1991-6639-2021-6-104-214-221
27. Kozlov, A.V. Teslya, A.B. Ivashchenko, A.A.: Creating an indicator system to survey the digitalization process of a national economy. Izv. Vyss. uchebnyh Zaved. Ser. Jekonomika, Finans. i Upr. Proizv. **1**, 97–107 (2021). https://doi.org/10.6060/ivecofin.20214701.522

Enhancing Teachers' Digital Competence for Professional Development in Distance Mode

Marine Gurgenidze[1]([✉]) [iD], Nana Makaradze[1] [iD], Tatia Nakashidze-Makharadze[1] [iD], Anna Karmanova[2], Zhanna Nikiforova[2] [iD], and Victoria A. Sheleiko[2] [iD]

[1] Batumi Shota Rustaveli State University (BSU), Batumi, Georgia
`marine.gurgenidze@bsu.edu.ge`
[2] Peter the Great St. Petersburg Polytechnic University (SPbPU), Saint Petersburg, Russian Federation

Abstract. The teaching profession is dynamic and requires constant development. By introducing and prioratising an effective professional development system, school facilitates the introduction of innovations. The term "professional development" refers to an orderly, continuous, and intensive approach to improving teacher's work efficiency with the ultimate goal of further enhancing student achievement which involves three interrelated stages: study of specific needs, planning and implementation of relevant activities, evaluation of the obtained effect. The most popular activities are trainings with the core concept of digitalization, which involves developing teachers digital competence and skills using digital tools. During the pandemic, the practice of offering various types of online trainings for teacher professional development has gradually increased. Different digital educational platforms were introduced. Above mentioned online trainings/webinars were the best solution to maintain the continuity of teachers' professional development, however, this process posed a number of challenges to the pedagogical community. The purpose of the present work is, to identify the strengths and weaknesses of distance training, evaluate its results and define ways to increase efficiency. Research methods: surveys, interviews, focus groups. The research was conducted in 3 stages: an online survey of teachers, an interview with 14 school principals and a focus group with trainers/representatives of training organizations. Research outcomes: Though teacher development programs were problematic in terms of intensity, outdated topics, teachers lack of digital competence, poor internet connection, lack of implementation and evaluation of the training experience, the flexibility and availability of attendance, access to the materials enhanced teachers readiness and motivation. On the basis of the research and analysis that highlight the current situation recommendations are made which will add practical value to the study.

Keywords: Professional development · Online trainings · Digital platforms · Digital tools · Digital competence · Training evaluation

© Springer Nature Switzerland AG 2022
D. Rodionov et al. (Eds.): SPBPU IDE 2021, CCIS 1619, pp. 277–291, 2022.
https://doi.org/10.1007/978-3-031-14985-6_20

1 Introduction

The teaching profession is dynamic and requires constant development, the essence of which is the constant development and improvement of professional knowledge and personal skills. By introducing an effective professional development system, the school will be able to facilitate the introduction of innovations. The school management is obliged to properly assess the existing needs for professional development and to constantly allocate appropriate resources for these purposes. Moreover, professional development should be one of the main priorities of the school and an integral part of the strategic development plan.

When planning professional development, it is useful to use the following strategies: extended working day, increase of working days, summer trainings, replacement of teachers, use of weekends, etc. Self-analysis (reflection) of one's own practice is a particularly important skill for professional development [1, 2].

Professional development goals can be achieved in a variety of ways, but when planning them, it is important to keep in mind that a specific event should aim to acquire and improve knowledge and skills as needed. To meet the needs of professional development, the school should select the activities that best suit its specifics and conditions. These are: collaboration between school and university, professional development in any form/at any time, project development, conferences, collaboration with other schools, sharing experiences with colleagues, mentoring (For this it is necessary to train expert teachers so that they can mentor, conduct professional dialogue and make assessments), Special courses/trainings/webinars offered by non-governmental organizations or government agencies [1, 2].

Simons, P., & Ruijters, M. C. [3] state that two requirements are required for professionals. The first is to take care of self-development and to develop and support learning in students, while the second is integrity. If these two requirements are met, then teachers must develop four qualities: first, they must have theoretical knowledge and be able to put it into practice; Second, they need an action plan and a desire to improve their pedagogical work based on reflection; Third, they must be experts in their field and seek and implement innovations in their own practice, both individually and collectively; Fourth, they must have a professional framework, ie they must belong to a professional community that copes with difficulties as a result of collective work. If teachers meet these two requirements or have these four qualities, they, as recognized professionals and can enjoy greater autonomy and authority. Teachers, in addition to their own professional development, should support the learning of colleagues. Thus, they can create professional learning communities in which they are constantly seeking and sharing each other's experiences and improving their skills [4, 5].

By introducing an effective professional development system, the school will be able to facilitate the introduction of innovations. In order to regularly introduce innovative teaching methods, improve the teaching-learning process, establish research-based teaching practices, meet students' interests and needs, improve student attendance and enhance achievement - the school must pay special attention to the professional development of colleagues. The school management is obliged to properly assess the existing needs for professional development and to constantly allocate appropriate resources for these purposes [6]. Moreover, professional development should be one of the main priorities of the school and an integral part of the strategic development plan. According to Bates "Ideally the state or province Council of Universities or Colleges, or school boards, should get together and develop a comprehensive system of training for all teachers and ensure that such programs are continually updated."

Teacher professional development is directly related to school success. If the school is considered as an organizational unit where the role of the teacher as a leader is important, then its professional development is one of the indicators of the school's success. The professional development of a teacher depends on all kinds of professional activities that the teacher is engaged in. However, professional development is often equated only with special training programs and webinars, which is wrong. Such a vision significantly hinders the development of the organization/its employees. Professional development is a broader concept. It is a kind of framework within which the daily activities of the organization should take place. Trainings/webinars are just one specific component of this process and not the only means of professional development.

The term "professional development" refers to an orderly, continuous, and intensive approach to improving teacher's work efficiency with the ultimate goal of further enhancing student achievement. Teacher professional development can serve several purposes. Including: (1) updating of subject knowledge; (2) updating skills, attitudes, and approaches to address new learning objectives, new circumstances, and education research; (3) to enable teachers and schools to make new changes in the teaching process following the curriculum; (4) exchanging information and knowledge between teachers and scientists, entrepreneurs and researchers, and (5) increasing the effectiveness of weak teachers [OECD 1998] [20].

The professional development of school teachers should be promoted, first of all, by the school principal himself. It is their responsibility to develop professional development programs and to ensure every employees active involvment according to their professional needs and requirements. When developing continuing professional development programs, the school principal should ensure that they meet the needs of the school. Thus, programs must always be implemented with particular efficiency and real results must be ensured. It is important to develop a convenient schedule and evaluate the results adequately, especially when working in distance mode.

2 Discussion and Findings

The professional development process involves three interrelated stages. These are: evaluating needs, planning and implementation of specific professional development activities, evaluation of the obtained effect. In a successful organization, this cycle is continuous and creates a solid foundation needed to maintain competitiveness and quality at a qualitatively new, higher level [7, 8].

"Professional development programs for teachers should aim to increase professional competence in at least one of the following areas:

1. Knowledge of the subject;
2. Use of new technologies in the education process;

3. Evaluation strategies;
4. National priorities of the education system;
5. Methods and curriculum."

After defining the main directions of professional development, it is necessary to outline specific measures that will enable the teacher to achieve the desired results by deepening skills and knowledge. It is also important to determine how the results will be evaluated; In order to effectively manage the evaluation process, it is necessary to develop appropriate criteria for the evaluation process. Even the most effective professional development measure will not bring the desired result if it is not tailored to specific needs. Should a school principal know why a teacher needs professional growth in a particular case? How will his professional development benefit the school? How effectively were the teacher's professional development activities selected?

"Several important factors contribute to the professional development of teachers". In particular:

The teacher is considered an active student (he/she should always be in the process of searching and learning);

It is a long, time-consuming process where teachers learn for a long time;

It is perceived as a process where specific issues are discussed;

It is closely related to school development;

The teacher should apply the acquired knowledge in practice;

"It is closely linked to the collaborative process."

Teacher professional development can be considered successful if:

Combines different ways to improve education;

Applys an individual development plan;

Student assessment results are successful;

The teacher correctly identifies the existing needs;

A professional development plan is developed based on the student's basic learning needs and serves to solve common problems;

Allows teachers to collaborate with colleagues both on and off school;

Promotes current and future professional development;

Integrates the principles of adult education;

Provides sufficient time and resources;

The performance of the teacher will be positively evaluated according to the results of the students' achievements;

Teacher professional development takes place mainly on a school basis. Because the teacher has more opportunities to apply the knowledge in practice at school. However, given the modern requirements, the school principal should actively involve teachers in the ongoing education process. It assists teachers in fulfilling the learning goals and objectives set out in the national and school curricula [9–11].

The school administration is obliged to explain to the staff that in order to develop professionaly and educate the students, it is important to allocate adequate time for professional development and to participate fully in the programs they need. "Professional development in any form is essential at all levels. The main starting point of the learning process is the student and the result achieved. The school leader, as an educational leader, has a responsibility to nurture and promote a strong collaborative, democratic school-based school culture in which strive for quality student education and school-based teacher professional development is paramount".

When planning professional development, it is useful to use the following strategies: providing time for teachers' for development built in workday, summer trainings, providing class coverage from other teachers, allocating time on weekends, etc.

Professional development goals can be achieved in a variety of ways, but when planning them, it is important to keep in mind that a specific event should aim to acquire and improve knowledge and skills as needed [12, 13]. To meet the needs of professional development, the school should select the activities that best suit its specifics and conditions. These are:

Cooperation between school and university - Within the framework of cooperation between school and university, it is possible to offer special training/retraining courses for teachers and administration staff;

Professional development in any form/at any time - such an approach is useful for any school subject. Development can be accessed in a variety of formats, including distance learning courses and/or other media.

Development of projects - One of the means of professional development is also the development of special educational projects, which will be directly related to the existing needs of school development.

Conferences - Participating in conferences is a good way to raise knowledge and exchange ideas for both teachers and administrators.

Collaborating with other schools - Collaborating with schools (roundtables, conferences and other events) is an effective approach not only for one school-specific professional development but for all schools across the municipality.

Sharing the experience of colleagues - In the process of observing the activities of colleagues and sharing their experience, the teacher observes the practice of his colleague, and then gives feedback. In order for observation to be beneficial to both parties, it is essential that there is trust between colleagues and a desire for mutual assistance.

Mentoring - Working with a successful and experienced teacher as a mentor is one of the most effective tools for professional development for beginners and less experienced teachers. This requires the training of expert teachers so that they can mentor, conduct professional dialogue and make assessments. Mentoring can be done in a variety of ways, such as by organizing regular meetings, observing lessons, and so on.

Special courses/trainings/webinars offered by non-governmental organizations or government agencies - It is the responsibility of the school administration to ensure that information about such courses/trainings/webinars is obtained and disseminated in the school.

Among the specific professional development activities, the most popular today is training, which involves equipping employees with new knowledge and skills, as well as deepening existing knowledge. Training is the most common form of knowledge acquisition. Traditional training is very close to the lesson process - the trainer (field expert, professional) tries to convey specific factual information to the listener and develop practical skills by using different methods of adult teaching. Quite often, this process takes place away from the workplace so that the training participants can concentrate as much as possible and be actively involved in the training program.

During the pandemic crisis, the practice of offering various types of online training and webinars for teacher professional development has gradually increased. This, on the one hand, was the best solution to maintain the continuity of teachers' professional development, however, on the other hand, this process posed a number of challenges to the pedagogical community [14, 15].

Given the importance of the issue, it is essential to determine, in particular, what are the strengths of distance training and what are its challenges? In the current period, does this form of professional development achieve the set goal and what results has it shown? What needs to be maintained and what needs to be changed in terms of distance training planning/implementation? What is the attitude of teachers and school principals towards distance learning?

These questions formed the basis of the research conducted in the secondary schools of Adjara region.

The main objectives of the study are: to identify the strengths and weaknesses of distance training, to determine the results of online training and to identify ways to increase efficiency.

3 Methodology and Data Analysis

The study of the strengths and weaknesses of the distance training is essential to enhance teachers' professional development. The object of given research are 321 teachers of public schools in Adjara region.

The methods that were used to achieve the set goals: Survey, interview (with school principals), focus groups (with trainers/representatives of training organizations).

The research was conducted in 3 stages. In the first phase of the research, an online survey of teachers was conducted. In the second stage, an interview with 14 school principals was conducted through interviews [16]. In the next phase of the research, a focus group was conducted with trainers/representatives of training organizations.

In the first phase of the research, an online survey of teachers was conducted.

To the question "How intense are the online trainings?" 75.21% of the respondents indicated high intensity. 20.79% - above average, 4% - below. These indicators allow us to think that not all teachers are equally involved in the process due to unequal opportunities or lack of desire. It is also noteworthy that the teachers of the city schools are more involved in the trainings (Fig. 1).

The response to the question about the duration of the trainings show that both long-term trainings are held - for a few weeks or a whole year and short-term trainings - from 1 to 5 days.

In response to the question "Which day of the week is mostly allocated for trainings?" respondents note that meetings are scheduled both on weekdays (after work hours) and on weekends. 68.2% of the surveyed teachers notice in the comments that there are cases when you do not leave any day of the week free, due to which they do not have chance to relax and are tired at the beginning of the new week. This may adversely affect the quality of the learning process.

„How Intensive are online trainings?"

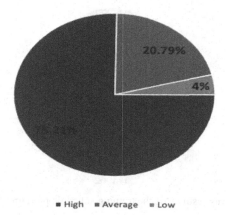

■ High   ■ Average   ■ Low

Fig. 1. Survey results: "How intensive are online trading?"

The response to the question "Is there a coincidence of different training times?" 57% of the surveyed teachers indicates that there are cases when two (in rare cases - more) coincide in the training/meeting time. The comments indicate that at this time teachers have to record attendance using two technical means, hindering the process of fully understanding the material presented at the trainings. Teachers are able to supplement their knowledge by listening to meeting records (if any), but at the expense of extra time and reduced rest time (Fig. 2).

"Is there a coincidence of different training times?"

■ Yes   ■ No

Fig. 2. Survey results: "Is there a coincidence of different training times?"

The response to the question "Is the training schedule pre-agreed with you?" show that the training organizers only in certain cases (12.3%) agree schedule with listeners. Basically (87.7%) in case the listeners have to adapt to the offered schedule. We think it is important to agree on a schedule with the trainees at the planning/organizing stage of the training, which will reduce the likelihood of several trainings coming together, increase the effectiveness of the training and have a positive impact on its results (Fig. 3).

"Is the training schedule pre-agreed with you?"

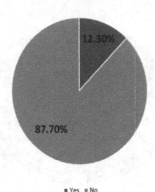

Fig. 3. Survey results: "Is the training schedule pre-agreed with you?"

The response to the question "How do you assess the productivity of the trainings in terms of your professional development?" respondents indicated that some of the information presented at the training is related to topics already familiar to them. Consequently, such trainings will not be able to take important steps for their development. However, there is also the practice of conducting trainings on innovative and valuable issues (Fig. 4).

"How do you assess the productivity of the training in terms of your professional development?"

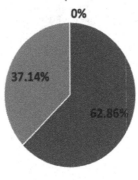

Fig. 4. Survey results: "How do you assess the productivity of the training in terms of your professional development?"

In response to the question "What are the strengths of online training and what are the challenges you face during online training?" teachers consider the strengths of the ability to engage in training from anywhere, to save finances (road, hotel, etc.), to communicate with experienced trainers, to re-listen and view the reviewed material when needed, if necessary.

44.75% consider schedule inconsistency as a challenge, which often results in two or more training sessions coinciding.

For 17.5%, the difficulty is the lack of skills to work on different electronic platforms. Because not all platform skills are well developed, they believe that a platform that is well-owned by all members of the group should be selected before the training, or that the training organizers should consult on how to use it before the meeting.

30.5% consider the insufficient frequency of the Internet as a challenge, which is why they are involved in the process with significant delays.

For 15.34% the obsolescence and malfunction of technical means poses a problem.

37.85% consider the increase of the number of trainings as a problem. Respondents notice that in such a situation they often experience a lack of free time and at the same time, in a short time they have to listen/understand a lot of information and face difficulties in transposing and reflecting.

75.5% name stress as a challenge due to working online, find it difficult to cope with stress and try to minimize or not be active during the training.

In general, overwork and stress is a very important problem because more work than an individual can actually overcome will inevitably lead to fatigue, exhaustion, occupational stress, and decreased productivity. Risks in this regard should be considered and appropriate preventive measures should be taken.

To the question "What would you change about the organization and content of online training?" Teachers consider it necessary:

- Schedule to be agreed in advance with the group;
- Determine the number of training courses for individual trainees to avoid fatigue and reduced productivity;
- When determining the content of the training, the material should optimally be selected to enable not only the analysis of new material, but also the effective transfer into practice and appropriate reflection.

At the next stage, an interview with 14 school principals was conducted through interviews. The initial version of the questionnaire was based on the analysis of the results of the teachers' research. Respondents indicated that the ability to conduct trainings in online format has greatly increased their number. The number of trainings organized by the public sector, as well as projects and programs planned under various programs has increased. We inquired whether the details of the training (target group, time, duration) were agreed with them, it was found that in some cases they participate in the selection of the target group of the training, the duration and time of the event are determined by the organizers. Teachers also disagree less about this. Trainings are scheduled during non-working hours and today and thus do not interfere with the learning process. Respondents pointed to the excessive number of online trainings and did not rule out that this, due to the development of fatigue, may have affected the motivation of teachers in addition to reducing productivity. They observed cases when teachers refused to participate in the training during the formation of the training group. There were cases when a teacher involved in a long-term (for example one-year) program had to be replaced.

They do not link this to just the fatigue factor. It is noticed that teachers are motivated to participate in the trainings by trainings that will directly affect their career advancement (the hours spent within the training will be recognized as credits). During the interview, the principals highlighted the lack of practice in using the knowledge gained during the trainings in the classroom, citing the fact that the knowledge gained during the trainings was not piloted and evaluated by the trainers. Also, a large proportion of the trainings have less practical component, which does not prevent a large part of the trainees from being in a passive role. According to the respondents, the trainings should be more focused on developing the practical skills of the trainees, especially in the case of long-term trainings [17, 18].

In the next phase of the research, a focus group was conducted with trainers/representatives of training organizations. First of all, it should be noted that the composition of the focus group was mixed, which was due to the diversity and abundance of organizations/providers providing teacher training. Representatives of both state (31.7%) and private sector/programs/projects (41.1%) and non-governmental (27.2%) organizations participated in the focus group. As we can see, the private sector is particularly interested in distance learning, and the main reason for this is the lower demands for the private sector/programs/projects and less responsibility for training outcomes. Consequently, the answers to the questions asked within the focus group were also quite different.

The answer to the question "On what principle do you choose the target group of the training?" Mostly depended on type of training organization: the private sector training group voluntarily registers for the announced training or the training group is based on a preliminary survey/surveys. As for non-governmental sector, they conducts various trainings within different projects. Accordingly, they purposefully plan trainings for representatives of a specific field. As for the public sector, as the study revealed, it mainly carries out the state order and is less involved in the selection of training target groups. The time of the training is agreed directly with the trainees after the start of the training and the communication between the two parties, however, due to the number of trainees in the group, which is less limited in online mode and sometimes averages 20–25 trainees, full agreement can not be reached [19].

Naturally, training organizations and trainers response to the question "What is the attitude of teachers towards online training?" They believe that online trainings are much more convenient and flexible for the trainees, however, they also emphasize that although the positive attitude of the teachers is felt during the summarizing of the trainings, the answers in the training evaluation questionnaire are mixed.

On the question "What challenges did the trainer face during the online training?", Almost the entire focus group participants highlighted the problem of trainees' digital competencies. Trainers find it particularly problematic for participants to have insufficient skills to use the platforms that teachers have had to deal with when switching to distance learning. Almost all of them cited the ability to use Teams as an example, which was required for all public schools in Georgia from the first day of transition to distance learning, although the massive use of this platform was spontaneous, without any preparatory work and training. On the progress and results, and this requires extra time and effort from the trainer.

The training organizations/trainers are ultimately satisfied with the results of the trainings, as evidenced by their answers to the question "How do you evaluate the effectiveness of online trainings in terms of results?". As they point out, the trainings mainly achieve the set goal and desired results, however, they also note that the trainings do not involve checking/evaluating the training results directly in the field - in the classroom and therefore do not have information on how the knowledge gained in the trainings is implemented directly in the classroom. The focus group revealed that pre- and post-tests are rarely used in training, which is one of the best ways to measure training outcomes.

Regarding the question "What would you change about the organization and content of online trainings?", The focus group participants noted that they have the opportunity to make changes directly to the organization of trainings with each new training group, which, of course, they can not say about the content of trainings. The public and nongovernmental sector mainly has a strictly written content of trainings, while the private sector is entirely focused on research and plans the content of trainings on the basis of preliminary and post-training surveys.

Effectively planned and result-oriented training significantly contributes to the professional development of the teacher, which in turn increases student achievement in learning. "In general, the professional development of teachers will be effective if it is based on research. Surveys should focus on the outcome of each student. It is essential that the teacher constantly monitors, analyzes, and identifies the relationships between the strategy he or she uses and the benefits to the students: "What will they learn, how will they learn, and how will my student benefit if I use particular teaching method mastered by me? Therefore, the effectiveness of professional development is determined not only by the degree of mastery of this or that strategy by the teacher, but also by its impact on students' learning and outcomes." In this difficult path, teachers make changes in their pedagogical practice as a result of research-based professional development. The reflexive teacher should always ask himself the following questions: "What do my students know and what should they know? In what areas should I improve my professional knowledge and skills so that my students can achieve their learning goals?" What should they be able to do and what can they do? etc."

Lastly and most importantly as Bates A.W. notes: "Although governments, institutions and learners themselves can do a great deal to ensure success in teaching and learning, in the end the responsibility and to some extent the power to change lies within teachers and instructors themselves."

4 The Analysis of Research Outcomes

The intensity training programs in remote mode is quite high, which causes the trainees to be overwhelmed and sometimes stressed [1, 2]. In fact, the training schedule (date, time) is not agreed in advance with the school administration and the trainees, online trainings often coincide in time, and at this time teachers have to record attendance using two technical means, the complete understanding of the material presented at the trainings is hindered. Teachers try to fill up their knowledge by listening to re recording (if the meeting was recorded), but at the expense of allocating additional time and reducing rest time. To achieve desired outcomes trainings should be planned meticulously.

The schedule should be agreed with the school administration and the trainees which will reduce the likelihood of several trainings overlapping and increase the effectiveness of the training and have a positive effect on its results. Also, the number of training courses for individual trainees should be adjusted in order to avoid cases of their fatigue and decreased productivity [1, 2].

In terms of professional development, the productivity of the trainings does not always reach the desired level - not all trainings are based on important news, part of the information presented at the training refers to topics already familiar to the trainees. Therefore, such trainings cannot enhance teachers professional development. However, our research revealed the practice of conducting innovative content trainings too;

According to the results of the research, the strengths of online training are considered to be the ability to participate in the training from any place, saving money (travel, accomodation expenses, etc.), chance to communicate with experienced trainers, rewatch and discuss material again when necessary in case of a video recording of the training; The challenges of online trainings are considered to be the schedules, trainees digital incompetence, the insufficient frequency of the Internet, due to which the trainees engage in the process with significant delays, the age and malfunction of technical means, the excessive increase in the number of trainings, the stress associated with working in the online mode; In order to improve the quality of online trainings, it is important to develop trainees digital skills of using different platforms.

Less practice of using the knowledge gained in online trainings in the classroom is considered a problem, due to the fact that the knowledge gained during the trainings is not piloted and evaluated by the trainers; A large portion of the trainings have less of a practical component, which does not prevent a large part of the trainees from being in a passive role.

Trainings should be more focused on the development of trainees' practical skills, especially in the case of long-term trainings;

The results achieved within the trainings and their evaluation are of the utmost importance, to determine the extent to which it was possible to raise the knowledge and develop the skills of the trainees, to determine/evaluate how well the training trainees mastered the material provided and to what extent they transfer the acquired knowledge in the educational process;

It is important to evaluate the effectiveness of the trainings by the trainee - self-evaluation (what I learned and how my practice changed), evaluation of the knowledge gained by the trainee, to determin what the person actually learned by participating in a specific process. Pre-test and post-test can be a nice solution to this problem.

As one of the most important criteria for evaluating the effectiveness of the training course is the practical application of the knowledge gained by the trainee, it is important to observe the work process in order to measure the results of the training.

Teachers are motivated to participate in those online trainings that have a direct impact on their career advancement (recognition of hours spent within the training in the form of credits).

5 Conclusion

Based on the analysis of the research results, we can make the following conclusions:

- The teaching profession is dynamic and needs constant development. The essence of professional development is the continuous development and improvement of professional knowledge and personal skills.
- By introducing an effective system of professional development, the school will be able to promote the introduction of innovations. The teaching-learning process is improved, the research-based teaching practice is established, the interests and needs of the students are satisfied, and the academic performance of the students is improved.
- The process of professional development involves three interrelated steps. These are: needs research, planning-implementation of specific measures of professional development, evaluation of the obtained effect.
- To ensure the need for professional development, cooperation between the school and the university should be of utmost importance; professional development in any form/at any time; development of projects; conferences; cooperation with other schools; sharing the experience of colleagues; mentorship; Special courses/trainings/webinars offered by non-governmental organizations or government agencies.
- Training is the most popular of the specific events/activities of professional development.
- In the conditions of the pandemic crisis, the practice of offering different types of online training and webinars for the professional development of teachers gradually increased.
- The advantages of online trainings are the ability to engage in training from anywhere, save finances (travel, accommodation, etc.), interact with experienced trainers, and videotape the reviewed material as needed;
- Challenges of online trainings are considered to be: inconsistency of training schedule with the trainees; Lack of skills to work in different electronic platforms; Insufficient frequency of the Internet, due to which the trainees have significant delays in the process; The intensity of distance learning is quite high, which causes overload of the trainees; Stress related to working in online mode; Not all the trainings are based on introducing innovative topics; There is no piloting and evaluation of the knowledge gained within the trainings by the trainers; Most of the trainings do not include a practical component; Less practice of using the knowledge gained in online trainings in the classroom.

6 Recommendations

- It is important to agree on a schedule with the school administration and participants at the planning/organizing stage of the training, which will reduce the likelihood of several trainings overlapping, increase the effectiveness of the training, and have a positive impact on its outcomes.
- Also, the number of training courses for individual trainees should be adjusted to avoid cases of their fatigue and reduced productivity.

- The most important thing is the results achieved during the trainings and its evaluation, to determine the extent to which the trainees' knowledge and skills were developed, to determine/evaluate how well the trainees mastered the material provided and how well they transfer the acquired knowledge in the learning process.
- It is important to evaluate the effectiveness of the training by the trainee - self-assessment (what I have learned and how my practice has changed), assessment of the knowledge gained by the trainee, or to determine what a person has actually learned by participating in a particular process. To assess this, pre-testing and post-testing are noteworthy. The difference between the answers given to the two tests at different times (before and after the training) reflects the effect that the training course had.
- As one of the most important criteria for evaluating the effectiveness of a training course is the application of the knowledge gained by the trainee in practice, it is important to observe the work process in order to measure the training results.
- Trainings should be more focused on developing participants' practical skills, especially in the case of long-term training.
- In order to improve the quality of online training, it is important to develop the skills of teachers to use different platforms.

References

1. Liu, A., Liu, N., Wang, A.: Why can't rural schools retain young teachers? An analysis of the professional development of rural school teachers in China: taking teachers in rural western China. Soc. Sci. Humanit. Open. **5**, 100238 (2022). https://doi.org/10.1016/J.SSAHO.2021.100238
2. Nelimarkka, M., Leinonen, T., Durall, E., Dean, P.: Facebook is not a silver bullet for teachers' professional development: anatomy of an eight-year-old social-media community. Comput. Educ. **173**, 104269 (2021). https://doi.org/10.1016/J.COMPEDU.2021.104269
3. Simons, P., Ruijters, M.C.: The real professional is a learning professional. In: Billett, S., Harteis, C., Gruber, H. (eds.) International Handbook of Research in Professional and Practice-based Learning. Springer International Handbooks of Education, pp. 955–985. Springer, Dordrecht (2014). https://doi.org/10.1007/978-94-017-8902-8_35
4. Hennessy, S., et al.: Technology use for teacher professional development in low- and middle-income countries: a systematic review. Comput. Educ. Open. **3**, 100080 (2022). https://doi.org/10.1016/J.CAEO.2022.100080
5. Kim, D., Long, Y., Zhao, Y., Zhou, S., Alexander, J.: Teacher professional identity development through digital stories. Comput. Educ. **162**, 104040 (2021). https://doi.org/10.1016/J.COMPEDU.2020.104040
6. Chaaban, Y., Arar, K., Sawalhi, R., Alhouti, I., Zohri, A.: Exploring teachers' professional agency within shifting educational contexts: a comparative study of Lebanon, Qatar, Kuwait, and Morocco. Teach. Teach. Educ. **106**, 103451 (2021). https://doi.org/10.1016/J.TATE.2021.103451
7. Mendoza, N.B., Cheng, E.C.K., Yan, Z.: Assessing teachers' collaborative lesson planning practices: Instrument development and validation using the SECI knowledge-creation model. Stud. Educ. Eval. **73**, 101139 (2022). https://doi.org/10.1016/J.STUEDUC.2022.101139
8. El Shaban, A., Egbert, J.: Diffusing education technology: a model for language teacher professional development in CALL. System **78**, 234–244 (2018). https://doi.org/10.1016/J.SYSTEM.2018.09.002

9. Çamlıbel-Acar, Z., Eveyik-Aydın, E.: Perspectives of EFL teacher trainers and pre-service teachers on continued mandatory distance education during the pandemic. Teach. Teach. Educ. **112**, 103635 (2022). https://doi.org/10.1016/J.TATE.2022.103635

10. Martin, A., Partika, A., Castle, S., Horm, D., Johnson, A.D.: Both sides of the screen: Predictors of parents' and teachers' depression and food insecurity during COVID-19-related distance learning. Early Child. Res. Q. **60**, 237–249 (2022). https://doi.org/10.1016/J.ECR ESQ.2022.02.001

11. Heikkilä, M., Iiskala, T., Mikkilä-Erdmann, M.: Voices of student teachers' professional agency at the intersection of theory and practice. Learn. Cult. Soc. Interact. **25**, 100405 (2020). https://doi.org/10.1016/J.LCSI.2020.100405

12. Tang, H.: Teaching teachers to use technology through massive open online course: perspectives of interaction equivalency. Comput. Educ. **174**, 104307 (2021). https://doi.org/10.1016/J.COMPEDU.2021.104307

13. Eshchar-Netz, L., Vedder-Weiss, D., Lefstein, A.: Status and inquiry in teacher communities. Teach. Teach. Educ. **109**, 103524 (2022). https://doi.org/10.1016/J.TATE.2021.103524

14. Segal, A.: Story exchange in teacher professional discourse. Teach. Teach. Educ. **86**, 102913 (2019). https://doi.org/10.1016/J.TATE.2019.102913

15. Prenger, R., Poortman, C.L., Handelzalts, A.: Factors influencing teachers' professional development in networked professional learning communities. Teach. Teach. Educ. **68**, 77–90 (2017). https://doi.org/10.1016/J.TATE.2017.08.014

16. Shoiynbayeva, G.T., Shokanov, A.K., Sydykova, Z.K., Sugirbekova, A.K., Kurbanbekov, B.A.: Methodological foundations of teaching nanotechnology when training future physics teachers. Think. Ski. Creat. **42**, 100970 (2021). https://doi.org/10.1016/J.TSC.2021.100970

17. Gaudin, C., Chaliès, S.: Video viewing in teacher education and professional development: a literature review. Educ. Res. Rev. **16**, 41–67 (2015). https://doi.org/10.1016/J.EDUREV.2015.06.001

18. Hordvik, M., Fletcher, T., Haugen, A.L., Møller, L., Engebretsen, B.: Using collaborative self-study and rhizomatics to explore the ongoing nature of becoming teacher educators. Teach. Teach. Educ. **101**, 103318 (2021). https://doi.org/10.1016/J.TATE.2021.103318

19. Ching, C.C., Hursh, A.W.: Peer modeling and innovation adoption among teachers in online professional development. Comput. Educ. **73**, 72–82 (2014). https://doi.org/10.1016/J.COMPEDU.2013.12.011

20. Distance Learning Management: A Practical Guide for School Administrators. The Georgian Association of School Administrators prepared the textbook. Editor-in-Chief: Gia Murghulia, Tbilisi (2021)

Digital Transformation Trends
in the Government and Financial Sector

Artificial Intelligence System for Financial Risk Prediction in the Banking Sector

Nikolay Lomakin[1]([✉]) [iD], Aleksandr Rybanov[2] [iD], Anastasiya Kulachinskaya[3] [iD],
Elena Goncharova[2] [iD], Uranchimeg Tudevdagva[4] [iD], and Yaroslav Repin[2] [iD]

[1] Volgograd State Technical University, Avenue V.I. Lenina, 28, Volgograd 400005, Russia
tel9033176642@yahoo.com
[2] Volga Polytechnic Institute (Branch), Volgograd State Technical University, St. Engels, 42a,
Volgograd Region, Volzhsky 404121, Russia
[3] Peter the Great St. Petersburg Polytechnic University,
Polytechnicheskaya, 29, St. Petersburg 195251, Russia
[4] Technische Universität Chemnitz, Chemnitz, Germany

Abstract. The aim of the study was to put forward and prove the hypothesis that using the AI system it is possible to obtain a forecast of the share of overdue loans in the bank's portfolio. Based on the study, the following results were obtained. Theoretical foundations of the analysis and forecasting of financial risk in the banking sector under conditions of market uncertainty have been studied. The novelty of the study lies in the fact that the share of overdue loans in the bank's portfolio can be predicted based on the use of the developed artificial intelligence system - perceptron. The practical significance is that the perceptron AI system can be recommended for practical use. The study showed that the total loan portfolio of Russian banks in 2020 grew by 13.8% to 63.2 trillion rubles. The share of overdue debt on loans decreased over the past year from 11.9 to 11%. However, the problem with the quality of loans remains relevant. As a result of this project, the perseptron program was developed to predict the dynamics of the share of overdue loans in the portfolio of a commercial bank, which was formed on the Deductor platform. It was revealed that the share of overdue loans of commercial banks is influenced by many factors, including the factors included in the AI system. The perseptron program has been developed to predict the dynamics of the share of overdue loans in the portfolio of a commercial bank.

Keywords: Financial risk · Market uncertainty · Loan portfolio · Perceptron · Bad loans · Money

1 Introduction

1.1 Review of Existing Research

The relevance of the study lies in the fact that the presence of overdue debt in the loan portfolios of commercial banks on loans to legal entities, individual entrepreneurs and individuals is currently an important problem and requires the development of modern

© Springer Nature Switzerland AG 2022
D. Rodionov et al. (Eds.): SPBPU IDE 2021, CCIS 1619, pp. 295–306, 2022.
https://doi.org/10.1007/978-3-031-14985-6_21

methods for its forecasting. In their article, Haoran S. and Boyan V. presented the results of a study on the credit risk assessment of an online network loan based on gradient-based decision tree (GBDT) [10]. Zhibin, L. measured the factors affecting the risk of default of the borrower in P2P network lending [33] Many scientists have devoted their works to credit risk issues, including Wenxue C., Yonghao L., Guanxiang, Z. and Huiling, Z. (2017) [30], Wenbin H. (2016) [29], moreover Wang, M. and Yang, H. (2021) [28].

The study of scientific research materials allows us to conclude that the problem of forecasting overdue loans in commercial banks is relevant. A hypothesis has been put forward and proved that with the help of the AI system, it is possible to obtain a forecast of the share of overdue loans in the bank's portfolio.

In the theoretical part of the study, the main issue was to determine methodological approaches in the use of various financial risk measure indicators, including VaR, Shortfall and SaR.

In the empirical part of the study, the main task was to find out the reasons why there was a change in the resultant indicator - the share of overdue loans in Russian commercial banks.

It is well known that financial risk is a risk that is associated with the probability of loss of financial resources, in particular, cash. Humanity faced the problem of minimizing financial risks simultaneously with the appearance of money circulation, with the emergence of various kinds of monetary relations. For example, in relations: investor - issuer, creditor - borrower, seller - buyer, exporter - importer and others, financial risks are an integral part, especially in conditions of market uncertainty [24].

As practice shows, market uncertainty is expressed as certain conditions in which the process of making economic decisions takes place, changes in which are difficult to predict and evaluate. The incompleteness of information has always been and remains, therefore, market uncertainty cannot be eliminated at all, but its degree can be reduced.

The scientific gap concerns the problem that there is no reliable method to obtain a successful forecast of the share of non-performing loans in a bank's loan portfolio in the face of market uncertainty.

Many scientific studies have been devoted to the issues of reducing the risk of financial losses and reducing overdue debts in the loan portfolio of commercial banks. So, for example, according to Parikova E.I. important is the use of statistical analysis to manage the amount of overdue debt of commercial banks in the Russian Federation [21]. According to experts, the Russian banking system during periods of crisis is characterized by a situation where the accumulation of overdue debt continues for quite a long time [25].

Thus, during the crisis of 2008–2009, the peak of growth in overdue debt occurred in May–June 2010, and after the crisis of 2014–2015, the maximum level of overdue debt was recorded in August 2016.

According to the requirements of the Bank of Russia [20], in order to control capital adequacy after the procedures for distributing capital by types of risks, areas of activity and divisions of a credit institution, it is recommended to form a system of limits [2].

This makes it possible to coordinate strategic decisions on expanding the bank's presence in various market segments with an approved risk appetite and to ensure that the volume of risks that a credit institution can take on in different areas of its activity is limited.

The process of setting strategic limits is one of the most important processes in risk management, which contributes to the diversification of risks and the maintenance of complex strategic management mechanisms.

For a credit institution with RAROC can be valued using the following formula:

$$RAROC = (E - EL) / EC \qquad (1)$$

where: MRC (market risk capital) - unexpected losses of market risk;
ORC (operational risk capital) - unexpected losses of operational risk.

As practice shows, the difficulty in determining RAROC is the calculation of the economic capital estimate, which corresponds to the amount of capital required to cover the total financial risk with a probability of 99.9%. Historically, in the early stages of calculating RAROC, the amount of capital required to cover the inherent risk of the activity was determined as the amount of funds needed to cover unforeseen losses due to various risks. So, if there are such risks characteristic of a credit institution as market, credit, operational, the value of economic capital will be determined as follows:

$$RC = MRC + CRC + ORC, \qquad (2)$$

Where: E - is net profit;
EL - expected losses;
EC - is the economic capital required to cover unexpected risks.

As practice shows, a simple summation of individual risk factors cannot be an adequate assessment of the total risk, since it proceeds from the full correlation of losses from the realization of risks among themselves, which does not correctly reflect reality. Therefore, to estimate economic capital, the use of more advanced aggregation methods is required [26].

Thus, a comprehensive assessment of financial risk can be represented as some aggregate distribution of losses of several types of risk, therefore, taking into account possible relationships between them, the capital to cover it will be reflected in the VaR indicator of this total distribution. As you know, in some cases the probability of a loss can be very small, but the amount of loss is so great that the result of an unfavorable outcome can be catastrophic. In such cases, in the decision-making process, the decision maker (DM) may neglect the risk itself, due to the fact that the probability of its occurrence is very small and thus may make a mistake.

This risk, due to catastrophic consequences, is a serious danger to the financial condition. Naturally, in such cases, there is a need for risk assessment, with which it would be possible to take into account the magnitude of possible losses. One such method of assessing financial risk is the so-called SaR method (Shortfall-at-Risk, Average Loss). That is, the SaR method is used along with the Value at Risk (VaR), which is based on the determination of the functional relationship of the risk occurrence probability. This SaR method is widely used by commercial banks in order to assess the magnitude of possible financial losses. Calculations show that six largest banks operate in the Russian credit market, their market share is 65.92% (32.37% of which is Sberbank). There are clear leaders in the banking services market, while other market participants lag far behind in key indicators. The level of market concentration is high, as 98% of banks account for about a third of the market share. Studies show that the forecasting of overdue debts in the portfolios of commercial banks is relevant and of great practical importance.

2 Methods for Studying the Dynamics of Overdue Debt in the Loan Portfolios of Commercial Banks

2.1 Methods for Analyzing the Dynamics of Arrears

The article used such research methods as: monographic, analytical, RAROC, VaR and SaR methods have been studied.

2.2 Prediction Method

To obtain a forecast of the share of overdue loans in the bank's portfolio, an artificial intelligence system was used – perceptron.

3 The Results of the Study

3.1 The Main of Factors Affecting Bad Debts

The analysis showed that in December 2020, the portfolio of loans provided by banks to small and medium-sized businesses (SMEs) continued to grow and already in January 2021 amounted to 5.8 trillion rubles. In general, according to the results of the analysis, in 2020, SMEs received loans for 7.6 trillion rubles. At the same time, in December, the volume of loans issued was the highest in the last two years and amounted to 942 billion rubles. At the same time, the value of the weighted average interest rates on loans in rubles in December 2020 decreased compared to December 2019: for loans for up to 1 year - up to 8.10% per annum, for long-term loans - up to 7.62% per annum. Accordingly, the share of overdue debt on such loans decreased over the past year from 11.9 to 11% [27].

According to experts, the Russian banking system during periods of crises is characterized by a situation where the accumulation of overdue debt continues for quite a long time. Thus, during the crisis of 2008–2009, the peak of growth in overdue debt occurred in May–June 2010, and after the crisis of 2014–2015, the maximum level of overdue debt was recorded in August 2016.

Problems with the quality of loans remain relevant for mortgage loans. Mortgages continue to play the role of a retail lending driver, despite the current upward trend in interest rates. Studies have shown that the dynamics of assets, capital, client funds and the total loan portfolio of the banking sector in the crisis year of 2020 turned out to be significantly higher than those of 2019. At the same time, such growth is due not only to the revaluation of foreign exchange assets and liabilities. To a certain extent, the assistance of state programs and measures to support the population and business influenced.

The total loan portfolio of Russian banks in 2020 grew by 13.8% to 63.2 trillion rubles. Its dynamics in three out of four quarters was positive: in the first quarter - 6.5%, in the second quarter the total loan portfolio decreased by 0.8%, in the third and fourth quarters - increased by 6.6% and 1.0%, respectively. The dynamics of the loan portfolio clearly shows the policy of tightening anti-coronavirus restrictions and subsequent recovery when they are relaxed [9].

In 2020, the volume of the corporate loan portfolio of Russian banks increased by 5.4 trillion rubles, or 14.3%, the retail loan portfolio - by 1.97 trillion rubles, or 16.6%. The same dynamics was shown by the volume of loans issued to individuals by the five largest retail lenders: an increase over the year by 16.6%, or 1.97 trillion rubles (in 2019 - by 17.5%, or 1.77 trillion rubles).

There are many factors that in a certain way affect the amount of bad loans in the banking portfolio. Among them are such as the demand for borrowed funds due to the COVID-19 pandemic, the dynamics of the bank interest rate, the level of creditworthiness of the bank's client, the change in the level of the Central Bank's requirements for the quality of the loan portfolio, and others.

According to the literature, the three main macroeconomic factors that affect the development of overdue loans are - the GDP (Louzis D.P. et al.) [16].

– unemployment: (Rinaldi and Sanchis-Arellano);
– rates (Lending-Interest-Exchange) Berge and Boye [4].

The goal of banks is to maintain optimal credit risk, since its minimization requires the creation of certain financial reserves. It is well known that the percentage of overdue or bad loans always takes place and it affects the amount of interest income of a credit institution. It is advisable to consider how this indicator has changed over 10 years. The dynamics of the growth rate of assets of the banking sector of the Russian Federation and the dynamics of overdue loans is shown below (Fig. 1).

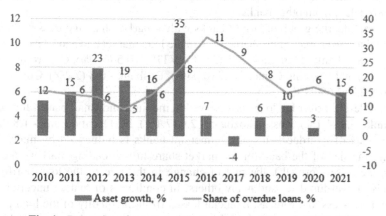

Fig. 1. Dynamics of assets and share of overdue loans in 2010–2021

The distribution of assets in the banking services market is also uneven. According to the Central Bank of the Russian Federation, out of 104.5 trillion rubles total assets 86.1 trillion accounts for the 30 largest banks in the country.

Distribution diagram of overdue loans of Russian banks for 2020–2021 shown below (Fig. 2).

According to the chart data, in the process of reducing overdue loans, their share in the loan portfolio does not decrease in such a way that one could speak of some kind of dependence.

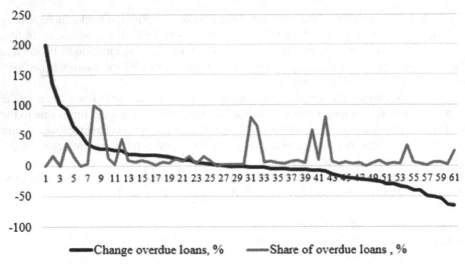

Fig. 2. Diagram of overdue loans of Russian banks for 2020–2021

Moreover, in the middle part of the graph, one can observe bursts of growth in overdue loans on loans in certain problem banks, for example, TCS Bank (Tinkoff. Credit Systems) 100%, BM-Bank 90%, Investtorgbank 80.6%, which is explained by the action of other factors not taken into account, including attracting "bad" clients with restructured debt from other banks.

For example, the group of largest banks with a market share includes the following banks, which have a maximum share of - % in the loan market and a low level of overdue loans (%): Sberbank of Russia - 23.5 (2.8%), VTB - 10.5 (3.4%), Gazprombank −4.8 (2.5%), National Clearing Center −1.7 (0.04%), Rosbank - 0.8 (3.2%), Credit Bank of Moscow - 2.2 (2.6%) [9].

A high level of overdue loans is observed in medium and small banks, for example, Alfa-Bank - 3.2 (4.1%), Rosselkhozbank - 2.6 (7.1%), FC Otkritie Bank - 1.8 (9.7%).

The share of overdue loans of commercial banks is influenced by many factors, including the size of the bank (or its market share in the lending market), the bank's growth rate (assets growth), the rate of change in the size of the loan portfolio, the dynamics of overdue debt, and many others. In conditions of market uncertainty, it is important to assess and forecast financial losses from the quality of the loan portfolio, or the share of overdue loans. To predict the amount of credit risk, it is advisable to use the AI-system - perceptron.

3.2 Perseptron

The main source of income for banks is the payment of interest on loans by its customers. Issuing loans is a risky activity, as there is always a risk of loan default.

In order to predict the level of risk, it seems appropriate to form a numerical mathematical model - a neural network. The scheme of operation of the multilayer perceptron used in the work is presented below (Fig. 3).

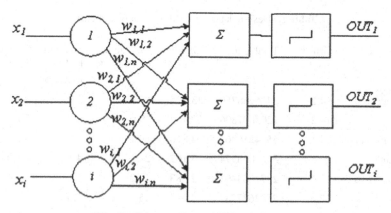

Fig. 3. Scheme of a multilayer perceptron

Let J - is the number of perceptron layers, $W_j = \left(w_1^j, w_2^j, \ldots w_K^j \right)$ – is the weigh matrix of the j-th layer, $K = K(j)$ - is the number of neurons in j-th layer, w_k^j – vector of weights of the k-th neuron of the j-th layer, $W = \left(W_j \right)_{j=1}^{J}$.

Then the output of each layer can be represented by the formula:

$$x_{j+1} = \varphi \left(W_j x_j \right), j \in [1..(J-1)], \tag{3}$$

$$\varphi(z) = \begin{cases} \text{ReLU}(z), \textit{if } j < J, \\ \sigma(z) = \frac{1}{1+\exp(-z)}, \textit{if } j = J, \end{cases} \tag{4}$$

In this case, the result of predicting the GDP $\tilde{\imath}$ (s) is determined as follows:

$$\forall s \in S \ \tilde{\imath}(s, W) = x_J \in [0, n] \quad \textit{if} \quad x_1 = f(s). \tag{5}$$

A simple perceptron neural network can have a structure that consists mainly of a single layer of artificial neurons connected by weights to multiple inputs. The perceptron neural network was proposed by a team of authors as a result of a scientific study.

To predict the amount of credit risk, it is advisable to use the AI-system - perceptron. There are four parameters at the input layer of the perceptron in percent: asset growth, market share, change in the loan portfolio, dynamics of overdue loans. The output layer has one parameter: the forecast for the share of overdue loans in percent.

The data of 62 Russian commercial banks for the period 2019–2020 were used in the process of forming the data set of the AI model. A fragment of the AI-system dataset is presented below (Table 1).

The architecture of the neural network, in addition to the input layer, has two hidden layers, and an output layer with a single parameter (Fig. 4).

The perceptron neural network was trained by the method of error backpropagation during 10,000 epochs. The trigger function is sigmoid. The AI system has been successfully formed.

Table 1. Design dataset for AI-system (fragment)

Parameters	Growth assets, %	Total loans,	Market share, %	Change in portfolio, %	Share of bad loans, %	Changing of bad loans, %
Sberbank	14.2	27069687503	23.525	14.9	2.8	−16.2
VTB	18.2	12038018969	10.462	9.0	3.4	5.7
Gazprombank	12.1	5534216262	4.810	9.1	2.5	−1.5
Alfa-bank	26.5	3661058974	3.182	28.1	4.1	−5.0
Rossedkhozbank	13.6	2972234401	2.583	9.2	7.1	−4.6
Moscow bank	12.6	2542677782	2.213	15.7	2.6	−1.7
Bank FK Otkritie	25.6	2076568446	1.805	24.8	9.7	−8.1

Source: author, based on materials [26]

Asset growth, %

Market share, %

Change in the loan portfolio, %

Dynamics of overdue loans, %

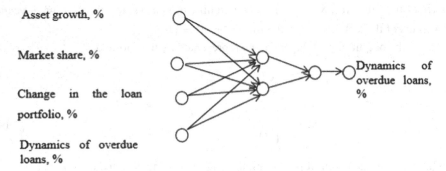

Dynamics of overdue loans, %

Fig. 4. Graph of perseptron

The generated AI-model allows you to get the predicted value of overdue loans under the influence of factors. Let us substitute the values of the parameters into the AI model, for example, for the Post-bank at the end of 2021, namely: Asset growth 11.3%, Market share 0.401%, Change in the loan portfolio 1.5%, Dynamics of overdue loans 27.2% and get a forecast for the share of overdue loans of 13.6108% (Fig. 5).

Field	Meaning
Input	
9.0 Growth of assets, %	11,3
9.0 Market share, %	0,401
9.0 Change in loan portfolio, %	1,5
9.0 Dynamics of overdue loans, %	27,2
Output	
9.0 Forecast share of overdue loans, %	13,6108129999649

Fig. 5. Calculating a predictive value using the what-if function

If we take into account that the actual value was 12.6, then we can conclude that the prediction accuracy is high, since the error rate was 1.2159%.

4 Discussion

It seems appropriate to compare the results obtained by us within the framework of the study with the results of other authors who conducted similar studies.

4.1 The Problem of Assessing and Reducing Financial Risk

In contrast to the approach used in this article, for assessing and minimizing financial risks, some authors have proposed a wider set of financial mathematics tools. Felmer and Sheed proposed quantile hedging, minimum risk deficit hedging, and optimal quadratic hedging [6].

An important problem remains the issue of assessing and reducing financial risk. Of scientific interest is the study of Eugene F. and Macbeth D. who considered it necessary to consider risk as a category in which profitability and equilibrium are observed [5]. Frazzini and Pedersen took into account the role of the beta portfolio of financial instruments [7].

Practice shows that the use of artificial intelligence systems allows solving a wide range of problems. Important in the development of the banking system is the study of such a factor as banking innovations, which can reduce credit risks. Thus, in the work of a team of authors, the method of analyzing hierarchies in the study of banking innovations in the digital economy is considered [15].

4.2 AI-Systems for Predict the Overdue Loans

Like the authors of this article, who focused on the study of the influence of the factorial sign - the share of overdue loans on the resultant sign - the change in the value of overdue loans, the results of studies by other authors also show a tendency that as the share of overdue loans grows, there is a weak trend aimed at increasing their absolute values.

In the works of other authors, artificial intelligence systems are also widely used, and AI systems are increasingly used in the field of finance and lending.

Neural networks show their effectiveness for assessing financial risks. For example, the SAR method has been successfully applied to assess the financial risks in SiU8 futures trading using a neural network based on the SAR method [14].

Khaldi R. et al. proposed to predict BTC volatility using a comparative study of parametric and non-parametric models [11]. Atzeni M. et al. used frame-based resources to analyze financial sentiment [3]. Marques A.I. et al. used to form MCDM models based on rankings in financial management and analysis applications and emerging issues [18]. Ghatasheh N. et al. investigated ensemble methods that are cost-sensitive in predicting bankruptcy. The approach proposed by the authors is applicable when working with an extremely unbalanced data distribution [8].

Neural networks used in practice are constantly becoming more complex. For example, Abbas S. with co-authors, proposed for practical application Multi-user detection using fuzzy logic, enhanced by an adaptive back-propagation neural network, [1]

Mohamed Kh. Sh. with co-authors proposed for scientific research a modified neural network with a higher order feed-forward with smoothing regularization, [19] Xu Y. et al. proposed an Improved Artificial Neural Network based on an intelligent optimization algorithm to obtain a practical result [31].

In foreign literature, the problem of non-performing loans is treated as a problem that arises exogenously. The effort of the academic community and industry professionals is to develop a synthetic and holistic approach to problem loans that includes the steps from creation to resolution [22].

The most interesting, in our opinion, are the results on the problem of non-performing loans obtained by Jiahao Wang with co-authors. Under these conditions, according to the authors, a technology is needed to predict the probability of a repeated payment based on limited collection data.

It is known, that in the initial form of data intended for training a neural network, there are many data elements that contain both useful and useless information. The authors formed a CBOW (Continuous Bag of Words Model) based on Hierarchical Softmax in word2vec to train texts segmented by words and network structure.

With word2vec, they got a series of semantically related words that could be new keywords, and their respective degrees of similarity if the keyword is entered. Thus, the data processing proposed by scientists and the extraction of features addressed to data on overdue financial debt are effective for predicting the probability of repayment of samples.

The application of artificial intelligence opens up broad prospects for solving the problem of non-performing loans in the banking sector. Thus, based on the above, we can conclude.

5 Conclusion

Based on the study, the following conclusions can be drawn.

1. A hypothesis has been put forward and proved that with the help of the AI-system, it is possible to obtain a forecast of the share of overdue loans in the bank's portfolio.
2. For the full implementation of multi-level and dynamic tasks related to analysis, forecasting, generalization of initial information on a complex managerial problem related to financial risk management under conditions of market uncertainty, artificial intelligence systems can be successfully used, especially in the context of digitalization of the economy.
3. The application of artificial intelligence opens up broad prospects for solving the problem of non-performing loans in the banking sector.

It is important to outline what future directions of research are.
Among the future directions of research should be noted:

1) Predicting financial risks using decision trees and deep learning neural networks [12, 17, 34].
2) Application of credit risk prediction models based on XGBoost and graph-based deep neural network [13, 23, 32].

Acknowledgments. The research was partially funded by the Ministry of Science and Higher Education of the Russian Federation under the strategic academic leadership program 'Priority 2030' (agreement 075-15-2021-1333, dated 30 September 2021).

References

1. Abbas, S., et al.: Multi user detection using fuzzy logic empowered adaptive back propagation neural network. Neural Netw. World 381–401 (2019)
2. ARB Coordinating Committee for Banking Quality Standards Guidelines for organizing the functioning of a quality management system in a commercial bank (draft, version 2.1 dated 27 December 2010). https://arb.ru/b2b/docs/koordinatsionnyy_komitet_arb_po_standa rtam_kachestva_bankovskoy_deyatelnosti_met-412161/. Accessed 1 July 2022
3. Atzeni, M., Dridi, A., Reforgiato, R.D. Using frame-based resources for sentiment analysis within the financial domain. Progr. Artif. Intell. 7(4), 273–294 (2018)
4. Berge, T.O., Boye, K.G.: An analysis of bank's problem loans. Norges Bank Econ. Bull. 78(2), 65–76 (2007)
5. Eugene, F. Fama, J., MacBeth, D.: Risk, return and equilibrium: empirical tests J. Polit. Econ. 81(3) (1973)
6. Felmer, G., Shid, A. Introduction to stochastic finance. Discrete time/Per. from English. - M.: MNTsMNO, p. 496 (2008)
7. Frazzini, A. and Pedersen, L.H. Betting Against Beta NBER Working Paper. - p. 220.(2010)
8. Ghatasheh, N., et al.: Cost-sensitive ensemble methods for bankruptcy prediction in a highly imbalanced data distribution: a real case from the Spanish market. Progr. Artif. Intell. 9(4), 361–375 (2020)
9. Good year. How much did banks earn on lending in 2020. Banki.ru research. https://www.banki.ru/news/daytheme/?id=10943547. Accessed 1 July 2020
10. Haoran, S., Boyang, W. Research on credit risk assessment of online network credit based on GBDT. ACM International Conference Proceeding Series. pp. 103–107 (2020)
11. Jiahao, W., Liang, Z., ShenEmail, G., ZhuYuhuai, Z. Preprocessing and feature extraction methods for microfinance overdue data. In: CCF Conference on Big Data. Big Data pp. 23–43 (2018)
12. Khaldi, R., El Afia, A. Chiheb, R. Forecasting of BTC volatility: comparative study between parametric and nonparametric models progress. Artif. Intell. 8(4), 511–523 (2019)
13. Kristóf, T., Virág, M.: EU-27 bank failure prediction with C5.0 decision trees and deep learning neural networks. Res. Int. Bus. Fin. 61, 101644 (2022)
14. Liu, J., Zhang, S., Fan, H.: A two-stage hybrid credit risk prediction model based on XGBoost and graph-based deep neural network. Expert Syst. Appl. 195, 116624 (2022)
15. Lomakin, N.: Financial risk assessment in the siu8 futures trading using neural network based on the SAR-method. In: Sukhomlin, V., Zubareva, E. (eds.) Convergent 2018. CCIS, vol. 1140, pp. 156–162. Springer, Cham (2020). https://doi.org/10.1007/978-3-030-37436-5_14
16. Lomakin, N.I., et al.: Method of analysis of hierarchies in the study of banking innovations in the digital economy. Int. Res. J. 5(107), 25–29 (2021). Part 3
17. Louzis, D.P., Vouldis, A.T., Metaxas, V.L.: Macroeconomic and bank-specific determinants of non-performing loans in Greece: a comparative study of mortgage, business and consumer loan portfolios. J. Bank. Fin. 36(4), 1012–1027 (2012)
18. Maoguang, W., Hang, Y. Research on personal credit risk assessment model based on instance-based transfer learning. In: Intelligence Science III, pp.159–169 (2021). https://doi.org/10.1007/978-3-030-74826-5_14

19. Marqués, A.I., García, V., Sánchez, J.S.: Ranking-based MCDM models in financial management applications: analysis and emerging challenges. Progr. Artif. Intell. **9**(3), 171–193 (2020). https://doi.org/10.1007/s13748-020-00207-1

20. Method of analysis of hierarchies in the study of banking innovations in the digital economy. Int. Res. J. **5** (107). Part 3, 25–29 (2021)

21. Mohamed, K., Wei, W., Yan, L.: A modified higher-order feed forward neural network with smoothing regularization. Neural Netw. World **27**(6), 577–592 (2017)

22. Ordinance of the Bank of Russia No. 3624-U dated 15 April 2015. On the requirements for the risk and capital management system of a credit institution and a banking group System Garant. https://base.garant.ru/71057396/. Accessed 1 July 2022

23. Parikova, E.I.: Statistical analysis of overdue debts of commercial banks of the Russian Federation, Text: Direct Young Sci. **12**(116), 1397–1399 (2016). https://moluch.ru/archive/116/31606/. Accessed 1 July 2022

24. Patsis, P., Liapis, K., Galanos, C.: A synthetic and holistic approach of the non-performing loans: from the creation to the solution. In: Nermend, K., Łatuszyńska, M., Thalassinos, E. (eds.) CMEE 2019. CMS, pp. 103–135. Springer, Cham (2021). https://doi.org/10.1007/978-3-030-67020-7_7

25. Rinaldi, L., Sanchis-Arellano, A. Household debt sustainability: what explains household non-performing loans? An empirical analysis Google Scholar (2006)

26. Risk management: bank risk management system. https://www.vtb.ru/akcionery-i-investory/raskrytie-informacii/upravlenie-riskami/. Accessed 7 Jan 2022

27. The banking system is stable, but questions remain. https://www.acraratings.ru/research/2213. Accessed 7 Jan 2022

28. The Central Bank pointed to a noticeable increase in problem debts of the population in banks. https://www.rbc.ru/finances/22/06/2020/5ef0d4f59a7947c4734cc1a7. Accessed 1 July 2022

29. The portfolio of loans to small and medium-sized businesses for 2020 grew by 22.6\% https://cbr.ru/press/event/?id=9619. Accessed 1 July 2022

30. Wang, M., Yang, H.: Research on personal credit risk assessment model based on instance-based transfer learning. IFIP Adv. Inf. Commun. Technol. **623**, 159–169 (2021)

31. Wenbin, H.: Research on the influencing factors of P2P online lending success rate in China. J. Xiamen Univ. (Philos. Soc. Sci. edn. 3), **5**, 136–146 (2016)

32. Wenxue, C., Yonghao, L., Guanxiang, Z., Huiling, Z.: Personal credit risk assessment model and empirical analysis based on the fusion of GBDT and logistic regression. Manag. Modern. **37** (2), 1–4 (2017)

33. Xu, Y., He, M.: Improved artificial neural network based on intelligent optimization algorithm. Neural Netw. World **28**(4), 345–360 (2018)

34. Zhang, Y., Wang, D., Chen, Y., Shang, H., Tian, Q.: Credit risk assessment based on long short-term memory model. In: Huang, D., Jo, K.-H., Figueroa-García, J.C. (eds.) ICIC 2017. LNCS, vol. 10362, pp. 700–712. Springer, Cham (2017). https://doi.org/10.1007/978-3-319-63312-1_62

35. Zhibin, L.: Measurement of influencing factors of borrower is default risk in P2P network lending. J. Xinjiang Univ. Fin. Econ. **4**, 30–38 (2018)

36. Zhu, B.: Research on credit scoring model based on transfer learning. Oper. Res. Manag. Sci. J. **1** (2015)

Assessing the Relationship Between Public Spending on Higher Education and a Country's Readiness for Digitalization

Olga Chemeris[1]([✉]) [iD], Victoria Tinyakova[2] [iD], Yaroslav Lavrinenko[3] [iD], and Xingyuan Sun[4] [iD]

[1] Peter the Great St. Petersburg Polytechnic University,
29 Polytechnicheskaya St., St. Petersburg 195251, Russia
`o.s.pogarskaya@gmail.com`
[2] State University of Management, Moscow, Russia
[3] Voronezh State Technical University, Voronezh, Russia
[4] Beijing Urban Construction Design and Development Group Co. Limited, Beijing, China

Abstract. Most countries around the world, in pursuit of efficiency and readiness for digitalization, ensure the interaction of government, business and the population, spending significant funds on science and higher education. The digitalization of the economy is also a consequence of the innovative activity of universities, but not only as centers of education or science, but also as centers of innovation creation. To get a quantitative assessment of the effectiveness of such countries' spending, the authors analyzed all 132 countries from the Global Innovation Index (GII), which is a widely recognized indicator of the innovativeness of the economy and characterizes, among other things, the readiness of countries to digitalization. A distinctive feature of this study is the use of the GII as a kind of tool to measure the level of innovativeness of the country's economy, which is determined in the current environment by digital transformations, as well as the identification of factors influencing it. The article uses calculated indicators that are not directly included in this rating, which allows to reduce dependence on it and increase the level of reliability of the results. The study revealed a strong correlation between the amount of public spending per student and the level of innovativeness of the economy. The top 20 countries in the world were determined by this criterion, it is possible to adopt their experience in the development, where digital technology is a tool that contributes to the growth of innovation of the economy of the modern state.

Keywords: Digitalization · Digital economy · Innovation · Government spending · Higher education · Innovative activities

1 Introduction

Recently, there has been an increased interest of scientists and practitioners in identifying the factors and conditions that ensure the innovative development of the country, which is

© Springer Nature Switzerland AG 2022
D. Rodionov et al. (Eds.): SPBPU IDE 2021, CCIS 1619, pp. 307–324, 2022.
https://doi.org/10.1007/978-3-031-14985-6_22

associated with the readiness for digitalization. The level of innovativeness of a country's economy is an indicator of its competitiveness and future well-being [1–4]. Currently, there is no doubt that intensifying the development of the digital economy is the basis of the innovative level of the country, which is the higher education system [5–7], which has a dual role. On the one hand, it is designed to train the necessary personnel for the digital economy [8–10], and on the other hand, it is the environment in which innovations should be born.

In order to assess the level of innovation activity in a particular country in comparison with other countries, an annual Global Innovation Index has been formed since 2007 [11]. Many countries around the world, when designing development strategies, take into account the scores received in this rating and strive to improve their positions in the Global Innovation Index [12, 13].

The rating is based on two sub-indices: investment in innovation and innovative products. The sub-indices formally reflect different flows: the input and output of innovations in the economy. The subindex of investment in innovation includes: development institutions, human capital and research, infrastructure, market conditions and business experience. Innovation output subindex: results in knowledge and technology, innovative products and services.

The purpose of this study was to examine the impact on the country's readiness to digitalization through public spending on higher education.

A distinctive feature of the study is the use of the Global Innovation Index as a kind of tool to measure the level of innovativeness of the country's economy, determined in the current environment by digital transformations of all spheres of human life, as well as the identification of factors influencing it.

Besides, the research pursues the purpose of estimation of efficiency of the state expenses on higher education in a paradigm of innovative economy. It is important to identify not only those countries, which spend a lot of funds, but also those, which spend these funds most effectively.

A number of scholars have attempted to address similar issues in their research, confirming the relevance of this study. Thus, Jovanka Damoska Sekuloska [14, 15] considered higher education as the basis for increasing innovation potential. But her research was limited to several Balkan countries and Eastern European countries: Albania, Bosnia and Herzegovina, Macedonia, Montenegro, Serbia, Czech Republic, Poland, Hungary, Slovenia, and Slovakia. Jovanka Damoska Sekuloska used the Higher Education Index and the Global Innovation Index as the basis for the study. The Higher Education Index is taken into account in calculating the Global Innovation Index, so there is a mutual influence. In her study, Jovanka Damoska Sekuloska identified the impact of higher education on innovation in the economy and determined that the level of economic development and the level of correlation between the index of higher education and innovation are in direct relation. The more innovatively developed the economy, the closer the relationship between the economy and innovation.

The authors Yurii Chentukov, Volodymyr Omelchenko, Olha Zakharova and Tamara Nikolenko [16] similarly assess the correlation between the U21 index of higher education competitiveness and a number of other indicators of macroeconomic indicators. In their work they analyze only 11 countries and come to the conclusion that there is a high correlation between the quality index of higher education and a number of selected indicators from the Global Innovation Index. The disadvantage of the work is again a small sample (11 countries) and the use of indicators that are dependent on the final Global Innovation Index.

The authors Agostino Menna, Philip R. Walsh, Homeira Ekhtari [17, 18] evaluated the correlation of 770 indicators and 242 relationships between them, which shows the enormous amount of work done by scientists. However, in the study, they again included only 35 countries from the OECD. During the study, the authors noted that the large input volume of data showed a low level of correlation with the final Global Innovation Index.

The article below presents the results of the authors' study of the relationship between the number of points that countries scored on the Global Innovation Index and a number of indicators related to public spending on education in general, higher education in particular, and scientific research.

2   Materials and Methods

The study used data from The world bank, UNESCO and official portals of individual governments [18–22]. The analysis was subjected to 132 countries of the world, which are included in the Global Innovation Index 2021. Understanding the process of innovative development in the context of digital transformation as a long-term evolutionary process, it is impossible to use data for one selected year as the only criterion of government performance in the field of innovation, so the authors of the study considered the average number of points of each country in the GII rating for 4 years: from 2018 to 2021.

Another problem encountered in the selection of data was the lack of background information on individual countries. The information base of the study was made up of data from The World Bank, but even this extensive base cannot be called complete. Information for some years was missing, and for some countries we had to use alternative sources and government reports.

Data for the six-year period (2014–2020) from The World Bank was averaged. In some cases, the averaging period began in 2005. Most often, the lack of data was observed in the least economically and innovatively developed countries, which provided minimal impact on the results of the overall calculations.

The authors selected the following baseline indicators from a variety of indicators:

- Expenditure on primary education (% of government expenditure on education);
- Expenditure on secondary education (% of government expenditure on education);
- Expenditure on tertiary education (% of government expenditure on education);
- Government expenditure on education, total (% of GDP);
- Research and development expenditure (% of GDP);
- Expense (% of GDP), GDP (current US$);
- GDP per capita (current US$);
- Population, total;
- Students, total.

The biggest difficulty was finding information about the indicator "Students, total". First, there is no single database on the number of students in each country. Second, there are different approaches to estimating the number of students by country. Some countries do not count the total number of students, but the number of students enrolled in the first year. Other countries do not count the number of students as such, or researchers have not been able to obtain reliable data.

The initial data generated for the calculations are presented in Appendix. Appendix presents the following indicators: average country position for 2018–2021, education per capita (current US$), tertiary education per capita (current US$), research and development expenditure per capita (current US$), expanse per capita (current US$), tertiary education per student (current US$).

Once again, we would like to emphasize that Appendix presents information on 132 countries, which is a kind of unique data set. Previously, other researchers have stopped at some limited sample. The authors of the paper decided to fill this gap of previous researchers.

3   Results

In the study, the authors determined the average and median expenditures on education, specifically on higher education, and on research per capita. In addition, the average level of expenditure per student and the average level of expenditure of the country as a whole per 1 inhabitant were determined. An example of the initial data for the calculation, the average and median values are presented in Table 1.

The top 10 countries in the GII have twice as many points as other countries on average, and spend on average 3.5 times as much on education. The top 10 countries already spend 7.9 times more on higher education, and per student spending is 4 times higher. Based on the data presented in Table 1 above, we can see a certain correlation between the scores of the global innovation index of countries and the level of spending on education.

The study conducted a correlation analysis to establish the relationship between the amount of points received by the country in the Global Innovation Index ranking and the indicators contained in Appendix. Table 2 presents the indicators assessing the quality of the established relationships.

The data in Table 2 allow us to conclude that there is a sufficiently high correlation between the analyzed indicators. The highest correlation was found between government spending on research and development and the number of points that the country scored in the Global Innovation Index.

The authors of the study confirmed the hypothesis about the impact of higher education on countries' readiness for digitalization, in particular on the position of countries in the Global Innovation Index ranking. An important part of the study was painstaking work to collect data on the number of students by country for subsequent calculations. As a result, a strong correlation was found between it and the innovativeness of the economy.

Note to Table 3. The following column designations are used in the table: 1.1 – place of countries with the highest public expenditures per student; 1.2 and 2.2 – country

Table 1. Example of baseline expenditures on education, higher education, and students

Country	Points in the GII ranking	Education per capita, USD	Tertiary education per capita, USD	R&D expenditure per capita, USD	Expanse per capita, USD	Tertiary education per student, USD
Switzerland	66,81	3 872	999	2 522,2	13 302	24 957
Sweden	63,08	3 748	996	1 759,8	17 291	17 749
United States	60,78	2 694	737	1 463,6	12 712	19 724
Netherlands	60,53	2 673	829	936,8	19 755	17 147
United Kingdom	60,25	2 304	471	709,3	16 876	8 410
Finland	58,72	3 061	916	1 534,2	17 669	13 589
Singapore	58,15	1 499	527	1 099,5	7 066	2 029
Denmark	57,92	4 636	1 321	1 668,9	22 608	24 090
Germany	57,52	2 074	548	1 206,6	12 511	16 984
Korea, Rep	57,15	1 159	237	943,1	5 715	6 156
Average TOP-10	60,09	2772	758	1 384	14 551	15 084
Median TOP-10	59,49	2684	783	1 335	15 089	17 066
Russia	**36,94**	**440**	**96**	**118,1**	**2 865**	**4 466**
Average	34,99	789	178	254	4 556	3 757
Median	32.60	268	48	22	1 260	338

Table 2. Results of correlation analysis[a] (Compiled by the authors)

Model	R	R2	Adjusted R2	Std. Error	F
Education per capita (current US$)	0,770	0,592	0,589	0,840	188,784
Tertiary education per capita (current US$)	0,744	0,553	0,550	0,841	161,006
Research and development expenditure per capita (current US$)	0,860	0,740	0,738	0,719	370,212
Expanse per capita (current US$)	0,800	0,639	0,636	0,730	230,274
Tertiary education per student (current US$)	0,757	0,573	0,569	0,805	174,228

[a] Dependent Variable: country's points in the GII ranking

scores in the GII rating; 1.3 and 2.3 – place of country in the GII rating; 1.4 and 2.4 – GII rating countries; 1.5 – country public spending per student in USD; 2.5 – country public

Table 3. Top 20 countries from the GII (Compiled by the authors)

1.1	1.2	1.3	1.4	1.5	2.1	2.2	2.3	2.4	2.5
1	51,05	19	Norway	36 796	1	51,05	19	Norway	1768
2	54,53	12	Hong Kong	35 965	2	57,92	8	Denmark	1321
3	66,81	1	Switzerland	24 957	3	66,81	1	Switzerland	999
4	57,92	8	Denmark	24 090	4	63,08	2	Sweden	996
5	54,26	14	Ireland	19 922	5	58,72	6	Finland	916
6	60,78	3	United States	19 724	6	60,53	4	Netherlands	829
7	63,08	2	Sweden	17 749	7	50,95	20	Iceland	814
8	50,82	21	Austria	17 465	8	53,06	17	Canada	807
9	60,53	4	Netherlands	17 147	9	50,82	21	Austria	761
10	57,52	9	Germany	16 984	10	60,78	3	United States	737
11	53,06	17	Canada	14 089	11	31,82	70	Kuwait	699
12	58,72	6	Finland	13 589	12	54,26	14	Ireland	663
13	49,74	23	Australia	13 574	13	49,74	23	Australia	644
14	54,32	13	France	12 764	14	49,75	22	Belgium	626
15	46,88	29	Spain	10 824	15	48,84	26	New Zealand	594
16	48,84	26	New Zealand	10 502	16	57,52	9	Germany	548
17	50,95	20	Iceland	10 200	17	58,15	7	Singapore	527
18	54,21	15	Japan	9 914	18	54,32	13	France	509
19	37,73	42	Greece	8 982	19	60,25	5	United Kingdom	471
20	60,25	5	United Kingdom	8 410	20	54,53	12	Hong Kong	437
...	...	...	...	...	...	...	...	...	...
36	36,94	46	Russia	4 466	51	36,94	46	Russia	96

expenditures per student in USD. U.S. dollars; 2.5 – government spending on higher education per capita

The analysis of Table 3 shows that for some countries there is a certain discrepancy between the amount of money spent and their positions in the GII ranking. One example is Kuwait, which ranks 11th in expenditure on tertiary education and 70th in the GII. Another example is Spain, which ranks 15th in spending per student but only 29th in the GII rankings.

The differences in states' spending on education, higher education (per capita), and public spending (per student) that are reflected in Table 4 suggest different efficiencies.

An interesting example of the efficiency of public spending is the UK, which is not even in the top 10 countries in terms of spending, but ranks 5th in the ranking of innovativeness of the economy. Another positive example is South Korea and China. On the other hand, we see indicators in Norway, which in 3 out of 4 indicators is in first

Table 4. Input data for comparative analysis (Compiled by the authors)

Rank in the GII rating	Points in the GII ranking	Country	Rank of education spending per person	Rank of spending on higher education per person	Rank of spending on R&D per person	Rank of spending per student
1	66,81	Switzerland	5	3	1	3
2	63,08	Sweden	6	4	2	7
3	60,78	United States	10	10	7	6
4	60,53	Netherlands	12	6	17	9
5	60,25	United Kingdom	16	19	21	20
6	58,72	Finland	7	5	5	12
7	58,15	Singapore	22	17	14	45
8	57,92	Denmark	2	2	3	4
9	57,52	Germany	20	16	12	10
10	57,15	Korea, Rep	31	31	16	27
11	55,29	Israel	21	22	6	24
12	54,53	Hong Kong	26	20	29	2
13	54,32	France	18	18	18	14
14	54,26	Ireland	8	12	19	5
15	54,21	Japan	25	27	11	18
16	53,99	China	71	66	38	56
17	53,06	Canada	17	8	20	11
18	51,96	Luxembourg	3	21	4	21
19	51,05	Norway	1	1	8	1
20	50,95	Iceland	4	7	10	17
21	50,82	Austria	13	9	9	8
22	49,75	Belgium	9	14	15	22
23	49,74	Australia	11	13	13	13
24	49,67	Estonia	35	32	31	28
25	48,88	Czech Republic	36	34	28	35
26	48,84	New Zealand	15	15	23	16
27	48,20	Malta	24	26	34	23
28	47,14	Cyprus	27	24	43	25

(*continued*)

Table 4. (*continued*)

Rank in the GII rating	Points in the GII ranking	Country	Rank of education spending per person	Rank of spending on higher education per person	Rank of spending on R&D per person	Rank of spending per student
29	46,88	Spain	28	25	25	15
30	46,02	Italy	23	30	24	31
31	44,78	Slovenia	29	29	22	29
32	44,52	Portugal	33	33	30	32
33	43,42	Hungary	43	45	33	44
34	42,54	Malaysia	53	38	42	26
35	42,39	United Arab Emirates	30	121	26	68
36	42,18	Slovak Republic	41	37	36	38
37	41,88	Latvia	39	42	46	37
38	41,35	Bulgaria	63	65	53	50
39	40,71	Poland	44	39	41	39
40	40,43	Lithuania	42	36	35	34
41	38,28	Croatia	46	46	39	30
42	37,73	Greece	37	23	32	19
43	37,73	Vietnam	98	90	87	48
44	37,63	Thailand	72	70	64	54
45	36,96	Ukraine	75	61	67	53
46	**36,94**	**Russia**	**55**	**51**	**37**	**36**
47	36,89	Turkey	58	48	47	49
48	36,48	Romania	61	55	56	40
49	36,25	Montenegro	131	131	57	
50	35,94	India	108	86	79	65

place in terms of costs, but in the ranking of the GII is only 19th place. Let us analyze the position of the Russian Federation in the ranking under consideration (Table 5).

We can see that in the ranking with Russia there are countries that spend less public money, but are higher in the ranking. Some examples are Ukraine and Thailand. On the other hand, the example of Greece, which spends 3.2 times more on higher education than Russia, but in the ranking are higher by only four positions or one point.

Table 5. Comparison of Russia and neighboring countries in the GII ranking (Compiled by the authors)

1	2	3	4	5	6	7	8	9	10	11	12
41	38,28	Croatia	579	119	112,9	5 386	5 961	46	46	39	30
42	37,73	Greece	843	304	178,4	11 329	8 982	37	23	32	19
43	37,73	Vietnam	84	13	6,8	–	1 866	98	90	87	48
44	37,63	Thailand	208	38	24,0	991	1 558	72	70	64	54
45	36,96	Ukraine	186	57	22,3	1 109	1 567	75	61	67	53
46	**36,94**	**Russia**	**440**	**96**	**118,1**	**2 865**	**4 466**	**55**	**51**	**37**	**36**
47	36,89	Turkey	360	115	80,5	3 244	1 826	58	48	47	49
48	36,48	Romania	323	81	43,8	3 072	2 989	61	55	56	40
49	36,25	Montenegro	–	–	39,7	–		131	131	57	
50	35,94	India	51	15	11,1	232	374	108	86	79	65
51	35,85	Chile	565	115	47,0	2 619	1 913	48	47	52	47

Note to Table 5. The table uses the following column designations: 1 - place in the GII rating; 2 - the sum of points in the GII rating; 3 - country; 4 - spending on education per person/USD; 5 - spending on higher education per person/USD; 6 - spending on research per person/USD; 7 - total state expenditure per 1 person/USD; 8 - spending on higher education per student/USD. /USD; 8 - spending per student/USD; 9 - ranking of education spending per person; 10 - ranking of higher education spending per person; 11 - ranking of research and development spending per person; 12 - ranking of spending per student. All of the "expenditures" in the table are government expenditures

Each country has its own efficiency of public spending relative to the Global Innovation Index. In the table below we have calculated the comparative efficiency by correlating the average public spending on higher education per person and the average spending per student. The top 50 economies of the Global Innovation Index were chosen as the basis of the study (Table 6).

Assessing the costs of higher education and their efficiency, we notice that the undisputed leaders are Great Britain, Singapore, Germany, South Korea, Israel, and Japan. By identifying the countries that spend funds on higher education and students more effectively than others and are among the best, it is possible to adopt their experience in developing and improving innovation activities. Digital technology is a tool for the growth of innovativeness of the modern economy, and each country has its own way and peculiarities of forming an innovative economy, but the role of universities on this path is undoubtedly great.

Table 6. The effectiveness of the GII "score" relative to public spending on higher education and students (Compiled by the authors)

Rank in the GII rating	Country	"Cost" of one point in relation to the cost of higher education per person	"Cost" of one point in relation to the cost of one student, USD
1	Switzerland	15,0	373,6
2	Sweden	15,8	281,4
3	United States	12,1	324,5
4	Netherlands	13,7	283,3
5	United Kingdom	7,8	139,6
6	Finland	15,6	231,4
7	Singapore	9,1	34,9
8	Denmark	22,8	416,0
9	Germany	9,5	295,3
10	Korea, Rep	4,1	107,7
11	Israel	5,8	134,1
12	Hong Kong	8,0	659,6
13	France	9,4	235,0
14	Ireland	12,2	367,2
15	Japan	5,3	182,9
16	China	0,9	23,8
17	Canada	15,2	265,6
18	Luxembourg	7,1	159,2
19	Norway	34,6	720,8
20	Iceland	16,0	200,2
21	Austria	15,0	343,6
22	Belgium	12,6	163,0
23	Australia	12,9	272,9
24	Estonia	4,3	122,5
25	Czech Republic	3,8	93,2
26	New Zealand	12,2	215,0
27	Malta	5,9	162,6
28	Cyprus	6,4	148,2
29	Spain	6,3	230,9

(*continued*)

Table 6. (*continued*)

Rank in the GII rating	Country	"Cost" of one point in relation to the cost of higher education per person	"Cost" of one point in relation to the cost of one student, USD
30	Italy	5,9	125,7
31	Slovenia	6,1	133,5
32	Portugal	4,7	119,7
33	Hungary	2,9	54,8
34	Malaysia	3,3	163,6
35	United Arab Emirates	–	–
36	Slovak	3,6	78,1
37	Latvia	3,2	84,4
38	Bulgaria	1,2	43,7
39	Poland	3,5	79,4
40	Lithuania	4,0	117,9
41	Croatia	3,1	155,7
42	Greece	8,1	238,1
43	Vietnam	0,4	49,5
44	Thailand	1,0	41,4
45	Ukraine	1,6	42,4
46	Russian Federation	2,6	120,9
47	Turkey	3,1	49,5
48	Romania	2,2	82,0
49	Montenegro	–	–
50	India	0,4	10,4

4 Discussion

In most countries innovations are born in the leading universities, so it is interesting to study the experience of the universities themselves, their level of funding, both by the state and the private sector. The structure of cost distribution and the level of endowment of students and professors attract attention. All this may be considered in further research. The digitalization of the economy is also a consequence of the innovative activity of universities, but not only as centers of education or science, but also as centers of innovation creation.

The results obtained by the authors, indicating a high correlation between the scores in the Global Innovation Index rating and the level of spending on education, confirm the dependence of innovative development of the economy with the level of spending on education. In her study, Jovanka Damoska Sekuloska indirectly confirmed the high correlation between the index of higher education and the GII index.

Yurii Chentukov, Volodymyr Omelchenko, Olha Zakharova, Tamara Nikolenko found a high correlation between the U21 Higher Education Competitiveness Index and macroeconomic indicators from the Global Innovation Index. Indirectly, this emphasizes the high correlation between the level of higher education and the level of innovativeness of the economy, which implies digitalization.

On the other hand, there is a certain gap in the research of innovativeness of the economy and expenditures on higher education, which was filled by the authors of this study. The relationship between the financing of education, higher education and the level of development of innovativeness of the state economy was determined.

By evaluating the experience of leading innovative economies in developing higher education and catalyzing the innovative activity of universities, it is possible to form one's own path and minimize the number of mistakes on it.

5 Conclusions

The goal of this study to examine the impact of public spending on higher education on the country's readiness for digitalization as a whole has been achieved. This study complements previous studies. It covers the whole set of countries from the Global Innovation Index ranking. The article uses calculated indicators that are not directly included in the GII ranking, which reduces dependence on it and increases the level of reliability. To quantify the effectiveness of these expenditures, we analyzed 132 countries from the Global Innovation Index (GII), which characterizes, among other things, countries' readiness for digitalization. The study revealed a strong correlation between the amount of public spending per student and the level of innovativeness of the economy. Thus, a strong correlation was found between the country's spending on higher education and research and its position in the Global Innovation Index ranking.

The Global Innovation Index rating is a universally recognized indicator of the innovativeness of the economy, which implies its digitalization. As a result of the study it was possible to find out which innovative economies of the world spend funds more effectively, and which ones - less effectively. The top 20 countries of the world were identified by this criterion, and it was found that the most efficient spending countries are Great Britain, Singapore, Germany, Israel and Japan.

The authors continue their study by evaluating the leading universities as centers of innovation: the structure of their income and expenditures, the degree of state participation, the level of expenditures on staff, professors and students. The modern economy implies innovation in a digitized environment. Innovative economies are made by high-class specialists who graduated from universities, and universities themselves not only create the basis for future digital innovations, but are also their centers.

Appendix

See Table 7.

Table 7. Public spending on education, higher education, and research per person and per student (Compiled by the authors)

Country position (2018–21)	Country	Education per capita, USD	Tertiary education per capita, USD	R&D expenditure per capita, USD	Expanse per capita, USD	Tertiary education per student, USD
1	Switzerland	3 872	999	2 522,2	13 302	24 957
2	Sweden	3 748	996	1 759,8	17 291	17 749
3	United States	2 694	737	1 463,6	12 712	19 724
4	Netherlands	2 673	829	936,8	19 755	17 147
5	United Kingdom	2 304	471	709,3	16 876	8 410
6	Finland	3 061	916	1 534,2	17 669	13 589
7	Singapore	1 499	527	1 099,5	7 066	2 029
8	Denmark	4 636	1 321	1 668,9	22 608	24 090
9	Germany	2 074	548	1 206,6	12 511	16 984
10	Korea, Rep	1 159	237	943,1	5 715	6 156
11	Israel	1 978	322	1 474,3	12 991	7 413
12	Hong Kong	1 388	437	291,3	4 845	35 965
13	France	2 187	509	874,1	18 914	12 764
14	Ireland	2 965	663	846,5	21 223	19 922
15	Japan	1 416	286	1 317,2	6 609	9 914
16	China	238	50	113,3	1 043	1 286
17	Canada	2 262	807	813,4	8 050	14 089
18	Luxembourg	4 260	367	1 576,0	41 377	8 272
19	Norway	5 974	1 768	1 444,5	29 602	36 796
20	Iceland	4 184	814	1 325,7	20 416	10 200
21	Austria	2 584	761	1 342,5	21 677	17 465
22	Belgium	2 840	626	982,5	18 871	8 112
23	Australia	2 677	644	1 148,1	13 757	13 574
24	Estonia	913	216	258,7	6 188	6 086
25	Czech Republic	850	184	315,0	6 699	4 558
26	New Zealand	2 387	594	454,9	12 175	10 502
27	Malta	1 454	287	151,4	11 825	7 838

(*continued*)

Table 7. (*continued*)

Country position (2018–21)	Country	Education per capita, USD	Tertiary education per capita, USD	R&D expenditure per capita, USD	Expanse per capita, USD	Tertiary education per student, USD
28	Cyprus	1 353	303	96,6	9 652	6 983
29	Spain	1 300	294	369,7	9 438	10 824
30	Italy	1 454	270	431,8	14 644	5 785
31	Slovenia	1 240	273	467,3	9 842	5 978
32	Portugal	1 101	210	281,0	9 218	5 330
33	Hungary	662	127	166,4	6 037	2 378
34	Malaysia	469	141	100,6	1 766	6 958
35	United Arab Emirates	1 240	–	345,1	1 658	0
36	Slovak	674	153	119,8	6 683	3 296
37	Latvia	731	135	82,9	6 195	3 535
38	Bulgaria	290	50	45,4	2 401	1 809
39	Poland	636	141	104,5	4 574	3 232
40	Lithuania	671	163	126,6	4 913	4 769
41	Croatia	579	119	112,9	5 386	5 961
42	Greece	843	304	178,4	11 329	8 982
43	Vietnam	84	13	6,8	-	1 866
44	Thailand	208	38	24,0	991	1 558
45	Ukraine	186	57	22,3	1 109	1 567
46	Russia	440	96	118,1	2 865	4 466
47	Turkey	360	115	80,5	3 244	1 826
48	Romania	323	81	43,8	3 072	2 989
49	Montenegro	–	–	39,7	–	–
50	India	51	15	11,1	232	374
51	Chile	565	115	47,0	2 619	1 913
52	Serbia	248	71	44,1	2 331	–
53	Costa Rica	606	127	45,0	2 454	5 262
54	Mongolia	159	18	7,1	799	326
55	Mexico	465	91	39,4	2 026	2 778

(*continued*)

Table 7. (*continued*)

Country position (2018–21)	Country	Education per capita, USD	Tertiary education per capita, USD	R&D expenditure per capita, USD	Expanse per capita, USD	Tertiary education per student, USD
56	Moldova	193	33	10,3	825	1 583
57	Philippines	76	9	3,1	363	–
58	Georgia	114	14	8,3	975	1 299
59	South Africa	395	51	55,3	2 058	1 140
60	Brazil	528	93	107,3	3 135	1 719
61	Qatar	2 473	–	338,8	–	–
62	North Macedonia	162	–	15,2	1 433	–
63	Iran	185	46	23,7	968	1 167
64	Uruguay	542	131	51,1	4 049	–
65	Mauritius	355	30	27,3	1 802	795
66	Armenia	100	12	8,4	771	394
67	Saudi Arabia	1 137	–	85,8	5 753	–
68	Colombia	271	56	13,7	1 693	1 089
69	Tunisia	264	68	26,3	1 124	2 773
70	Kuwait	2 145	699	49,5	12 046	–
71	Belarus	303	58	38,4	1 775	2 011
72	Peru	185	28	5,7	1 047	–
73	Brunei	1 099	276	95,2	–	–
74	Bosnia and Herzegovina	–	–	7,3	1 793	–
75	Morocco	155	31	19,4	776	–
76	Panama	337	75	16,7	1 543	–
77	Argentina	537	104	57,7	2 561	2 613
78	Bahrain	573	140	22,6	–	–
79	Jamaica	276	52	–	1 351	–
80	Oman	800	138	35,8	–	–
81	Kazakhstan	280	36	16,9	1 479	–
82	Jordan	126	26	21,8	1 101	–

(*continued*)

Table 7. (*continued*)

Country position (2018–21)	Country	Education per capita, USD	Tertiary education per capita, USD	R&D expenditure per capita, USD	Expanse per capita, USD	Tertiary education per student, USD
83	Azerbaijan	136	17	10,5	1 168	–
84	Kenya	74	11	7,6	289	–
85	Albania	150	30	5,1	1 005	–
86	Indonesia	98	14	5,5	477	1 197
87	Dominican Republic	200	29	---	938	–
88	Lebanon	154	43	–	1 925	–
89	Paraguay	166	39	4,1	654	573
90	Sri Lanka	65	12	3,8	541	–
91	Tanzania	32	8	3,4	123	–
92	Kyrgyz	64	8	1,7	276	–
93	Trinidad and Tobago	705	–	11,7	5 219	–
94	Egypt	105	–	13,6	819	–
95	Botswana	544	176	29,4	2 021	–
96	Uzbekistan	106	–	3,2	269	–
97	Rwanda	26	5	4,3	122	–
98	Ecuador	243	87	16,2	–	–
99	Namibia	412	100	12,1	1 504	902
100	Senegal	64	18	5,7	251	350
101	El Salvador	129	12	3,6	788	–
102	Cabo Verde	175	27	2,4	875	–
103	Tajikistan	36	3	0,8	0	–
104	Cambodia	18	1	1,2	119	–
105	Guatemala	107	13	1,5	446	–
106	Pakistan	29	7	4,3	–	–
107	Honduras	123	19	0,6	465	–
108	Nepal	29	3	1,6	121	–
109	Ghana	93	20	5,1	339	–

(*continued*)

Table 7. (*continued*)

Country position (2018–21)	Country	Education per capita, USD	Tertiary education per capita, USD	R&D expenditure per capita, USD	Expanse per capita, USD	Tertiary education per student, USD
110	Bolivia	185	–	4,0	607	–
111	Uganda	16	2	2,1	85	–
112	Malawi	19	5	–	77	–
113	Madagascar	13	1	0,4	46	–
114	Côte d'Ivoire	117	19	–	248	–
115	Cameroon	41	4	–	173	–
116	Zimbabwe	53	10	–	213	–
117	Algeria	262	71	13,2	–	–
118	Bangladesh	21	3	–	102	–
119	Nigeria	70	–	3,0	–	–
120	Mali	27	5	2,7	97	–
121	Mozambique	30	4	1,6	106	–
122	Burkina Faso	30	5	1,6	92	–
123	Lao PDR	40	7	–	–	–
124	Ethiopia	28	12	1,6	58	–
125	Zambia	50	7	2,1	251	–
126	Benin	35	7	0,0	–	–
127	Togo	27	5	1,6	99	–
128	Niger	17	2	–	–	–
129	Guinea	17	6	–	–	–
130	Myanmar	25	4	0,5	198	–
131	Angola	68	–	0,8	526	–
132	Yemen	61	–	–	–	–

References

1. Didenko, N., Skripnuk, D., Kikkas, K., Kalinina, O., Kosinski, E.: The impact of digital transformation on the micrologistic system, and the open innovation in logistics. J. Open Innov. Technol. Mark. Complex. **7**, 115 (2021). https://doi.org/10.3390/joitmc7020115
2. Fanta, A., Wachira, E.W., Sándor, D.: The Determinants of Innovation Performance; An Income Based Cross-Country Comparative Analysis Using Global Innovation Index (GII) (2021). https://doi.org/10.21203/rs.3.rs-955254/v1
3. Kanke, A.A., Morozova, N.I., Tinyakova, V.I.: Restarting the education model in the digital economy. In: Popkova, E.G., Ostrovskaya, V.N., Bogoviz, A.V. (eds.) Socio-Economic

Systems: Paradigms for the Future. SSDC, vol. 314, pp. 1043–1051. Springer, Cham (2021). https://doi.org/10.1007/978-3-030-56433-9_109

4. Levchenko O., Tkachuk O., Tsarenko I., Levchenko O., Tkachuk O., Tsarenko I.: The role of universities and their research work in generating innovation (2018). http://dspace.kntu.kr.ua/jspui/handle/123456789/8541

5. Bril, A.R., Kalinina, O.V., Ilin, I.V.: Economic analysis of projects in the improvement of the HR management system of enterprises. In: Proceedings of the 29th International Business Information Management Association Conference, pp. 2268–2277 (2017). https://doi.org/10.3390/joitmc7020105

6. Ilin, I.V., Levina, A.I., Ershova, A.S., Efremova, M.A.: Methodology for the transition to a digital enterprise. Econ. Entrepreneurship. (2021). https://doi.org/10.34925/EIP.2021.131.6.229

7. Ilin, I.V., Levina, A.I., Dubgorn, A.S.: Digital transformation as a factor in shaping the architecture and IT architecture of an enterprise. Sci. J. NRU ITMO Ser. Econ. Environ. Manage. 50–55 (2019). https://doi.org/10.17586/2310-1172-2019-12-3-50-55

8. Sohn, S.Y., Kim, D.H., Jeon, S.Y.: Re-evaluation of global innovation index based on a structural equation model. Technol. Anal. Strateg. Manage. **28**, 492–505 (2016). https://doi.org/10.1080/09537325.2015.1104412

9. Todeva, E.: The global innovation index as a measure of triple helix engagement. In: Abu-Tair, A., Lahrech, A., Al Marri, K., Abu-Hijleh, B. (eds.) THS 2018. LNCE, vol. 43, pp. 119–134. Springer, Cham (2020). https://doi.org/10.1007/978-3-030-23898-8_10

10. Erceg, A., Sekuloska, J.D.: E-logistics and e-SCM: How to increase competitiveness. E-logistics i e-SCM: Jak zwiększyć konkurencyjność, Logforumthis Link Disabled **15**(1), 155–169 (2019). https://doi.org/10.17270/J.LOG.2019.323

11. Sekuloska J.D.: Increasing efficiency through digital digitization of public services. Comput. Sci. Technol. 45

12. Damoska Sekuloska, J.: Higher education as a pillar In increasing innovation capacities. Econ. Manage. **19**, 241–247 (2014). https://doi.org/10.5755/j01.em.19.3.8125

13. Chentukov, Y., Omelchenko, V., Zakharova, O., Nikolenko, T.: Assessing the impact of higher education competitiveness on the level of socio-economic development of a country. Probl. Perspect. Manage. **19**, 370–383 (2021). https://doi.org/10.21511/ppm.19(2).2021.30

14. Menna, A., Walsh, P., Ekhtari, H.: Identifying enablers of innovation in developed economies: a national innovation systems approach. J. Innov. Manage. **7**, 108 (2019). https://doi.org/10.24840/2183-0606_007.001_0007

15. Dölarslan, E.A., Koçak, A., Walsh, P.: Perceived barriers to entrepreneurial intention: the mediating role of self-efficacy. J. Dev. Entrepreneurship Link Disabl. **25**(3), 2050016 (2020). https://doi.org/10.1142/S1084946720500168

16. World Bank Open Data|Data. https://data.worldbank.org/. Accessed 02 Sept 2021

17. The UNESCO Institute for Statistics. http://data.uis.unesco.org/. Accessed 01 Sept 2021

18. Knoema. https://knoema.com/. Accessed 01 Sept 2021

19. Statista - The Statistics Portal for Market Data, Market Research and Market Studies. https://www.statista.com/. Accessed 01 Sept 2021

20. Tinyakova, V.I., Morozova, N.I., Ziroyan, M.A., Falkovich, E.B.: Monitoring of human resources and a new educational structure for training specialists as key factors to reactivate the system of consumer cooperation in Russia. Amazonia Investiga **7**(17), 353–359 (2018)

21. Kalugin, V.A., Pogarskaya, O.S., Malikhina, I.O.: The principles and methods of the appraisal of commercialization projects of the universities innovations. World Appl. Sci. J. **25**(1), 97–105 (2013). https://doi.org/10.5829/idosi.wasj.2013.25.01.7029

22. Data Lab - Federal Finance Data Visualizations. https://datalab.usaspending.gov/, Accessed 02 Sept 2021

23. Our World in Data. https://ourworldindata.org/. Accessed 02 Sept 2021

The Introduction of Digital Technologies to Participatory Design in the Public Spaces Formation

Svetlana Pupentsova[1]([✉]) [ID], Alexandr Demin[2] [ID], Alina Kirilyuk[2] [ID], and Victoria Pupentsova[2] [ID]

[1] Peter the Great St. Petersburg Polytechnic University, Polytechnicheskaya, 29, 195251 St. Petersburg, Russia
pupentsova_sv@spbstu.ru

[2] St. Petersburg State University of Architecture and Civil Engineering, 4 Vtoraya Krasnoarmeiskaya, 190005 St. Petersburg, Russia

Abstract. The relevance of the topic is confirmed by the compliance of the study with the sustainable development goals formulated at the UN Summit, and the development of socially oriented spaces design in Russia, based on an analysis of the preferences and opinions of the residents. The subject of the research is modern digital technologies and a participatory design in the formation of public spaces in towns. Aim of the work: development of tools for participatory design in the formation of urban public spaces in towns; analysis of methods and tools of participatory design. The scientific and scientific-practical significance of the work lies in: generalization of the world and Russian experience of participatory design; in identifying approaches and methods of participatory design; in developing a methodology for creating a trusting environment in the design of public urban spaces in small towns. The results of the work are presented in the form of academic reflection of both local and worldwide experience in the use of participatory design tools, the analyzed techniques and methods used in participatory design, the described type of experience in the use of participatory design tools in the area improvement project in Kingisepp, Leningrad Region. The authors came to the conclusion that effective digital methods of participatory design should include: targeting in social networks; mailing by e-mail and in private messages; activities on the development of the territory; film screenings, lectures; a post in the official accounts of the administration in social networks; survey on a dedicated website.

Keywords: Modern digital technologies · Network technologies · Online participatory design tools · Urban public spaces · Architectural environment design

1 Introduction

Sustainable Development Goals were confirmed in September 2015 at the UN Summit in New York. The proposed goals include reducing hunger, inequalities and poverty, preservation of the planet's resources, creating an ecosystem that promotes economic

© Springer Nature Switzerland AG 2022
D. Rodionov et al. (Eds.): SPBPU IDE 2021, CCIS 1619, pp. 325–342, 2022.
https://doi.org/10.1007/978-3-031-14985-6_23

growth, and sustainable consumption and production, comfortable conditions for education, decent work, and living. Sustainable Development Goals have been confirmed by 193 countries for implementation by 2030.

Sustainable development goals can be achieved through new methods and tools for the integrated assessment of environmental, social, economic, and cultural qualities in urban areas. For the rapidly expanding anthropogenic environment under current urbanization conditions, sustainability includes the design and placement of buildings and infrastructure in accordance not only with environmental principles but also with the interests and preferences of citizens. Participatory design methods can promote solving this problem, as they are based on an analysis of the needs of local residents. This approach becomes more and more common in developed countries. In Russia, this method is not widespread yet: pilot projects appear in some places only.

The relevance of the topic is confirmed by the compliance of the study with Sustainable development goals formulated at the UN Summit, and the development socially-oriented spaces design in Russia. The latter is done basing on the analysis of the preferences and opinions of the residents.

The scientific and practical significance of the work lies in the following fields: generalization of the world and Russian experience of participatory design; identifying approaches and methods of participatory design; developing a methodology for creating a trusting environment in the design of public urban spaces in towns, which is distinguished by the formulated principles of participatory design, an updated list of portals helping to carry out participatory design, and a developed classification of online participatory design tools.

The subject of the research is participatory design in the formation of urban public spaces in towns. In Russian practice, a locality with a population of less than 50,000 people is called 'town'. Frequently these are single-industry towns and/or satellite towns of the nearest major city.

The theoretical and methodological basis for writing this work are the works by H. Sanoff [1], J. Jacobs [2], participation design pioneers. The contribution of M. Alberti and L. Susskind [3], well-known promoters of these methods, also could be noted. Comparative analysis of tactical urbanism and participatory design presented by the authors M. Lydon and A. Garcia [4], J. Sasser [5] и D. Campo [6]. The creation of an ecosystem of a trusting environment in the design of territories, that contributes to the sustainable development of cities and the creation of a "smart city" system can be found in the works by M. Singhania and N. Saini [7], Jha et al. [8], P. Sankowska [9], Wann-Ming Wey and Ti-Ching Peng [10], A. Radziejowska and B. Sobotka [11], Al Ridhawi et al. [12], Y. Nurulin et al. [13]. The formation of urban public spaces in the concept of sustainable development of cities was given great attention by J. Sasser [5], D. Campo [6]. This issue was also discussed on the examples of Shenyang authors Wen Wu and Yiquan Wang [14] Tokyo (Chenghao Yang and Tongtong Liu) [15], Belgrad (T. Vukovic et al.) [16]. The issue of the need to involve residents in the design of public spaces is discussed in the works by Atiqul Haq et al. [17], Y. Peng, You Tao Feng, and H.Timmermans [18], M. Piaggio [19]. Authors A. Kozlov [20], T. Kharlamova [21], S. Gutman et al. [22, 23] explores the problems of a human-centered approach with the possibility of obtaining feedback from the local population in the design of urban public spaces in Russia.

The results of the work are presented in the form of studied foreign and domestic experience in the use of participatory design tools, analyzed techniques and digital methods used in participatory design on the example of a square development project in Kingisepp, Leningrad Region. The results of this study can be applied for designing public spaces in towns.

The aims of the work are the development of digital tools for participatory design in the formation of public spaces in small towns and analysis of methods and tools of participatory design.

2 Materials and Methods

2.1 Research Methodology

The idea of creating a comfortable urban environment with the involvement of citizens is spreading wider and wider. Participatory design arose in the 1980s in Porto Alegre, the capital of Rio Grande do Sul, Brazil's southernmost state. The successful experience of Porto Alegre was replicated many times, first in Brazil, then in other countries, and in the 2000s in Russia.

The term "participatory design" was first coined by Henry Sanoff. [24]. He noted that "participatory design" can be defined as "a design process involving residents, local communities, activists, representatives of administrative structures, local businesses, investors, representatives of the expert community and other parties interested in the project for jointly determining the goals and objectives of the development of the territory, identifying true problems and people's needs, collaborative decision-making, conflict resolution, and project effectiveness increasing."

The first activities resembling participatory design originated in the 1960s. Trade unions in Scandinavia created a "cooperative design" movement [25] for participating in the development of technological systems, affecting their work. At the same time, in New York, Jane Jacobs explored the city's communities, fought to preserve them, and wrote about her experiences in "The Death and Life of Great American Cities" [2].

By 2010, the international standard for participatory design ISO 9241-210: 2010, based on the principle of "user involvement in design and development" was ratified. Nowadays, this approach is gradually being introduced into the design process, but there are certain difficulties in organizing surveys and taking into account the opinions of residents and future users. Therefore, carried out by the authors aggregating of foreign and domestic experience, comparative analysis of the tools and methods of a human-oriented approach in design will help future researchers in the formation of urban public spaces in towns.

2.2 Theoretical Fundamentals

The theoretical and methodological basis for writing this work are numerous works of various authors. A review of prominent examples of participatory design and tactical urbanism is by M. Lydon and A. Garcia. Their work [4] presents a detailed set of tools for designing, planning, and implementing projects, including how they can be adapted to local needs and challenges.

Research [7] calls on the regions to develop policies that promote the implementation of the ESG concept and shift the priorities of the city's development towards the formation of a trusting environment. Document [8] options for using modern technologies for urban planning are discussed to create smart and sustainable cities with a trusting environment for communicating with the population. Article authors [9] pay attention to the role of "smart government" and the definition of current, city-specific demand for an administrative system based on information and communication technologies when creating a trusting environment. In the study [10] indicators of the sustainability of cities and smart cities are determined and the directions for the development of intelligent, sustainable, and inclusive strategies for urban environmental planning and design are assessed. Authors A. Radziejowska and B. Sobotka in work [11] pay attention to the fact that residents of towns are not only beneficiaries, they must participate in the creation of urban public spaces. An overview of the applications of the smart city environment for involving users in design and development is given in [12].

J. Sasser [5] and D. Campo in the article [6] pay attention to the role of activists in the formation of urban public spaces in small towns. In the work [2] proposes to use a modified surveillance strategy implemented for the Jane Jacobs neighborhood in the West Village. In the study [14], using the example of the city of Shengyang (China), a tool to identify residential areas with poor accessibility to open urban public spaces is proposed. The authors Wen Wu and Yiquan Wang note that increasing the capacity of urban public open spaces promotes healthy and sustainable urban development. In the study [15] two projects in downtown Tokyo are compared and background information on creating an urban public space that caters to the preferences of local residents is provided. In the article [16] the impact of spatial transformations on urban life is investigated, namely, the issue of individual and group satisfaction is discussed, using the example of public open spaces in Belgrade. In the article [17] the issue of the need to involve residents in the design of public spaces is discussed. The authors [18] note that a survey of residents and an assessment of external comfort can provide valuable information about the quality of urban public spaces. The study [19] will help in the development of urban planning policy, providing insight into the impact of urban green spaces on the value of fixed assets and people's well-being.

The issue of the digitalization of two megacities of Russia with the possibility of obtaining feedback from the local population when designing urban public spaces is revealed in the work [20]. In the article [26] examples of a human-oriented approach are considered in cases of reorganization of former production areas into comfortable living and recreation areas. In the article [21] the author T. Kharlamova considers the need for active implementation of monitoring as a management tool in the process of urban planning. This will ensure the creation of effective information support for the sustainable development of modern cities, confirmed in the work of M. Laskin [27]. A human-centered approach to the design of regions is considered by S. Gutman et al. in works [22, 23], where it is proposed to use an index with established indicators of the socio-economic development of the region.

We have considered numerous articles which confirm the relevance of our study. The works on specific examples we have studied show that the involvement of residents in the design contributes to improving the quality of the created environment and the sustainable development of urban areas. But in the analyzed works, there is no analysis of the tools and methods for involving the residents in the design.

Therefore, the authors of this article have a methodology for creating a trusting environment in the design of public urban spaces in towns, which is distinguished by the formulated principles of participatory design, an updated list of portals that help to carry out participatory design, and a developed classification of online participatory design tools.

2.3 The Main Provisions of the Proposed Methodology for Creating a Trusting Environment in the Design of Public Urban Spaces in Towns

The developed methodology includes the basic principles of participatory design; classification of online participatory design tools developed by the authors; an integral assessment of participatory design methods. The main stages of the proposed methodology of applying modern digital technologies and creating a trusting environment in the design of public urban spaces in small towns are:

1. Pre-creating a trusting environment in the design of public urban spaces in small towns.

    1.1 The accumulated experience in co-design generalizing, the principles formatting.
    1.2 An approach (approaches) to the revitalization of small towns selecting
    1.3 Selection of co-design methods and tools on the basis of a classification developed by the authors.
    1.4 Co-design methods integral evaluating

2. Gathering and analysis of information necessary to create a trusting environment in the design of public urban spaces in small towns.

    2.1 Planned activities conducting.
    2.2 Processing and analyzing data, if necessary, carrying out additional activities to facilitate communication between different public institutions and organizations and involve them in the work on the urban environment.
    2.3 Public opinion summarizing and proposals for the design of public urban spaces in small towns formulating.
    2.4 Competitive selection of the projects of public urban spaces in small towns, offering the selection of the best and the most popular projects among the citizens in and out picking amongst the projects.

Let us dwell on each stage in detail.

Generalization of the world experience of participatory design. The successful first experience of participatory design in Porto Alegre has been replicated many times. Achieving the goals of urban sustainable development fuels an increased interest in involving citizens in the design of urban public spaces. Below there is the list of the most successful experiences in the implementation of participatory design.

Public participation in design of the urban environment in Japan is a relatively new idea, but this movement reflects the determination and confidence of people. Henry Sanoff was invited as a design consultant for citizen participation projects in cities in Japan. [24], initiated by the urban community development organization Nippon Seinenkan Foundation. The project included the revitalization of the historic shopping street in Arakawa and the protection and revitalization of the historic city of Ohiya.

The history of recreating the canals of the 17th century in The Hague (Netherlands) began atypically. The driving force was a local Shirin Poik.

An analysis of the numerous works presented above made it possible to identify the main principles of participatory design:

- ensuring an unambiguous link between the contribution made by the public and the impact on the decision;
- the right to the complicity of all people who are affected by the decision under discussion;
- search for the best form of organization for the participatory process for participants/stakeholders;
- providing participants with all the information necessary for qualified and meaningful participation;
- recognition and communication of the needs and interests of all participants;
- involvement of all potentially affected or interested in decision making;
- communicating to the participants how their contribution to the discussion affected the final result.

Participatory design approaches in towns. The character of the city, the sense of place is shaped by its architectural style, surrounding natural landscape, cultural diversity, materials used, and many other features that distinguish one place from another. The relationship of these elements is decisive for the identity of the environment, so towns need support, especially from urban planners. The four main approaches to the revitalization of small towns, which reveal new opportunities for old territories and buildings, are indicated in Fig. 1.

The process of understanding problems, setting goals, and forming strategies for change begins with informing citizens. Revitalization implies knowledge of the internal conditions and external factors that can affect the development of certain areas or small towns. Such studies are called "environment scanning", they include SWOT analysis (strengths, weaknesses, opportunities, threats).

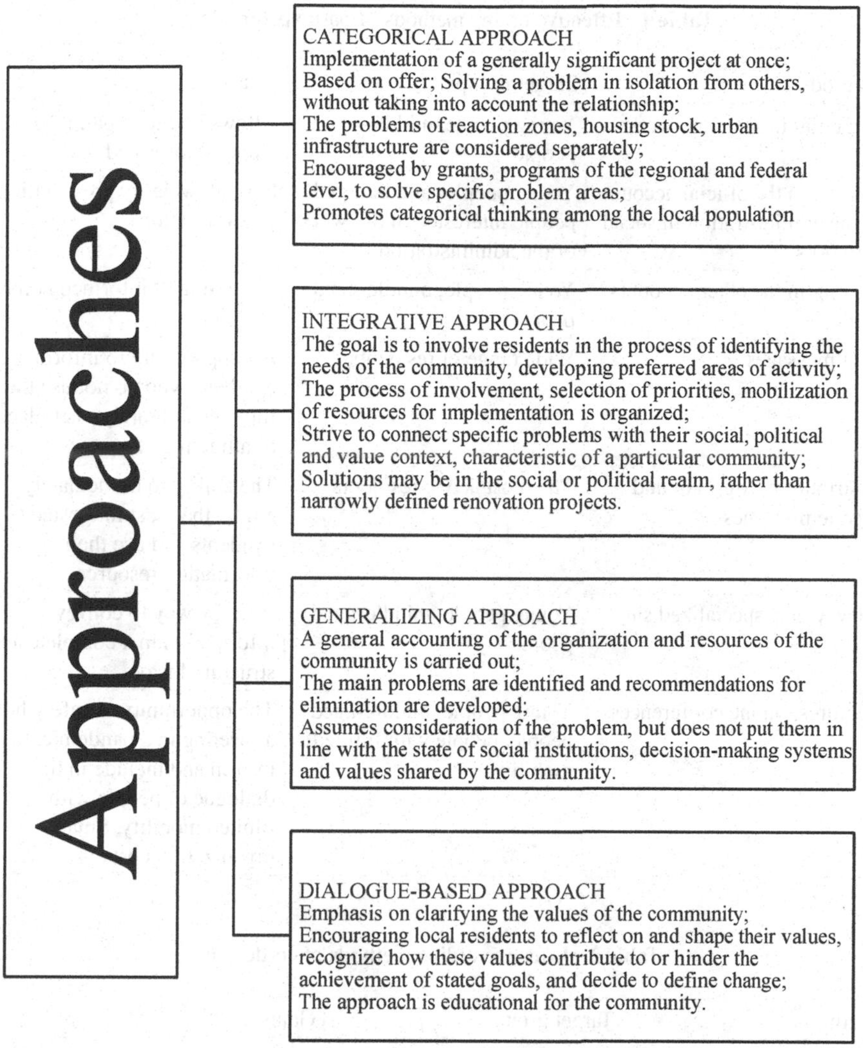

Approaches

CATEGORICAL APPROACH
Implementation of a generally significant project at once;
Based on offer; Solving a problem in isolation from others,
without taking into account the relationship;
The problems of reaction zones, housing stock, urban
infrastructure are considered separately;
Encouraged by grants, programs of the regional and federal
level, to solve specific problem areas;
Promotes categorical thinking among the local population

INTEGRATIVE APPROACH
The goal is to involve residents in the process of identifying the
needs of the community, developing preferred areas of activity;
The process of involvement, selection of priorities, mobilization
of resources for implementation is organized;
Strive to connect specific problems with their social, political
and value context, characteristic of a particular community;
Solutions may be in the social or political realm, rather than
narrowly defined renovation projects.

GENERALIZING APPROACH
A general accounting of the organization and resources of the
community is carried out;
The main problems are identified and recommendations for
elimination are developed;
Assumes consideration of the problem, but does not put them in
line with the state of social institutions, decision-making systems
and values shared by the community.

DIALOGUE-BASED APPROACH
Emphasis on clarifying the values of the community;
Encouraging local residents to reflect on and shape their values,
recognize how these values contribute to or hinder the
achievement of stated goals, and decide to define change;
The approach is educational for the community.

Fig. 1. The main four approaches to the revitalization towns

Basic methods of participatory design. The greatest effectiveness of the participatory design is achieved, among other things, by widening information and involvement of various groups of residents. To do this, you can use various online and offline tools, choosing and combining them depending on the conditions. Effective tools to involve certain groups are presented in Table 1, Table 2.

Table 1. Effective online methods of participatory design.

Methods	Target group	Goals
Targeting in social networks	Young people, middle-aged people	Allows you to expand the circle of informed
Posting in the official accounts of the administration in social networks	Young people, middle-aged people interested in the work of the administration	Formal, weighty presentation of information
Posting in the other accounts	Young people, middle-aged people	Increasing of informed number
Text messages	Wide range of residents	An opportunity to inform residents who do not use the Internet and rarely visit places of attraction
Distribution by e-mail and private messages	The most active residents	The ability to immediately attract the most interested residents and use their information resource
Survey on a specialized site	Young people, middle-aged people	An easy way to convey information in a complete and structured way
Lectures, online conferences	Young people, middle-aged people, people with limited mobility	The opportunity to safely hold a meeting in a pandemic, to inform and include in the dialogue of people with limited mobility. Small organization costs

Table 2. Effective offline methods of co-design.

Methods	Target group	Goals
Television broadcasting	Wide range of residents	Formal, weighty presentation of information. The ability to visualize the subject of discussion
Publishing in newspapers, magazines	Middle-aged people, elderly	Formal, weighty presentation of information. Possibility of long-term storage and re-examination of information. The possibility of distribution through mailboxes, stands in places of attraction (MFC, office buildings, educational institutions)

(*continued*)

Table 2. (*continued*)

Methods	Target group	Goals
Radio broadcasting	Wide range of residents. Post office, bank, MFC - suitable for middle-aged and elderly people. Educational institutions - for youth, families with children, teachers	Possibility of acquaintance of listeners with organizers
Flyers, posters, questionnaires at important points in the district	For a wide range of residents. Post office, bank, MFC - suitable for middle-aged and elderly people. Educational institutions - for youth, families with children, teachers	Formal, weighty presentation of information. Possibility to conduct a survey using questionnaires located in the waiting areas
Leaflets in mailboxes, posters in porches, courtyards of residential buildings	For a wide range of residents	The largest audience coverage
Events on the subject of survey/development of the territory	Wide range of residents	Possibility of acquaintance of listeners with organizers Possibility of focus-groups planning Increasing the interest of residents in the urban environment
Film shows, lectures	Wide range of residents	Informing residents about the possibilities of participatory design, modern areas of improvement. Increasing the interest of residents in the urban environment
Focus-groups, organized meetings	Pre-selected groups of residents	Deep research into the needs of different population groups
Game, art meeting	Pre-selected groups of residents	The ability to simulate various scenarios for the use of space for a deeper immersion of residents in the design, generation of new ideas, unity of groups
Souvenirs of improvement programs, information resources	Wide range of residents	Increasing the interest of residents in the urban environment, the work of the administration, public associations
Volunteer home visits	For elderly and disabled people	Opportunity to inform and collect opinions of people with limited mobility

The application of some of the above methods requires cooperation with local authorities, business, information resources, which helps to establish links between various public institutions and organizations and involve them in working on the urban environment.

Based on the monitoring of open Internet sources, the authors developed a classification of the most common online participatory design tools (Fig. 2).

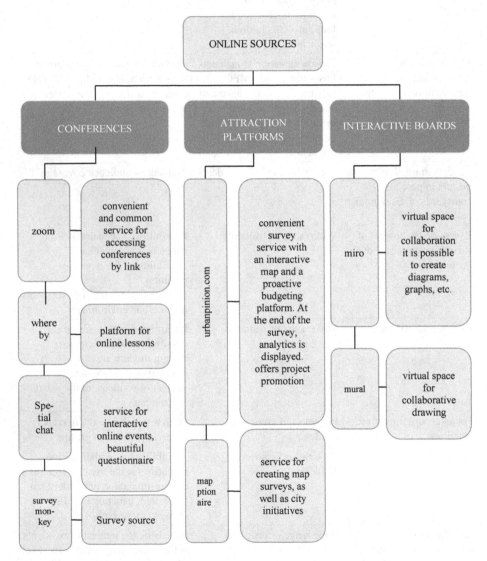

Fig. 2. The main four approaches to the revitalization towns

Thus, according to this classification, it will be easier for researchers to navigate the variety of online portals and choose the most optimal one for themselves.

Integral evaluation of participatory design methods. For a comparative analysis of participatory design methods, we use a scoring method, where we evaluate on a three-point scale according to two criteria: the complexity of the method and feedback from residents. Points are proposed to be placed by experts. Table 3 provides a scale for evaluating methods.

Table 3. Effective online methods of participatory design.

Labor intensity		Feedback	
Score	Description	Score	Description
1	Preparation requires the involvement of professionals, high cost	1	Up to 10% of the residents involved in the event showed back contact
2	Preparation required, middle cost	2	From 10 to 30% of the residents involved in the event showed back contact
3	No special preparation required, low cost	3	More than 30% of the residents involved in the event showed back contact

The effect (E) of the event is proposed to be calculated as the product of scores for labor intensity and feedback. Accordingly, the maximum effect of the method corresponds to Emax = 9, and the minimum effect is equal to Emin = 1. The integral assessment is proposed to be calculated by the formula:

$$K = ((Ei - E_{min})/(E_{max} - E_{min}). \tag{1}$$

Let us give an example of the application of the proposed methodology and the calculation of an expert assessment for a participatory design in the city of Kingisepp within the framework of the Hackathon project from the Competence Center of the Leningrad Region.

3 Results

3.1 Participatory's Design Academic Reflection Summary

As a part of the Hackathon project by the Competence Center of the Leningrad Region we tested participatory design in Kingisepp. The team consisted of mentors and students. The project for the improvement of the territory adjacent to the city culture center in Kingisepp, developed by the authors, can be found at the link.

Let's present examples of participatory design and initiative budgeting in Russia in the form of Table 4.

According to statistical data as of 2020, in the constituent entities of the Russian Federation there is a tendency to increase the number of projects created with the participation of citizens. The number of these projects has exceeded 290. The growth of this

Table 4. Participatory design and proactive budgeting projects.

Location	Project name	Description
Sosnovyi Bor	Playground	Sports ground with 4 different sections, presented in the form of a butterfly (for different age categories)
Kazan	Boulevard "Belye Tsvety"	The facility is located on the site of a former truck stop. It consists of many functional areas and sites, which allows you to hold various events in this area
Izhevsk	"Open garden"	Space for family leisure and organization of city events
Yakutsk	"Future generations Park"	This facility has several open areas for work, playgrounds, an amphitheater and a skate park
Moscow	"Dacha in the yard"	Yard on Norilsky street, with many trees and shrubs separating playgrounds and recreation areas
Sertolovo	Sports ground	Sports zone for high-grade leisure of children and teenagers. The area was 240 square meters. The facility has 5 exercise machines and 2 sports complexes

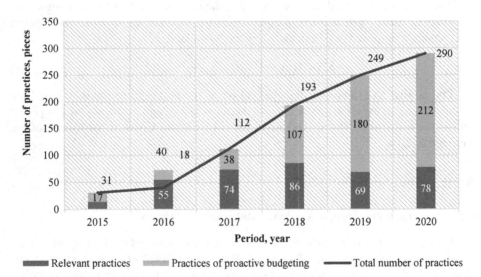

Fig. 3. Dynamics of related relevant practices at all levels from 2015–2020.

indicator has been observed over the last five years. The dynamics of this parameter is clearly shown in Fig. 3.

For example, in 2020, there were 78 projects implemented using related practices, and 212 using initiative budgeting. Thus, the share of projects implemented through initiative budgeting increased over the period from 2015 to 2020 by 18%.

3.2 Approbation of the Methodology for Choosing Methods of Participatory Design on the Example of the City of Kingisepp, Leningrad Region

The principles developed within the Kingisepp project are presented in Sect. 2.3. For the revitalization, an integrative approach was chosen, with the most accessible methods and tools to involve the residents of Kingisepp in the process of discussing the area near the Kingisepp City House of Culture improvement project. In Fig. 4 we present the results of an integrated assessment of the methods of participatory design of the Kingisepp project, combined with an assessment of a possible model based on expert estimates for towns.

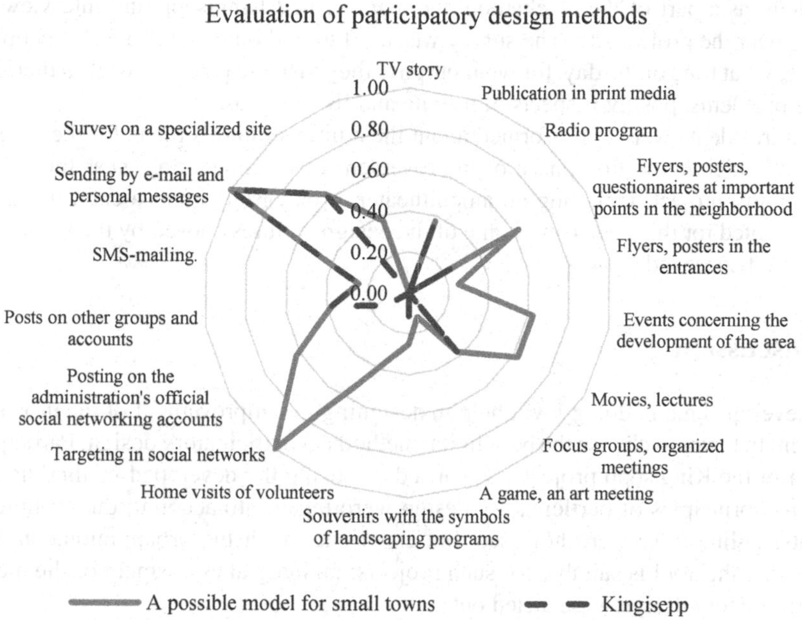

Evaluation of participatory design methods

Fig. 4. Classification of online participatory design tools

As a result of comparative analysis, effective methods of participatory design of a possible model for assessing participatory design methods for towns, with an integral coefficient above 0.63, include: targeting in social networks; mailing by e-mail and in private messages; flyers, posters, questionnaires at important points in the region; activities on the development of the territory; films, lectures; a post in the official accounts of the administration in social networks; survey on a dedicated website.

In the above list of effective and less effective methods of a possible model for small towns, the methods used in the Kingisepp project are highlighted in italics.

As inefficient methods of participatory design for a possible model of towns, with an integral coefficient below 0.25, we expertly identified the following TV story; broadcast; game, art meeting. As inefficient methods of participatory design for a possible model of small towns, with an integral coefficient below 0.25, expertly identified: TV story; broadcast; game, art meeting. For each project, the set of methods depends on the allocated budget and tasks.

3.3   Gathering and Analyzing Information to Design the Area Near the Kingisepp City House of Culture Improvement Project

Hackathon organizers offered participating architects the results of local residents online surveys on the territory at 4 Karl Marx Ave improvement. (territory near the City House of Culture). The survey involved 335 participants. As a part of the survey, residents were asked to choose functions and elements of improvement from a prepared list and to enter their own suggestions in a special line.

Then, as a part of the Hackathon, the team visited Kingisepp and interviewed 50 people near the project site. The survey was used to find out what groups of people use the site, what time of the day, for what purpose they visit the place, as well as their views on the problems, positive aspects of the site and its future use.

The residents were not informed about the administration's plans for the neighboring site, which is the first phase of improvement of the single area near the MCC. A landscaping project, including an amphitheater, a playground and a café, has already been adopted for this site. Thus, some of the design features chosen by the townspeople duplicated approved project.

4   Discussion

The developed methodology will help in designing the improvement of the urban environment in towns to choose the best digital methods of participatory design. Participatory design in the Kingisepp project was carried out using the developed methodology: all the basic principles of participatory design were taken into account; due to time constraints, online tools were not used, but experience with the urbanpinion.com portal shows that this tool is suitable for such projects; an integral assessment of the methods of participatory design was carried out.

Figure 4 shows an integral assessment of the recommended online methods for the implementation of digital technologies in participatory design in the public spaces formation and separately highlighted the methods used in the Kingisepp project. The limited time allocated for the collection of information in the project "Hackathon" did not allow to apply such effective methods as targeting in social networks, events on the topic of territory development, film screenings and lectures, notification of the population through flyers and posters. The survey proved to be an extremely inefficient and at the same time labor-intensive tool. Residents had a hard time agreeing to take part in the survey and were reluctant to give answers. Some of them were not interested in the improvement of the site because they visit it rarely, others were not in the mood to discuss the questions asked and complained about the quality of the domestic urban environment in general, the level of cleanliness in the city, the development of neighboring areas, etc. In other words, the results of the pedestrian survey include a significant number of responses from residents who are not part of the initiative groups. Also, this format gives respondents insufficient time to formulate their answers; for this reason, many answers are incomplete or random. Most respondents described the area as safe, despite the lack of lighting and coverage of walkways, potholes, and the proximity of the site to an industrial area. This can probably be explained by the low requirements of small town residents for the quality of the urban environment, which makes it difficult to co-design. It also turned out that most residents are not aware of the history of the site, despite the fact that it is located in the historic center of town.

The project of the central square of Kingisepp improvement, developed with the main methods of co-design, won first place in the category "The best solutions for the city of 20–50 thousand people" and was presented on a single platform for voting 47.gor odsreda.ru. In 2022, the city administration launched a project to improve Kingisepp's central square.

After analyzing the experience of participatory design of domestic and foreign specialists, methodology, and tools, as well as trying to apply the knowledge gained in practice (Project of the territory near the Kingisepp City House of Culture improvement), we developed the following recommendations:

1. Involvement of a larger audience. A combination of online and offline methods would make it possible to inform the elderly about the project and to attract more young and middle-aged people.
2. Preparatory work with enterprising citizens. Lectures on modern landscaping, the safety of the urban environment, and the history of the city could draw public attention to the project and form the basis for discussion.
3. Correct formulation of the issues under discussion. Shifting the focus of the discussion from the project to other topics is a common problem of participatory design, as it is difficult for residents to move from discussing pressing issues to discussing city development initiatives. In order to solve this problem, there are several methods, including the following:

   - education of the population - publications on the topic of urbanism and urban planning, examples of high-quality improvement, advice on how to develop the territory on your own;
   - the correct message in the posts and description of the portal – architect/activist must immediately indicate that they are accepting initiatives about the territory development, but complaints about problems should be received by some other methods;
   - territories development competitions - this stimulates citizens to submit ideas and will help to develop dialogue, discussion, and voting.

Continuation of the story, regularity of communications. The territory development is a continuous and complex process, so it is important not only to collect opinions and implement some of them but also to continue the joint development of the renovated territory. Citizens should be informed in advance of what the next steps of the project will be, including providing a platform – an online portal, a local newspaper, or any other suitable resource – that will allow citizens to regularly check the participatory design progress, track the status of initiatives, and understand what will happen, how the implementation process is going, what will happen to the territory in the future. Also, the creation of long-term ties with the city community will make it possible to single out a group of the most active residents who are ready to cooperate with the administration and architects in other projects.

It is also important to realize that good ideas arise when a dialogue with the authorities is established and the most pressing problems are resolved. Being aware of these factors, residents are more calmly involved in the development of the territory, realizing that they will be heard, and even pressing problems such as replacing a bad container site with a new one will be resolved in any case and a situation will not arise when the budget is spent on creating an incredible park, while the population is experiencing a host of other problems.

5 Conclusion

Human-centered design or participatory design increases the effectiveness, accessibility, and efficiency of working in the urban environment. In this work, foreign and domestic experience of participatory design in towns was analyzed, as well as our own experience of participatory design in Kingisepp within the framework of the Hackathon project from the Competence Center of the Leningrad Region.

Numerous studies considered in the work confirm the relevance of the study. The relevance of the topic is also confirmed by the compliance of the study with the goals of sustainable development formulated at the UN Summit, and the development in Russia of the direction of designing a socially-oriented space based on an analysis of the preferences and opinions of the inhabitants themselves.

The authors of this article have developed a methodology for creating a trusting environment in the design of public urban spaces in small towns, which is distinguished by the formulated principles of participatory design, an updated list of portals that help to carry out participatory design, and a developed classification of online participatory design tools. The developed methodology was tested in the project for the improvement of the territory adjacent to the urban culture center in Kingisepp, where all the basic principles of participatory design were taken into account.

The authors came to the conclusion that effective digital methods of participatory design should include: targeting in social networks; mailing by e-mail and in private messages; activities on the development of the territory; film screenings, lectures; a post in the official accounts of the administration in social networks; survey on a dedicated website.

Possible directions for future research may be based on a trusting eco-environment development and the principles of participatory design usage in the design of smart city systems design.

Acknowledgments. The research is partially funded by the Ministry of Science and Higher Education of the Russian Federation under the strategic academic leadership program 'Priority 2030' (Agreement № 075-15-2021-1333 dated 30.09.2021).

References

1. Lang, J., Burnette, C., Moleski, W., Vachon, D.: Designing for human behavior: architecture and the behavioral sciences (1974)
2. Litscher, M.: Jane Jacobs: the death and life of great American cities. In: Eckardt, F. (eds) Schlüsselwerke der Stadtforschung. Springer, Wiesbaden (2017). https://doi.org/10.1007/978-3-658-10438-2_22
3. Alberti, M., Susskind, L.: Managing Urban Sustainability: An Introduction to the Special Issue (1996)
4. Lydon, M., Garcia, A.: The next American city and the rise of tactical urbanism. In: Tactical Urbanism. Island Press, Washington, DC (2015). https://doi.org/10.5822/978-1-61091-567-0_3
5. Sasser, J.: Tactical urbanism: short-term action for long-term change, by Mike Lydon and Anthony Garcia. J. Urban Aff. **39** (2017). https://doi.org/10.1111/juaf.12287
6. Campo, D.: Tactical urbanism: short-term action for long-term change. J. Urban Des. **21** (2016). https://doi.org/10.1080/13574809.2016.1167534
7. Singhania, M., Saini, N.: Institutional framework of ESG disclosures: comparative analysis of developed and developing countries. J. Sustain. Finance Invest. (2021). https://doi.org/10.1080/20430795.2021.1964810
8. Jha, A.K., Ghimire, A., Thapa, S., Jha, A.M., Raj, R.: A review of AI for urban planning: towards building sustainable smart cities. In: Proceedings of the 6th International Conference on Inventive Computation Technologies, ICICT 2021 (2021)
9. Sankowska, P.J.: Smart government: an European approach toward building sustainable and secure cities of tomorrow. Int. J. Technol. **9** (2018). https://doi.org/10.14716/ijtech.v9i7.2517
10. Wey, W.-M., Peng, T.-C.: Study on building a smart sustainable city assessment framework using big data and analytic network process. J. Urban Plann. Dev. **147** (2021). https://doi.org/10.1061/(asce)up.1943-5444.0000704
11. Radziejowska, A., Sobotka, B.: Analysis of the social aspect of smart cities development for the example of smart sustainable buildings. Energies 14 (2021). https://doi.org/10.3390/en14144330
12. Al Ridhawi, I., Bouachir, O., Aloqaily, M., Boukerche, A.: Design guidelines for cooperative UAV-supported services and applications. ACM Comput. Surv. **54** (2022). https://doi.org/10.1145/3467964
13. Nurulin, Y., Sergeev, V., Skvortsova, I., Kaltchenko, O.: Energy efficiency in urban districts: case from polytechnic university. In: Devezas, T., Leitão, J., Sarygulov, A. (eds.) The Economics of Digital Transformation. SESCID, pp. 211–225. Springer, Cham (2021). https://doi.org/10.1007/978-3-030-59959-1_14
14. Wu, W., Wang, Y.: Evaluation and promotion of the service capacity of urban public open spaces based on improving accessibility: a case study of Shenyang city, China. Chin. Geogr. Sci. **31**(6), 1045–1056 (2021). https://doi.org/10.1007/s11769-021-1238-0
15. Yang, C., Liu, T.: Urban public space regeneration in Tokyo's urban center by urban renaissance. Open House Int. **46** (2021). https://doi.org/10.1108/OHI-03-2021-0062
16. Vukovic, T., Salama, A.M., Mitrovic, B., Devetakovic, M.: Assessing public open spaces in Belgrade – a quality of urban life perspective. Archnet-IJAR **15** (2021). https://doi.org/10.1108/ARCH-04-2020-0064
17. Atiqul Haq, S.M., Islam, M.N., Siddhanta, A., Ahmed, K.J., Chowdhury, M.T.A.: Public Perceptions of Urban Green Spaces: Convergences and Divergences (2021)
18. Peng, Y., Feng, T., Timmermans, H.J.P.: Heterogeneity in outdoor comfort assessment in urban public spaces. Sci. Total Environ. **790** (2021). https://doi.org/10.1016/j.scitotenv.2021.147941

19. Piaggio, M.: The value of public urban green spaces: measuring the effects of proximity to and size of urban green spaces on housing market values in San José, Costa Rica. Land Use Policy **109** (2021). https://doi.org/10.1016/j.landusepol.2021.105656

20. Kozlov, A., Teslya, A., Kankovskaya, A., Bagaeva, I., Krolas, P.: Comparative analysis of the level of digital infrastructure development: Case of two Russian urban agglomerations. In: IOP Conference Series: Materials Science and Engineering (2020)

21. Kharlamova, T.: Monitoring as an instrument of Sustainable Urban Development. In: MATEC Web of Conferences (2018)

22. Gutman, S., Kozlov, A., Rytova, E., Zaychenko, I.: The application of the fuzzy set theory to counting a regional innovative development indicators: the case of the Yamal region of the Russian Federation. In: Proceedings of International Conference on Soft Computing and Measurements, SCM 2015 (2015)

23. Kozlov, A.V., Rytova, E.V., Gutman, S.S., Zaychenko, I.M.: The valuing of the indicator of a regional industrial development: the fuzzy logic approach. In: Proceedings of the 19th International Conference on Soft Computing and Measurements, SCM 2016 (2016)

24. Sanoff, H.: Collaborative design processes. J. Archit. Educ. **33** (1979). https://doi.org/10.1080/10464883.1979.10758204

25. ITONAGA, K.: Low impact developments and eco-villages in U.K. and Scandinavia. J. Rural Plann. Assoc. **19** (2000). https://doi.org/10.2750/arp.19.19-suppl_211

26. Pupentsova, S.V., Alekseeva, N.S., Stroganova, O.A.: Foreign and domestic experience in environmental planning and territory management. In: IOP Conference Series: Materials Science and Engineering (2020)

27. Laskin, M.B.: Multidimensional log-normal distribution in real estate appraisals. Bus. Inf. **14** (2020). https://doi.org/10.17323/2587-814X.2020.2.48.63

Author Index

Printed in the United States
by Baker & Taylor Publisher Services

Printed in the United States
by Baker & Taylor Publisher Services